Spotlight
on FCE

Jon Naunton and John Hu[...]

Student's Book

HARROW COLLEGE
EFL CENTRE

HEINLE
CENGAGE Learning

Australia • Brazil • Japan • Korea • Mexico • Singapore • Spain • United Kingdom • United States

Spotlight on FCE Student's Book
Jon Naunton and John Hughes

Publisher: Bryan Fletcher
Development Editor: Karen Jamieson
Assistant Editor: Amanda Cole
Project Manager: Howard Middle
Content Project Editor: Natalie Griffith
Art Editor: Natalie Griffith
Manufacturing Buyer: Helen Mason
Marketing Manager: Marcin Wojtynski
Text Designer: Co Studio and Oxford Designers & Illustrators
Cover Designer: Thomas Manss & Company and Co Studio
Photo Researcher: Suzanne Williams/ Pictureresearch.co.uk
Illustrator: Paul Cemmick, Mark Draisey, Mark Duffin, Oscar Gimenez, Doug Nash, Jacquie O'Neill, Peters & Zabransky
Audio: Martin Williamson, Prolingua Productions
Printer: Canale

Cover image: Erol Taskoparan|egotrips.de

© 2009 Heinle, Cengage Learning

ISBN 978-1-4080-0762-4

Heinle
High Holborn House, 50-51 Bedford Row
London WC1R 4LR

Cengage Learning is a leading provider of customised learning solutions with office locations around the globe, including Singapore, the United Kingdom, Australia, Mexico, Brazil and Japan. Locate our local office at:
international.cengage.com/region

Cengage Learning products are represented in Canada by Nelson Education, Ltd.

Visit Heinle online at **http://elt.heinle.com**
Visit our corporate website at **www.cengage.com**

Authors' acknowledgements
The authors would like to acknowledge and thank the following people: Bryan Fletcher, Karen Jamieson, Amanda Cole, Ceri Jones, Howard Middle, Natalie Griffith, Vic Forrester and Chris Wenger.

Printed in Singapore
2 3 4 5 6 7 8 9 10 11 10 09

Contents

	Vocabulary	Grammar	Use of English
Unit 1 **Friends and family**	• Family connections • Key word: *like* • Phrasal verbs: relationships • Describing relationships • Keeping a vocabulary notebook	• Present tenses • State and dynamic verbs • Present perfect simple and present perfect continuous	• Paper 3, part 3: Word formation
Unit 2 **Jobs and work**	• Jobs and work • Key word: *as* • Phrasal verbs: jobs and applications • Suffixes	• Making comparisons • Rules for comparing	• Paper 3, part 1: Multiple-choice cloze • Paper 3, part 3: Word formation
Unit 3 **Sport and leisure**	• Sport and pastimes • Key word: *time* • Verb + noun collocations	• Obligation and necessity	• Paper 3, part 4: Key word transformations • Paper 3, part 3: Word formation • Paper 3, part 2: Open cloze
Unit 4 **Nature and animals**	• Animals • Key word: *look* • Phrasal verbs: *look* • Adjectives and prepositions	• The grammar of phrasal verbs • Countable and uncountable determiners	• Paper 3, part 3: Word formation • Paper 3, part 1: Multiple-choice cloze • Paper 3, part 4: Key word transformations
Unit 5 **A good story**	• Books and films • Key word: *thing* • Verbs of manner	• Gradable and non-gradable adjectives • Narrative tenses	• Paper 3, part 1: Multiple-choice cloze • Paper 3, part 2: Open cloze
Unit 6 **Transport and travel**	• Travel • Key word: *just* • Phrasal verbs: travel • Confusable words • Particles and meaning in phrasal verbs	• Expressing the future	• Paper 3, part 4: Key word transformations • Paper 3, part 2: Open cloze
Unit 7 **Technology**	• Inventors and inventing • Key word: *to* • Phrasal verbs: inventing, computers, technology • Dictionary skills	• Verbs followed by gerund or infinitive	• Paper 3, part 3: Word formation • Paper 3, part 2: Open cloze • Paper 3, part 4: Key word transformations
Unit 8 **Crime and social responsibility**	• Crime and criminals • Key word: *get* • Phrasal verbs: *get*	• Relative clauses: defining and non-defining • Informality and formality in relative clauses	• Paper 3, part 2: Open cloze • Paper 3, part 1: Multiple-choice cloze

Reading	Listening	Speaking	Writing
• *Family soap operas* • Paper 1, part 3: Multiple matching • *Gossip* • Paper 1, part 2: Gapped text	• Talking about people • Listening for general meaning • Paper 4, part 1: Multiple choice	• Asking and answering questions • Paper 5, part 1: Conversation (spoken questions)	• Paper 2, part 1: Compulsory letter or email
• *Volunteer work* • Paper 1, part 3: Multiple matching	• Talking about jobs • Paper 4, part 1: Multiple choice	• Comparing • Paper 5, part 3: Two-way conversation	• Paper 2, part 2: Letter of application
• *Eccentric sports* • Paper 1, part 2: Gapped text	• *Free time* • *The early history of football* • Paper 4, part 2: Sentence completion + part 3: Multiple matching	• Expressing ability • Comparing photographs • Paper 5, part 2: Individual 'long turn'	• Paper 2, part 1: A review
• *A dog's life* • Paper 1, part 3: Multiple matching	• *Animals and humans* • *Almost human?* • Paper 4, part 2: Sentence completion + part 3: Multiple matching + part 4: Multiple choice	• Comparing photographs • Paper 5, part 2: Individual 'long turn'	• Paper 2, part 1: Compulsory email (giving advice)
• *The bangle* • Paper 1, part 1: Multiple choice	• *Great adaptations* • Paper 4, part 2: Sentence completion + part 4: Multiple choice	• Tenses	• Paper 2, part 2: A short story • Sequencing
• *Dream holidays* • Scanning • Paper 1, part 3: Multiple matching	• *Travel and visits* • Travel arrangements • Paper 4, part 1: Multiple choice	• Organising a schedule • Discussing options • Discussing your travels	• Paper 2, part 2: A report
• *Robot revolution* • Paper 1, part 2: Gapped text	• *Intelligent robots* • Paper 4, part 2: Sentence completion	• Suggesting and recommending • Exchanging ideas, expressing and justifying opinions • Paper 5, part 3: Two-way conversation	• Paper 2, part 2: A review
• *Crime and punishment* • Paper 1, part 3: Multiple matching	• *Stopped by the police* • *Social responsibility* • Active listening • Paper 4, part 3: Multiple matching + part 4: Multiple choice	• Paper 5, part 3: Two-way conversation	• Paper 2, part 2: An article

Reading	Listening	Speaking	Writing
• *All mouth* • Paper 1, part 2: Gapped text	• *Eating out* • *In the dark* • Paper 4, part 3: Multiple matching + part 4: Multiple choice	• Expressing preferences • Talking about the past	• Paper 2, part 2: An opinion essay
• *Crop circles* • Paper 1, part 1: Multiple choice	• *Out of the blue* • Paper 4, part 2: Sentence completion + part 3: Multiple matching	• Guessing and speculating • Paper 5, part 2: Individual 'long turn'	• Paper 1, part 2: Compulsory email (Informal exchange) • Fluency and accuracy
• *Pocket money* • Paper 1, part 3: Multiple matching	• *Money habits* • Paper 4, part 1: Multiple choice	• Expressing regret, giving advice and making suggestions	• Paper 2, part 1: An opinion essay • Giving arguments 'for and against'
• *Weather forecasts* • Paper 1, part 2: Gapped text	• *Natural disasters/Hurricanes* • Paper 4, part 3: Multiple matching + part 2: Sentence completion + part 4: Multiple choice	• Activating your knowledge • Criticising and complaining	• Paper 2, part 1: A discussion-type essay
• *The paparazzi* • Paper 1, part 1: Multiple choice • Strategies for unknown vocabulary	• *A news report* • *What's on TV?* • Paper 4, part 2: Sentence completion + part 3: Multiple matching	• Reporting • Agreeing on what to watch • Paper 5, part 3: Two-way conversation	• Paper 2, parts 1+2: Checking and editing your work
• *Fashion victim* • Paper 1, part 1: Multiple choice • Writer's overall attitude	• *Crazes* • *School uniform* • Paper 4, part 1: Multiple choice + part 4: Multiple choice	• Challenging • Paper 5, part 3: Two-way conversation + part 4: Collaborative task	• Paper 2, part 2: A descriptive essay
• *Genuine fakes* • Paper 1, part 2: Gapped text sentences • *Festivals* • Paper 1, Part 3: Multiple matching	• *Statues* • *Living traditions* • Paper 4, part 3: Multiple matching + part 4: Multiple choice	• Adverbs in conversation	• Paper 2, part 2: An article
• *A dream island* • Paper 1, part 1: Multiple choice	• *Design and colour psychology* • Paper 4, part 4: Multiple choice	• The Speaking Paper: all four parts	• Paper 2, part 1: Compulsory email (giving advice)

What are the differences between the old exam and the revised exam?

You are probably wondering what the differences between the old and revised exam are. There are still five papers, but overall the exam has been reduced in length. A question type has been lost from each of Paper 1 (Reading) and Paper 3 (Use of English). The number of questions in each part may be slightly different, but essentially there are few differences between the old and the new exam.

Revised Exam	Old Exam
1 **Paper One: Reading** (1 hour) • Part 1 Multiple choice (8 questions) • Part 2 Gapped text sentences (7 questions) • Part 3 Multiple matching (15 questions)	**1 hour 15 minutes** • There are now three rather than four parts (questions). • The matching exercise where candidates matched headings to paragraphs has disappeared.
2 **Paper Two: Writing** (1 hour 20 minutes) • Part 1 Compulsory letter or email (120–150 words) • Part 2 One question from four – Non-transactional letter, report, essay, review, story (110–180 words). Question 5 based on set text.	**1 hour 30 minutes** • Students now write emails. • The word length for part 1 is now shorter. • Students can now write a 'Review' in Part 2.
3 **Paper Three: Use of English** (45 minutes) • Part 1 Multiple-choice lexical cloze (12 questions) • Part 2 Open cloze (12 questions) • Part 3 Word formation (10 questions) • Part 4 Key word transformations (8 questions)	**1 hour 15 minutes** • The number of questions have been reduced in part 1, 2 and 4. • Old part 5, sentence correction, where students identified an extra and unnecessary word has disappeared.
4 **Paper Four: Listening** (approximately 40 minutes) • Part 1 A series of eight short unrelated extracts from monologues or exchanges between interacting speakers. There is one multiple choice question per extract. • Part 2 A monologue or text involving speakers. Sentence completion (10 questions). • Part 3 Five short unrelated monologues. Multiple matching (5 questions). • Part 4 A monologue or text involving interacting speakers. Multiple choice questions (7 questions).	**40 minutes (approximately)** • This paper is unchanged, however the old 'who said what' format of part 4 has disappeared. • Emphasis has been placed more on candidate's understanding of attitude and opinion.
5 **Paper Five: Speaking** (14 minutes) • Part 1 A conversation between interlocutor and each candidate (spoken questions). • Part 2 An individual 'long turn' for each candidate, with a brief response from the second candidate (visual and written stimuli, with spoken instructions). • Part 3 A two-conversation between the candidates (visual and written stimuli, with spoken instructions). • Part 4 A discussion on topics related to Part 3 (spoken questions).	**14 minutes** • The only change is that there are now written prompts with the photos and pictures in parts 2 and 3 which students use when speaking.

Spotlight on FCE: Introduction

Spotlight on FCE is a new preparation course for students intending to take the Cambridge ESOL First Certificate in English examination. The course is based on the new Cambridge exam guidelines for December 2008 and onwards.

Approach of the book

The sixteen units of *Spotlight on FCE* will take you from no knowledge of the First Certificate exam through to thorough preparation for the day of the exam! The book also assumes you would like to continue improving your overall level of English. For this reason *Spotlight on FCE* approaches your success in two ways: preparing exam candidates and preparing language students.

Preparing for the exam

The Student's Book helps you to develop the skills you need to be successful in the exam. You will learn about all parts of the exam papers and make use of exam techniques which previous successful candidates have used.

Exam spotlight feature

These boxes on the unit pages provide valuable information and advice on different parts of the exam. They explain what the examiner is looking for, but also draw attention to certain key skills and techniques that successful candidates have used in past exams. Many of these spotlight boxes require you to complete a short exercise which focuses you on task achievement.

Use of English

Spotlight on FCE includes a special focus on the *Use of English* paper, with full explanations on strategies for approaching the questions and guided practice in the units, as well as extra practice in the Review section at the end of each unit. It will also improve your level of English. The book develops skills for reading, writing, speaking and listening as well as expanding knowledge of grammar and vocabulary.

Spotlights

This feature offers advice on how to develop the four skills (reading, writing,

listening and speaking) as well as focusing on specific grammar and vocabulary points.

➡ There is also a summary *Wordlist* on pages 234-237.

Phrasal verbs

In order to pass the First Certificate exam you will need a good range and understanding of phrasal verbs. You will find exercises on these types of verbs in the units as well as an explanation of the grammar of phrasal verbs in unit 4.

➡ Also note the *Phrasal Verb Reference* on pages 232–233.

Approach to writing skills

The writing sections in the units look at each of the types of writing you might have to produce in Paper 2 of the exam. In this section you are presented with a writing question. To help you understand what is required, you are taken systematically through various steps before being asked to complete the task. In addition, these sections help to develop various writing skills including planning, developing good paragraph structure and checking and editing. Look out for the *Writing Checklist* feature.

➡ You can also refer to the *Writing Guide* on pages 199–206 for information on the main types of writing in the exam and some samples of pieces of writing.

Key word

Most units include a key word feature. These are common words that you will be familiar with. This feature looks in more detail at the grammar and use of these words including collocations and fixed expressions.

Approach to grammar

If you are taking the First Certificate exam you should already have been introduced to the main areas of English grammar and so *Spotlight on FCE* starts to contrast

grammatical areas.

➡ Each grammar section in the units is referenced to the comprehensive *Grammar Reference* on pages 165–186. As well as giving more detailed descriptions of the grammar, this section includes further practice exercises.

Speaking

There are plenty of opportunities for you to speak, with discussion questions included throughout the units. The Speaking section presents useful functions and expressions which you will use in real life but these are also practised in the context of an exam-type task. The audio CD also includes examples of the Speaking test for students to listen to. Unit 16 has a special feature on the speaking test.

➡ *Speaking Files* on pages 187–198 contain even more practice and useful expressions.

Listening

The listening exercises are presented in the style of the listening questions in the First Certificate exam, with all four parts of the paper covered. There are questions to help develop the necessary skills and strategies along with useful advice and tips.

Reading

There are a wide variety of reading texts in order to reflect the diversity of the exam. As well as giving you plenty of exam practice, the reading texts should create discussion and help you to develop a wider knowledge of vocabulary.

Finally, don't forget to use the accompanying *Exam Booster* workbook which provides further practice in all of these areas as well as a focus on pronunciation and a DVD of the Speaking test.

Jon and John

Overview of the exam

The First Certificate in English examination consists of five papers, each worth an equal 40 marks of the maximum 200 marks. Grades A, B and C represent a pass grade. Grades D and E are a fail. It is not necessary to achieve a satisfactory grade in all five papers in order to receive a final passing grade.

PAPER 1 (1 HOUR)

Reading
- three parts (a variety of texts and comprehension tasks).
- You must answer all three parts.
- 30 questions in total (You have one hour).
- You receive two marks for each correct answer in Parts 1 and 2, and one mark for each correct answer in Part 3.

Part 1: Multiple choice
You read a text and answer eight multiple choice questions. Each question has four possible answers (*A, B C* or *D*).

Part 2: Gapped text
Sentences are missing from a text and you must decide where to put them. There are seven sentences in the question but you can only use five.

Part 3: Multiple matching
You read one or more texts (often four shorter texts) and match prompts to parts of the whole text. There are 15 prompts.

SPOTLIGHT ON FCE

PAPER 1
See the following pages for Exam Spotlights on Paper 1: 11, 18, 28, 38, 48, 66, 88, 108, 128, 139, 148, 158.

PAPER 2 (1 HOUR 20 MINUTES)

Writing
- two parts.
- You must answer both parts.
- two questions to answer in total (You have one hour 20 minutes).
- You receive equal marks for each question.

Part 1: Write a letter or email
This part has one question and you must answer it. You read some text and respond with a letter or email. Your answer must be between 120-150 words.

Part 2: Write an article, an essay, a letter, a report, a review or a story
This part has four possible questions and you answer one only with between 120–180 words:
Questions 2–4 can ask you to write an article, an essay, a letter, a report, a review or a story. You read about a situation and then write a response using the correct type of text.
Question 5 also asks you to write similar types of texts but based upon the set reading text that you can study for the exam (optional).

SPOTLIGHT ON FCE

PAPER 2
See the following pages for Exam Spotlights on Paper 2: 12-13, 22-23, 32-33, 42-43, 46, 52-53, 62-63, 72-73, 82-83, 92-93, 102-103, 112-113, 122-123, 132-133, 142-143, 152-153, 161.

PAPER 3 (45 MINUTES)

Use of English
- four parts.
- You must answer all four parts.
- 42 questions in total (You have 45 minutes).
- You receive one mark for each correct answer in Parts 1, 2 and 3, and two marks for each correct answer in Part 4.

Part 1: Multiple-choice cloze
This is a cloze test with twelve gaps and four possible options for each one.

Part 2: Open cloze
This is a cloze test with twelve gaps. You complete each gap with one word.

Part 3: Word formation
You read a text with ten gaps. At the end of each is a word stem. You must change the form of the word and complete the gap.

Part 4: Key word transformations
There are eight questions. Each question has a lead-in sentence. Then a key word is given. You must use this word in a second gapped sentence so it has the same meaning as the first.

SPOTLIGHT ON FCE

PAPER 3
See the following pages for Exam Spotlights on Paper 3: 16, 31, 34, 40, 56, 144.

PAPER 4 (APPROXIMATELY 40 MINUTES)

Listening

- four parts.
- You must answer all four parts.
- 30 questions in total (approximately 40 minutes).
- You receive one mark for each correct answer in all four parts.
- Text types: you hear four different sets of recordings (monologues or interacting speakers). Monologues could include answerphone messages, radio documentaries, announcements, instructions, news, lectures, reports, speeches, advertisements and stories. Interacting speakers could include conversations, interviews, discussions, quizzes and transactions. After you listen, you have five minutes to write your answers onto the answer sheet.

Part 1: Multiple choice

You listen to eight short unconnected recordings. Each one is 30 seconds long. For each recording you answer a question with three answers to choose from.

Part 2: Sentence completion

You listen to someone talking or a conversation. It lasts about three minutes. You have to complete ten sentences with words you hear on the recording.

Part 3: Multiple matching

There are five short recordings and you match five questions to the correct option. There are six possible options.

Part 4: Multiple choice

You listen to a longer text with more than one speaker. You have seven questions: each one has three options to choose from.

SPOTLIGHT ON FCE

PAPER 4

See the following pages for Exam Spotlights on Paper 4: 10, 26, 30, 46, 86, 96, 100, 107, 120, 127.

PAPER 5 (APPROXIMATELY 14 MINUTES)

Speaking

- four parts.
- You must answer all four parts.
- You take the speaking test with another candidate.
- The interlocutor (examiner talking to you) asks you questions and gives you prompts (pictures and words) which you may have to talk about or discuss with the other person.
- You are assessed on your performance throughout.

Part 1: Conversation between interlocutor and each candidate (asking and answering)

This is general interactional and social language – a conversation between the interlocutor and each candidate. You will answer questions on topics such as home, family, and personal interests. This part will last approximately three minutes.

Part 2: An individual 'long turn' for each candidate with a short response from the second candidate

You look at two photographs and the interlocutor asks you to talk about them (describing, comparing and giving an opinion). The other candidate listens then has to respond at the end of your talk. Each candidate's turn should last approximately one minute, with a further 20 seconds given for the other candidate to respond and comment on what you have said.

Part 3: A two-way conversation between the candidates, with a decision-making task

Both candidates are given spoken instructions with written and visual stimuli. You work together in a collaborative task (exchanging ideas, expressing opinions, agreeing and/or disagreeing, speculating, suggesting, evaluating, reaching a decision through negotiation). Your discussion should last three minutes.

Part 4: A discussion on topics related to the collaborative (Part 3) task

The interlocutor now joins in the discussion (from Part 3) and asks further questions to each candidate so it is a three-way conversation lasting four minutes. The focus here is expressing and justifying opinions, and agreeing and/or disagreeing.

SPOTLIGHT ON FCE

PAPER 5

See the following pages for Exam Spotlights on Paper 5: 5, 9, 21, 32, 41, 71, 97, 162-163.

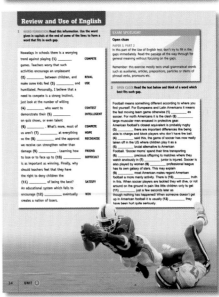

First Certificate Exam Glossary

Article: a piece of non-fictional writing, usually forming part of a magazine or newspaper.

Cloze test: a type of gap-filling task in which whole words have been removed from a text. Candidates must replace the missing word.

Coherence: language which is coherent is clear and planned well. All the parts and ideas should form a unified whole.

Collaborative task: the section in the Speaking task in which candidates engage in discussion and work towards a negotiated outcome of the set task.

Discourse: written or spoken communication.

Email: an electronic letter, usually less formal in language than a letter.

Essay: a structured piece of writing on a specific topic.

Gap-filling item: any type of item requiring the candidate to insert some written material into the spaces in the text. This material may include letters, numbers, single words, phrases, sentences or paragraphs. The response may be selected from a set of options, or supplied by the candidate.

Gapped text: candidates are required to decide from where in a given text, seven sentences have been removed.

Gist: the central theme/meaning of the text.

Interlocutor: the Speaking Paper examiner who conducts the test and makes an assessment of each candidate's performance.

Key: the correct answer to an item.

Key word: the word which must be used in an answer to an item in the Use of English Paper, part 4.

Letter: a written message addressed to a person or organisation. Usually sent through the post.

Long turn: the section in the Speaking Paper allowing a candidate to talk uninterrupted for a period of time. They will produce an extended piece of discourse.

Multiple choice: a task where candidates are given several possible answers, with only one being correct.

Multiple-choice cloze: a text which has gaps in which every gap represents a missing word or phrase. The text is followed by sets of words or phrases. Each set corresponds to a gap.

Multiple matching: a task in which a number of questions or sentence completion items are set. They are generally based on a reading text. The responses are provided in the form of a word or phrase bank. Each of these responses can be used an unlimited number of times.

Neutral style: no specific features of formality or informality to distinguish the writing style at an FCE level appropriate for compositions.

Open cloze: a type of gap-filling task in which whole words have been removed from a text. Candidates must replace the missing word. Candidates are not given a set of words from which to choose.

Options: the individual words in the set of possible answers for a multiple choice item.

Paraphrase: to use different words to convey the meaning of something.

Phrasal verb: a verb which takes on a new meaning when followed y a certain adverb or preposition.

Prompt sentence: the complete sentence given as the opening or closing line of a story in the Writing Paper, part 2.

Sentence completion: a section in the Listening paper in which candidates need to listen to the text and complete the sentences.

Set text: a piece of literature chosen for study.

Short story: a piece of fiction dealing with only a few characters and incidents.

Register: the tone of a piece of writing. It should be appropriate for the task and target reader.

Review: a critical evaluation of a book, film, play, etc.

Rubrics: the instructions to an examination question which tell the candidate what to do when answering the question.

Stem word: the word at the end of each line in the Use of English Paper, part 3. This word should form the basis for the word that has to be formed.

Transactional letter: a letter written in response to a request or to initiate action. A letter of complaint is transactional, a letter of advice is not.

Word formation: candidates are required to fill a gap by forming an appropriate word by using a given stem word.

1 Friends and family

MAIN MENU

Vocabulary:	family connections; describing relationships; key word: *like*
Grammar:	present tenses
Speaking:	asking and answering questions
Reading:	*Family soap operas; Gossip*
Listening:	talking about people
Writing:	a letter or email

EXAM MENU

Reading:	gapped text; multiple matching
Writing:	compulsory letter
Use of English:	word formation
Listening:	multiple choice
Speaking:	conversations

Getting started

1 Work in pairs. Ask and answer these questions to find out about your partner. Keep a note of their answers.

QUESTIONNAIRE

1 Where are you from? What do you like about living there?
2 Do you work or are you a full-time student?
3 Who are the most important people in your life? Why?
4 Tell me about your best friend.
5 How much time do you spend with family or friends?
6 Do you prefer to spend time on your own or with other people? Why?
7 Tell me about a holiday you enjoyed recently.
8 Do you like the same TV programmes as the rest of your family?
9 How do you normally find out news? On TV, on the Internet or in newspapers?
10 Tell me about a website you often visit.
11 What do you like doing in your free time or on holiday?
12 Why is learning English important to you?

EXAM SPOTLIGHT

Conversation: asking and answering questions

PAPER 5, PART 1

In this part of the speaking test, you will be asked questions like the ones in the questionnaire.

2 Categorise the questions from the questionnaire under the headings below. There may be more than one possibility.

A Likes and dislikes   C Personal experiences   E Work and learning
B Places   D Media   F Relationships

3 Work in pairs. Think of one more question for each topic heading A–F above. Ask your partner your questions.

4 Tell the class about the person you interviewed.
Example:
Marco likes watching TV and reading books in his free time. His favourite website is ...

Reading: family soap operas

1 Families have enjoyed watching TV together for over 50 years. Find out how much TV people in your class watch. Who watches the most?

2 Work in groups. Discuss:
- What kind of TV shows do you like watching?
- Do you like soap operas?
- Are they popular in your country?

3 Work in pairs. Read about soap operas (texts A–D opposite) from four different countries. Then complete these two sentences about them.

I'd like to see [name of soap opera] because ...
[name of soap opera] is probably the worst because ...

Ask your partner what they think. Do you agree?

4 MULTIPLE MATCHING Which text (A–D) do these sentences refer to? The text may be chosen more than once.

1 The families in this soap are neighbours. __B__

2 This soap includes a character that became richer. _____

3 This soap features a mother and three brothers. _____

4 This country has adapted a soap from another country. _____

5 This soap created arguments off-screen as well as on. _____

6 This country imports many of its soaps from another country. _____

7 One star is using her fame to start another job. _____

8 The family in this soap is split geographically. _____

9 This soap is about moving from one country to another. _____

5 Discuss. Do soap operas reflect real life?

SOAPS
Around the World

A POLAND

Zlotopolscy (The Golden Poles) is a soap based around the main members of the Zlotopolscy family. That's Barbara, her sons Marek, Waldek and Kasper, plus their wives and children. But the family is divided. Some of the relatives live in a small town and the other half live in Warsaw. *The Golden Poles* forms part of the Polish soap industry which is one of the biggest in the world. Poles have a particular love for Brazilian soaps and many people regularly listen to the second-longest running radio soap opera in the world called *The Matysiak Family*. It has been broadcast since 1956.

B GERMANY

Germans have been watching *Lindenstrasse (Linden Street)*, the country's favourite soap opera, since it began over 1,000 episodes ago. Set in Munich, it isn't so much about individual characters but more about extended families living on top of, or next door to, each other. Another German soap, *Verbotene Liebe (Forbidden Love)*, is a version of the Australian soap *Sons and Daughters*. In it all sorts of people including twins, cousins, half-brothers and stepsisters, spouses and their offspring all fall in love with people they aren't supposed to fall in love with!

C INDIA

Apart from the fact that *Kyunki Saas Bhi Kabhi Bahu Thi* (*Because Once a Mother Was a Daughter-in-Law*) has a title which is longer than most soap operas, the basic ingredients of this Indian TV series follow those of every other soap opera – it's about a family! It began over 1,250 episodes ago with the heroine, Tulsi, marrying into the wealthy Virani family. Tulsi, who was poor before she joined the family, is always arguing with her mother and sisters-in-law. Recently the serial jumped 20 years forward and introduced a new generation of siblings. The latest news from the series is the real-life news that Smriti Irani, who plays Tulsi, has recently started a career in politics.

D BRAZIL

In a country which loves its soap operas, the series *América* won 64 percent of Brazil's TV audience every night by the time it finished. It told the story of a tough but vulnerable girl called Sol from Rio de Janeiro who travels to Miami in search of 'the American dream'. She left behind her parents as well as her fiancé, Tião, who rode bulls at the rodeo. As well as being popular, *América* was controversial. Many people criticised the show for presenting an idealised view of the USA and for encouraging illegal immigration.

Vocabulary: family connections

1 Find words in the text which mean the same as 1–12 below.

1 husband or wife ____*spouse*____
2 your child or children _____
3 a brother who shares just one parent with you _____
4 the daughter of your father's new wife _____
5 opposite of nuclear family _____
6 wives of your husband's brothers _____
7 your future husband _____
8 all the members of your family including the ones who don't live with you _____
9 two children born at the same time to the same mother _____
10 the sons and daughters of your parents' brothers and sisters _____
11 your husband or wife's mother _____
12 your brothers and sisters _____

2 Work in pairs. Think of a friend's family or a family you know very well. Perhaps it's a family on TV! How many of the words above can you use to describe them? Tell your partner.
Example:
There are five people in the family who live next door to me. There's a mother and father, twin boys and a baby ...

Key word: *like*

1 Match the answers (a–e) to the questions (1–5).

1 What's your brother like? __*b*__
2 Does he look like you? _____
3 What does he like doing at the weekend? _____
4 Do you like him? _____
5 Do you think he would like to come out with us sometime? _____

a I like him a lot.
b He's quite serious and quiet when you first meet him but he relaxes when you get to know him.
c Yes, I'm sure he would.
d Yes, we're both dark haired with blue eyes.
e He likes going to the cinema or sometimes eating out.

2 Work in pairs. Tell your partner the name of someone you know very well; for example, a member of your family or your closest friend. Now take turns to ask and answer questions 1–5 in exercise 1 about that person.
Example:
A: My sister's name is Alison.
B: Does she look like you?
A: Not at all. She has blue eyes and light brown hair. Does your sister look like you? ...

Grammar: present tenses

1 Compare the uses of the present simple and the present continuous tense in these pairs of sentences. Answer the questions for each pair with *a* or *b*.

1 a Some of the relatives live in a small town.
  b Some of the relatives are living in Warsaw for the next few months.
  1 Which sentence describes something true all the time? _____
  2 Which sentence describes a temporary situation? _____

2 a Tulsi is always arguing with her mother and sisters-in-law.
  b Tulsi always argues with her mother and sisters-in-law.
  1 Which sentence describes something that is generally true? _____
  2 Which sentence emphasises the repetition (of something negative)? _____

3 a Sol travels to Miami in search of the American dream.
  b Sol is travelling to Miami.
  1 Which sentence describes a story? _____
  2 Which sentences describes something true at the moment of speaking? _____

GRAMMAR SPOTLIGHT

State and dynamic verbs

There are many verbs that are usually only used in the present simple. However, verbs such as *be, like, believe, understand* and *know* describe states. We rarely use state verbs in the continuous form.

Example:
I understand the lesson today. (✓)
NOT *I'm ~~understanding~~ the lesson today.* (✗)

Note this exception:
a My uncle is annoying. (✓)
b My uncle is being annoying. (✓)

Sentence *a* describes a permanent *state*. Sentence *b* describes something true at the moment of speaking.

➡ Grammar Reference (Section 12.4) page 181

2 Work in pairs. Tell your partner about ...

- your daily routine during the week.
- something you are always arguing about with members of your family or with close friends.
- what you are currently studying or working on.
- some of the current changes in your life or in your local area.
- a book or film you have read or seen recently. Describe what happens.

3 Read this email and check the verbs in each line carefully. Some are correct but some are incorrect. Delete any mistakes and write the correction. See the example.

To: Milan Spasovski
From: Rona Kalodikis
Subject: My friend from Greece

Dear Milan,

Thanks for your email. ~~It's being~~ *It's* great to hear from you again! It's interesting to hear that your family moves house. I'm hoping they'll like their new home and it's wonderful that you're starting university.

I write to ask you a favour. A friend of mine from Greece wants to come to Britain in three weeks. It'll be his first time. His flight lands at 3pm on June 15th but his tour doesn't starting until the 16th. Would it be possible for you to meet him and let him stay at your flat for the night? His English isn't very good but he has a great sense of humour and he is looking rather like Brad Pitt!

Anyway, let me know if you are not having time.

Love,

Rona

4 **Compare the use of verbs in these sentences. Answer the questions for each sentence.**

1 a The Indian soap began over 1,250 episodes ago.
  b The Indian soap has begun over 1,250 episodes ago.
  c Hurry up! The Indian soap has just begun.
  1 Which sentence is wrong? _____ Why?
  2 Can you identify the tenses in sentences a and c?

2 a They've already watched 1,000 episodes of *Lindenstrasse*.
  b They've been watching *Lindenstrasse* since it began.
  1 Which sentence emphasises the duration of the activity? _____
  2 Which sentence emphasises a number or result? _____

3 a How long have you been watching *América*?
  b Have you ever watched *América*?
  1 Which asks about an activity which started in the past and continues in the present? _____
  2 Which asks about an experience which happened sometime in the past? _____

GRAMMAR SPOTLIGHT

Present perfect simple and present perfect continuous

With some verbs (e.g. *work*, *live*) there is little or no difference in meaning between the present perfect simple and the present perfect continuous.

Example:
I've lived there for three years. = *I've been living there for three years.*

If the action is quite recent or short in duration, the speaker is more likely to say *I've been working here for a week* rather than *I've worked here for a week*.

→ Grammar Reference (Section 12.4) page 181

Conversation

PAPER 5, PART 1

5 **Read the transcript below of the conversation between the interlocutor and the candidate at the beginning of the speaking test. Choose the correct present form.**

Examiner: First of all I'd like to know something about you, Dorota. Where (1) *are you/have you been* from?

Candidate: Poland. I (2) *am living/live* in a small town called Nowy Targ.

Examiner: And how long (3) *do you live/have you lived* there?

Candidate: I (4) *have lived/am living* there all my life though (5) *I'm/I've been* studying English in Torun at the moment.

Examiner: Have you ever (6) *studied/been studying* any other languages?

Candidate: Yes. I (7) *studied/have studied* German for two years when I was at school.

Examiner: OK. So what (8) *do/are* you and your family most *enjoy/enjoying* doing at home?

Candidate: We all (9) *like/are liking* skiing. My family always (10) *go/have gone* skiing each winter in a place called Zakopane which is near us.

Examiner: And what's the most exciting thing (11) *you've ever done/you've ever been doing*?

Candidate: Oh, that's a difficult question. Erm ... well, currently (12) *I take/I'm taking* a course in mountain rescue.

6 **🎧 1.1 Listen to another candidate in the speaking test. He makes some mistakes with present tenses. Can you identify them? Check your answers afterwards in Tapescript 1.1 on page 207.**

Speaking:
asking and answering questions

PAPER 5, PART 1

1 **Work in pairs. Practise a similar conversation. One of you is the interlocutor (examiner) and asks the questions from the dialogue in exercise 5 above. The other person is the student.**
Example:
A: *First, I'd like to know something about you. Where do you live?*
B: *I live in Italy, quite close to Rome.*

Close this book and answer in your own words.

9

Listening: talking about people

1 🎧 1.2 Listen to four conversations. Which speaker (1–4) has …?

- met the person
- seen the person

EXAM SPOTLIGHT

Listening for general meaning

PAPER 4, PART 1

In the listening test, you hear the recording twice.
Use the first time of listening to understand general meaning and the second for specific detail. The listening task below is similar to the First Certificate exam, but there are only four questions here. In the exam there are eight.

2 🎧 1.2 **MULTIPLE CHOICE** Listen to the four conversations again. For questions 1–4, choose the best answer (**A, B** or **C**).

1 Who are the two people talking about?
   A a friend
   B a customer
   C a manager

2 What is Nigel to the two speakers?
   A an old friend
   B a boyfriend
   C an acquaintance

3 Who is the woman criticising?
   A the TV show
   B the children
   C the parents

4 What is the woman telling her friends about?
   A some gossip
   B a TV show
   C her two brothers

Vocabulary:

describing relationships

Phrasal verbs

1 Read sentences 1–9 below. Replace the words in *italics* with the phrasal verbs from the box. Write the verb at the end of the sentence. Make any necessary changes.

get on with	let down	put up with	fall out	stand by
break up with	look after	get back together	ran into	

1 I don't know how long I can *tolerate* her. _____

2 All the staff *like her and are friendly to* her. _____

3 I *met* Kim *by chance* the other day. _____

4 She wants to *end the relationship with* him. _____

5 They *have arguments* over everything. _____

6 She always leaves him and then a week later they *start their relationship* again. _____

7 There was a mother and father on the show who still *take care of* their three grown-up children. _____

8 They never do anything around the house and *always disappoint* them *by not doing what they should do*. _____

9 She said she would *be loyal to* him whatever happened.

_____

SPOTLIGHT ON VOCABULARY

Keeping a vocabulary notebook
Phrasal verbs are used a lot in English so learn as many as you can. Here are some ideas for writing them down in a notebook to help you remember them.

Write a synonym: *put up with = tolerate*
Write it in your own sentence:
I can put up with hard work if it's useful.
Where does the object go?
I let her down. NOT ~~I let down her.~~

Write vocabulary in groups according to …

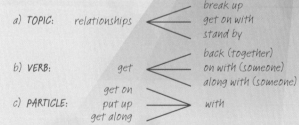

2 Find out what these phrasal verbs mean using a dictionary, and write them in your vocabulary notebook.

make up with	take after
go along with	look up to

Reading: gossip

1 **Discuss. Do you enjoy gossip?**
- Have you heard some interesting gossip recently?
- Can gossip be a good thing?

2 **GAPPED TEXT SENTENCES Read the article below. Five sentences have been removed. Choose from sentences A–E to fill each gap.**

A Conversely, (*to what?*) a mutual liking for the speaker produced less of a connection.

B Now scientists in the USA are telling us that there's nothing better for you than a bit of a moan about someone.

C The results (*of what?*) showed that sharing negative attitudes about others helps create friendship.

D They (*who?*) have concluded it is a mistake to believe that only shared positive attitudes promote closeness.

E Afterwards, the participants (*which participants?*) talked to someone they had never met before about the two characters (*which characters?*).

3 **Underline the three adjectives in the text which describe relationships.**

4 **Complete this table with the adjective or noun form of the word.**

Adjective	Noun
close	
	friendship
difficult	
	strength

5 **Write words from the table in these questions.**

1 Are you a person who has lots of friends or do you have one or two really _____ friends who you can share your feelings with?

2 Do you have brothers or sisters? How _____ is your relationship with them? Do you ever argue or find it _____ to get on with them?

3 What do you value most in a _____?
Do you have any _____ making friends?

6 **Work in pairs. Practise asking and answering the questions in exercise 5.**

Gossip is good for you

Have you heard some interesting news about someone recently? Is it true? Do you care? People enjoy sharing gossip with friends but it often leads to difficulties or feelings of guilt. **(1)** _____ These experts have discovered that spreading gossip can help make people have close relationships and can, in fact, be a way of releasing tension.

The team of psychologists from the University of Oklahoma first questioned two groups of students aged 16 to 25 about views shared with their close friends.

(2) _____ On the other hand shared attitudes towards movies, activities and beliefs tended to be positive.

In another part of the study 31 men and 74 women were asked to listen to a recorded conversation between two fictional characters, Brad and Melissa. **(3)** _____ They discussed what they had liked or disliked about the couple and if they preferred one to the other. The scientists found that partners developed a friendly relationship if they both agreed they disliked the speaker. **(4)** _____

'If there is a positive side to gossip, we believe it is that shared, mild negative attitudes towards others can build a strong relationship' said the researchers. **(5)** _____

Writing: a letter or email

Understanding the task
PAPER 2, PART 1

In this part of the writing test, you have to write a letter or an email.

1 **Read the exam question below. Check you understand the task by answering these questions first:**
- What do you have to write? An email or a letter?
- What information must you include? Is this given or do you create it?
- How long will it be?
- What could you lose marks for?
- Do you expect Renate's letter to be formal or informal?

Exam question

You have received a letter from your English-speaking friend, Renate, who is planning to visit you. Read it and the notes you have made on it then write a letter back to Renate in 120–150 words, using your notes. You must use gramatically correct sentences with accurate spelling and punctuation in a style appropriate to the situation.

Dear ...

It was great to talk on the phone last week about my visit to your country. I'm really sorry that you won't be home when I visit but it's great that your brother can meet me at the airport and let me stay at his house. I'll only stay a couple of days and then travel round the country.

say where →

As I only have ten days, where would you recommend I visit? And also what is the best way to travel? Is it expensive to hire a car?

← *Yes, recommend alternative*

This is a good idea! →

One other thing, I'd like to bring your brother a present. What do you think he'd like? Maybe he'd like some of my country's famous chocolates.

Anyway, I must go now.
Best wishes,
Renate

Describe your twin brother →

PS What does your brother look like? How will I recognise him at the station?

Starting and ending a letter

The level of formality affects how you start and end a letter:

Start		End
Dear Sir/Madam	→	Yours faithfully
Dear Mr Brown	→	Yours sincerely/Best regards
Dear Renate	→	Best wishes

→ Writing Guide, page 199

2 **Look at the two letters on the next page. Two students have answered the exam question above. Read the letters and decide:**

	Letter A	Letter B
• if the letter includes all the relevant information.	☐	☐
• if the letter is the correct length. (120–150 words)	☐	☐
• which letter is too formal.	☐	☐

LETTER A

Dear Renate,

Further to your last letter, I apologise that I will be unavailable to see you. However, my brother is looking forward to meeting you. He is my twin brother so he looks very similar to me. I am sure that he would be delighted to receive chocolates.

With regard to visiting my country, I would strongly recommend that you see the main palace in the capital city. It has beautiful gardens and a museum. Unfortunately, hiring a car is very expensive but public transport is normally reliable.

There are lots of places to visit. If you go to the north, you should go walking in the mountains and there is also skiing at that time of year. My brother will also accompany you to some places of interest during your stay.

I look forward to hearing from you again before you leave.

Yours sincerely ...

LETTER B

Dear Renate,

Thanks for your letter. I'm really sorry that I won't be here to see you but my brother is looking forward to meeting you. He's my twin brother so he looks very similar to me. I'm sure he'd be happy to get chocolates. Anyway, if he doesn't eat them, I will!

About visiting my country, you should see the main palace in the capital city. It has beautiful gardens and a museum. The bad news is that hiring a car is very expensive but public transport is normally reliable so use that.

There are lots of places to visit. If you go to the north, go walking in the mountains and there's also skiing at that time of year. I'm sure my brother will take you to some interesting places while you are with him.

Speak to you soon.

Best wishes ...

3 Write in the missing expressions below for formal and less formal letters. Find the missing expressions in Letter A (formal) and B (less formal).

Refer to previous letter:	Formal:	Further to your ...
	Less formal:	(1)
Apologise:	Formal:	I apologise ...
	Less formal:	(2)
Give good news:	Formal:	(3)
	Less formal:	He'd be happy ...
Make reference:	Formal:	(4)
	Less formal:	About ...
Recommending:	Formal:	I would strongly recommend ...
	Less formal:	(5)
Refer to future contact:	Formal:	(6)
	Less formal:	(7)
End the letter:	Formal:	(8)
	Less formal:	(9)

4 Here are some more formal and less formal words from letters. Match the two synonyms and decide which is usually more appropriate for a letter to a friend.

inform	verify	receive	request	want
↘ ask for		unavailable	help	check
tell	busy	assist	get	require

5 Now answer the exam question on page 12. Write an informal letter to Renate about where and how to travel in *your* country and describe *your* brother (if you don't have a brother, invent one!)

WRITING CHECKLIST

Letters

After you write, always check your work. Check the grammar, vocabulary, structure and layout. Another good way to check your work is to swap with a partner and comment on each other's writing. For your letter you could use this checklist to help you.

The letter ...	Yes (✓)	No (✗)
• begins and ends appropriately (*Dear ...*, *Best wishes*, ...).	☐	☐
• uses 120–150 words only.	☐	☐
• includes all the information in the handwritten notes.	☐	☐
• is written with the correct level of formality.	☐	☐
• uses paragraphs (at least three).	☐	☐

Review and Use of English

1 **WORD FORMATION** Use the word given in capitals at the end of some of the lines to form a word that fits in the gap in the same line.

A recent study has concluded that

(1) _____ to friends and solid **CLOSE**

(2) _____ may help you stay healthier **RELATION**

and live longer. (3) _____ already **PSYCHOLOGY**

knew that having good companions helps

mental well-being but this new data

says that a strong (4) _____ also **FRIEND**

extends life expectancy. The (5) _____ **RESEARCH**

were particularly surprised by their

(6) _____ because it was more true of **DISCOVER**

friends than family, perhaps because we

share (7) _____ problems or express **PERSON**

our likes and (8) _____ more **LIKE**

freely with friends. So, if you like the

idea of (9) _____ a few extra years, **LIVE**

why not ring your mates now or even

renew a few old (10) _____ who you **ACQUAINT**

haven't seen for a while.

2 **Read sentences 1–8 below. What is the relationship of the speaker to each person? Write the word.**

1 She's my mother's sister. _____

2 I'm related to her on my father's side. She's the daughter from my father's first marriage. _____

3 We aren't identical but she was born on the same day as me to the same mother. _____

4 That's the son of my brother and his wife. He's only three. _____

5 I was engaged to her at the time but it didn't work out. _____

6 That woman in the photograph was my father's mother but she isn't alive now. _____

7 Ben's the same age as me. He's my father's sister's son. _____

8 I'm very polite to my wife's mother but we've never really liked each other. _____

3 The word in brackets is missing from the sentence. Write it in the correct position. Look at the example.

Example:
            'd
I ⋀ like to have a coffee, please. ('d)

1 She looks just her mother. (like)

2 The two boys are playing tricks on the rest of the family. (always)

3 I never really got with my brother-in-law. He annoyed me. (on)

4 You've really let me this time by not doing what I asked. (down)

5 I'd say she's still her twenties. (in)

4 Rewrite the first sentence using the word in bold. Do not change the form of the word.

1 I'm writing about your letter.
   regard
   I'm writing _____ letter.

2 See you next week.
   forward
   I _____ you next week.

3 I think you should go to the sea.
   recommend
   I _____ to the sea.

4 The reason I'm writing is about your phone call.
   further
   _____ phone call, I am writing
   to …

5 Read the responses below to some of the questions on page 5. They each contain one mistake. Remember that it's easy to make mistakes when you are nervous! Correct each sentence. Look at the example.

Example:
          'm
I ⋀ from Greece.

1 I like play tennis at the weekend.

2 I must to learn English for my job.

3 Me and my friends often make parties.

4 My family; this are the most important people to me.

5 For my last holiday I go to America with my family.

6 I rather spend time with my friends.

7 My best friend is Suzanne. I spend a lot of time with him.

8 I love snowboarding and I can also skiing.

9 The English is spoken all over the world so it's very important.

2 Jobs and work

Getting started

1 Do you dream of being a celebrity? What would you be famous for? Acting, singing, or perhaps for having your own TV chat show?

2 If you can't be a celebrity yourself, you could work for one. Which of these jobs would suit you best?
- a bodyguard
- a butler or housekeeper
- a chauffeur (driver)

3 What personal qualities do you need to do this kind of work?

4 Imagine that your friend has seen the job advertisement below in the newspaper and has written this list of reasons to apply. Look at the list and write some disadvantages.

Wanted

Personal assistant to work with Hollywood celebrity. You

I'll be able to ...
- travel around the world
- borrow their clothes
- drive around in a limo
- have a luxury lifestyle
- mix with the rich and famous
- go to opening and gala nights

5 Work in pairs. One of you is applying for the job.
The other should try to convince him/her that it's a bad idea.
Example:
A: *I'll be able to travel the world.*
B: *Yes, but you'll be away from your friends and family too much.*

Use of English:
multiple-choice cloze

Multiple-choice cloze

PAPER 3, PART 1

In this part of the Use of English test, you read a text with 12 gaps and have to decide which answer (A, B, C or D) best fits each gap. The types of words missing from the text include: present/past participles, verbs, collocations, part of a fixed expression, linkers and conjunctions, adjectives, a part of a phrasal verb, and adverbs.

1 Read the first sentence from a text and the two answers with explanations.

Assistant to the stars

It stands to **(1)** _____ that a city like Los Angeles, which is home to the rich and famous, is also where you **(2)** _____ the Association of Celebrity Personal Assistants (ACPA).

1	A reason	B truth	C argument	D discussion
2	A look	B search	C find	D see

1 Answer A is correct. It's part of the expression:
it stands to reason

2 Answer C is correct. Answers A and B would need the preposition _for_ after them (_look for, search for_). D is wrong because you can't _see_ an association.

2 Now read the rest of the article and answer questions 3–12.

Celebrity personal assistants are a unique group among Hollywood professionals. **(3)** _____ the lawyers and agents who rub shoulders with the stars and **(4)** _____ millions, personal assistants (PAs) are not paid well. They typically earn about $56,000 a year which, **(5)** _____ their round-the-clock obligations, isn't much by Hollywood standards. As for the job description, it's also **(6)** _____ from glamorous. Responsibilities include **(7)** _____ laundry, fetching groceries and paying bills. So what's the attraction? One celebrity PA says,'I don't **(8)** _____ myself a vain or superficial person, but it would be **(9)** _____ to say that we all don't like being close to someone that's powerful.' But not everyone is qualified for the job. Rita Tateel teaches would-be assistants to the stars and begins her lessons with some **(10)** _____ truths: 'You must be in good health at all times, because you are **(11)** _____ a celebrity's life. If you get sick their life can't just stop. And you need to be flexible and able to **(12)** _____ in all kinds of hours. You have to be a can-do person. If there's one word that celebrities don't want to hear, that word is "no".'

3	A Despite	B Unlike	C However	D Similarly
4	A take	B make	C pay	D give
5	A being	B received	C given	D spend
6	A far	B just	C such	D still
7	A making	B doing	C having	D fixing
8	A think	B know	C describe	D consider
9	A lie	B honest	C wrong	D true
10	A such	B hard	C advice	D heavy
11	A running	B dealing	C getting	D working
12	A take	B adapt	C get	D put

Vocabulary: jobs and work

Suffixes
We often add suffixes to words for job titles.

1 Combine the words in A with the suffixes in B and make job titles. More than one suffix may be possible

A   **B**

(wait)	journal	teach	act		ee	or	ist	(ress)
music	assist	employ			er	ian	ant	

2 Make job titles from these words with a suffix:
conduct   manage   art   paint   write   electric

3 Can you think of any jobs which do not combine a suffix with an existing word?
Example: _doctor, cook_

4 **Work in pairs. Take turns to be Student A and B.**

Student A

Imagine you have one of the jobs from the the Vocabulary Spotlight on page 16. Answer Student B's questions but don't say what your job is.

Student B

Interview A about his/her job and guess the job. Don't ask what the job is. Ask these (or similar) questions:

• What's your typical day like?

• Do you require special skills for this job?

• Which parts of your job do you dislike?

• What benefits do you have in your job (e.g. health insurance, a company car)?

5 **Choose between the words in *italics* to complete these sentences.**

1 We read candidates' CVs and discuss which ones might be *convenient/suitable*. Then we invite them to come for an *interview/interrogation*.

2 Personal *qualities/qualifications* such as enthusiasm and motivation are just as important as formal *education/qualifications*.

3 This job *notice/advertisement* looks really interesting.

4 We have a (an) *overtime/flexitime* system at work. We all work 35 hours a week but can organise exactly when we work those hours.

5 The company *recruits/applies* six graduates on its management *employee/trainee* programme.

6 We were forced to *make her redundant/sack her* because she kept arriving late.

7 The Minister of Health was forced to hand in his *notice/resign* over the hospital scandal.

8 The *salary/wages* isn't great but there are *perks/pay rises* such as health insurance and other benefits.

6 **Write sentences with the words and phrases from exercise 5 that you didn't use.**

Phrasal verbs

7 **Complete the sentences by making phrasal verbs using the particles in the box. More than one may be possible.**

back	for	out	with	in	on	down	off

1 If you would like to apply for the job, simply fill _____ the online application form.

2 Petra deals _____ some of our most important clients and handles their accounts.

3 He is looking _____ staff. He always takes _____ extra staff during the holiday season.

4 I sent _____ my CV and a letter of application but they never wrote _____.

5 Terrible news ... the factory is laying _____ three hundred people; the jobs are going overseas.

6 They offered me the job but I turned it _____ when I found _____ the salary was too low.

Listening: talking about jobs

1 **⌂ 2.1 Listen to eight people talking about jobs. Which speakers (1–8) ...?**

1 say the name of their job

2 explain how they got the job

3 describe what the job involves

PAPER 4, PART 1

2 **⌂ 2.1 MULTIPLE CHOICE Listen again and choose the best answer (*A*, *B* or *C*).**

Speaker 1: How did she first find out about the job opportunity?
A through a friend
B from a job agency
C from a charity

Speaker 2: Why did he choose this kind of work?
A because his father did it
B because he likes working on farms
C because it was well paid

Speaker 3: Why did she get the job?
A because very few people want to work in advertising and marketing
B because she attended an interview
C because the interviewer was her old boss

Speaker 4: What is his main responsibility?
A attending meetings
B writing up the sports results
C reporting the local news

Speaker 5: What does she think about training?
A It's a waste of time.
B It's useful.
C It's more useful than learning on the job.

Speaker 6: What was her problem when she first started?
A Some staff didn't like her.
B She didn't have the right skills and abilities for the job.
C Some staff didn't believe she had the right skills and abilities.

Speaker 7: What does the employee want?
A a pay rise
B a company car
C overtime

Speaker 8: Where does the artist work?
A he doesn't say
B on TV
C from home

Reading: volunteer work

1 Discuss in pairs:

- What are the differences between the jobs in the pictures below?
- What type of person chooses these kinds of jobs?
- Which would you prefer to do?

2 **Read the text about an organisation with volunteers who work in different parts of the world, and the four case studies (A–D). Underline in the text the answers to these questions.**

1 What qualities does the organisation want to develop in people?

2 What qualifications do Felicia and Amira have?

3 What is Rebecca's previous work experience?

4 What skills and abilities did Holly improve?

EXAM SPOTLIGHT

Multiple matching

PAPER 1, PART 3

In this part of the reading test you read four short texts and choose one answer for each of the 15 questions. You might have to find specific information from the text or understand the opinion and attitude of the writer.

3 **The first four questions below have been answered for you. Read the Raleigh International text again and underline the words in each part which give the answer.**

Which person ...
1 read about Raleigh on the website? *Person D*
2 already had a career before joining Raleigh International? *Person B*
3 will begin university next year? *Person A*
4 didn't travel abroad for her gap year? *Person C*

4 **Now find the answers in the four texts for questions 5–15.**

Which person ...

5 has become more patriotic? _____

6 has children? _____

7 learned to understand other people's views? _____

8 was keen to do something she wasn't used to? _____

9 helped to teach people? _____

10 prefers people to possessions? _____

11 communicated between volunteers and local people? _____

12 was surprised that making meals for lots of people would be a useful skill?

13 helped to make a place for local children? _____

14 admits missing home? _____

15 made the most use of her previous experience? _____

5 **Imagine you are going to volunteer for Raleigh International. Make a list of your qualifications, work experience (paid or unpaid) and skills and abilities that are relevant. Tell your partner about them.**

WHAT IS RALEIGH INTERNATIONAL?

Raleigh International began in 1978 with the purpose of running youth projects from ships circumnavigating the globe. The aim was to develop self-confidence and leadership in young people, through their participation in adventure, scientific exploration and community service. What began as a short project grew into a permanent operation with volunteers of all ages coming from all over the world. Now read about the work of its volunteers.

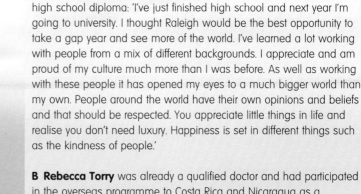

A Felicia Royaards, 19, from The Netherlands, joined a Raleigh International overseas programme to Costa Rica after finishing her high school diploma: 'I've just finished high school and next year I'm going to university. I thought Raleigh would be the best opportunity to take a gap year and see more of the world. I've learned a lot working with people from a mix of different backgrounds. I appreciate and am proud of my culture much more than I was before. As well as working with these people it has opened my eyes to a much bigger world than my own. People around the world have their own opinions and beliefs and that should be respected. You appreciate little things in life and realise you don't need luxury. Happiness is set in different things such as the kindness of people.'

B Rebecca Torry was already a qualified doctor and had participated in the overseas programme to Costa Rica and Nicaragua as a programme doctor: 'Having worked as a doctor in England for three years without a break, I decided to take three months out to do something different. Someone recommended Raleigh International's overseas programmes for my sons and in researching it I saw that Raleigh needed medics too and I thought "Why not me too?" As a medic, my responsibilities were broad, ranging from training both staff and programme participants in health, hygiene and first aid to providing on-site medical support. As a medic I relied heavily on the medical and telephone consultation skills from my experience as a doctor in England. More generally, my experience as a parent and teacher helped in working with the young people. An ability to cook for large numbers meanwhile proved unexpectedly valuable.'

C Amira Yahaya, 21, from Kuala Lumpur in Malaysia, took a break between completing her degree at university and finding work, to join a Raleigh programme in her own country: 'I heard about Raleigh International through my Careers Advisory Service at university. As a Malaysian, I wanted to find out more about different aspects of my country. I also wanted to see how I reacted when put in different, quite extreme, situations as well as playing different roles within a team of individuals. One of my jobs was to act as a go-between for the group and the local community, which improved my knowledge of translating and the different ways of life in my country. I also learnt the basic skills of working on a building site and one of my most enjoyable moments included seeing the kindergarten for a local village go up.'

D Holly Murphy, 20, Canadian, took a break after her studies to join a Raleigh overseas programme: 'I was looking for volunteer work abroad and came across Raleigh International on the Internet. I didn't really know what to expect, apart from the fact that it was likely to be hard work. I hoped the programme would give me a better understanding of my strengths and weaknesses and would give me the opportunity to develop my abilities to work in a team as well as improving my leadership skills. For the first few days I found life in the programme fairly difficult. We had to adjust to the accommodation, Malaysian culture, homesickness, fatigue and various other differences. My highlight was socialising with villagers. They gave me a skirt, made me a necklace and often gave us lunch. On a personal level I feel I have improved my communication skills, and find that I now listen to others more readily before speaking.'

Grammar: making comparisons

1 Work in pairs. Look at the two adverts below. Which job would you prefer? Why?

RECEPTIONIST WANTED

Enthusiastic, friendly person with excellent interpersonal skills required for agency for actors.
Duties include meeting and greeting visitors, answering calls and some general secretarial responsibilities.

- Salary: €30,000 per year
- Hours: 35 hours a week minimum (9 to 5)
- 25 days holiday per year
- Experience not necessary as full training provided
- Regular opportunities for overtime
- Company pension scheme available

PA (Personal Assistant) wanted
Experienced PA required to support busy actor. You need to be flexible and have experience in planning and organising, and be available to travel at any time – including at weekends. You will work a flexible 40-hour week with a basic salary of €45,000 with pension scheme and health insurance. Bonuses and overtime are also paid. 20 days holiday per year.

---

2 Read these sentences comparing the two jobs. Some contain incorrect information. Check the information in the job adverts and rewrite any incorrect sentences.

1 This receptionist is much better paid than the PA.
2 The receptionist's holidays aren't as long as the PA's.
3 The PA receives the best perks and benefits.
4 As PA, the harder you work, the more likely you are to receive a bonus.
5 The PA doesn't need as much work experience.

GRAMMAR SPOTLIGHT

3 Complete these rules using sentences 1–5 in exercise 2.

Rules for comparing

1 Add _____ or -est to a comparative or superlative form of a one-syllable adjective.
2 Use *more* or _____ with adjectives of more than two syllables.
3 Use _____ + adjective + _____ to show something is similar or equal to.
4 Use _____ before a superlative adjective.
5 With two comparatives we often use *the ..., the ...* .
6 Some adjectives/adverbs are irregular:
  good → _____ → best

➡ Grammar Reference (Section 5) page 168

---

4 🎧 2.2 Listen to two people discussing the jobs in the advertisements on the left. Write in the missing words in their conversation.

A: Anything in the paper today?
B: Nothing much. Though there are a couple of jobs that might interest you.
A: Well they (1) *can't be any worse than* the others I've seen.
B: This one is for thirty thousand a year which is (2) _____ your old job.
A: Well I used to do (3) _____ overtime so actually that isn't (4) _____ much.
B: Oh, it says here 'opportunities for overtime', so it's probably (5) _____ the same.
A: Yes. It sounds OK. What is it?
B: Receptionist and they provide training.
A: But my last job was (6) _____ responsible than that. And I know how to answer the phone and all that stuff.
B: All right. I'm just trying to help.
A: Sorry, but it's just that I don't want to do something that isn't (7) _____ skilled than what I was doing before.
B: Well here's one. 'Personal Assistant. Forty-five thousand', so it's easily (8) _____ your last job and you have plenty of experience in planning and organising. Oh, and you get to travel ...

5 The words in 1–8 in exercise 4 all modify the comparison. Write them in the three categories below:

Large difference: *very much, a great deal,* _____,
_____, _____,

Small difference: *a little, slightly, not quite as,*
_____, _____

No difference/equal: *no ... than,* _____,
_____

6 Work in pairs. Compare yourselves using the list below. You will need to find out the information below from each other.

- size of family
- when you both learnt to ride a bike
- your height
- number of holidays per year
- approximate distance walked per day

Now make comparisons using the information. Use words from exercise 5 to describe the size of the difference.
Example:
My family isn't quite as big as yours.

---

7 Write the missing words in this article. All the words are connected with making comparisons.

HELP WANTED!

Surveys show that more and (1) _____ young people plan to work a great (2) _____ longer than people have in the past. In fact, the majority expect to continue working beyond (3) _____ most typical retirement age of 65. The reasons are that most people's pension won't be worth as much (4) _____ it is now and we are living (5) _____ longer than ever before. Some companies are also looking for (6) _____ experienced employees, so a new recruitment website in America actually targets a (7) _____ older workforce. The boss of one company using the site commented: 'This sector of the workforce is a (8) _____ easier one to employ because they already understand the needs of business and they are often (9) _____ at jobs which require greater concentration (10) _____ their younger counterparts.'

Key word: *as*

1 Read the sentences (a–e) which contain the word *as* and match them to the meanings (1–5).

1 compares appearance _____
2 compares the present with the past _____
3 compares qualities _____
4 compares two actions at the same time _____
5 compares the past with the present _____

a He's as tall as me.
b I earned as much in my last job as I do now.
c She was arriving as I left.
d He's as happy now as he ever was.
e She doesn't sing as well as you do.

2 Work in pairs. Make sentences to compare:
- the past and the present.
- your appearance and qualities.

USEFUL EXPRESSIONS

- *X is (much) better than Y …*
- *This seems like a better idea than …/the best (idea)*
- *I don't think it's anything like as (good) as …*
- *It looks fairly similar to …*
- *How do you think it compares to …?*

Speaking: comparing

1 Work in pairs. A local countryside charity has a group of 12 volunteers aged 18–21 coming to spend a weekend in your village. Discuss and compare each of the ideas in the pictures below. Decide which would be the most useful project for your village.

build cycle paths around the village

build a children's playground in the park

create walking trails through the woods near the village

make a skateboard park

put up nesting boxes for some rare owls

Writing: a letter of application

1 A letter of application is quite formal. Match the formal phrases (1–8) to the less formal phrases (A–H).

1 I am writing to …
2 I have recently completed …
3 I am particularly keen on …
4 In addition to this, I have always been interested in other countries and cultures …
5 I would be grateful if you could …
6 and inform me how to apply …
7 I look forward to hearing from you …
8 Yours faithfully,

A I've just done …
B Just a quick note to …
C Please …
D Best wishes,
E and let me know what to do next.
F And I like travelling …
G Be in touch …
H I like …

2 Becky Raven has replied to the advert below for volunteers for the journey of a lifetime.

THE JOURNEY OF A LIFETIME

We are looking for young enthusiastic people to spend six months on voluntary projects in different parts of the world. Projects include environmental work to improve coasts, teaching children your language and building paths in national parks around the world. You will be a highly self-motivated and resourceful person with the desire to improve the world you live in.

Write for an information pack and tell us about:

- your current situation and interests;
- your personal qualities and reason for applying;
- any previous work experience (including voluntary work).

Read Becky's letter opposite. The grammar and vocabulary is correct but the letter could be much better. A teacher has written comments on it. Read the comments (in red) and rewrite the letter.

3 Now turn to the Writing Guide, page 199. Read the new version of Becky's letter. Compare it with your ideas.

4 You have seen the advert below. Write your reply in 120–180 words.

WORK ON A SUMMER CAMP IN THE USA

We are looking for young enthusiastic people to spend the summer working as volunteers on one of our many summer camps for children (aged between 8 and 16). You should be able to help organise team games and activities such as painting and pottery.

The camps are in over ten different states. You receive free accommodation and a salary. At the end of your six-week placement, you will also have time to travel around the USA.

Write for an information pack and tell us about yourself and why you would like to apply.

WRITING CHECKLIST

Letters

After you write, check your work. Check grammar and vocabulary, but also check the structure and layout. Swap your answers with a partner and use the checklist below to comment on each other's writing.

	Yes (✔)	No (✗)
• The letter contains at least three paragraphs.	☐	☐
• The first paragraph gives the reason for writing.	☐	☐
• The second paragraph tells the reader about you.	☐	☐
• The third paragraph asks for some action.	☐	☐
• The letter is written in an appropriate style.	☐	☐
• It includes the correct number of words.	☐	☐

(1) Are you sure it's a man who's reading this letter? What if it's a woman?

(2) Where did you see the information? In a newspaper advert? Say where you saw it.

(3) You have used the verb 'do' three times in this paragraph. Can you use some other verbs?

(5) Use paragraphs. The first paragraph in a formal letter of application will say why you are writing. The middle paragraphs will give more information about you and why you want to apply. The final paragraph requests some action.

(8) Maybe your parents should go and you should stay at home! This isn't a good enough reason.

(4) In formal writing, try not to use words like 'but' or 'and' at the beginning of a sentence.

(6) This is interesting and relevant. Can you give some more detail?

(7) Like in (6). Give some more detail.

(9) This sounds like an order. Can you be more polite?

(1)

Dear Sir,

(2)

I'm writing about 'The Journey of a Lifetime'
(3)
because I've just done my studies at school
(4)
and will go to University. But I don't want to

do my degree in Business Studies or start my

career yet so I'd like to do a gap year to have
(5)
a good time and see the world. I like mountain

biking and sailing. This year at school I was
(6)
involved in getting money for some local children
(7)
and I also worked on the school drama festival.

I enjoy meeting people and I want to do one of
(8)
your gap year projects because my parents think
(9)
it would be good for me. So send me your

information pack and tell me how to apply.

(10)
Thanks a lot.

Becky Raven

(10) This is very informal. We'd only use it in an email or a letter to a friend. What's a more formal way to end a letter?

Review and Use of English

1 Delete the odd one out in each group of words below.

> RECRUIT: hire, employ, resign, take on

> PAY: salary, wage, perk, income

> QUALIFICATION: degree, diploma, First Certificate, title

> QUALITIES: hard-working, determination, patience, designing

> SKILLS: giving notice, programming computers, translating, managing people

2 WORD FORMATION Use the word given in capitals at the end of some of the lines to form a word that fits the gap.

> VOLUNTEERS NEEDED FOR SUMMER WORK
>
> We are a volunteer (1) _____ and every   **ORGANISE**
>
> summer we offer 50 young (2) _____   **RECRUIT**
>
> the chance to join us in helping to provide
>
> holiday fun for many (3) _____ who   **CHILD**
>
> could not normally have a holiday.
>
> No specific (4) _____ are necessary. You   **QUALIFY**
>
> just need the (5) _____ to look after kids   **ABLE**
>
> and organise activities. Our (6) _____   **SELECT**
>
> procedure involves three stages. First, fill
>
> in our (7) _____ form online. Then we'll   **APPLY**
>
> invite you to an (8) _____ weekend   **ASSESS**
>
> where you work with others. If you are
>
> (9) _____ we'll finally ask you to provide   **SUCCESS**
>
> two (10) _____ from people who have   **REFER**
>
> known you well for more than two years.

3 Choose the correct word (in *italics*) in a-h.

a I'm interested *in/of/for* this job because I like working with people.

b Compared to me, my sister is much better *in/at/than* using computers.

c I would like to apply *by/on/for* the position of PA.

d I look forward *by/to/about* hearing from you.

e They're very keen *about/with/on* travel so a gap year is a good idea.

f She's responsible *for/of/to* checking the cars for problems.

g The successful candidate will deal *for/with/on* customers on a daily basis.

h If it doesn't improve, he'll probably give *up/over/on* the job.

4 MULTIPLE-CHOICE CLOZE Read the text below and decide which answer (*A*, *B*, *C* or *D*) best fits the gap.

Formula for career success

'Since the end of January I haven't eaten any chocolate,' Lisa Lilley says proudly. This isn't (1) _____ to her job as technology manager in Shell's Formula One team, but it tells us about how she works. Her team-mates, most of whom are men, challenged her to (2) _____ up chocolate and she has done it. This (3) _____ is partly responsible for Lilley's rise to a (4) _____ role with Ferrari.

The most exciting (5) _____ of the job is working at the races. Last year she attended her first one at Imola, the Italian track that hosts the San Marino Grand Prix, (6) _____ the famous red suit and ear defenders for the first time, an (7) _____ that left her nearly lost for words: 'It's an incredible feeling to be part of a phenomenal team.' Something she'd first seen as a career (8) _____ has become a passion. 'I became enthusiastic through work. I never had a big interest in it before, but now when I'm not at a race I watch it on TV.'

But what is it like working in such a male-dominated environment? 'I don't notice it,' she says. 'The Ferrari team have (9) _____ me feel so welcome. Because I have a technical role at the track it wouldn't matter whether I was male or female; you have to gain respect for (10) _____ good at your job.' Next year she will (11) _____ about 200 nights away from home with the team. 'At the moment, I'm loving it. The Ferrari team is like an extended (12) _____,' she says.

1	A connected	B part	C defined	D described
2	A put	B resign	C eat	D give
3	A food	B taste	C determination	D intelligence
4	A simple	B position	C crucial	D heavy
5	A way	B piece	C part	D quality
6	A changing	B wearing	C buying	D showing
7	A experience	B qualification	C application	D interest
8	A job	B chance	C opportunity	D position
9	A had	B did	C made	D were
10	A staying	B being	C applying	D wanting
11	A move	B work	C drive	D spend
12	A family	B partnership	C life	D interview

3 Sport and leisure

Getting started

1 Work in pairs or small groups. Look at the pictures below and match them with the sports and games in the box. Which is the most ancient one?

| croquet | beach volleyball | synchronised swimming | | wrestling | tug of war |
| chess | snowboarding | tenpin bowling | darts | archery | sailing |

Which ones do you think ...
- are Olympic sports?
- used to be Olympic sports, but no longer are?
- have never been Olympic sports?

2 Work in pairs. Choose one of the sports above which has never been an Olympic event. Think of three arguments that you could use to convince the Olympic committee to include it in the next Olympic Games. Tell the class.

→ Information File 3.2, page 230

USEFUL EXPRESSIONS

I think/I'd like to suggest that chess should become an Olympic sport.

It deserves to be an Olympic sport because ...

- To begin with/First of all it is very skilful/ beautiful to watch/exciting.

- Next ...

- Finally ...

Vocabulary: sport and pastimes

1 Look at the verbs and activities in the boxes. Decide which verbs go with which activities.

Verbs:
do   play   go

Activities:
bowling   tennis   sailing
karate   archery   golf

SPOTLIGHT ON VOCABULARY

Verb + noun collocations
Collocations are words that always go together to the exclusion of other words. Study these examples:
We **have** a good time.   NOT   We **do** a good time.

2 Make pairs of other verbs and activities from the ones in *Getting started* on page 25.

3 Choose the correct word (in *italics*) in sentences 1–14.
1 My favourite *play/game* is chess.
2 In my free time I like to play *violin/the violin*.
3 Model making is a marvellous *hobby/sport*. It helps me *pass/spend* the time.
4 Try to *hit/kick* the ball with your racquet.
5 We *scored/let in* a goal in the last minute and lost.
6 Kirsten keeps on *winning/beating* me at table tennis.
7 Don't play tennis when the *pitch/court* is wet.
8 Look at this lovely trophy Justine has *gained/won*.
9 I am a big *fan/spectator* of American football.
10 Hooligans attacked rival *supporters/pitches*.
11 Chess, mahjong and backgammon are three complicated board *pastimes/games*.
12 Beckham used to play *for/against* Manchester United, but then he moved to Real Madrid.
13 We were *lost/beaten* in the semi-finals.
14 It is time for you to *practise/practice* your service.

4 Read 1–5 below. Fill in the gaps with words from the box.

bat	chess	pitch	darts	court	shuttlecock
ball	puck	field	foot	soccer	backgammon
racket	tennis	badminton			

1 You need a net or a goal: _____, _____, _____

2 You play on these: _____, _____, _____

3 You need a board: _____, _____, _____

4 You hit the ball with these: _____, _____, _____

5 You hit these: _____, _____, _____

Listening: free time

Multiple matching

PAPER 4, PART 3
In this part of the listening test, you listen to five people talking about a similar topic. You have to decide who says what, by matching each speaker to a prompt. Often the answer isn't directly stated; instead you have to arrive at the meaning by putting together different parts of what you've heard. Study the example in exercises 1 and 2 below.

1 In exercise 3 you are going to listen to five people talking about sport and leisure. Before you listen, read the prompts (A–F) below.
Which speaker …?
A gives examples of unsporting behaviour _____
B is doing something his/her parents wouldn't approve of _____
C achieved an ambition _____
D underestimated the difficulties he/she would face _____
E used to play extreme sports _____
F sometimes does charity work _____

2 Now read what Speaker One said. Notice the highlighted words and the notes. Which sentence, A–F in exercise 1, best describes what the speaker said?

Speaker One: 'Well, when I was a kid my hobby was collecting football stickers. You know, for the World Cup, or the League – you put them in an album and try and get all the players for all the teams. They sell them in packets – you've got half a dozen stickers in each one. There were always three or four I could never find. One year, there was just one player I needed – Roberto Carlos, that's right. Well in the end I got him by swapping fifteen of my spare stickers for just one of him – but it was worth it. I completed the whole album for the first and last time. Now and again, I look at it and feel the same pride.'

speaker introduces the topic

a regular problem

the challenge he faced

achievement

feeling of pride and satisfaction

Roberto Carlos Brazil

Key word: *time*

1 Complete the sentences by joining a beginning (1–6) with an ending (a–f).

1 The meeting was a complete *waste of time*;

2 Thanks for inviting me; ...

3 How do you spend ...

4 We see Marina *from time to time*; ...

5 Nowadays it's so quiet but ...

6 I'll never forget *the first time* I used chopsticks;

a your *free time*?

b *once upon a time* this was the busiest port in the country.

c I made a complete fool of myself, dropping food all over the table!

d we talked for three hours but nothing was decided.

e I had a really *good time*.

f maybe once at New Year and twice during the summer.

2 Continue the second sentence so that it has a similar meaning to the one above it. In each sentence, use a phrase which includes the word *time*.

1 I had never been bowling before.

It was the _____ had ever been bowling.

2 To be honest I didn't learn anything from the experience.

The whole experience was an absolute _____.

3 Now and again we go to the theatre.

We go to the theatre from _____.

4 Our local team used to be in the first division, but not any more!

Once _____ our team was in the first division.

5 What sort of things do you do when you're not working or studying?

How do you _____?

6 I really enjoyed myself a lot last Saturday.

I had a _____ last Saturday.

3 Work in groups. Tell each other ...

• when something you did was a total waste of time.

• about the very first time you did a sport or leisure activity.

• about something you do or a place you go to from time to time.

• what life in your country/region was like once upon a time.

• about what you do in your free time (in the evenings or at weekends).

3 ∩ **3.1** MULTIPLE MATCHING Listen to five speakers and decide who says what by matching them (1–5) with sentences A–F in exercise 1. There is an extra sentence you do not need.

4 Work in pairs. Turn to Tapescript 3.1 on page 208 and underline the clues and vital information which helped you to identify the speaker.

5 Think of a sport or activity you have played. Write a short speech about it. Give your speech. The class should guess what you are talking about.

Reading: eccentric sports

1 Quickly read through the text and find the names of the sports or activities shown in the photographs.

2 Choose from the sentences (A–H) the one which fits each gap (1–7). (Use the words in blue and red to help you.) There is one extra sentence which you do not need to use.

A Finland hosts one event in which success depends on creativity rather than strength.

B So the 'wife' can be one's own, or a neighbour's, or from even further away.

C We aren't likely to see them in the Olympics just yet.

D Some competitors have wanted to throw their own, but that's against the rules.

E For example, the wife carrying competition has its roots buried deep in an old local tradition – the 19th century practice of wife stealing.

F This obviously doesn't please the local Finns, who have been wife-carrying for centuries.

G These finalists must perform a compulsory one-minute song as well as a song of their own choice.

H Contests in, for instance, wife carrying, swamp soccer, and endurance sauna sitting attract hundreds of competitors every year from around the globe.

ECCENTRIC SPORTS

In the past decade or so, Finland has become host for a number of unusual sporting competitions. (1) __H__ In many of these events, the winner – or winners – will be crowned as world champions.

Common to most of these pursuits is their origins in Finnish folk heritage. (2) ____ Intelligence or social skills are not required for success but power, stamina, and courage are vital. What, then, are these strange sports? Here are a few of the most popular ones.

The Wife Carrying World Championships have been held in the small town of Sonkajärvi, central Finland, since 1992. The winners are the couple who complete the course in the shortest time. To make it more difficult, two dry and two metre-deep water obstacles have been added. Competition rules also state that men can choose any woman over the age of 16 to be their partner for the event. (3) ____ The competition is usually dominated by Estonian pairs. (4) ____

Finland, being the home of Nokia, is the obvious place to organise the Mobile Phone Throwing World Championships. This year, a record 3,000 spectators watched the competition in Savonlinna, eastern Finland. The mobile phones used in the competition are provided by the organisers and fitted with batteries. (5) ____ And the prize for the longest throw? A new mobile phone.

(6) ____ For the past decade, the northern Finnish town of Oulu has gathered imaginary guitar heroes to the annual Air Guitar World Championships. In recent years, more than 15 nationalities have been represented in this light-hearted competition. ('Air guitar' is the art of pretending to play along to a rock solo with nothing but an imaginary guitar and the fitting facial expressions.) Most contestants are national champions sent to Oulu by their local air guitar associations. (7) ____ Judges are looking for originality, technique, stage charisma, artistic impression and, obviously, 'airness'.

Overall, even though the Finns are sometimes described as being reserved, no nation taking itself too seriously could come up with these amazing sports!

Grammar: obligation and necessity

→ Grammar Reference (Section 11) page 176

1 Complete the sentences by joining a beginning (1–7), with an ending (a–g).

1 You really *must* watch tonight's final ... _____
2 Jason *has to* make sure the players are fit as ... _____
3 I *must* buy some tickets for the match ... _____
4 Players *mustn't* deliberately commit fouls ... _____
5 You *don't have to/needn't* programme the DVD as I've ... _____
6 Fans *aren't supposed to* take drinks into the stadium ...

_____
7 You*'d better* finish your homework quickly ... _____

a already set it up.
b if you want to watch the match later.
c he is the team's trainer.
d or insult each other on the pitch.
e because it's going to be the best for years!
f but a lot of people do.
g otherwise there won't be any left.

2 Which of the forms in *italics* in exercise 1 is used to ...?

say something is absolutely forbidden _____
talk about a rule which may not be respected _____
say that something isn't necessary _____
give a threat _____
give an order to yourself _____
describe a responsibility which is part of someone's job _____
makes a strong recommendation _____

3 Put sentences 1–3 below into the past simple and the future simple tenses.

1 She *has to* sell tickets. _____
2 We *must* post that letter. _____
3 You *don't have to* come. _____

→ Grammar Reference (Section 12) page 178

4 Study *a* and *b* below and complete rules 1 and 2 by choosing between *needn't have done*, or *didn't need to*.

a *I didn't need to* buy any equipment, so I didn't/but I did anyway.
b *I needn't have bought* any equipment. I wish I had known it wasn't necessary.

1 We use '_____' **both** for when we did OR didn't do something which was necessary.
2 We use '_____' **only** for situations where we did something we later discover wasn't necessary.

5 What would you say in these two situations?

1 You took your own lunch but lunch was provided.
2 You didn't have to wear running shoes, so you didn't.

6 ∩ 3.2 Listen to situations 1–5 and respond using expressions of obligation and necessity from exercise 1.

7 Work in groups. Study the rules of air guitar.

• Which things are absolutely compulsory?
• What are the things you have to/don't have to do?
• What isn't permitted?

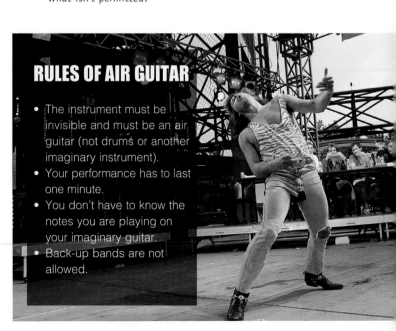

RULES OF AIR GUITAR

• The instrument must be invisible and must be an air guitar (not drums or another imaginary instrument).
• Your performance has to last one minute.
• You don't have to know the notes you are playing on your imaginary guitar.
• Back-up bands are not allowed.

Listening: the early history of football

1 Discuss. Which of these football quotations do you agree or disagree with? Do you think that players, managers and fans can care too much about winning?

> 'Some people think football is a matter of life and death ... I can assure them it is much more serious than that.' *Bill Shankly, Liverpool, Football club manager*

> 'Football? It's the beautiful game.' *Brazilian footballer, Pele*

2 🎧 3.3 Jessica Sawyer is an expert on the early history of football. She is being interviewed by Marcus Hanks. Listen to part A and answer questions 1–7 by choosing between answers A and B.

1 According to Jessica ...
  A football has had an uninterrupted history.
  B the Ancient Egyptians used their feet to play with balls.
2 The Chinese played ...
  A with a rubber ball.
  B with a ball filled with feathers.
3 The Chinese game ...
  A had a military purpose.
  B was simply for pleasure.
4 What was tlatchi like?
  A Tlatchi was a mixture of other sports.
  B Tlatchi was similar to the football we play today.
5 Tlatchi was played ...
  A on an outside court.
  B in front of an exclusive audience.
6 When a player put the ball in the basket ...
  A the teams changed ends.
  B the game automatically ended.
7 Sometimes in tlatchi, the losing team ...
  A could be executed.
  B became slaves.

Sentence completion

PAPER 4, PART 2

In this part of the Listening test, you listen to a conversation or talk and complete some notes you are given.

3 🎧 3.4 Listen to part B on the history of football, and correct a candidate's answer:

> People played different kinds of football across Europe during **(1)** *The Medium Ages*.
> Jessica tells us that the Anglo-Saxon version of football was called kicking **(2)** *the Anglo's Head*.
> The Italians developed a version of the game they called **(3)** *calcia*.
> Jessica says that two big differences between the Italian and English game were that the Italians wore beautiful costumes and played in proper **(4)** *groups* whereas in England **(5)** *no one* could join in because whole villages used to take part!

Follow these steps:
- Exploit the title, *The Early History of Football*, to predict what will be said.
- Try to guess what kind of information is missing in the gaps.

Remember:
- No marks will be given for wrong or incomplete answers.
- When a word is spelt out, you must write it correctly.

4 🎧 3.5 **SENTENCE COMPLETION Now listen to part C and complete the notes below.**

> The English game ended when someone kicked the ball **(6)** _____ of the other team's captain.
> Jessica says sometimes there wasn't a winner because people were tired or it **(7)** _____ to continue. Some kings of England and the Lord Mayor of London **(8)** _____ football. The kings wanted people to do their **(9)** _____ instead.
> Jessica thinks that football is just an excuse for bad behaviour; in Ancient Rome there were **(10)** _____ hooligans who often killed each other!

Speaking: expressing ability

➜ Grammar Reference (Section 11) page 176

1 Study sentences a and b below and answer questions 1 and 2.

   a She *could run/was able to run* for miles when she was young.

   b After weeks of practice she *was able to* complete the routine.

   1 Which refers to general abilities in the past? _____

   2 Which describes a specific occasion when she achieved something difficult? _____

2 Read the sentences below. Tick (✓) where we can use both *was able to* and *could* to complete these sentences.

   1 We're in luck! I *could/was able to* get some tickets for the final. _____

   2 They *could/were able to* pass the ball for ages without letting it fall to the ground. _____

   3 I looked everywhere for my racket but I *couldn't/wasn't able to* find it. _____

   4 I was delighted when finally I *could/was able to* stand up on my skis. _____

3 These two sentences are similar in meaning but what is the difference in their grammar?

   1 We managed to score a goal.

   2 We succeeded in scoring a goal.

4 Work in groups. Tell the others in your group about a time when you succeeded at something that was difficult, using some of the expressions from the list below. Think about:

- a sporting achievement
- an academic success
- learning a new and difficult skill

> **USEFUL EXPRESSIONS**
>
> - *I'll never forget/I'll always remember the time/when I learned to ski …*
> - *That reminds me of the time when I first learned how to …*
> - *At first I couldn't/wasn't able to …*
> - *In the end/Finally I managed to (do)/succeed in (doing) …*

Use of English: key word transformations

Key word transformations

PAPER 3, PART 4

In this part of the Use of English test, you have to rephrase sentences using a key word for each sentence. You can only use between **two** and **five** words, including the key word. Study the two examples and the explanations which follow:

Example 1
Fans shouldn't take food into the stadium.
supposed (*the key word*)
Fans **aren't supposed to take** food into the stadium.
Explanation:
Supposed to is similar to *should* and is used passively.

Example 2
Every so often we go to a premier league match.
to (*the key word*)
From **time to time** we go to a premier league match.
Explanation:
Every so often means *occasionally*. *From time* **to time** means *every so often*.

1 KEY WORD TRANSFORMATIONS Complete the second sentence so that it has a similar meaning to the first sentence. Do not change the word given. Use between two and five words including the word given.

   1 I took my football boots but it wasn't necessary.
     taken
     I _____ my football boots.

   2 If I were you, I'd take a waterproof jacket.
     had
     You _____ take a waterproof jacket.

   3 In his free time Wayne builds model planes.
     spends
     Wayne _____ model planes.

   4 Smoking is prohibited in this building.
     supposed
     You _____ in here.

   5 Rita knows how to walk on her hands.
     at
     Rita _____ on her hands.

   6 I found snowboarding too difficult.
     able
     I _____ to snowboard.

Speaking: comparing photographs

EXAM SPOTLIGHT

Individual 'long turn'

PAPER 5, PART 2

In this part of the Speaking test, you have to describe and contrast a pair of photographs for about one minute ('having an individual long turn'). It's very important to listen carefully to the interlocutor's questions.

1 🎧 **3.6 Listen to the interlocutor's instructions. What does she ask Kasia to do? Turn to Tapescript 3.6 on page 209 to check.**

2 🎧 **3.7 Now listen to Kasia's answer. How well does she answer the interlocutor's question?**

3 🎧 **3.7 Listen again to Kasia as she describes the photographs to the interlocutor, and complete these sentences.**

1 ... they are _____ you can see at a festival or a children's party ...

2 ... there's a _____ wall, the _____ you put air in ...

3 ... he has a suit with that sticky _____, maybe.

4 It is like that Japanese sport, the one _____ play.

4 **How does Kasia describe and explain the following ...?**
- an inflatable wall
- Velcro®
- the Japanese sport of sumo

5 **Work in pairs. Turn to Information File 3.1 on page 228 and talk about these new photographs in a similar way. Take it in turns to be the interlocutor (asking the questions) and the candidate (speaking for about one minute).**

Writing: a review

1 **Discuss. Do you like attending public events with large crowds? Look at the photographs. Have you ever been to large public events like these?**

2 Read these sentences from different reviews. Is the adjective correct (✓) or incorrect (✗)? Decide and then make any necessary corrections to the incorrect ones. Look at the example in number 1.

Example: *interesting*

1 We had a really ~~interested~~ night out (✗)
2 The crowds were so exciting – they couldn't stop cheering and shouting. ( )
3 Dinner was very enjoyed. You should have come with us. ( )
4 I find most TV very boring. Only the news is worth watching. ( )
5 My taste in food is quite various. I tend to try most things. ( )
6 We saw this fascinating film about the life of penguins at the cinema. ( )
7 The clowns were very fun. They made us laugh! ( )
8 I liked the show but my friend wasn't impressed. ( )

3 Choose four adjectives from the box and describe the two public events opposite in exercise 1.

Example:
The circus came to our town and the clowns were really funny.

funny	physical	interesting	loud	colourful
exciting	attractive	atmospheric	fantastic	huge
varied	complicated	well-designed	important	exotic

4 Read extracts from three reviews. Complete each extract with a suitable word from the box above. There may be more than one possibility.

(A)

If you missed Captain Big Top's circus visit last week to our town, you missed the most (1) _____ event of the year – possibly of the decade! The day began with a (2) _____ parade down the high street. The clowns came first and pulled people out of the crowd to join the celebrations – they were really (3) _____! Then came the circus leader called Captain Big Top, followed by all sorts of performers in (4) _____ costumes from around the world.

(B)

It was the first time I'd ever seen this type of sport so it was really (1) _____ to read about the game and find out the rules before I went. I don't think I would have understood otherwise because it's fairly (2) _____. The players are (3) _____ and when they play it's a very (4) _____ game. I'm amazed they don't get hurt more. Even if you don't like sport, American football is still very (5) _____ with all the singing and the cheerleaders dancing.

(C)

I couldn't believe how (1) _____ it was. There were some enormous speakers and you could hear all the way at the back of the stadium. The good thing was that you could see the band from anywhere because the stage was so (2) _____. I was surprised because they didn't just play all their recent hits. The songs were fairly (3) _____ with some from their early years. Anyway, they did three encores and then ended with my favourite song so it was a (4) _____ night!

PAPER 2, PART 2

5 You recently saw this notice for readers of an English-language magazine called *Leisure and Travel*. Read the notice then write a review of between 120 and 180 words. Use the checklist below to help you.

Reviews needed!

What are the most popular sporting or cultural events in your country? Write a review (of approximately 180 words) of an event you have been to and explain why tourists may be interested in it.

Include information on what the event was, how popular it was and why you would recommend it to visitors to your country.

The best reviews will be published in our next issue and receive a cheque for 50 euros.

WRITING CHECKLIST

Review
After you write, check your work. Check grammar and vocabulary, but also check the structure and layout.
For a review you could use this checklist to help you.

The review tells us ...	(✓)
• what the event is.	☐
• what the reaction of the audience was (and why).	☐
• why you would recommend it to tourists.	☐
• The review contains at least three paragraphs.	☐
• It includes a variety of adjectives.	☐
• It includes no less than 120 and no more than 180 words.	☐

➜ Writing Guide, page 201

33

Review and Use of English

1 WORD FORMATION Read this information. Use the word given in capitals at the end of some of the lines to form a word that fits in each gap.

Nowadays in schools there is a worrying trend against playing **(1)** _____ games. Teachers worry that such activities encourage an unpleasant **(2)** _____ between children, and make some kids feel **(3)** _____ and humiliated. Personally, I believe that a need to compete is a strong instinct, just look at the number of willing **(4)** _____ who want to demonstrate their **(5)** _____ on quiz shows, or even talent **(6)** _____ . What's more, most of us aren't **(7)** _____ at everything so the **(8)** _____ and the approval we receive can strengthen rather than damage **(9)** _____ . Learning how to lose or to face up to **(10)** _____ is as important as winning. Finally, why should teachers feel that they have the right to deny children the **(11)** _____ of being the best? An educational system which fails to encourage **(12)** _____ eventually creates a nation of losers.

COMPETE

RIVAL

USE

CONTEST

INTELLIGENT

COMPETE

HOPE

RECOGNISE

FRIEND

DIFFICULT

SATISFY

WIN

EXAM SPOTLIGHT

Open cloze

PAPER 3, PART 2

In this part of the Use of English test, don't try to fill in the gaps immediately. Read the passage all the way through for general meaning without focusing on the gaps.

Remember: This exercise mostly tests small grammatical words such as auxiliaries, articles, prepositions, particles or stems of phrasal verbs, pronouns etc.

2 OPEN CLOZE Read the text below and think of a word which best fits each gap.

Football means something different according to where you find yourself. For Europeans and Latin Americans it means the fast moving team game otherwise **(1)** _____ as soccer. For North Americans it is the clash **(2)** _____ large muscular men encased in protective gear. American football's closest equivalent is probably rugby **(3)** _____ there are important differences like being able to charge and block players who don't have the ball. **(4)** _____ said this, the game of soccer has now really taken off in the US where children play it as a **(5)** _____ brutal alternative to American football. 'Soccer moms' spend their time transporting **(6)** _____ precious offspring to matches where they watch anxiously in **(7)** _____ junior is injured. Soccer is also played by women **(8)** _____ professional league has its own galaxy of stars. This may explain **(9)** _____ most American males regard American football a more manly activity. There is **(10)** _____ truth in this. When soccer players are tackled they will dive, or roll around on the ground in pain like little children only to get **(11)** _____ just a few seconds later as though nothing has happened! When someone doesn't get up in American football it is usually **(12)** _____ they have been hurt quite seriously.

4 Nature and animals

Getting started

1 Work in pairs. Answer the questionnaire.

QUESTIONNAIRE

Why, oh why?

1 Why do cows lie down when it is going to rain?
   A so they won't get struck by lightning
   B to keep the grass beneath them dry
   C because rain makes them too heavy to stand

2 Why do some dogs chase their tails?
   A because they need exercise
   B to please their owners
   C because they are crazy

3 A bird in a cage hits its mirror with its head …
   A because it's fighting the bird in the mirror
   B because it is saying 'hello' to itself
   C to be friendly

4 What does it mean when a cat waves its tail gently from side to side?
   A it is about to jump
   B it is in a good mood
   C it has seen something which interests it

5 Why do bees come together in the spring?
   A to form another colony
   B to make honey
   C for protection

2 Share your answers with the rest of the class. What is the most popular explanation for each question?

3 Work in groups. Think of some other 'Why, oh why?' questions and share them with the rest of the class. See if anyone knows the answers.

Vocabulary: animals

1 Complete sentences 1–7 with words from the box.

pet	endangered	train	breed	tame
instinct	extinction	wild	prey	habitat

1 The Siberian tiger is a/an _____ species. It faces _____ within the next twenty years.

2 Some animals, such as pandas, are notoriously difficult to _____ in captivity.

3 Rachel has been asking for a/an _____ rabbit for ages but where could we keep it?

4 Human beings depend on reason more than _____.

5 It is better to study _____ animals in their natural _____ rather than in zoos.

6 You can _____ birds of _____ to do some amazing things.

7 Even though it looks _____, it could attack you without warning.

SPOTLIGHT ON VOCABULARY

Adjectives + prepositions

Adjective + preposition collocations are common in English and may be tested in the Use of English paper.

Example: *There's no need to be afraid **of/by/from** scorpions; their sting is less dangerous than we think.*

2 Match the adjectives in list A with prepositions from list B below.

A keen	aware	famous	allergic	fed up	interested
B to	on	in	with	of	for

3 Complete sentences 1–6 with an adjective + preposition collocation from exercise 1 above.

1 I wasn't _____ the time so I missed my riding lesson.

2 I'm really _____ our new dog; it keeps digging up the garden.

3 Australia is _____ its koalas and kangaroos.

4 Lucy has been _____ wildlife programmes since she was small.

5 I keep sneezing; I must be _____ the cat.

6 No, I don't want to hold him; I'm not very _____ snakes, I'm afraid.

Listening: animals and humans

PAPER 4, PART 3

1 🎧 **4.1 MULTIPLE MATCHING You will hear five speakers talking about animals and wildlife. Choose from the list (A–F) what each one is talking about. Use the letters only once. There is one extra letter you don't need to use.**

Which speaker talks about …?

A insects and problem-solving

B a particularly greedy pet

C the death of a pet

D the eating habits of an insect

E a badly behaved pet

F the beginning of an allergy

Speaker _____
Speaker _____
Speaker _____
Speaker _____
Speaker _____

2 🎧 **4.1 Work in pairs. Listen again and discuss these questions for each speaker.**

Speaker 1

1a How did the speaker feel about the circus?

1b What was he looking forward to most?

1c What were his symptoms?

Speaker 2

2a How long have scorpions existed?

2b Where can't we find them?

2c Where do they live?

2d How do they prepare their food?

Speaker 3

3a How does the speaker feel about guinea pigs?

3b What agreement did he make with his children and how well was it respected?

3c What happened when the first guinea pig died?

Speaker 4

4a Who gives the orders in an ant colony?

4b How successful are ants?

4c How has their behaviour inspired scientists?

Speaker 5

5a How many owners did the cat in the story have?

5b How did the owners find out that they shared Sid with other people?

5c Did Sid deserve his nickname?

Grammar: the grammar of phrasal verbs

1 Study sentences a–d below. Which phrasal verb in bold means …?

1 find/discover, often by chance _____

2 die _____

3 wait with excitement, anticipate with pleasure _____

4 disappoint _____

a I went into the garage and noticed one of them had **passed away**.

b They didn't want to **let** me **down** so they came over after dinner.

c You can even **come across** them between the bark of trees.

d I had really been **looking forward to** it.

2 Look again at sentences a–d in exercise 1. Which sentence …?

1 has a pronoun between the verb and its particle _____ (separable)

2 consists of three parts followed by a pronoun _____ (three part)

3 has a phrasal verb with no object _____ (intransitive)

4 has a pronoun after the second part of the phrasal verb _____ (transitive inseparable)

→ Grammar Reference (Section 12.3) page 180

3 Turn to Tapescript 4.1 on page 210 and look at the phrasal verbs in **bold**. Match the definitions in the table below to some of the phrasal verbs.

	Phrasal verb	Definition	Type
1		survive	
2		discover information after looking for it	
3		invent/have the idea for something	
4		endure/suffer an unpleasant experience	
5		perform/complete	
6		become extinct	
7		finish	
8		trick/deceive	
9		consider something as inferior	
10		be careful	

4 In pairs, decide which type each phrasal verb in the table above is.

5 Work in pairs. Study situations 1–8 below. Create comments using the phrasal verbs from the previous exercises.

Example:

Situation: You took a car to be repaired. At the garage they couldn't fix it because they didn't have the spare part that was needed.

Comment: *I'm really fed up. I took my car to the garage to be fixed but they couldn't carry out the repairs because they didn't have the spare part that the car needs.*

Situations and comments:

1 You've discovered an old painting in your attic, which used to belong to your grandmother.
You'll never guess what I (you continue) …………

2 You're really excited that your friend from Australia is coming to visit you.
I'm so glad that my friend is coming to visit us. I'm really (you continue) …………

3 A snobbish person you know thinks his new neighbour is inferior because he doesn't have an expensive sports car.
You really shouldn't (you continue) …………

4 A classmate promised to bring you back a grammar book you lent him. You are disappointed that he didn't do what he promised.
You forgot my book again? I needed it to do my homework this evening. You have really (you continue) …………

5 Your friend is back from her holiday. You tell her that unfortunately her favourite plant died while you were looking after it.
I'm afraid I've got some bad news to tell you. Your (you continue) …………

6 You and your friends gave money to someone who said she was collecting for a children's charity. You discover that the woman tricked you.
You remember we all gave money for children in Africa? Well, I'm afraid we (you continue) …………

7 You have been thinking of a theme for an end of term party. Tell everyone in your class your fantastic idea.
I've been thinking about the end of term party and I think I've (you continue) …………

8 You want to make people aware that global warming is melting the polar ice caps and polar bears may soon become extinct. What do you tell people?
Did you know that if we don't do anything about global warming (you continue) …………

Reading: a dog's life

1 Read what it says on the car sticker. What does it tell us about the driver? Do you know anyone who would say the same thing?

PAPER 1, PART 3

2 MULTIPLE MATCHING You are going to read a magazine article about four different pet dogs and their owners. For questions 1–15 below, choose from Lola (*L*), Burnie (*B*), Dolce (*D*), and Nancy (*N*).

Which dog …?

1 sleeps in a bed fit for a princess __*L*__

2 spends its time between two owners _____

3 is well-known _____

4 suffered from poor health _____

5 has an independent social life _____

6 has a perfume named after it _____

7 is a baby substitute _____

8 has a good relationship with its chauffeur _____

Whose owner(s) …?

9 didn't want it to travel with the luggage _____

10 would put future boyfriends in second place _____

11 recognises other people's disapproval _____

12 has a stepchild _____

13 has changed career through having a dog _____

14 likes to add extras to her pet's outfits _____

15 modified their home to make their pet's life easier _____

3 Discuss. Is it right to 'humanise' pets?

EXAM SPOTLIGHT

PAPER 1, PART 3

Read the texts all the way through for a general understanding. Read very carefully so you know what to look out for.

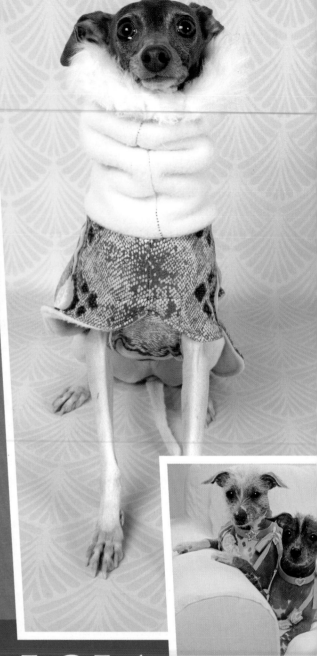

LOLA

Lola is the number one priority in my life. Her wardrobe alone is worth £20,000. Her clothes range from summery T-shirts to winter coats trimmed with fake fur. If she comes to a party with me, her nails are painted pink. The finishing touch is her perfume which I had made for her by a chemist. It's called *Lola Love* and costs £8 a bottle. Her bed, which is next to mine, is a £2000 four poster dog bed but she is also welcome into mine. She has special steps to climb up and her own cashmere blanket and pillow. Until two years ago it had never crossed my mind to get a dog but as soon as I saw Lola it was love at first sight. Within six months of having her, I gave up my £50,000 a year City job to open my own dog boutique and parlour called *Diva Dogs*. I am single at the moment but prospective boyfriends know that Lola comes first.

BURNIE

The doorbell rings and I finish putting Burnie into one of his favourite outfits. Then with a final brush of his hair he is ready for his lift to the office. Burnie travels by taxi with his favourite driver, Anthony, because they get on so well. He has the latest dog wardrobe from *Tabitha and Angus*, a speciality dog clothing retailer. He was quite ill as a puppy, and rather thin, so he needed clothes to keep warm. Richard and I bought Burnie two and a half years ago. I used to work for Richard and we were always telling him that he ought to have a dog – but he said that because he travels so much he couldn't look after a dog full-time. So we came up with the idea of a dog share. Burnie spends most weeks with Richard and I have him at weekends.

DOLCE

My husband and I would be lost without Dolce. She sleeps on a tiny pink bed between Rhys and I at night. She has beds in nearly every room of our flat and a huge heart-shaped cushion by the French windows. Rhys has a 13-year-old daughter from his previous marriage, Danielle, whom we both adore, but for the moment Dolce is our baby. The most we have ever spent directly on Dolce was our holiday to Florida last year. We flew first class so she could sit with us. Her ticket cost us around £500 but I couldn't bear to think of her sitting in the hold. I buy all her outfits from *Pet London*. She has around 60 outfits, all kept in her own wardrobe. She comes everywhere with me. When we went skiing in Val d'Isère she came too with her ski jackets. She hates wooden floors because they make her slide around, so we recently paid £5000 for the apartment to be carpeted.

NANCY

Nancy wants for nothing. She has her own perfume, *Canine*. Her most expensive item of clothing is a sheepskin jacket that cost £120. People may think that it's cruel to dress a dog in clothes, but Nancy adores it. Her wardrobe must be worth £1000. Some of my friends think I'm mad, but a lot think it's great fun. I love to accessorise her outfits and she has become rather famous. People come to our greengrocer's just to see what she is wearing. She is a very sociable dog and she happily goes to parties without me. People hold dog parties in places like Hyde Park, where all the dogs dress up and eat dog cakes. Nancy has a best friend, a dog called Missy Elliott, and they go off together or to see friends in the pub.

Listening: points of view

1 🎧 4.2 MULTIPLE MATCHING Three friends are discussing the reading text about dogs. Listen and decide who says what. Write *T* for Terry, *C* for Charlotte or *R* for Rebecca after each of the statements.
Who ...?

1 thinks that the dogs look lovely _____
2 thinks that it's crazy to spend so much on them _____
3 talks about hungry children _____
4 mentions the homeless _____
5 thinks it is immoral to spend money in this way _____
6 talks about the needs of the animals _____
7 supports the right of the owners to choose _____

2 🎧 4.2 Listen again. Look at the table below and tick (✓) the expressions that you hear.

Expressions	tick
Giving opinions I think/believe ... (that) As I see it ... From my point of view ... In my opinion ... As far as I'm concerned ...	
Agreeing and disagreeing I (quite/totally) agree ... Absolutely ...	
Giving someone else's point of view Marcus says ... Antonia thinks ...	
Disagreeing Yes, but ... I don't/can't agree ... I (completely/totally) disagree ...	
Acknowledging what the other person says I hear/understand what you're saying but ... I understand/respect your point of view but ... I see your point but ... I suppose (Terry) is right. That's true but ...	

3 Work in pairs. Brainstorm any other expressions you could add to the list in the table.

4 Work in groups. Discuss the following statements. Try to use as many expressions for giving opinions and agreeing and disagreeing as you can.
1 Zoos and circuses should be banned.
2 Animals should have the same legal rights as humans.
3 It is natural for people to be vegetarians.
4 We should never use fur and leather.
5 Experiments on animals are never justified.

Use of English: word formation

Word formation

PAPER 3, PART 3

In this part of the Use of English test, you transform a word to fit the context within a sentence. You must change the part of speech of the word in capitals.

Follow these **four steps**:

1 Read the text without concentrating on the gaps and make sure you understand the story.
2 Identify the part of speech of each word in capitals.
3 Decide into which part of speech you need to transform the word in capitals.
4 Finally, build the necessary word.

1 **Study the example below where the correct new word *has already been inserted into the text*, and read the explanations which follow.**

People may be able to have a close ¹**relationship** with large animals but be afraid of a tiny spider! On country walks we are ²**terrified** in case we see a snake. Yet, apart from a few ³**exceptions**, they present little real danger. European spiders are shy and ⁴**harmless** creatures so our fears are ⁵**imaginary**.	**RELATION** **TERRIFY** **EXCEPT** **HARM** **IMAGINE**

1 RELATION (personal noun) = *relationship* (concept noun). Use the noun suffix *-ship*. The gap comes after the adjective *close*, so we know we need a noun.
2 TERRIFY (verb) = *terrified* (participial adjective). We need to follow *to be* with an adjective. We have a choice of two participial adjectives: *terrifying* or *terrified*.
3 EXCEPT (verb) = *exception* (noun). *Few* comes before nouns. We make the noun by adding *-ion* to the verb.
4 HARM (noun/verb) = *harmless* (adjective). *-less* is a suffix meaning *without*. We need an adjective to describe the noun *creatures*.
5 IMAGINE (verb) = *imaginary* (adjective).

2 **Read the rest of the example and decide what the original word in capitals was.**

Sometimes our fears can become a ⁶**reality**. For most of us a wasp sting is an ⁷**unpleasant** experience. It is ⁸**painful** for a few minutes but then it is over. However, when a friend was stung by a wasp she had an ⁹**extremely** severe reaction which almost killed her. So even a simple sting can prove ¹⁰**deadly** to some people.

3 **Read the text below without concentrating on the gaps and, in pairs, explain the story in a few words.**

Chef Paul Stevens was in the kitchen of the restaurant where he worked when he was bitten on the hand by a giant spider. His first **(1)** _____ was to take its picture on his mobile to show his friends. However, when he started to feel ill he was taken to hospital. The doctors were **(2)** _____ in making a diagnosis and sent him home. When Paul felt worse he was rushed back to hospital. **(3)** _____ he still had his mobile with the photograph. This time doctors sent it to Bristol zoo where they identified his **(4)** _____ as a Brazilian Wandering Spider – one of the world's most **(5)** _____ arachnids. Its venom can kill 225 mice. In humans it can provoke an **(6)** _____ heartbeat and high blood pressure. In some instances it can even result in **(7)** _____. Happily, since the **(8)** _____ of an antidote nobody has died. At first nobody could explain the arachnid's **(9)** _____ in an English restaurant. Then they realised there was nothing **(10)** _____ about it – it had almost certainly hidden away in a box of bananas.

4 **Now follow the steps in the Exam Spotlight to fill in the table below.**

Word in CAPITALS	Part of speech of the word in CAPITALS	Part of speech of the new word	New word needed
1 REACT	*verb*	*noun*	*reaction*
2 SUCCESS			
3 LUCKY			
4 ATTACK			
5 POISON			
6 REGULAR			
7 DIE			
8 INVENT			
9 APPEAR			
10 MYSTERY			

Speaking: comparing photographs

1 🎧 4.3 Listen to the examiner's instructions about part 2 of the Speaking test. Write down exactly what the examiner says he wants the candidate to do with the photographs.

2 You are going to listen to a candidate called Beate talking about the photographs. Before you listen, in pairs, list the similarities and differences between the photos.

3 🎧 4.4 Listen and tick which points from your list Beate mentions. Does she say anything you forgot to say?

4 🎧 4.5 Now listen to the question the examiner asked Walter. How well do you think he answered it?

PAPER 5, PART 2

5 Work in pairs. Look at the photographs on page 229 and talk about them using some of the expressions in the Exam Spotlight above. Take it in turns to be the interlocutor (asking the questions) and the candidate (speaking for about one minute).

Key word: *look*

1 Complete these sentences from Listening 4.4, with *look*, or an expression which uses *look*.

1 In the photo on the left, there is a man … it _____ a policeman … (It's not very clear.)

2 … the dogs _____ tired.

3 It _____ they are going to be in a race …

2 Where necessary, correct these sentences.
1 The dog looks like a German Shepherd.
2 The dog looks like tired.
3 It looks as though it is going to bite.
4 It looks as like they are going to stop.
5 The photographs look as if similar.

3 Discuss. What words and forms follow *look* in exercises 1 and 2?

Phrasal verbs

4 Complete the sentences with a phrasal verb based on *look*. All of these verbs appear somewhere in this unit.

1 I can't find my keys. Can you help me look _____ them?

2 Looking _____ someone else's pet is always a big responsibility.

3 The police are looking _____ the problem posed by dangerous dogs.

4 I'm really looking _____ reading her new book about horses. Her last one was fascinating.

5 We shouldn't look _____ on people who live in smaller homes than *we* do. It's wrong.

Listening: almost human

1 **Discuss.** Many people believe that their pets behave in ways which are almost human. In groups, talk about any animals you know of which display almost human behaviour.

PAPER 4, PART 2

2 🎧 **4.6 SENTENCE COMPLETION** You will hear part A of an interview with Professor Helena Murray, an expert on animal behaviour. Complete the notes below.

Humans are mammals but there are three things which separate us from most other animals in our group:
(1) _____, (2) _____ (can think logically), and our capacity (3) _____.
Animals don't 'think'; instead they are governed by their (4) _____. We know if an animal recognises itself through the (5) _____ test. Chimpanzees can recognise their reflection as well as (6) _____.
During an experiment at a zoo in (7) _____ three elephants showed they recognised their reflections. They put (8) _____ their mouths! One of the elephants, called (9) _____, actually removed a mark from her face. However, people who believe that cats and dogs are self-aware are (10) _____.

PAPER 4, PART 4

3 🎧 **4.7 MULTIPLE CHOICE** Listen to part B of the interview and choose the best answer (*A, B* or *C*).

1 Dogs form such close relationships with humans because they
   A think like humans.
   B are pack animals.
   C can tell what humans feel.

2 How good are dogs at reading human expressions?
   A They're not as good as chimpanzees.
   B They're better than our closest relatives.
   C They're worse than dolphins.

3 What happens with the cup test?
   A chimpanzees simply guess
   B chimps and dogs have similar success rates
   C dogs get it right most of the time

4 What, according to Professor Murray, is the principal reason for this ability to read expressions?
   A a combination of human company and evolution
   B it is an instinct possessed by canines
   C any dog can quickly acquire this skill

5 Which dogs can read human expressions?
   A dogs raised from puppies, by humans
   B wolves
   C those with a history of domestication

6 What is special about the New Guinea singing dog?
   A It had never been tamed.
   B It had once lived alongside humans.
   C It had never been used in a scientific experiment.

7 The singing dogs experiment demonstrated that the ability to read human expressions
   A could easily be reactivated.
   B was passed from generation to generation.
   C could be lost.

Grammar: countable and uncountable determiners

1 **Choose between the words (in *italics*) in sentences 1–10.**
   1 The elephants did *several/all* surprising things.
   2 *All/every* mammals look after their young.
   3 *No/Many* change in behaviour was noted between the two groups.
   4 There is *few/little* difference between humans and other mammals.
   5 Almost *any/all* dog can perform this task.
   6 A great *number/deal* of time has been spent on researching it.
   7 How *much/many* importance does evolution have in this?
   8 Hardly *any/many* creatures display any kind of self-awareness.
   9 There are *a number/an amount* of key differences.
   10 A great *amount/number* of ink has been used.

➡ Grammar Reference (Section 7) page 171

Writing: an email

Giving advice

1 Jordan and Ashley are friends. Jordan has asked Ashley for some advice. Quickly read the exchange of emails on this page. Who are ...?
- Miranda
- Rick
- Auntie Jane

2 Ashley has received the email below from her friend, Jordan, which she has printed out and made some notes on. Write her reply, including the points she has made in the notes.

Dear Ashley,

I need some advice! Miranda and Rick keep asking for a pet. They won't be satisfied with a bird or a hamster in a cage any more. They want a *real* pet like a cat or a dog. Rick has even said he wants a horse! *what an idea!*

I suppose I have less excuse than other parents because I work from home but, even so, who would take care of a pet when I travel (which is about once a month at the moment)? *are they really?*

They're jealous of the other kids in their class: they say they've have got exciting pets and that it is unfair that they don't. The other problem is that my mother-in-law is allergic to long-haired cats so she would complain even more than usual if we had something which made her sneeze a lot. She's also scared of dogs. *maybe she'll come less often!!!*

Anyway, what would you do if you were me? I'm getting so bored and fed up with their demands.

Jordan

---

3 Read Ashley's reply to Jordan's email and complete it using words and introductory phrases from the box.

face it ...	as far as ...
believe ...	anyway ...
as for ...	basically ...
or else ...	obviously ...
first ...	I were you ...

Hi Jordan,

I remember when Daisy wanted a puppy. In the end we compromised with a rabbit. At **(1)** _____ she was delighted, but she soon lost interest. Let's **(2)** _____, rabbits don't do very much, do they? **(3)** _____, a horse is out of the question!

(4) _____, I think you should do one of two things. Either you should put up with them asking you for a pet and just not take any notice (after all, I am sure that not every child in their class has a pet). **(5)** _____, you could admit defeat and get a dog or cat. If **(6)** _____, I wouldn't go for a rabbit or guinea-pig as someone has to clean out their cages. **(7)** _____ me, that someone will be you!

And **(8)** _____ your mother-in-law being allergic, perhaps having a cat or dog might stop her from coming so often!!! **(9)** _____, hope this helps, although **(10)** _____ I'm concerned pets are nothing but trouble!
Ashley

4 Work in pairs. List the expressions used to ...
1 ask for and give advice.
2 consider and balance different options.

PAPER 2, PART 1

5 Read an email from Miranda (Jordan's daughter) to Auntie Jane about the pet problem, and plan a response. Write the reply.

Hi Auntie Jane,

I'm writing for your advice. Rick and I would really love a dog or a cat. Rick asked for a horse because he thought that way Mum would agree to a cat. Isn't that stupid!

You told us that when you were younger Granny and Grandpa were against you and Mum having a pet too. What happened in the end? How did you persuade them? How can we persuade Mum and Dad?

Love,

Miranda

WRITING CHECKLIST

Did you ...?
- write between 120 and 150 words ☐
- answer all the questions in Miranda's letter ☐
- include introductory phrases and expressions for this type of letter ☐

➔ Writing Guide, page 199-200

Review and Use of English

1 MULTIPLE-CHOICE CLOZE Read the text below and decide which answer (*A, B* or *C*) best fits each gap. Remember, in the exam you will have four words to choose from.

An eight-year-old peacock called Mr P has fallen in love with a row of red and white pumps at a petrol station. **(1)** _____ to a bird expert, peacocks are keen **(2)** _____ colourful objects and always return to the same place. A great **(3)** _____ of people come to fill up just to see him; however, **(4)** _____ local residents have complained because of the awful noise he makes. His owner says the sound made by the pumps is **(5)** _____ to that made by female birds looking **(6)** _____ a mate. Mr P and his two brothers were raised from eggs. All three are called Mr P because you can **(7)** _____ tell them apart. During the mating season Mr P **(8)** _____ up to 18 hours day by the pumps. Sometimes he is even away for a **(9)** _____ nights. His brothers, on the other hand, remain for **(10)** _____ of the mating season in their owner's garden where they are fascinated by **(11)** _____ bright object **(12)** _____ orange balls and kittens!

1	A For	B Further	C According
2	A on	B of	C by
3	A lot	B amount	C number
4	A several	B few	C all
5	A same	B similar	C almost
6	A forward to	B for	C into
7	A hardly	B nearly	C almost
8	A takes	B spends	C lasts
9	A few	B couple	C many
10	A nearly	B most	C every
11	A any	B no	C none
12	A such	B like	C as

2 KEY WORD TRANSFORMATIONS Complete the second sentence so that it has a similar meaning to the first sentence, using the word given. Do not change the word given. You must use between two and five words, including the word given.

1 I can't wait to see Martha again.

forward

I'm really _____ Martha again.

2 What do you think I should do?

were

What would _____ me?

3 Could you look after Rex while I'm away?

care

Could you _____ Rex while I'm away?

4 In my opinion cats make better companions than dogs.

am

As far _____ cats make better pets than dogs.

5 Human beings and chimpanzees aren't very different.

between

There is very _____ human beings and chimpanzees.

6 Look at that tree, it's going to fall.

as

That tree _____ it's going to fall.

7 We were quite disappointed that almost nobody came to the talk.

hardly

It was quite a _____ came to the talk.

8 Malcolm has had a good idea for a costume.

up

Malcolm has _____ a good idea for a costume.

3 Harriet has emailed her friend Josh for some advice about pets. Write his reply by replacing the words in bold with words and expressions from the box.

otherwise	anyway	basically	if I were you
as far as I'm concerned		all things considered	

(1) In your position I'd get a pedigree puppy; **(2) if not**, you could get an older dog from a refuge. There are practical considerations. **(3) The essential point is** who will look after it while you're at work? That's why **(4) in my opinion** cats are much less trouble than dogs. **(5) Taking everything into account** I'd go for a cat. **(6) That's all I've got to say**, the final decision is yours.

5 A good story

MAIN MENU

Vocabulary:	books and film; key word: *thing*
Grammar:	verbs of manner; narrative tenses
Speaking:	tense
Reading:	*The bangle*
Listening:	*Great adaptations*
Writing:	a short story

EXAM MENU

Reading:	multiple choice
Writing:	a story
Use of English:	multiple-choice cloze; open cloze
Listening:	multiple choice; sentence completion
Speaking:	two-way conversation

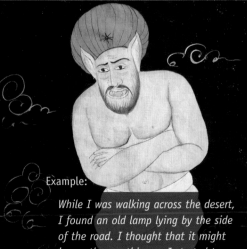

Example:

While I was walking across the desert, I found an old lamp lying by the side of the road. I thought that it might be worth something so I started to clean it. All of a sudden there was a flash and an enormous man came out of it!

Answer: Aladdin

Getting started

1 **Work in pairs or teams. Look at the pictures and try to identify the characters and the stories they come from. Then check your answers on Information File 5.1 on page 230.**

2 🎧 **5.1 Listen and match the speakers (1–4) with the characters.**

Speaker 1: _____ Speaker 3: _____
Speaker 2: _____ Speaker 4: _____

3 **Which of the stories in the pictures have you ...?**
- read as a children's story
- read in the original version
- seen on TV or at the cinema

4 **Work in groups. Think of two characters from fiction and write a paragraph about how they might describe themselves. When you are ready, read them out and see if the other groups can guess who you have described.**

45

Vocabulary: books and films

1. Work in groups. Brainstorm different types of books and literature (e.g. horror). Think of some books which have been turned into films (e.g. *Frankenstein*).

2. Complete sentences 1–14 with the words from the box. Make any changes necessary.

scene	narrator	scenery	series
chapter	fiction	villain	location
episode	classic	serial	heroine
set	character	plot	script
novel	mythology	playwright	novelist

1. My favourite TV _____ is *24*.

2. Shakespeare is England's most famous _____ and poet, and Dickens is probably England's best-known _____.

3. When they made a _____ of *Oliver Twist*, it was divided into eight one-hour _____.

4. *Vanity Fair* is considered a _____ work of English literature, but like many books at that time it was serialised for magazines. Writers had to produce several _____ each week

5. In addition to the hero and _____ there are lots of minor _____ who make an appearance.

6. This book has got one of the most complicated _____ I've ever come across. It's hard to work out who is who and what's happening!

7. The story was clever but the _____ was poor – some of the dialogues were terrible.

8. The _____, or storyteller, has an important role in this book.

9. The most moving _____ in the film is when Esther meets her mother for the first time.

10. The film was shot on _____ in Kenya; the _____ is absolutely amazing.

11. I don't like the version of *Romeo and Juliet* which was _____ in Miami.

12. Generally I prefer fact to _____ but I also love a good historical _____.

13. In the legend of *Robin Hood*, the _____, or 'bad guy' is the Sheriff of Nottingham.

14. One of my teachers used to read us Greek _____ which I really enjoyed.

3. Work in groups. Find out …
   - each other's favourite books and films.
   - the kinds of books and films the others in the group dislike and why.

Set book

PAPER 2, PART 2 (QUESTION 5)

In this part of the writing test, you have the opportunity to answer a question about one of the set books you have studied. **This is an optional question.**

Listening: great adaptations

Multiple choice

PAPER 4, PART 4

Between each part of the listening test there is a pause which gives you time to check your answers and to prepare for the next part of the test.

Reading all the questions beforehand will give you clues about what you are going to hear.

1. You will hear an interview with a scriptwriter who adapts books for TV and the cinema. What questions do you think the interviewer will ask? What do you think the scriptwriter will say?

3 ○ **5.3 SENTENCE COMPLETION** In Part B, Jacinta and Lorolei discuss some of the differences between literature and films, and the film adaptation of *Vanity Fair*. For questions 1–10, complete the sentences.

Jacinta thinks that sometimes film and cinema are better than the written word because film can be
(1) _____ in terms of time.
Sometimes descriptions in books can go on for
(2) _____. A lot depends on the filmmaker's correct choice of **(3)** _____.
For Jacinta, the main problem with film is that it cannot replace the **(4)** _____. Jacinta says it is possible to use **(5)** _____ from the page to tell the story but you can't do this with the narrator unless you use lots of **(6)** _____. *Vanity Fair* tells the story of Becky Sharpe and her desire to
(7) _____. Becky is a terrible person. In the book the narrator observes and comments on what's
(8) _____. Jacinta admits that
the film looked **(9)** _____
because of the fabulous scenes
and the breathtaking costumes.
However, the overall effect was
that the film was empty because
the **(10)** _____
was missing.

Key word: *thing*

1 The expressions in italics (1–6 below) are from the interview in the Listening section above. Look at Tapescript 5.2 on page 212. Match the expressions to their meaning (a–f).

1 *one thing led to another* _____
2 The director *made a really big thing of* the big formal dances _____
3 *All things considered* I'd rather adapt a classic ... for the small screen. _____
4 *I've got a thing for* Colin Firth, the actor who played the hero. _____
5 If you want to do *your own thing*, that's fine, but ... _____
6 Well, *the other thing of course is that* ... _____

a I have strong feelings for
b do what you want, how you want
c emphasised
d we shouldn't forget
e having taken everything into account
f one opportunity created another

2 ○ **5.2 MULTIPLE CHOICE** Listen to the interview with a scriptwriter who adapts books for TV and the cinema.
Listen to Part A. For questions 1–7, choose the best answers (A, B or C).

1 How did Jacinta become a specialist in adapting books for the cinema?
   A She realised she would never be a successful writer.
   B It happened by chance.
   C It had always been her ambition.
2 What does she need to know before she begins an adaptation?
   A which parts of the book she can cut
   B the medium and type of story
   C the audience she is writing for
3 Why does she prefer working on TV serials?
   A because it's less stressful
   B there are fewer problems with the budget
   C the adaptation can be more complete
4 According to Jacinta, what do people expect when they go to the cinema?
   A a gripping story
   B visual excitement
   C well-known stars
5 What does she think of the ballroom scenes in the big screen version of *Pride and Prejudice*?
   A They take time away from other parts of the story.
   B At times the attention to detail is poor.
   C People will enjoy them just as much if they watch them at home on TV.
6 Why does Jacinta prefer the TV version of *Pride and Prejudice*?
   A It pays particular attention to the ballroom scenes.
   B She likes the actor who played the hero.
   C It is old-fashioned.
7 How does Jacinta feel about changing the original story of the book she's adapting?
   A It gives adapters the chance to show their creativity.
   B She will do it if it improves the plot.
   C She's against changing the story.

Reading: the bangle

1 Novelist Alexander McCall Smith has written a series of charming stories set in modern-day Botswana. The main character, and heroine, of his books is Precious Ramotswe, a private detective and founder of the *No. 1 Ladies Detective Agency*. Read the extract opposite. Discuss which of the following titles would be the best choice for this extract, or think of a more suitable title of your own:

- *How to catch a thief*
- *The last honest woman*
- *A quiet cup of tea*

2 Work in pairs. Choose the correct answer (*A, B, C* or *D*) to questions 1–6, and say why the other options are wrong. Question 1 has been done as an example.

1 The woman in the market ...
   A was an ordinary shopper. *(wrong – she was a thief)*
   B knew someone was watching her. *(wrong – she had no idea Mma had seen her)*
   C wanted to buy some sunglasses. *(wrong – a trader tried to get her to buy some)*
   D distracted the stall keeper. *(correct – she pointed to something at the back of the stall so that the trader would have to turn around. In other words, she distracted him)*

2 What was Mma Ramotswe's reaction to what she had seen?
   A It contradicted her views on human nature.
   B She was quietly amused by it.
   C She thought the trader should be more careful.
   D She was shocked and prepared to act.

3 How did the woman behave after she had taken the bangle?
   A She argued noisily with the trader.
   B She returned to the previous stall.
   C She chatted to the trader about his wares.
   D The woman coolly moved away.

4 What did the waitress think when she saw Mma Ramotswe leave?
   A that she was a silly and forgetful woman
   B that Mma Ramotswe was trying to stop a crime from being committed
   C that she was just another dishonest customer
   D that she would return in a couple of minutes

5 How did Mma Ramotswe feel when the waitress stopped her?
   A that anyone can make a mistake
   B that she had done a terrible thing
   C that the waitress had made a reasonable assumption
   D robbed of the power of speech

6 After hearing Mma Ramotswe's explanation the waitress ...
   A blackmailed her.
   B realised an honest mistake had been made.
   C laughed out loud.
   D called the police.

7 While the waitress went for the bill, Mma Ramotswe ...
   A tried to discover who had seen the incident.
   B gave her side of the story to the woman next to her.
   C decided what to do next.
   D felt angry and humiliated.

8 The woman at the nearby table ...
   A disapproved of Mma Ramotswe's behaviour.
   B pretended not to notice what had happened.
   C wasn't that honest herself.
   D thought Mma Ramotswe was innocent of the crime.

3 Work in groups. Occasionally people are wrongly accused of doing something dishonest. Can you think of a time when this happened to you or to someone you know? What happened and what were the consequences?

Mma Ramotswe raised her tea cup to her lips and looked over the brim. At the edge of the car park, immediately in front of the café, a small market had been set up, with traders' stalls and trays of colourful goods. She watched as a man attempted to persuade a customer to buy a pair of sunglasses. The woman tried on several pairs, but was not satisfied and moved on to the next stall. There she pointed to a small piece of silver jewellery, a bangle, and the trader, a short man wearing a wide-brimmed felt hat, passed it across to her to try on. Mma Ramotswe watched as the woman held out her wrist to be admired by the trader who nodded encouragement. But the woman seemed not to agree with his verdict, and handed the bangle back, pointing to another item at the back of the stall. And at that moment, while the trader turned round to stretch for whatever it was she had singled out, the woman quickly slipped another bangle into the pocket of the jacket she was wearing.

Mma Ramotswe gasped. This time she could not sit back and allow a crime to be committed before her very eyes. If people did nothing, then no wonder that things were getting worse. So she stood up, and began to walk firmly towards the stall where the woman had now engaged the trader in earnest discussion about the merits of the merchandise which he was showing her.

"Excuse me. Mma."

The voice came from behind her, and Mma Ramotswe turned round to see who had addressed her. It was the waitress, a young woman whom Mma Ramotswe had not seen at the café before.

"Yes, Mma, what is it?"

The waitress pointed an accusing finger at her. "You cannot

run away like that," she said. "I saw you. You're trying to go away without paying the bill. I saw you."

For a moment Mma Ramotswe was unable to speak. The accusation was a terrible one, and so unwarranted. Of course she had not been trying to get away without paying the bill – she would never do such a thing: all she was doing was trying to stop a crime being committed before her eyes.

She recovered sufficiently to reply. "I am not trying to go away, Mma," she said. "I am just trying to stop that person over there from stealing from that man. Then I would have come back to pay."

The waitress smiled knowingly. "They all find some excuse," she said. "Every day there are some people like you. They come and eat our food and then they run away and hide. You people are all the same."

Mma Ramotswa looked over toward the stall. The woman had begun to walk away, presumably with the bangle still firmly in her pocket. It would now be too late to do anything

about it, and all because of this silly young woman who had misunderstood what she was doing.

She went back to the table and sat down. "Bring me the bill," she said. "I will pay it straightaway."

The waitress stared at her. "I will bring you the bill," she said, "but I shall have to add something for myself. I will have to add this if you do not want me to call the police and tell them about how you tried to run away."

As the waitress went off to fetch the bill, Mma Ramotswe glanced around her to see if people at the neighbouring tables had witnessed the scene. At the table next to hers, a woman sat with her two children, who were sipping with great pleasure at large milkshakes. The woman smiled at Mma Ramotswe, and turned her attention back to the children. She had not seen anything, thought Mma Ramotswe, but then the woman leaned across the table and addressed a remark to her.

"Bad luck, Mma," she said. "They are too quick in this place. It is easier to run away at the hotels."

Vocabulary: verbs of manner

Verbs of manner

We can bring a story to life by using verbs which describe more precisely how something was done.

1 **Find these verbs in the text on page 49 and decide which of the definitions (*a* or *b*) is best.**

1 *gasp*: (a) to breathe in with surprise (b) to make a disapproving noise

2 *stare*: (a) a short quick look (b) a long fixed look

3 *glance*: (a) a long look into the distance (b) a quick sideways look

4 *sip*: (a) to drink greedily in large mouthfuls (b) to drink slowly, appreciating each drop

2 **Read sentences 1–10 below and study the verbs they contain. Which verbs give a more precise meaning for …?**

a ways of looking: _____

b ways of drinking: _____

c a way of breathing: _____

d ways of walking/moving: _____

e ways of laughing: _____

1 He *sighed* with disappointment when he saw his examination results.

2 When they reached the top of the hill they *gasped*, and *gazed* in wonder at the valley below them.

3 Stop *slurping* your coffee. People are *staring* at us!

4 Those girls get on my nerves. They just sit at the back and *giggle* at stupid jokes.

5 They *staggered* towards the van carrying the heavy box between them.

6 We were so thirsty that we *gulped* down a whole bottle of water each.

7 The librarian *glared* at the children who were making too much noise.

8 We took our time and *strolled* along the beach in the warm sunshine, throwing stones into the waves.

9 Maurice heard the boys *sniggering* nastily when he fell over on the icy road.

10 After the match the losing team *limped* in pain back to the changing room.

3 **Look again at the sentences in exercise 2. Create a short definition for each of the verbs.**

Example: ***snigger:*** *to laugh in an unpleasant and unkind way at someone who looks foolish or who has hurt themselves*

4 **Work in pairs. Take it in turns to mime the different verbs. Be as dramatic as you like! Your partner must guess which verb you are miming.**

Grammar: narrative tenses

1 **Study this extract from the reading text and underline examples of:**

a the simple past.

b the past continuous.

c the past perfect.

> As the waitress went off to fetch the bill, Mma Ramotswe glanced around her to see if people at the neighbouring tables had witnessed the scene. At the table next to hers, a woman sat with her two children, who were sipping with great pleasure at large milkshakes. The woman smiled at Mma Ramotswe, and turned her attention back to the children. She had not seen anything, thought Mma Ramotswe, but then the woman leaned across the table and addressed a remark to her.

2 **In the extract above which tense is used to …?**

1 describe a single or sequence of completed actions _____

2 describe an action in progress _____

3 talk about an action further back in the past: 'past in the past' _____

➡ Grammar Reference (Section 12) page 178

3 **We use a form of the continuous to set the scene, or describe something which is or was in progress.**

Study sentences 1–4 below, which are based around the text on page 49. Underline examples of the past continuous and circle examples of the past perfect continuous.

1 She stole the bangle while the trader was searching through his wares.

2 The waitress challenged Mma just as she was leaving the café.

3 Mma Ramotswe realised that the kids' mother had been following everything.

4 It was a typically busy market day. People were looking at the stalls, traders were selling their goods and Mma Ramotswe was waiting for her tea to arrive.

4 **Which sentence from 1–4 …?**

a sets the scene and gives the background for the story _____

b describes a single completed action which happened while something else was going on _____

c describes an action which started further back in the past, which was still in progress later on _____

d an action which prevented an even earlier action from continuing/being completed _____

5 Work in pairs. Complete part one of the story below by choosing between the different narrative tenses you are given in *italics*. Discuss your answers.

Olivier and Isabelle **(1)** *were going/had been going* out ever since they **(2)** *were meeting/met* at university two years earlier. Olivier **(3)** *felt/was feeling* it was time to ask her to marry him so he **(4)** *bought/was buying* an engagement ring. He **(5)** *had been/was* determined to make a romantic proposal so he **(6)** *had prepared/was preparing* a delicious picnic in a surprise location. Driving his dad's Land Rover, Olivier **(7)** *was picking up/picked up* Isabelle who **(8)** *had waited/was waiting* impatiently outside her house. After **(9)** they *had driven/drove* for an hour Olivier **(10)** *was making/made* her cover her eyes with a scarf until they **(11)** *had been reaching/had reached* their final destination. Olivier **(12)** *had been driving/had driven* directly onto the sand! Boats **(13)** *had sailed/were sailing* across the bay as seagulls **(14)** *had dived/dived* beneath the waves. It **(15)** *had been/was* simply perfect!

6 Continue the story with a suitable narrative tense.

They **(16)** .... (eat) the picnic that Olivier **(17)** .... (prepare) and **(18)** .... (drink) champagne. He **(19)** .... (give) her the ring when he **(20)** .... (notice) his bride-to-be **(21)** .... (already fall asleep). He **(22)** .... (yawn) sleepily too. Olivier **(23)** .... (have) a wonderful dream when he **(24)** .... (be woken) by Isabelle's scream. While they **(25)** .... (have) their nap the tide **(26)** .... (come in) and now the sea **(27)** .... (surround) them.

7 Work in pairs or small groups. Create an end to the story, using a range of narrative tenses. Look at the pictures on the right to give you ideas. Try to make at least eight more sentences. Imagine how ...
- they were rescued from the sea.
- Isabelle felt about Olivier afterwards.
- his father reacted when he saw the state of the car.

Speaking: tenses

1 Choose one of the adjectives in the Grammar Spotlight on page 53, and tell the class about an occasion when you felt this way. Make sure you use the correct tenses throughout your speech.

Writing : a short story

1 In the First Certificate writing test, there may be a question which asks you to write a story which begins or ends with some words you are given. Read this story which ends with the words *I have never been so embarrassed in my life* and find things which are wrong with the picture.

*On the occasion of the marriage
of our daughter, Sharon, to
Mr Hugo Ellery,
we have pleasure in inviting you to a wedding reception
at the Bayswater Hotel
from 15:30 on August 27th.*

Formal evening dress

*RSVP   Scott and Julia Thomas   28 Abbotstone Road,
London E4*

When I was in my twenties, my boss, Mr Thomas, invited me to his daughter's wedding reception. I was so delighted that I went out and bought a fabulous Italian beige suit. Afterwards, I found a matching beige shirt and a black tie in an expensive shop in Bond Street – I was determined to make a good impression. On the big day, I turned up at the smart London hotel where the reception was being held. I glanced admiringly at myself in the hotel's mirrors – I looked gorgeous.

However, the second after I had stepped into the reception I couldn't stop myself from gasping in horror. You see, even though it was only three in the afternoon on a hot summer's day everyone else was wearing formal evening dress. I realised that I hadn't read the invitation properly. There was a deathly quiet as everyone stared at me. As I sat down, children sniggered behind my back – I was mortified.

Worse was to come. For some reason, I had been feeling ill ever since breakfast. Then the meal began, and different courses kept arriving. First of all there was soup. Then some smoked salmon followed by a meat dish. After that there was cheese. By the time the bride and groom stood up to cut the wedding cake at around five o'clock I was feeling ghastly – I desperately needed some fresh air. I was staggering towards the exit when I passed out in the middle of the dance floor. When I came round, the first thing I saw was my boss's furious face glaring down at me 'Have you been drinking, Raymond?' he demanded. 'No, I haven't, Mr Thomas,' I protested, realising nobody actually believed me. I have never been so embarrassed in my life.

Sequencing

2 When we speak we often use *then* and *next* to put the events of the story in order. When we write we should vary how we sequence events to keep our readers interested. Read the notes and find further examples of the following in the story you have just read:

Then

1st action	2nd action
He received an invitation.	He bought a suit.

After

After may need to be followed by the gerund or the past perfect.

After receiving an invitation he bought a suit.

After that and **afterwards**

After that and *afterwards* are safer choices, as they are followed by the past simple.

He bought a suit **afterwards …/After that** *he bought a suit.*

3 Rewrite the short text below. Make it more interesting by using a variety of ways of putting actions in sequence.

Last weekend I got up late then I took the train to Barcelona, then I bought some shoes. I met my friend, Aranxa, in the shop, then I met my other friends in Catalunya Square. Everyone arrived then we had lunch, then we walked down the Ramblas to the sea. Then I bought ice-creams, then we went to the movies. Then I went home.

Gradable and non-gradable adjectives

Angry is a gradable adjective. We can modify it using *slightly, very, quite, extremely.*

Example: *I was extremely angry when I heard the news.*

Furious means *extremely angry* and is a non-gradable adjective. We can amplify meaning using *absolutely*:

I was **absolutely** *furious when I heard the news.*

4 Match a gradable adjective from box A, with its non-gradable partner from box B.

A

disappointed	pleased	embarrassed	tired
frightened	stupid	lovely	bad

B

ridiculous	devastated	mortified	exhausted
gorgeous	delighted	terrified	terrible

➜ Grammar Reference (Section 1.3) page 166

5 We often use non-gradable adjectives when we want to exaggerate.

Example:

A: Were you tired after the match?

B: I was absolutely exhausted!

Work in pairs. Create replies to the questions and sentences using non-gradable adjectives.

1 Did you feel embarrassed when you found out who he was?

2 She must have been disappointed with her results.

3 What's wrong? Are you feeling ill?

4 Were they pleased at the news?

5 Do I look stupid in this hat?

Create some further exchanges of your own.

6 We can add depth to a story through our choice of vocabulary. Find further examples of the following from the short story you have just read.

a non-gradable adjectives e.g. *furious* _____

b descriptive verbs e.g. *glanced* _____

c adverbs of manner e.g. *nastily* _____

7 Write a short story which can either begin or end with the words *It was a day which changed my life for ever*.

Short story

When writing a short story make sure you …

	Yes (✓)	No (✗)
• use a range of narrative tenses.	☐	☐
• include some direct speech (to make the narrative come to life).	☐	☐
• use a rich range of vocabulary, including verbs (to give the story character and interest).	☐	☐
• enrich descriptions with well-chosen adjectives and adverbs.	☐	☐
• use relative pronouns to combine clauses.	☐	☐
• use a variety of ways of putting actions in sequence.	☐	☐
• begin and end the story with the words given.	☐	☐

➜ Writing Guide, page 202

Review and Use of English

1 MULTIPLE-CHOICE CLOZE Read the text below and decide which answer (*A, B, C* or *D*) best fits each gap.

The Go Between by L.P. Hartley is my **(1)** _____ short novel. It is the story of **(2)** _____ innocence, and the tragic love affair of people **(3)** _____ a social divide. The **(4)** _____ character is a young boy called Leo, a pupil at a private school. During the long, hot summer of 1900 he goes to **(5)** _____ a rich classmate called Marcus at his family's magnificent country house. He immediately develops a **(6)** _____ crush on Marcus's elder sister, Marian. When Marcus falls ill, Leo is bored and Marian **(7)** _____ him deliver love letters to a farmer called Ted. Their meetings have to be secret **(8)** _____ to Ted's lower social position. **(9)** _____, Marian is engaged to be married to a gentleman. Poor Leo is used by the couple whose secret is finally revealed with the **(10)** _____ tragic consequences. The tale is narrated half a century later by a now **(11)** _____ Leo, whose chance of happiness disappeared forever after those terrible events. Not **(12)** _____ is the book a wonderful tale, but it was adapted into a haunting film directed by Joseph Losey.

1	A most	B best	C favourite	D quite
2	A gone	B lost	C disappeared	D vanished
3	A between	B over	C across	D from
4	A main	B great	C most	D primary
5	A stay	B maintain	C keep	D visit
6	A helpless	B useless	C hopeless	D helpful
7	A engages	B makes	C employs	D retains
8	A due	B because	C owed	D according
9	A While	B Although	C Moreover	D Yet
10	A most	B many	C very	D extremely
11	A ancient	B vintage	C antique	D elderly
12	A all	B yet	C only	D again

2 OPEN CLOZE Read the summary of *Pride and Prejudice* and think of the word that best fits each gap.

A recent opinion poll to choose Britain's most popular novel produced a surprising result. Rather **(1)** _____ the latest spy thriller, the book with the most votes was written **(2)** _____ an 18th-century novelist, Jane Austen. *Pride and Prejudice* describes the romance between Elizabeth Bennett and the snobbish Mr. Darcy. The book is full of brilliant observations **(3)** _____ society and social relationships of the period. However, voters' choices appear to have **(4)** _____ to do with a love of the printed word. When **(5)** _____ who had actually read the book, the survey produced another surprise: very few people, indeed **(6)** _____ anyone, had actually read the tale. **(7)** _____, they remembered the TV **(8)** _____ or the more recent film. Three explanations **(9)** _____ to mind. First of all, people wish that they had read it; secondly there is a nostalgia for a romantic age which was **(10)** _____ long ago. Or quite simply, **(11)** _____ their unromantic image, the British are in love with the idea of love. Perhaps we are **(12)** _____ to enter a new period of romance and courtship!

3 Put the verbs from the box into the appropriate column

slurp	giggle	glance	stagger	gaze	sigh	limp
glare	stare	sip	snigger	gasp	stroll	gulp

Ways of ...

laughing	walking/moving	breathing

looking	drinking

4 Which verbs in the table in exercise 3 mean ...?

1 to walk painfully or unevenly, as a result of an injury _____

2 to look at something in a fixed way for a long time _____

3 to look at someone angrily _____

4 to breathe in quickly and loudly, in surprise _____

5 to look quickly to the side _____

6 to walk in a slow and leisurely way _____

7 to drink slowly, a little at a time, enjoying the taste _____

8 to laugh unpleasantly at someone else's misfortune _____

9 to look far away into the distance _____

10 to drink noisily _____

11 to breathe out with disappointment or contentment _____

12 to walk with difficulty, moving from side to side due to carrying something heavy or being ill _____

13 to laugh in a silly way _____

14 to drink and swallow quickly in great mouthfuls _____

5 Turn the jumbled letters into non-gradable adjectives.

Example:

1	really angry	URIUFOS = *furious*
2	extremely pleased	LEGIHTDED = _____
3	very beautiful/lovely	OGSREGOU = _____
4	extremely embarrassed	ORFDMTIIE = _____
5	very frightened	ERTFRIIDE = _____

6 Transport and travel

Getting started

1 How do you travel to work or school? Which of these types of transport would you like to try?

2 Work in pairs. Think of two types of transport that you could combine into a new vehicle. What would you call it? Describe it to the class and explain why it might be useful.

3 Work in pairs. Ask and answer the following questions.
1 What's your favourite form of transport?
2 How good is public transport in your area? How could it be improved?
3 How do you think transport will change in the future?
4 What is the most interesting journey you've ever been on? Why?

Vocabulary: confusable words

1 **Choose the correct word (in *italics*) in sentences 1–7.**

1 They say that *travel/travels* broadens the mind, but I'm not so sure.
2 I haven't seen you for a while. Have you been away on your *travels/trips/journeys*?
3 We had a fascinating conversation during the *journey/travel*.
4 He is away on a short business *journey/trip/travel*. He'll be back on Thursday.
5 How long does it *last/take/need* to get there?
6 How *long/far* is it from Stockholm to Oslo?
7 The *voyage/flight* from London to Auckland takes about 26 hours.

2 **Work in groups. Discuss the differences between the following:**

1 a *package holiday* and a *holiday resort*
2 a *brochure* and a *guide book*
3 a *timetable* and an *itinerary*
4 a *commuter* and a *traveller*
5 a *souvenir* and a *reminder*
6 *heritage* and *sightseeing*
7 an *excursion* and a *trip*
8 a *tourist* and *tourism*

Listening: travel and visits

1 🎧 **6.1 Work in pairs. Listen to eight people talking in different situations. After listening, discuss answers to these questions.**

1 How clear are Sophie's plans?
2 What kind of job do you think Juan has?
3 How does Olga keep her travel costs to a minimum?
4 Who do you think Professor Heron is? Why is Blanka planning his visit so carefully?
5 How do you think Sebastian's mother will feel as she:
   (i) steps off the train?
   (ii) walks into the sitting room?
6 Where are Kim and David?
7 Why is Ray in Krakow?
8 How adventurous is Gemma really?

2 🎧 **6.1 MULTIPLE CHOICE Listen again. For questions 1–8 choose the best answer (*A, B* or *C*).**

1 You will hear a young person discussing her plans for the future. Which of these statements is true?
   A She is going to university soon.
   B She has discussed her plans with her parents.
   C She is planning to spend some time abroad.

2 You will hear Juan leaving a message for a colleague. What is the purpose of his message?
   A to say he is going to be late
   B to ask for help
   C to ask for directions

3 You will hear Sharon talking about what appeals to her about travelling. What do we find out about her?
   A She enjoys the unknown.
   B She likes to visit the well-known sites.
   C She hates being uncomfortable.

4 You will hear a manager briefing her colleagues about an important visitor. What do we learn about Professor Heron?
   A He doesn't mind where he speaks.
   B He refuses to go anywhere by plane.
   C He is a demanding person.

5 You will hear Sebastian talking to a group of family and friends. What is he organising?
   A a train journey
   B a wedding anniversary celebration
   C a surprise party

6 You will hear a couple, Kim and David, discussing their holiday. What do we learn?
   A Kim isn't pleased with David.
   B The brochure gave accurate details.
   C There isn't much night life.

7 Dagmara is discussing plans with Roy, an American colleague. What do we learn about Roy?
   A He would like a quiet evening in, or near the hotel.
   B He is expected to buy presents.
   C Roy doesn't enjoy sightseeing.

8 Gemma is in a restaurant in Rome. What do we learn from her choices?
   A She has adventurous tastes.
   B She doesn't like the special.
   C She is a vegetarian.

EXAM SPOTLIGHT

PAPER 4, PART 1

In this part of the listening test, you are tested on more than gist. You may need to listen for detail, but you may also be asked to understand people's relationships, attitudes and feelings.

Vocabulary: travel

Phrasal verbs

1 Complete the sentences by replacing the words in **bold** with one of the phrasal verbs from the box. Make any other necessary changes.

take ... out	show ... around	check in	put ... up
set off	pick ... up	drop ... off	meet up (with)
travel around	phone ... back	take off	turn up

1 There isn't anywhere to park. Is it OK if I just **leave you** in front of the hotel? _____
2 No problem. I can **register** on my own. I don't need anyone to take care of me. _____
3 We need to **leave** as early as possible if we want to miss the rush hour. _____
4 I'm coming to London next week. Can you **give me a bed** for a couple of nights? _____
5 Can you **return my call** on my mobile number? _____
6 I'll come and **collect you** at seven in front of the hotel. _____
7 When I was a student I used to **tour** the continent with an inter-rail pass. _____
8 You can't just **arrive unexpectedly** at someone's door without phoning first. _____
9 Why don't you let me **give you a guided tour of** the old city. You'll love it. _____
10 This evening we're **seeing** a group of old friends. _____
11 My flight should have **left the ground** an hour ago, but it has been delayed. _____
12 We'd like you to **go with us** to a restaurant this evening. _____

SPOTLIGHT ON VOCABULARY

Particles and meaning in phrasal verbs
Phrasal verbs consist of a stem (the verb) and one or two particles (adverb or preposition). Particles can have a central meaning which may help us understand the meaning of the phrasal verb.

Example: *around* has the idea of *here and there*.
I'll show you around = I'll show you here and there.

2 Using the verbs from exercise 1 match the particles *off*, *up* and *back* to the central meanings below;
1 return or repeat: _____
2 leave or begin: _____
3 collect or join: _____

3 What do you think it means if we ...?
1 pay someone back
2 kick off a football match
3 take up a new sport or hobby

---

4 🎧 6.2 Work in two or three teams. Listen to the definitions and shout out the phrasal verb or expression from the box below or in Vocabulary exercise 1.

give away	go for	put off
eat out	get away	freshen up

Speaking: organising a schedule

1 In many countries, towns and cities 'twin' themselves with similar places in other countries. How common is this in your country?

2 Work in groups. As part of the 'twinning programme', you are going to look after a family of foreign visitors from your twin city for the weekend. You have never met them before. They will be staying in a hotel. They are going to stay for three nights (Friday, Saturday and Sunday). Look at the information below and decide how you will entertain them. Create a programme for the weekend that will satisfy everyone.

Parents:
Mother: Sharon (age 45)
   Loves: sightseeing, clothes shopping, eating out
   Hates: fast food, sport
Father: Nick (age 47)
   Loves: sightseeing, traditional markets, eating out
   Hates: high street shopping

Children:
Lucinda: (age 17)
   Loves: shopping, the beach, dancing, fast food
   Hates: sightseeing
Alex: (age 14)
   Loves: swimming, watching sport, fast food
   Hates: sightseeing, eating out in restaurants

	Morning	Afternoon	Evening
Friday			Arrive by bus. Welcome party.
Saturday			
Sunday			Farewell party at hotel.

Grammar: expressing the future

→ Grammar Reference (Section 8) page 173

1 **Work in pairs. Study sentences a to d below. Identify the tenses in bold.**

a **I'm setting off** at three o'clock.
b His train **arrives** at four.
c **I'm going to take** a gap year.
d **I'll begin** with the artichokes and goat's cheese salad.

2 **Which sentence above ...?**

1 expresses an intention (something which has already been decided) _____
2 describes a personal plan _____
3 is a decision taken at the time of speaking _____
4 involves a timetable or a regular event _____

3 **Complete these two mini dialogues using will/shall or going to.**

1 *Martin:* What **(1)** _____ (we/do) this weekend, Phoebe?

Phoebe: I don't know. Why don't we invite Rebecca and Steven for dinner?

Martin: That's a great idea. I **(2)** _____ (phone) them straightaway.

2 *Carmen:* What **(3)** _____ (we/get) Harriet for her birthday?

Miles: I know, I **(4)** _____ (buy) her some flowers.

Carmen: Good idea! And I **(5)** _____ (get) her a box of her favourite chocolates.

Five minutes later ...

Paolo: Hi, everyone, have you thought about Harriet's birthday?

Carmen: Yes, Miles **(6)** _____ (buy) her some chocolates and I **(7)** _____ (get) her a box of her favourite chocolates.

4 **Study these three pairs of sentences and tick (✓) the ones that make predictions.**

1 a Be careful! Someone is going to get hurt. I can see it happening. _____
  b I'm going to meet him next Wednesday with Alexandra. _____

2 a You should give couch surfing a try. _____
  b I should get there at around seven. _____

3 a I'll email you the website details. _____
  b He'll be tired after the journey. _____

5 **Which sentence in exercise 4 ...?**

- gives advice _____
- is a spontaneous offer _____
- is an intention _____

6 **Study sentences a, b and c. Which one uses ...?**

1 the future perfect _____
2 the future in the past _____
3 the future continuous _____

a Kate *will be waiting* at the station.
b I didn't know it *was going to be* like this.
c He'll *have had time* to freshen up.

7 **Which sentence, a, b or c in exercise 6 describes ...?**

1 an action which is in progress at a point in the future _____
2 something that hadn't been predicted _____
3 something that has already happened by a point in the future _____

8 **Complete sentences 1–8 by changing the verb in brackets into the future continuous (*will be doing*), future perfect (*will have done*), or future in the past (*was going to do*).**

1 If we do nothing about it very soon, in another two or three hundred years Venice _____ (sink) beneath the waves.
2 My guess is that scientists _____ (already find) an environmentally friendly alternative to oil long before it runs out.
3 It's not your fault you're late. You didn't know that the car _____ (break down).
4 This time tomorrow we _____ (eat) seafood and _____ (watch) the sun set over Cascais beach.
5 By August he _____ (have) the same car for ten years.
6 Don't worry; I _____ (wait) for you at the end of the platform.
7 That's not fair. How was I to know that the restaurant _____ (be) full?
8 Hurry up, otherwise they _____ (eat) all the food by the time we get there.

9 **Some adjectives have a future meaning. Look at the adjectives (in *italics*) in sentences a–c below. Which sentence means ...?**

1 is expected/scheduled to _____
2 certain _____
3 highly possible _____

a She's *likely to* be feeling a bit sad.
b He's *bound to* want some time to himself.
c A taxi is *due to* pick us up.

10 **⌂ 6.3 Listen to information about eight situations. Using the most suitable way of expressing the future, decide what you would say in each situation.**

Listening: travel arrangements

1 You are going to hear three friends (Loïc, Tess and Marco) discussing travel arrangements from Birmingham in England to their holiday destination near La Rochelle in France. Work in groups. Look at the map. Discuss the different ways you think they could travel.

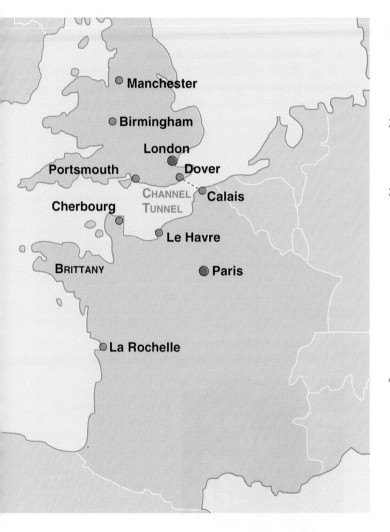

2 ∩ **6.4 Listen and decide who says what. Tick the name.**

Who ...?	Loïc	Tess	Marco
1 suggests taking the tunnel	☐	☐	☐
2 says the motorways will be expensive to drive on	☐	☐	☐
3 thinks flying or driving will cost about the same	☐	☐	☐
4 has never driven on the continent	☐	☐	☐
5 is unhappy with the way someone else drives	☐	☐	☐
6 suggests a night crossing	☐	☐	☐
7 is going to check prices	☐	☐	☐

3 Which travel option would you go for?

Speaking: discussing options

1 Study sentences 1–4 below, from the listening exercise opposite.

Which one ...?

a considers a condition and its consequence _____
b presents a possible option _____
c suggests an option of last resort/necessity _____
d suggests that something should be done _____

1 We could take the tunnel.
2 We could always hire a car if we need one.
3 We'd better make up our minds.
4 If we took a night crossing, it would give us a night's sleep.

2 Practise saying sentences 1–4 in exercise 1 above then answer these questions.
a Which word is stressed in sentence 2? _____
b What is 'd in sentence 3? _____

3 Compare these pairs of sentences (*a/b* and *c/d*) and answer the questions which follow.

a It's time for us to decide.
b It's time *we* decided. _____

c I'd rather get there as quickly as possible.
d I'd rather *we* got there as quickly as possible.

1 Which tense is used in the second halves of sentences b and d?
2 What happens when we use the personal pronoun (*we*) in sentences b and d?

4 Work in groups of three or four. Imagine that you are all going to take a short break in a foreign city. Using questions 1–8 below as a guide, organise a trip that will have something for everyone. Remember to give your opinion and make your own preferences clear. Use Tapescript 6.4 on page 214 as a guide if you need to.

1 Where will you go?
2 What time of year will you go? (Say why)
3 How will you get there? Give reasons.
4 Where will you stay?
5 How long will you spend there?
6 What will you do when you get there?
7 What special sights will you visit?
8 What will you do about food and eating arrangements?
9 How much money will you take?
10 What will you bring back as a souvenir?

Reading: dream holidays

1 **Discuss.** Where do you usually go on holiday? What would be your dream holiday destination? What do you like to do?

2 Quickly read about four travel destinations. Which one would you most like to go to? Which one would you least like to go to?

SPOTLIGHT ON READING

Scanning

When we scan a text, our eye passes over it quickly and focuses on key names, facts and figures. Scanning is a good way of approaching an information-rich text for the first time.

3 **Scan texts A–D and find out what the following names and numbers refer to:**

1973	$600,000	1935 Serengeti
1,149 miles	2,500 metres	Plaza Dorrego
El Viejo Almacén	600,000	

PAPER 1, PART 3

4 MULTIPLE MATCHING **Read the text again and for questions 1–15 below choose the correct destination (A–D). Each destination may be chosen more than once.**

Which place/travel experience …?

1 has to deal with a lot of letters _____
2 has encouraged the rebirth of a tradition _____
3 lets us witness an annual migration _____
4 is home to a world-famous dance _____
5 has links with a tragic artist _____
6 offers you a bird's-eye view of events below _____
7 has atmospheric bars and clubs _____
8 brings a children's dream to life _____
9 offers valuable prizes _____
10 is linked with a famous rescue mission _____
11 lets people who pay the most join one of the teams _____
12 allows you to watch amateur performers _____
13 has a place where you can buy presents _____
14 has a connection with a famous dog _____
15 offers you protection at night _____

5 **Work in pairs. Discuss with your partner which destination you would choose for a dream holiday. You can choose anywhere in the world. Tell the rest of the class and give your reasons.**

A The Iditarod: Anchorage, Alaska

For the ultimate experience of the Last Frontier, show up for the Iditarod, a gruelling sled-dog race across the Alaskan wilderness, from Anchorage all the way to Nome on the coast of the Bering Sea. Dogsledding had almost disappeared until 1973 when the first Iditarod was organised to revive the tradition and commemorate historical dogsledding events. One such historical event had taken place during the 1925 diphtheria epidemic in Nome when twenty riders (called *mushers*) and a sled team led by a legendary dog called Balto crossed the frozen landscape to fetch essential medicine for the town.

Today an average of 65 mushers and their teams come from as far away as Japan and Russia to compete for a share of the $600, 000 prize money, traversing 1,149 miles – a journey which usually takes between eight and fifteen days. The Iditarod has become the largest spectator event in Alaska. Along the way, entire towns turn out to cheer on the mushers and their teams. To get into the race yourself as an 'Iditarider' you can place a bid for a place on one of the mushers' sleds for the first 11 miles.

B Las Tanguerias de Buenos Aires

The Tango is Argentina's celebration of machismo, domination and tormented love, and it is in the very air the porteños (residents of Buenos Aires) breathe. This intricate and exquisite dance is the most authentic of Argentine creations. The tango's popularity has waxed and waned since the 1920s when the darkly-handsome singer, Carlos Gardel, drove the country wild before dying tragically in a 1935 plane crash.

A recent revival of tangomania confirms that this indigenous popular music has survived the era of rock and roll, and some of the large dance halls, such as El Viejo Almacén and Casa Blanca, still put on an emotion-packed nightly show with the country's finest tango dancers, singers and musicians. To see tango in its natural habitat – the classic small, smoky, dimly-lit tango bar where things don't start happening untill the other side of midnight – the casual Bar Sur is the place to go. On Sundays at the weekly flea market at the Plaza Dorrego, a number of amateur tanguistas perform spontaneous shows on street corners – with less polish, but from the soul.

C Safari: The Masai Mara, Kenya

The Masai Mara is nature's stage for what must be the most spectacular wildlife pageant on earth. Each year, when the rainy season ends in May, hundreds of thousands of wildebeests mass together. They are moving in search of greener pastures from the Serengeti in Tanzania north to the wide open grasslands of Kenya's Masai Mara. Along with migrating herds of zebra, antelope and gazelle, there are sometimes more than a million animals on the move at one time, and a horseback safari gives you a remarkable view of an animal kingdom unrivalled anywhere in Africa.

Riding through the unspoiled Loita Hills and the great rolling plains of the Mara, you'll pass through the manyattas (villages) of the nomadic Masai people who protect the animals they believe to be 'God's cattle'. Some ascents will reach 2,500 metres, providing spectacular views and open vistas. And while you marvel at the views, the staff go on ahead to set up camp in a lovely setting and have dinner and a hot shower ready for your arrival. They also keep watch throughout the sound-filled night to keep the wildlife at bay.

You can also view the endless expanse of the Masai Mara from a hot air balloon safari. At dawn, you ascend into a sky all shades of rose and orange. Masai villagers stand rooted as they watch you drift across the sky. The awesome magical stillness envelops you.

D Santa's village: Rovaniemi, Lapland, Finland

Rovaniemi, in Finland's Arctic Circle, is considered the gateway to Lapland. It is known for its indigenous, formerly nomadic, Sami people (once commonly known as 'Lapp'). Santa's village is how every child always imagines it to be – a snowy winter wonderland with a jovial Santa in attendance every day!

His busy workshops show how he keeps up with his toy-making, and the post office displays some of the 600,000 letters received every year from all over the world. About a third of these letters get answered. An irresistible gift shop provides a myriad of Yuletide presents that can be shipped back home with a Santa's village postmark, or, for a nominal fee, you can add your child's name to a list to receive a postcard from Santa. A nearby reindeer farm provides the chance for a Magic Sleigh Ride (though it's a ride that never leaves the ground!).

Vocabulary: words in context

1 Find the words and expressions in the reading text that mean:

Text A:
present yourself/appear _____
long, difficult and exhausting _____
where no one lives and nothing grows _____
encourage _____

Text B:
filled with emotional pain _____
increased and decreased _____ and _____
with little light to see by _____
where you can buy old things cheaply _____

Text C:
a colourful display _____
grassland for food _____
watch in wonder _____
extremely impressive _____

Text D:
lived there for a long time/original _____
friendly and cheerful _____
small amount of money _____
too many to count, huge number _____

2 Make adjectives from the following:

legend _____   spectacle _____

remark _____   protect _____

3 Make adjectives that mean:

the opposite of spoilt: _____   without a rival: _____
can't be resisted: _____   without end: _____

4 Make nouns from the following:

still _____   celebrate _____
attend _____   popular _____
dominate _____   shipped _____

Speaking: discussing your travels

1 Imagine that you have just come back from a visit to one of the places in the reading text. In groups, ask and answer questions about your trip. Use the questions and comments below to help you.

Questions
I haven't seen you for a while. Have you been away?
Oh really? Whereabouts?
What was special about it?
What exactly did you do/see?
So what was it like -ing?
How did it feel to ...?
Tell me more about ...
What will you remember most about your trip?

Comments
That sounds fun/scary.
Wow! Amazing!
How fascinating/interesting, etc ...
What a wonderful/frightening experience!

Key word: *just*

1 Study the word *just* in sentences 1–6 below and match them to the meanings (a–f). Write the letter next to the sentence.

1   I arrived *just* as the train was leaving. _____
2   There'll be *just* a short delay while we wait for clearance to take off. _____
3   I'm afraid the bus has *just* left. _____
4   The flight is *just* about to board. You'd better hurry. _____
5   With all the traffic on the roads, cycling to work is *just* as fast as taking the car these days. _____
6   We're *just* leaving. Are you coming with us? _____

a   a short time ago
b   a small amount (of time)
c   something equal to something else
d   at this moment
e   exactly the same time
f   something almost happening

2 These sentences are all correct but you can add the word *just* to modify their meaning. Write in *just*, as shown in the example.

Example:

just

Can I have a little sugar with that, please.

1   My car is as fast as yours.
2   I'm about to switch this off. Did you need to use it?
3   You've missed him I'm afraid. He'll be back at two.
4   Hold on, he's walking through the door as we speak.
5   I'll need a minute of your time, if that's OK.

3 Think of a comment using *just* for situations 1–5.

1   Your friend Stephanie went home 30 seconds ago. Someone has phoned to speak to her. Suggest they call back tomorrow.
2   You want to go on an expensive holiday with a friend. You've compared the price in two different travel agents. Both have given you the same price. Tell your friend.
3   You are walking out the door when your teacher asks to speak to you. You want to get home quickly to watch your favourite programme on TV. Politely explain to your teacher why you'd like to go home.
4   Your dinner is in the oven and will be ready in a couple of minutes. Your friend phones you. Explain and promise to phone back when you've eaten your meal.
5   Your friend has asked you to help her. You are finishing an email, then you'll be free.

Writing: a report

1 Discuss. Do you ever raise money for local projects or charities? What methods can you use to raise money?

2 Megan Green has been to a meeting to discuss how to raise money for new computers for her children's school. She has sent an email to her friend Joanna. Read Megan's email and answer these questions:

a   How many ideas did people at the meeting come up with? What was the problem with each?
b   What did they decide in the end?

To: joanna.sinclair@gremlin.com

From: Megan Green

Subject: replacement computers

Hi Joanna,

Hope you're feeling a bit better today. I thought I'd just summarise everything for you here to bring you up to date.

A lot of parents came, and teachers too, and everyone had plenty of different ideas. Mavis Walsh came up with the idea of a sponsored bike ride, but after a long discussion we dropped it in the end because it would be too dangerous on busy roads for young kids. Someone else suggested a sponsored walk but people thought this was a bit old-fashioned. Mr Harrison put forward the idea of a pageant, with lorries decorated as floats. We were all excited about that idea but Adrian Fox's dad said it would be too hard to get the lorries. I had the idea for a boat race on the river – people liked it but again were worried about safety. In the end we went with the idea of a sponsored walk. It's a bit boring, I know, but at least it's safe, easy to organise and a good way of making money.

I have agreed to create the sponsorship form, and Mr Fox is going to handle the money side of things. We'll need lots of volunteers to be stewards and I'm counting on you to sort out drinks and things! Is that OK? I'll send you my report when I've written it.

Give me a ring if you've got any questions.
Get well soon!

Megan

---

3 Read Megan's report below. Match the sections 1–5 to these subheadings A–E.

A Future action _____
B Two further proposals _____
C The safest option _____
D Purpose of this report _____
E Initial ideas _____

4 What differences do you notice between the email and the report's … ?

- layout and organisation
- vocabulary
- expressions

<u>Ideas for raising money for school computers</u>

1 _____

The aim of this report is to present the ideas that were discussed at the well-attended meeting of the parents' and teachers' association held on 25th January at 7p.m. The meeting was to discuss ways of raising money to purchase replacement computers. A number of proposals were made.

2 _____

One suggestion was the organisation of a sponsored bicycle ride. However, following discussions, it was decided a ride on roads would be dangerous for younger children. Consequently this idea was dismissed.

3 _____

The next proposal was for a pageant on the theme of English history with children travelling on decorated floats. A further idea was to organise a boat race on the river. Even though both ideas were greeted with enthusiasm, it was decided that the parade would be difficult to organise on account of the lorries while the boat race was unsuitable on safety grounds.

4 _____

Those present returned to the idea of the sponsored walk. On balance, it was agreed that a sponsored walk, while not the most imaginative choice, was the most acceptable. Moreover, it was felt that it would raise the money required.

5 _____.

Mrs Megan Green agreed to create a sponsorship form and Mr Fox accepted the role of treasurer. Volunteers will be required to act as stewards and to provide refreshments for the event.

---

5 Reports are usually more impersonal than emails or letters. Read the report again and find out how Megan makes her report 'impersonal'.

SPOTLIGHT ON WRITING

Report writing

PAPER 2, PART 2

We use subheadings in reports to summarise what each part of the report is about. Subheadings also help the reader to find the information they need quickly.

6 Imagine that you are reading a report about homelessness among young people. Discuss what you would expect to read under subheadings 1–5. The first one has been done as an example.

1 Introduction: *Homelessness – a growing problem among young people*
2 The results of family breakdown:
3 Fear and friendship on the streets:
4 The dangers of street life:
5 Back into the community:

7 Work in groups. People in your town have set up a committee to consider ways to raise money to pay for equipment for a children's hospital in Africa. You are the committee. Discuss four or five ways to involve the local community in raising money for the project. Decide on the best one/s.

8 Write a report about your meeting that is similar to the one you read earlier. For a list of further useful expressions, turn to page 203.

WRITING CHECKLIST

Report

After writing a report, make sure it contains …

	Yes (✓)	No (✗)
• sections with subheadings.	☐	☐
• between 120 and 180 words.	☐	☐
• an introduction and conclusion.	☐	☐

➡ Writing Guide, page 203

Review and Use of English

1 Fill the gaps using each of the words from the box just once.

take   last   trip   far   journey   travel   need

1 A How was your _____ here today?
   B Not too bad, although there was a lot of traffic.
   A Oh dear, so how long did it _____ you?
   B Forty-five minutes.
   A Really? And how _____ away do you live?
   B Just five kilometres.
   A Oh dear!
2 C How long does the film _____?
   D Just under two hours. Are you ready to go?
   C Not quite. I _____ another five minutes,
      if that's OK?
3 E What was your _____ to Sweden and Norway like?
   F It was fine, but business _____ is always the
      same; airports, meetings and hotels. Not much fun!

2 KEY WORD TRANSFORMATIONS **Complete the second
sentence so that it has a similar meaning to the first
sentence. Do not change the word given. You must use
between two and five words only, including the word given.**

1 I think you should find a job.
   time
   It's _____ job.
2 I'll call the moment I have some news.
   soon
   I'll call _____ I have some news.
3 I've never driven on the left before.
   ever
   It's the first _____ on the left.
4 How long does the journey last?
   take
   How _____ to get there?
5 I'd prefer us to go to the seaside.
   we
   I'd _____ to the seaside.
6 You ought to get some travel insurance.
   better
   You _____ get some travel insurance.
7 Why don't we take the train?
   always
   We _____ the train.
8 It's time for us to decide.
   made
   It's time _____.

3 OPEN CLOZE **Read the text below and think of a word that
best fits in each gap. Use only one word in each gap.**

Christopher Bohm and Elke Verheugen have started
a business called 'Teddy in Munich'. Basically, it's a
service that provides vacations for teddy bears. People
who feel that their teddy bears deserve a little time
away can send their **(1)** _____ to Christopher and
Elke. Once there, the bears **(2)** _____ treated to
a one-week vacation in Munich **(3)** _____ their
owners, to relax and unwind from the stressful hustle
and bustle of their busy lives. **(4)** _____ part of
the vacation, the teddy bear will visit popular tourist
attractions, including *Hofbräuhaus*, a world
(5) _____ tavern with a generous menu of beers.
There is also a focus on Bavarian traditions, including
a standard trip to a local beer garden. The bears can
also **(6)** _____ brought to the language laboratory
(7) _____ they will learn the basics of the German
language … starting with *bier und brezn* (beer and
pretzels). In **(8)** _____ to the standard tour,
the teddy bears can opt for extracurricular activities.
Adventurous bears can go bungee jumping or
paragliding. Other bears can choose a **(9)** _____
demanding activity, such as fishing or golf.
(10) _____ the vacation, Christopher and Elke
will take pictures so that the bear can have its very
(11) _____ photo journal to take home and show
to its owner. The vacation, including photo journal,
(12) _____ 99 euros for local bears and 149 euros
for out-of-towners.

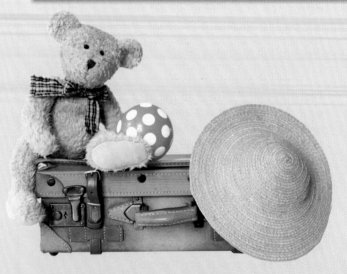

4 Discuss. **Would you send your teddy bear on holiday? Can you
think of a new idea for an interesting new holiday company
like 'Teddy in Munich'?**

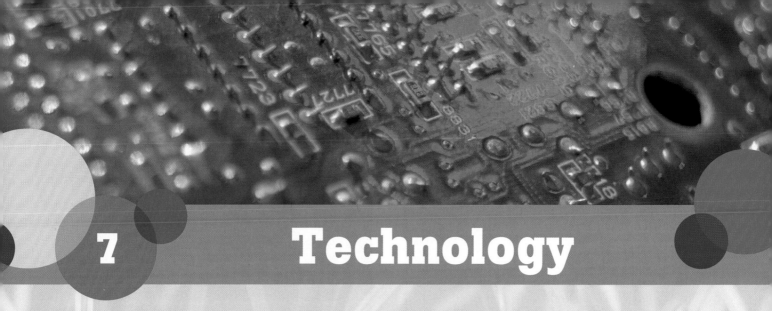

7 Technology

Getting started

1 **Discuss. Look at the pictures. In a recent poll these items were included as the world's worst inventions. Why do you think they were chosen? Which do you think were voted the worst three? See Information File 7.1 on page 230 for the answers.**

2 **Work in groups. Make a list of the world's best ten inventions. Compare your list with other groups. Try to agree on the number one best invention.**

Reading: robot revolution

1 Work in pairs. Look at the two photos on the right, and discuss these questions:
- Where might you expect to see this kind of transport?
- Why do you think the invention on the right might be an improvement?

2 Here are four pieces of advice about part 2 of the Reading test. However, one gives bad advice. Which one? Can you rewrite it?
1 Try to predict from the title what the text will be about.
2 Pay special attention to pronouns to help you.
3 Don't read all the text before you start to fill in the gaps.
4 When you're sure, transfer your choices to the answer paper.

3 **GAPPED TEXT SENTENCES** You're going to read about a man who invents robots. Seven sentences have been removed from the text. Choose from the sentences (A–H) the one which fits each gap (1–7). There is one extra sentence which you do not need to use.

A 'At that time, I didn't even know the term "robot",' Wu said.

B More recently, his house burnt down from his experiments.

C A newer model named Number Six is a monkey-like robot with magnetised feet which enables it to crawl slowly up metallic walls.

D He has now come up with one that will walk like a human being.

E At 42 years of age he has destroyed his family home, been seriously burned and ended up £5,000 in debt.

F He dreams his robots may become like the compass, gunpowder and the umbrella, all of which China pioneered the use of, before exporting them to Europe and the rest of the world.

G As for his next robot, Mr Wu is unsure.

H The inventor has already earned around £200 for a mechanical grasshopper, while a high-tech company has shown interest in Number Eight.

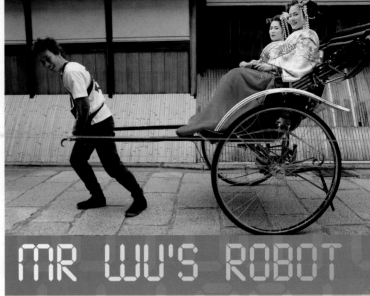

MR WU'S ROBOT

If you met Wu Yulu from Tongzhou, China, and father of two, you'd probably just think you were meeting a farmer. He appears to be quite poor and perhaps wouldn't be regarded by many people as a success story. (1) _____ But Mr Wu, who left school at 14 and has no formal technical training, is a part-time inventor who creates robots to help people reduce their time spent on doing jobs like the housework. What's even more amazing is that these 'labour-saving robots' are all created from scrap he comes across in rubbish dumps.

His brain children, which are all developed during long nights spent in his garden shed with only his imagination as a guide, include Number Five, a one-metre-tall humanoid robot capable of walking, changing light bulbs, lighting cigarettes and pouring tea. (2) _____ Like all of Mr Wu's inventions, it is made out of bits of old metal, tape and second-hand batteries.

Although a man of few words, the farmer will admit that his ultimate robot is a virtual human. 'It would have a brain that could think, and arms and legs like a real person.' Mr Wu also hopes that his creations may one day join a long list of Chinese inventions. (3) _____ With funding and support, Mr Wu believes his robots could similarly revolutionise everyday life and change the way we work.

You might doubt Mr Wu's self-belief but you certainly can't question his unstoppable enthusiasm, which has now lasted for over 25 years. In that time he thinks he has made at least

REVOLUTION

25 robots. He came up with the idea for his first robot while watching people walking and studying the motion of their bodies. (4) _____ 'But in my spare time from farming, I'd pick up anything that could be used in those movable things.'

Despite a number of setbacks, he has never thought of giving up. Once he went to hospital after trying out a new invention. It exploded and he still has scars on his hands and arms. (5) _____ 'I was left with nothing,' he said. With a new house costing 90,000 yuan, Mr Wu's long-suffering wife, Dong Shuyan, has started a private kindergarten in an attempt to pay off the family's loans. She describes her husband as 'child-like' in his obsession with inventions, though she is philosophical about her burden.

'When we got married, everyone warned me he would care more about his robots than about me,' she said, but Ms Dong is also optimistic about her husband's new plan to start selling the patents for his robots. (6) _____ 'He has so much talent,' said his wife, 'he should at least be able to make some money out of it.'

His latest 'robot rickshaw' took a year to build. The 1.8-metre-tall robot pulls a rickshaw and is operated by the driver operating a hand-held control. After its batteries have charged for six hours the robot can walk for eight kilometres, approximately one step every three seconds. (7) _____ 'There are so many good things in life, and any of them could become the basis for my robots.'

3 Work in groups. Discuss these questions.
1 What's your opinion of Mr Wu?
2 How would you describe Mrs Wu?
3 Mr Wu believes that *many good things in life could become the basis for a robot*. Do you agree with him?

Vocabulary: inventors and inventing

Phrasal verbs

1 Match the highlighted phrasal verbs in the article to these definitions:

a collect _____

b think of (something) _____

c test _____

d stopping/quitting _____

e find by accident _____

2 The following sentences include some words from the text about the Chinese inventor. Choose the correct word (in *italics*) in sentences 1–7. Use the text to help you.
1 Both the USA and Russia were *pioneers/prototypes* of space exploration.
2 Scientists have suffered a number of *drawbacks/setbacks* in their search for a cure.
3 The sad thing is that his *imagination/obsession* has virtually destroyed his family life.
4 This new method is a great *invention/innovation* in language learning.
5 I've had an amazing *brainwave/brainchild* for a new car.
6 My new robot has passed all the necessary *tests/experiments* and is ready to go on sale.
7 This is an amazing *breakthrough/breakdown* that has provided hope to millions of bald people.

3 Now complete these sentences using the incorrect words in exercise 2. The sentences are not in the same order.
1 One of the _____ of being married to an inventor is that they are always working.
2 The lack of progress on the project was due to a _____ in communication.
3 Before a company launches a new device, they need to make a _____.
4 Science is very important but I don't agree with doing _____ on animals.
5 The _____ of the compass meant that sailors no longer had to navigate by the stars.
6 This computer game is amazing. The person who designed it must have an incredible _____.
7 His latest _____ is a baseball cap with built-in headphones.

Listening: intelligent robots

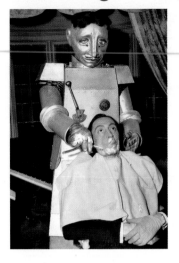 

1 Discuss. If you designed a robot, what would you like it to do? What would it look like?

PAPER 4, PART 2

2 🎧 7.1 SENTENCE COMPLETION Listen to an interview with a professor on the topic of robots of the future. For questions 1–10 below complete the sentences.

Old black and white science fiction films used to show robots that were dangerous and would attack
(1) _____. Nowadays, you can see robots in our
(2) _____. The Japanese are developing them to look after both **(3)** _____. Rather than have robots around the house, the interviewer thinks most of us would rather talk to a **(4)** _____.

Professor Witfield doesn't agree that humans don't like talking to **(5)** _____. Humans might prefer robots to ordinary computers because we then wouldn't have to stare at a **(6)** _____. Witfield thinks there is a problem with letting robots have **(7)** _____.

Unlike the past, robots in the future will be capable of making **(8)** _____.

Professor Witfield thinks the effect of computers now being able to think for themselves means that we need to have a
(9) _____.

If governments use robots in the army they need to consider **(10)** _____.

3 Discuss. Do you think the kinds of robots Professor Whitfield describes are a good idea? Should we have 'intelligent' robots?

Grammar: verbs followed by the gerund or the infinitive

➡ Grammar Reference (Section 9) page 174

1 Sentences 1–9 are from Listening 7.1. Write the verbs in brackets as gerunds or infinitives. Look at the examples in sentences 1 and 2.

1 We all remember _watching_ (watch) those old black and white science fiction films at the cinema with androids and robots.

2 As soon as you saw a robot you expected _to see_ (see) them go crazy.

3 Do we risk _____ (have) our day-to-day life controlled by machines that think for themselves?

4 Don't you think most people would prefer _____ (communicate) with a real person?

5 The Japanese have succeeded in _____ (develop) household robots for some time ...

6 A human being isn't designed _____ (look) at a screen all day ...

7 But we've also heard a lot about scientists who've managed _____ (make) robots with intelligence.

8 I would like _____ (see) a real public debate take place on how this will affect society in the future.

9 Governments should consider _____ (use) robots ethically.

2 🎧 7.2 Listen to check your answers in exercise 1.

3 Work in pairs. Decide which form (gerund, infinitive or both) would follow these verbs and match them to the categories in the Grammar Spotlight on page 69.

afford	try	decide	mind	enjoy	like
look forward to	want	finish	seem	would like

GRAMMAR SPOTLIGHT

Verbs followed by the gerund or the infinitive

Remember:

1 Some verbs are always followed by the gerund (*risk having* …).

2 Some verbs are always followed by the infinitive (*expect to see* …).

3 Some verbs may be followed by either the gerund or the infinitive with little difference in the meaning (*start attacking/start to attack*) or a big difference in meaning (*remember to watch/remember watching*).

4 Verbs + preposition are always followed by a gerund: *succeeded in developing*.

5 Verbs such as *like* and *prefer* can be followed by the infinitive or the gerund. When we add *would* (*would like, would prefer*), use the infinitive only: *I'd like to meet at nine*.

4 The verbs in 1–7 below can be followed by either the gerund or the infinitive but with a big difference in the meaning. Complete each pair with the correct form of the verb in brackets.

1 A She always remembered _____ her medicine before she went to bed. (*take*)

B She remembered _____ a drink from the glass and then she fainted. (*take*)

2 A He stopped _____ at the map because it was out-of-date. (*look*)

B He stopped _____ at the map because he was lost. (*look*)

3 A I regret _____ you that your delivery will be late. (*tell*)

B I regret _____ you now because you've told everyone else. (*tell*)

4 A Forget _____ about tomorrow! Worry about now! (*think*)

B Don't forget _____ about what you'd like to work on next week. (*think*)

5 A I had a difficult pupil in my class who went on _____ a famous celebrity. (*be*)

B I had a difficult pupil in my class who went on _____ difficult all through his life. (*be*)

6 A Sorry, I didn't mean _____ you from going out this evening. (*stop*)

B It meant _____ her from going out with her friends anymore. (*stop*)

7 A We tried _____ that question but it was too hard. (*answer*)

B We've tried _____ this question three times now and still can't get it right. (*answer*)

5 KEY WORD TRANSFORMATIONS Complete the second sentence so that it has a similar meaning to the first sentence, using the word given. Do not change the word given. You must use between two and five words, including the word given.

1 She hasn't smoked since 1996.

stopped

She _____ 1996.

2 Can I offer you a cup of tea or coffee?

like

_____ a cup of tea or coffee?

3 You don't like to work late, do you?

hate

You _____ you?

4 We've unsuccessfully answered this question three times already.

try

We've _____ this question three times already.

5 The student got the funding with some difficulty.

manage

The student _____ the funding, with some difficulty.

6 Do you remember Robby? He's a famous singer now.

went on

Robby _____ a famous singer.

7 Check your work carefully for spelling errors.

need

You _____ carefully for spelling errors.

8 I shouldn't have asked him to come.

regret

I _____ to come.

Key word: *to*

1 **The word *to* is missing. Write it into the sentences below.**

1 I look forward *to* seeing you.
2 What are you listening?
3 That's a terrible thing say!
4 Is she old enough ride a bike?
5 Remember call me when you get there.
6 Take a coat. It's sure rain.
7 Do you have leave so soon?
8 We're afraid go out in the dark.
9 OK. Let's get down some work now.
10 I'd rather talk face face than on the phone.

2 **Work in pairs. Here are six responses containing *to*. Think of six sentences that would receive each response. Then say the sentence to your partner. Can he/she give the correct response?**

What a horrible thing to say!
In order not to be late.
To be honest, I think you're right.
But I've got too much to do.
I'm sorry to hear that.

GRAMMAR SPOTLIGHT

Dictionary skills

Use your dictionary to help you learn verb patterns. Look at this example from the *Collins Cobuild Intermediate Dictionary*. How many verb patterns are there which contain the word *to*?

ask/aːsk, aesk/ **(asks, asking, asked) 1.** v-t If you **ask** someone something, you say something in the form of a question because you want some information □ *'How is Frank?'* he asked. □ *I asked him his name.* □ *I wasn't the only one asking questions. She asked me if I'd already had my dinner.* **2.** v-t If you ask someone to do something, you tell them that you want them to do it. If you ask to do something, you tell someone that you want to do it. *We had to ask him to leave.* □ *I asked to see the Director.* **3.** v-i If you ask for something, you say that you would like it. If you ask someone, you say that you want them

Look up the following verbs in your dictionary. How many have verb patterns which contain the word *to*?

say	tell	manage	forget	like

Vocabulary: computers and technology

Phrasal verbs

1 **Replace the words in bold in sentences 1–6 with the phrasal verbs in the box. Make any other necessary changes to the sentence.**

plug in	set up	log in to	hack into	click on	back up

1 To **enter** the website you need to type your username and password.
2 The bank has said that someone **illegally accessed** their computer records.
3 Just **put the arrow here and press** this icon twice to run the program.
4 Next, you need to **insert** this cable to connect it to the printer.
5 Did you **make a copy of** these documents?
6 Have you seen the website my school has **created**?

2 **Categorise these computer words under the headings Hardwear, Email and Internet.**

keyboard	inbox	online	mouse
worldwide	carbon copy (cc)	web	screen
homepage	attachment	subject	links

3 **Discuss. What's your favourite website? Why do you like it? Have you ever set up a website?**

4 **Work in pairs. You will each read about one person. Make notes in the table below about them.**

Student A: Turn to Information File 7.2 on page 230
Student B: Turn to Information File 7.3 on page 231

	Rebekka	Alex
What kind of background did this person have?		
When did he/she come up with the initial idea?		
How did he/she use the Internet?		
What has happened as a result?		

5 **Now find out from your partner about their person and complete the table.**

6 **Discuss. What are the similarities between the two people? Do you know about other people in your country who have been successful because of the Internet?**

Speaking: suggesting and recommending

1 🎧 **7.3 Listen to a web designer describing how to make a simple home page. Make notes about his recommendations using the headings below.**

- Name

  _____

- Links

  _____

- Icons

  _____

- Other features

  _____

- Contact

  _____

2 Discuss. Do you agree with the speaker's recommendations? What do you think makes a good website?

3 The sentences below are from Listening 7.3. Match a beginning (in A) to an ending (in B).

A
1 Let's _____
2 How about _____
3 Perhaps _____
4 Make sure you know _____
5 It's also important _____
6 It should be a name that's _____
7 I strongly recommend _____
8 Don't forget that _____
9 It's also worth _____
10 It's a good idea to _____

B
a that you include links to other sites.
b why you want a website.
c remembering that the more features and effects you have ...
d links can take the form of words that you click on.
e you could even start an e-business.
f advertising your local club?
g set up a website.
h give a contact email.
i to choose a good name.
j easy to remember.

4 🎧 **7.3 Listen again to check.**

5 Which words and phrases in sentences 1–10 in exercise 3 are followed by ...?

1 to infinitive _____

_____

2 the -ing form _____

_____

3 the bare infinitive _____

_____

Example:
Let's ... + bare infinitive
How about + -ing form

6 Choose one of the topics below. You are an expert in that topic. Make a list of three things to remember.
- riding a bike for the first time
- finding useful information on the Internet
- choosing a mobile phone
- memorising new English words
- designing a room in a house

7 Now work in pairs. Explain to your partner what is important to remember about your subject. Make suggestions and recommendations.

EXAM SPOTLIGHT

Exchanging ideas, expressing and justifying opinions

PAPER 5, PART 3
In this part of the speaking test, it's important to respond appropriately to your partner when they make a suggestion or recommend something.
Here are some useful phrases:
- *That's a good idea.*
- *Sure.*
- *Yes, I think so too.*
- *Right.*
- *I know what you mean, but ...*
- *Yes, but ...*
- *And we could also ...*

PAPER 5, PART 3

8 Your local town wants to set up a website to let people know about its news and events. On the main homepage there is space for two photographs that will represent what the site is about and help to attract lots of visitors.

- **Work in pairs.**

- **Discuss the possible photographs that the townspeople have donated on page 72.**

- **Then try to agree on the best two.**

Writing: a review

1   Discuss in pairs. Do you like playing computer games? If you answer, 'yes', tell your partner what makes a good or bad game. If you don't like them, explain why not to your partner.

2   A friend of yours is enthusiastic about computer games and she regularly writes reviews of different games for the college magazine. She has just bought a new game (*Goldfinder 3*) and has made some notes about it. Read her notes. Does she like the game?

THE STORY AND LOCATIONS
Not very original – you have to find treasure and fight monsters (as usual!)
Set in caves and mountains – needs to be more varied with jungles and cities.

GRAPHICS
These are fantastic and very realistic.
Monsters and creatures are scary.

ENTERTAINMENT VALUE
Provides many hours of fun. Most expensive game currently in the shops.

OVERALL
Well above average.
Much better than Goldfinder 1 and 2.

3 Finish her review of *Goldfinder 3* below by completing information from the notes in exercise 2.

> The aim of the new computer game 'Goldfinder 3' is to (1) _____ which isn't very
> (2) _____. All the locations are set
> (3) _____ and really it should be
> (4) _____.
>
> Nevertheless, the graphics are (5) _____ and it's worth playing just because the monsters
> (6) _____. One other thing I really like is that the game provides (7) _____ even if it is (8) _____.
>
> So, overall I'd recommend the game as it's
> (9) _____ and (10) _____.

4 Read extracts from four reviews. What is being reviewed?

> Aside from the <u>rather confusing plot</u> and <u>a bit of a slow start</u>, this ends up being <u>a real page turner</u> with <u>a nice twist</u> that <u>keeps you guessing</u> until the end.

> As <u>blockbusters</u> go, this <u>isn't 'edge of your seat' stuff</u>. It's probably worth seeing if you like sitting back in your armchair to <u>be wowed</u> by <u>great special effects</u>, but by the end you <u>don't care what happens</u> to any of the characters in the <u>less than gripping</u> storyline.

> With only one <u>really catchy</u> track at the beginning that you'll <u>find yourself singing</u> along to in the car and then nine more which <u>your grandmother might listen to</u>, I recommend you just download the first song and forget the rest.

> One thing I really liked about the homepage is that it's <u>easy to navigate.</u> Some of the graphics are a <u>bit retro</u> and look like they are left over from the 90s but the links are all <u>up-to-date</u> and overall it's much better than other similar …

5 Look at the underlined phrases in the reviews. Label them either positive (+) or negative (-).

6 Work in pairs. Use some of the underlined phrases from exercise 4 in full sentences. Tell your partner about a book, film, music CD/download or website you have read, seen, heard or visited recently.

7 Now write your own review of a website, book, film or music CD that you like. Structure your review in a similar way to the one in exercise 3, with three paragraphs. Use some of these expressions to help:

Introducing your review
The aim/purpose of this review is to …
My favourite is …
One book/film/website/CD I really like is …
An interesting book/film/website I read/saw/visited recently was …

Describing the main features and what you like about them
One thing I really like about it is …
It's worth visiting/reading/seeing/listening to because …

Describing what needs improvement
It should …
It isn't very …
One thing that could be improved is …
It needs more …

Final comments
Overall, I (strongly) recommend …
(Nevertheless) it's much better than …
To summarise, I'd say that …

WRITING CHECKLIST

A review

After you write, always check your work. Check the grammar or vocabulary and also the structure and the layout. Another good way to check your work is to swap with a partner and comment on each other's writing. For your review you could use this checklist to help you.

The review …	Yes (✓)	No (✗)
• includes no less than 120 and no more than 180 words.	☐	☐
• includes three to four paragraphs.	☐	☐
• introduces the website, film, book or music.	☐	☐
• introduces the main features and what they are for.	☐	☐
• describes what you like.	☐	☐
• describes what needs improvement.	☐	☐
• makes a final summary comment.	☐	☐

➜ Writing Guide, page 201

Review and Use of English

1 Match the word on the left to a suffix on the right. How many different words can you create?

Example: *invent – inventor – invention – inventing*

hack	terror	manage
engine	govern	compute
electric	educate	consult
secure	expert	

Suffixes:

-er -ant -ism -or
-ion -ing -al -ment
-ity -ise

2 **WORD FORMATION** Read the text about Ankit Fadia from India. Use the word given in capitals at the end of some of the lines to form a word that fits in each gap.

An Indian teenage **(1)** _____ expert who helped the police and the **(2)** _____ to protect itself from people attacking their **(3)** _____ is turning down job offers in order to complete his degree. Ankit Fadia, 18 and son of an electrical **(4)** _____ , said he would prefer five years at Stanford University to becoming a highly-paid **(5)** _____ .

Ankit has spread his technical **(6)** _____ across the world including giving lectures to **(7)** _____ . institutions and software companies. Last month he was in Singapore giving advice on cyber **(8)** _____ . Once he's finished his studies, Ankit intends to start a **(9)** _____ firm. In his spare time he likes listening to rock music and reading books on **(10)** _____ .

HACK

GOVERN

COMPUTE

ENGINE

CONSULT

EXPERT

EDUCATE

TERROR

SECURE

MANAGE

3 Choose the correct word (in *italics*) in sentences 1–10.

1 I remembered *to work/working* with him when we were both living in London.
2 They *managing/tried* to get the engine running.
3 Would you enjoy *to visit/visiting* this kind of place?
4 In most cases, doctors have *succeeded/managed* in discovering a remedy for this kind of disease.
5 How about *make/making* our own website instead of paying a designer.
6 It's probably worth *to ask/asking* her if she'd like to help at the party. We can't just assume that she will.
7 They were late because they stopped *to do/doing* some shopping on the way home.
8 Did you *remind/remember* Julia to call her mum?
9 Don't *recall/forget* you have an appointment later.
10 I strongly recommend *to try/trying* this game out.

4 Read the text below and think of a word which best fits each gap. Use only one word in each gap.

Dancing robot copies human moves

Japanese researchers **(1)** _____ created a dancing robot capable of imitating a routine, with no **(2)** _____ for rehearsals. The robot HRP-2 can copy **(3)** _____ moves of a human dance teacher through video motion capture technology. **(4)** _____ example, HRP-2 watched dance instructor Hisako Yamada performing a Japanese folk dance and accurately reproduced her performance **(5)** _____ minutes later. One use for such robots might be **(6)** _____ keep the knowledge of traditional Japanese folk dances alive as fewer humans **(7)** _____ maintaining the skills to perform them. However the robots are unlikely to replace ballerinas **(8)** _____ time soon. As one folk dancer said: 'My impression **(9)** _____ that there would still be a human element lacking. The robot would still look, for the want **(10)** _____ a better word, robotic.'

8   Crime and social responsibility

Getting started

1   Look at the crimes in the photos. How serious do you think they are? Give each a score from 1 to 6 ... (1 = least serious, 6 = most serious).

shoplifting

computer hacking

dropping litter

mugging

bank robbery

speeding

2   Which punishment below do you think was given for each crime in the photos? Say why.
- ten years in prison
- pay a fine of €100
- do community service for 40 hours
- attend a talk by the police on how to drive safely
- probation for one year
- an 18-month prison sentence

Check your answers in Information File 8.1 on page 230.

3   Discuss. Do you think the punishments in exercise 2 were fair? Would you change any of them?

Reading: crime and punishment

1 Discuss. What do you think the crime might be in each picture below?

1 2 3 4

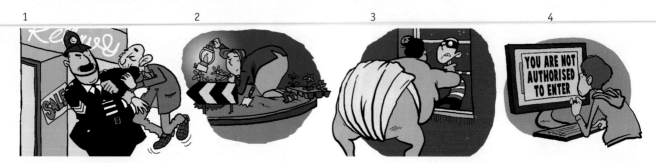

2 Read the text below and match the illustration to the crime.

POLICE WATCH

Your monthly round-up of the mad, bad and not-so-dangerous crimes from around the world.

A

One way to impress your future employer

A 14-year-old boy whose favourite pastime was hacking into the confidential computer records of banks and government organisations was finally caught by police last week. However, rather than receive a prison sentence or fine, the child-criminal has now been offered a job with a software developer specialising in anti-virus programs. The company that made the job offer said the boy had more than met their requirements, but one government minister commented that this kind of reward set a bad example for other youngsters thinking of breaking into systems. The software company defended its decision saying the boy had shown real initiative and that this approach to the crime would be more effective than sending him to juvenile prison.

B

When is a crime not a crime?

Do you often think that your town may benefit from more green spaces? Would you prefer fewer roads and buildings in favour of trees and flowers instead? If your answer is 'yes', then you might be surprised to hear about the local council in the English town of Blakenthorpe, which is currently trying to arrest people for 'planting flowers'. It all began when flowers and plants started appearing at road sides and areas around the city. The town council, which is responsible for green spaces in Blakenthorpe, has blamed 'Green Vandals' for doing some 'midnight gardening'. However, the council and police shouldn't expect much help from local residents who say this is the best kind of vandalism. As one person said, 'These so-called law-breakers are just doing the job that our local council should be doing. I wish them the best of luck!'

C

Lock me up – now!

Many burglars are probably prepared to deal with alarms or maybe one or two large dogs at the front door but a burglar in Osaka, Japan, had a surprise when he broke into a house where 15 sumo wrestlers were staying the night. Shiro Morioka, 42, had broken in through the back of the house and climbed into a bedroom in the middle of the night. He was in the process of looking for something to steal when he met a 130-kilo sumo wrestler. That would have been bad enough but Mr Morioka was even more horrified to find that the whole house was full of sumo wrestlers. 'First I was caught by a massive man. When the lights turned on, I was surrounded by sumo wrestlers,' Mr Morioka told reporters. He instantly surrendered himself and was relieved when the police took him away to the safety of a police cell.

D

A criminal whose bark was worse than his bite!

Police arrested a 76-year-old man last night for shoplifting and also accused him of attacking a police officer. The man had tried to escape by biting the officer. Unfortunately, he'd left his teeth on his bedside table at home. The pensioner, who tried to steal some trousers from a shop, sank his gums into the officer's arm – but it had no effect and the policeman was unhurt. A spokesperson for the police said, 'He had forgotten to put his false teeth in.' Journalists had arranged to have an interview with the ageing shoplifter but it was later reported that he was unavailable for comment. However, it is believed that he may simply be incapable of answering any questions without his teeth in!

3 MULTIPLE MATCHING For questions 1–15 choose the crime (A–D) from the text. Each crime may be chosen more than once.

Which criminal ...?

1 wanted to be arrested _____

2 didn't want to be arrested _____

3 benefited from the crime _____

4 illegally connected to another computer _____

5 hadn't remembered something _____

6 has the support of other people _____

7 might encourage further crime _____

8 had a hobby _____

9 wanted some new clothes _____

10 is doing someone else's job _____

11 hadn't expected to meet so many people _____

12 illegally entered a building _____

13 has improved something _____

14 hasn't been caught yet _____

15 tried to hurt a policeman _____

Vocabulary: crime and criminals

1 Use words from the text on page 76 to help you complete this table.

Crime	Person	Definition
shoplifting	(1) _____	stealing from (2) _____
(3) _____	vandal	damaging property
burglary	(4) _____	stealing by (5) _____
(6) _____	hacker	breaking into (7) _____

2 Match these other crimes to their definitions:

arson — threatening someone to make them give you money

theft — stealing such as robbery or burglary

forgery — deliberately setting fire to property

kidnapping — copying something such as money, important documents or paintings

smuggling — attacking and stealing from someone in the street

blackmail — taking someone (e.g. a child) and asking for money (from the family)

mugging — carrying and not declaring items through customs

3 Which is the odd word out in each of these lists?

A theft, speeding, burglary, shoplifting

B capture, imprison, release, arrest

C judge, detective, jury, prosecution

D police officer, thief, mugger, smuggler

E arson, burglary, blackmail, vandalism

Key word: *get*

1 Replace the word *got* with the correct form of these verbs.

understand	is	receive	arrest	annoy
force	meet	capture	arrive	manage

1 The police *got* him for shoplifting and attacking an officer. _____

2 He *got* ten years in prison for the crime. _____

3 I don't *get* how someone can do that to someone else. _____

4 By the time the police *got* there, the burglars were miles away. _____

5 We didn't *get* around to going to the public meeting. _____

6 What *gets* me is that the judge let him go with only a fine! _____

7 The police were determined to *get* the thieves. _____

8 Local people *got* together to discuss the problem of vandalism in the area. _____

9 He held a gun to my head and *got* me to open the safe in the bank. _____

10 Joe *got* robbed on his way to work. _____

2 Work in pairs. Complete these phrases about crime in your country. Tell your partner.

What gets me is that ...   I don't get how ...

Phrasal verbs

3 Complete sentences 1–5 with participles from the box.

away	into	away with	up to	out

1 The three men got _____ in a blue van.

2 I can't believe they got _____ the robbery and no one saw them.

3 It's very quiet. What do you think the children are getting _____?

4 The 42-year-old got _____ such a mess with the police.

5 If I help you, what do I get _____ of it? How much money do I make?

4 Think of two more phrasal verbs with *get* and make a sentence. Tell your partner.

Listening: stopped by the police

1 🎧 **8.1 MULTIPLE MATCHING You will hear five different people talking about why they were recently stopped by the police. Choose the reason from the list (A–F). Use the letters only once. There is one extra letter which you do not need to use.**

Speaker 1: _____

Speaker 2: _____

Speaker 3: _____

Speaker 4: _____

Speaker 5: _____

A driving along the wrong street

B breaking the speed limit

C witnessing a crime

D being mistaken for someone else

E driving in the wrong direction

F shoplifting at a supermarket

Grammar: relative clauses

GRAMMAR SPOTLIGHT

Relative clauses

Relative clauses add information to the main clause. Read these three sentences from the article on page 76. The relative clauses are underlined:

Sentence 1: A 14-year-old boy <u>whose favourite pastime was hacking into the confidential computer records of banks and government organisations</u> was finally caught by police last week.

Sentence 2: The company <u>that made the job offer</u> said the boy had more than met their requirements.

Sentence 3: The town council, <u>which is responsible for green spaces in Blakenthorpe</u>, has blamed 'Green Vandals' for doing some midnight gardening.

There are **two types** of relative clause:

Sentences 1 and 2 contain a **defining relative clause** because the writer feels the information is essential. Note that you can replace the pronouns *who* or *which* with the pronoun *that*.

Sentence 3 contains a **non-defining relative clause** because the information isn't essential but the writer wants to give some extra or background information. This clause is always punctuated with commas. Note that you cannot replace the pronoun *who* or *which* with the pronoun *that*.

1 There are four more sentences containing relative clauses in the article on page 76. Can you find them? Which of the clauses are *defining* and which are *non-defining*?

➡ Grammar Reference (Section 13) page 182

2 Combine the pairs of sentences below with a defining relative clause. Use the words in brackets.

1 That's the policeman. He caught the burglar. (*who* or *that*).

   That's the policeman that/who caught the burglar.

2 He's the one. He was seen at the scene of the crime. (*who* or *that*)

   _____

3 This is the shop. We said we'd meet in this shop. (*where*)

   _____

4 Do you know the reason? What was the reason he couldn't come? (*why*).

   _____

5 Over there is the building. The building was destroyed by fire last night. (*which* or *that*)

   _____

6 The woman is waiting for you in reception. Her car was stolen. (*whose*)

   _____

7 Do you remember the time? You could walk down the streets safely at night. (*when*)

   _____

3 Now read five sentences with non-defining relative clauses. Each one has at least one mistake (including punctuation). Can you correct them?

1 The shoplifter, he had only been released from prison a week ago was caught on camera.

2 The house, that had a security system, has been burgled three times.

3 The town, over half a million people live, is one of the safest in the country.

4 A retired policeman, that had left the police force in 2005, was accused of forgery yesterday at the High Court.

5 The factory which employs 200 people, caught fire in strange circumstances.

GRAMMAR SPOTLIGHT

Informality and formality in relative clauses

To be more informal you can leave out the pronoun in some defining relative clauses. Leave out *who, which* or *that* if it is the object of the verb in the relative clause:

The witness ~~who~~ I interviewed admitted it was her.

Do you have the money ~~which~~ you borrowed?

Do you have the money ~~that~~ you borrowed?

We often leave out *why* and *when* as well:

Do you know the reason ~~why~~ he left?

He'll never forget the night ~~when~~ he met a sumo wrestler.

To be more formal we replace certain pronouns with others: *whom (who), in which (where), for which (why), on which (where).*

*The suspect, **whom** police questioned for over six hours, is now free.*

*Is this the house **in which** you grew up?*

4 Write in a pronoun or preposition in sentences 1–5. Look at the examples:

> *which*
> *Where's the pen / I lent you yesterday?*
>
> *in*
> *This is the building / which a famous murder took place.*

1 Which date was it we all went out to that club?

2 Do you understand the reasons why you are going to prison?

3 The neighbour I mentioned is still causing problems.

4 Do you know the reason she called?

5 The suspect says he was away on business the night which the crime was committed.

5 Read the pairs of sentences about a prisoner. Use relative clauses to change sentences and form a news article about him.
Example:
Dragan Boskovic, who wanted to wish his girlfriend a happy birthday, escaped from a jail in Montenegro.

1a Dragan Boskovic escaped from a jail in Montenegro.

1b He wanted to wish his girlfriend a happy birthday.

2a He escaped over a wall.

2b It was over three metres high.

3a He went straight to his girlfriend's house.

3b He spent the evening there.

4a He finally explained his reasons to the police.

4b They arrested him two hours later.

5a 'I hadn't been able to call her on the prison phone to say "happy birthday".'

5b 'The phone was broken.'

6 Turn to Information File 8.2 on page 230 and read the original news story about this prisoner. Compare it with your own.

7 Now write three sentences about some news you heard recently. Do not use any relative clauses. Swap sentences with your partner and rewrite your partner's sentences by adding relative clauses to make it more interesting.

1 _____

_____

2 _____

_____

3 _____

_____

8 Read the article below. Choose between the correct words (in *italics*) in 1–8.

MAN FINED OVER CIGARETTE

A man, to (1) *whose/whom* a £75 fine was given for dropping cigarette ash, has finally agreed to pay it. Richard Jones, (2) *who/that* was smoking a cigarette on his local high street, was seen by local councillor Rona Keeting. The town councillor reported the cigarette to police (3) *which/when* she described as 'dripping ash'. The local magistrate of Hemden in Lincolnshire, the town (4) *in/on* which Mr Jones lives, ordered him to pay a penalty notice (5) *what/which* required settlement within 14 days. Mr Jones ignored the order so was requested to appear in court. As a result he has paid the fine but told local reporters that he can't understand the reason (6) *why/when* other people (7) *who/for which* drop chewing gum or litter don't receive similar treatment. Councillor Rona Keeting said 'Neither Hemden, (8) *who/which* has a clear policy on littering, nor the citizens of Hemden will tolerate behaviour of this kind.'

Use of English: open cloze

1 Read this article about being a 'Freegan'. Think of the word which best fits each gap. Use only one word in each gap.

A matter of choice

GREEN ISSUES

They don't need (1) _____ do it but for environmental and ethical reasons they choose to. These are Freegans: an organisation (2) _____ members live off other people's rubbish. 'I (3) _____ perfectly well afford to buy food,' says author Tristram Stuart. Yet his aim isn't to save money but to (4) _____ a political point.

Researchers estimate (5) _____ a quarter of all food waste that goes (6) _____ landfills is still edible. And the waste, according (7) _____ the Freegans, isn't limited (8) _____ to food. 'By recovering the things that have been thrown away by retailers, offices, schools, homes, hotels or places like that by going (9) _____ their rubbish bins,' says the website (www.freegan.info), 'freegans (10) _____ able to obtain books, toiletries, magazines, newspapers, videos, kitchen appliances, carpets, musical instruments ...' and the list goes (11) _____.

But beware, searching through the bins behind your local supermarket isn't (12) _____ anyone with a weak stomach and is often illegal.

2 Read the text in exercise 1 again. As you read complete these sentences about the article. Then compare and discuss your responses with your partner.

1 I found it really interesting that _____

2 One thing that surprises me is that _____
_____

3 I think what they are doing is really _____
_____

4 I would/wouldn't become a Freegan because _____
_____

Listening: social responsibility

1 🎧 8.2 Listen to an interview with a woman involved with 'Freecycling'. Find out one similarity and one difference between:
- Freegans and Freecyclers.
- Freecyclers and recyclers.

2 🎧 8.2 MULTIPLE CHOICE Listen to the radio interview again. For questions 1–7, choose the best answer (*A*, *B* or *C*).

1 Why is Connie on the radio programme?
   A in order to inform listeners about freecycling
   B because Geoff wanted to interview her
   C to find out more about recycling

2 The Freecycle Network was originally set up
   A by Connie to help her local town.
   B as an alternative to recycling.
   C to help protect a local area from waste.

3 The government
   A hasn't been involved with freecycling.
   B tried to stop freecycling.
   C wanted to make money from freecycling.

4 The emphasis is on
   A using everyday items again.
   B using reusable parts of household items.
   C selling everyday items you don't need anymore.

5 Total membership of the organisation
   A is only in the USA and Germany.
   B numbers nearly three million.
   C numbers over three thousand.

6 If you can't find a freecycler near you, Connie advises you to
   A join a local group.
   B set up your own community.
   C visit the website.

7 Items for freecycling must not
   A be for children.
   B be against the law.
   C have cost you anything to buy.

Speaking: showing you are listening

Active speaking

Taking part in a conversation means being an active listener as well as speaking effectively. It's important to show interest in what the other person is saying.

1 🎧 8.2 In the previous listening exercise on page 80, the presenter uses the following expressions to show Connie he is listening. Listen again and number these expressions in the order you hear them.

- OK. So ... _____
- Right. _____
- Sure. _____
- Wow! _____
- Sounds great. _____
- I see, but ... _____

2 Work in pairs. Take turns to describe the following:
- plans for your next holiday
- something not many people know about you
- how you get to your house
- something you would like to change about the world

If you are the person listening, remember to be an active listener by using some of the appropriate expressions from exercise 1.

PAPER 5, PART 3

3 Your local college intends to have one day when students raise money for a local charity. Look at the suggestions below. In pairs discuss each idea and decide which you think would be best.

Consider...
- the advantages of your choice.
- the disadvantages of your choice.
- what sort of preparation would be needed to hold your chosen event.

collect money in the street

have a sponsored walk

wash cars

have a fancy dress party

hold a talent show

have a sponsored cycle ride

Writing: an article

1 Work in pairs. Read the exam question below and one candidate's answer. How well do you think the candidate answers the question?

Exam question

Read this advertisement in a local newspaper and write the article.

We are looking for an article (120–180 words) that suggests **three** easy ways for our readers to produce less waste in their daily lives. Explain why this is an important issue and suggest three ways to help.

The writer of the winning article will receive a brand new bicycle!

Three easy ways to save you money and the planet

Have you ever stopped to consider how much you throw away every week? Producing less waste could save you money and, more importantly, save the natural resources of the planet.

Take, for example, plastic bags. Many people put their shopping in a bag and then throw the bag away. Why not simply take the old plastic bags back to the supermarket next time you shop and use them again? A second way to produce less waste is to give your unwanted things to charity. If you have old household appliances, books, DVDs and clothes, then take them to a charity shop. They will either resell the items or give them to people in need. Finally, start recycling products like glass bottles, cans and paper. Put these items into separate bins and take them to your local recycling centre.

So, next time you are about to throw something away ask yourself: Can I reuse this? Can someone else reuse this? Can it be recycled?

It's so easy.

EXAM SPOTLIGHT

PAPER 2, PART 2

If you write an article, opinion essay or review in the exam, it's important to:

- spend some time planning before you write.
- think of a title that will attract the reader's attention.
- have an opening sentence to interest the reader.
- use expressions to introduce each new idea;
  First .../ Another way is to ....

2 The candidate spent some time planning the answer in exercise 1 before writing. Below is part of the candidate's plan. Read the candidate's finished article again and write in the missing notes from the plan.

PLAN:

Why it's important:

_____

_____

One way to produce less waste:

_____

_____

A second way:

_____

_____

A third way:

_____

_____

---

3 Discuss. The candidate in exercise 1 used one of these titles for her article:

- How we can save the planet
- Why we shouldn't throw things away
- Three easy ways to save you money and the planet

Why do you think she chose the last title? Can you think of any other possible titles?

4 It is important to have an interesting opening sentence when writing an article. There are five common techniques used to write interesting opening sentences. Match the techniques in a–e to the example opening sentences (1–5).

a a question _____

b a general introduction to the topic _____

c a statistic or surprising fact _____

d create a point for discussion or argument _____

e a personal anecdote _____

1 The typical household probably produces around six bags of rubbish a week.

2 Have you ever stopped to consider how much you throw away every week?

3 There are many ways we can reduce the amount of household waste we produce.

4 One evening I was driving out of the city when I looked across at the sun falling behind what seemed like a giant mountain; in fact it was the city landfill.

5 Some people still say it is too difficult to recycle products and would prefer to throw them away.

5 The exam candidate in exercise 1 uses these expressions in the middle paragraph to introduce the three ways to produce less waste:

1 Take, for example, …

2 A second way to produce less waste is to …

3 Finally, …

Which of these expressions a–h are alternatives? Write 1, 2 or 3.

a First of all, there's _____

b And lastly … _____

c Alternatively you could _____

d You could also consider (-ing) _____

e For one thing, there's the problem of … _____

f Let's start with _____

g Thirdly, … _____

h Another easy way which takes no effort is to …

_____

6 Read the exam question below. Plan the article in the exam question by completing the notes below.

Exam question

You see this advertisement in a local paper. Write the article.

We are looking for an article (120–180 words) that suggests three easy ways to improve the local community. Explain why this is an important issue and suggest three ideas to help.

The winning article will receive a £50 book token!

PLAN:

Why it's important:

_____

One way to improve the community:

_____

A second way:

_____

A third way:

_____

PAPER 2, PART 2

7 Now write the article. Write your answer in 120–180 words in an appropriate style.

WRITING CHECKLIST

An article

After writing, check your work using this checklist.

	Yes (✓)	No (✗)
• Does the title attract attention?	☐	☐
• Is the opening sentence interesting?	☐	☐
• Is each 'idea' introduced with an expression (*first* … etc)?	☐	☐
• Does it have an introductory and concluding paragraph?	☐	☐

➡ Writing Guide, page 204

Review and Use of English

1 MULTIPLE-CHOICE CLOZE **Read the text below and decide which answer (A, B, C or D) best fits each gap.**

The government released **(1)** _____ figures for last year. Overall, the statistics show a fall in violent street crime **(2)** _____ as mugging. A police **(3)** _____ said that the number of arrests for robbery **(4)** _____ also increased. They also claimed that their work with local shop owners had reduced cases **(5)** _____ shoplifting and vandalism.

However, **(6)** _____-based crime continues to rise with 20% more cases than ever of hackers breaking **(7)** _____ files to access personal data on customers. George Maynard, a software analyst specialising **(8)** _____ computer security, believes this trend is unlikely to change in the near future. 'Hacking is here to stay and is potentially public **(9)** _____ number one.'

Finally, the figure attracting most attention is the increased **(10)** _____ to the rich and famous. The huge **(11)** _____ attention given to millionaire celebrities has meant their **(12)** _____ have become obvious targets for kidnappers ...

1	A detective	B crime	C number	D police
2	A like	B with	C such	D so
3	A criminal	B minister	C speaker	D spokesperson
4	A is	B was	C will	D has
5	A from	B of	C to	D in
6	A computer	B robber	C internationally	D password
7	A out of	B off	C up	D into
8	A in	B with	C for	D of
9	A against	B enemy	C terrorist	D crime
10	A problem	B rise	C threat	D stealing
11	A special	B media	C interest	D burglar
12	A possessions	B children	C houses	D accounts

2 **Which word is missing in each of these sentences?**

1 Sorry, I don't know he is. I'll get him to call you back.
2 I don't know the reason they haven't done their homework.
3 He's a politician has high principles.
4 Do you know he lives?
5 Can you tell me one you'd prefer?
6 The burglar was about to leave the police car arrived outside.

3 OPEN CLOZE **Read the text below and think of the word which best fits each gap. Use only one word in each gap.**

Burglars gave money to victim

Police **(1)** _____ currently looking for two burglars who broke **(2)** _____ a woman's apartment and then left her **(3)** _____ money. The woman, Filofteia Stefan, 86, told police **(4)** _____ two young men entered her apartment in the middle of the night wearing black masks.

(5) _____ then trashed her apartment in search **(6)** _____ valuables and money. She said the two men **(7)** _____ through everything, including tearing furniture apart, in their desperate search, but found only **(8)** _____ purse with the equivalent of 50p inside.

(9) _____ the end, realising that their victim was not wealthy, the burglars gave **(10)** _____ woman all of their loose change and left without taking anything! The victim **(11)** _____ now handed the money – a little more than £1 – to the police **(12)** _____ will carry out a fingerprint analysis on the coins.

4 **Use the word in capitals to complete each sentence. Change the form if necessary.**

1 Many _____ just do it for fun and for the challenge. **HACK**
2 The killer has been _____ for life without any probation. **PRISON**
3 Police say the _____ notes can be identified by a line across the left-hand side. **FORGE**
4 The _____ victim was in surprisingly good health when police found her. **KIDNAP**
5 Driving faster than 70 kph is _____ with a fine in my country. **PUNISH**
6 The _____ asked for $10,000 in return for the photographs. **BLACKMAIL**
7 The _____ got away with over €100,000 worth of jewels. **THEFT**
8 I don't think that dropping a cigarette should be _____. There are far worse crimes. **LEGAL**
9 Pirates and _____ used to use the caves along this coastline. **SMUGGLE**
10 They say the fire was the work of _____. **ARSON**

9   You are what you eat

MAIN MENU

Vocabulary:	food and drink; key word: *take*
Grammar:	forms of *used to* and *would*
Speaking:	expressing preferences; talking about the past
Reading:	*All mouth*
Listening:	*Eating out; In the dark*
Writing:	an opinion essay

EXAM MENU

Reading:	gapped text sentences
Writing:	an essay
Use of English:	open cloze; key word transformations
Listening:	multiple matching
Speaking:	two-way conversation

Getting started

1 Discuss. Morgan Spurlock made a film called *Super Size Me* about the effects of junk food on the body. Do you think it matters what you eat?

2 Read the questions (1–6) and match them to the speakers (a–f) below.
1 Are you careful about what you eat?
2 What food can't you do without?
3 How can world hunger be defeated?
4 What's your 'comfort food'?
5 Should governments encourage citizens to eat healthily?
6 If you knew you had one day left to live, what final meal would you choose?

a
It has to be tomato ketchup. Some people say it's not a food but I put it on everything.

c
What a horrible question, but if I had to choose, I think I'd go for steak and chips.

e
They try to make you feel guilty if you smoke and now they want to make you feel guilty about your weight. It makes me mad.

b
Whenever I feel depressed I go to the freezer and have a huge bowl of ice-cream.

d
Yes, I spend all my time counting calories. But each time I go on a diet, I lose three kilos then put on five!

f
The only way to feed the world is to grow genetically modified crops that can resist disease and grow in difficult conditions.

3 Discuss. How would you answer questions 1–6 in exercise 2 above?

Listening: eating out

1 Work in pairs. Tell each other how often you eat out and why.

2 🎧 9.1 You are going to listen to five different people talk about eating and eating out. Listen, and match speakers 1–5 to pictures A–E.

Picture A: Speaker _____

Picture B: Speaker _____

Picture C: Speaker _____

Picture D: Speaker _____

Picture E: Speaker _____

PAPER 4, PART 3

3 🎧 9.1 MULTIPLE MATCHING Listen again and match speakers 1–5 to descriptions A–F. There is an extra letter which you do not need to use.

Which speaker describes ...?

A a preference for ordinary, simple food _____

B the production of a traditional cheese _____

C a huge meal _____

D the finishing touches for a recipe _____

E dealing with a difficult waiter _____

F a mealtime in the olden days _____

Vocabulary: food and drink

1 Take an adjective from box A and pair it with an opposite from box B ('sweet' occurs three times in box A as it can have more than one opposite, depending on what it is referring to).

A
(adjectives)		
sweet	sweet	sweet
still	hot	rare
spicy	raw	tasty

B
(adjectives)		
sour	bland	bitter
cooked	mild	dry
cold		well-done
	sparkling	

2 Complete 1–10 using some of the adjectives from the boxes.

1 The bubbles go up my nose. That's why I always drink _____ water.

2 This recipe contrasts the sweetness of sugar and the _____ taste of vinegar.

3 The food in the canteen is so _____ and boring, so we add lots of ketchup to add some flavour.

4 How embarrassing. I didn't realise that gazpacho was a soup that you eat _____.

5 The curry was so _____ that I thought I was going to have to call the fire brigade.

6 I can't drink black coffee without sweetening it; I find it too _____.

7 Mm, this is delicious and really _____.

8 I'd like it _____, please; I don't like it pink in the middle.

9 I'm not that keen on sweet wine. I much prefer _____.

10 It's best to eat vegetables _____ as it preserves all the vitamins.

3 Using verbs from the box, complete the table.

(verb)						
sprinkle	fry	slice	mix	chop	peel	grate
boil	stir	grill	roast	add	bake	pour

Ways of cutting	Ways of cooking	Other verbs

4 Work in pairs or groups. Brainstorm as many words for different kitchen and cooking implements as you can, in one minute.

Example: *frying-pan, knife, bowl ...*

5 Complete the pairs of sentences using a single word which fits both gaps.

1a A three _____ lunch only costs €12 in that restaurant.

1b Magnus is going on a three-day _____ to learn how to cook Italian food.

2a The Mediterranean _____ is one of the healthiest ways of eating in the world.

2b Goodness me, I'll have to go on a _____ if I am going to wear these trousers again.

3a Truffles are _____ because they only grow in a few special places.

3b I love steak as long as it's quite _____.

6 Look at the pairs of words below. What is the difference between the words in each pair? Write a sentence for each word.
- a *receipt* and a *recipe*
- something *tasteful* and something *tasty*
- *cook* and *cooker*
- *greedy* and *ingredients*

7 Work in groups. Tell each other about ...
- your favourite recipe.
- something special made by a member of your family.
- your country's cuisine.

Speaking: expressing preferences

1 *Prefer* and *would rather* are similar in meaning but have different grammar. Look at sentences 1–5 below and choose the correct word (in *italics.*)

1 I *prefer/rather* chicken to beef.
2 I'd rather *have/to have* tea than coffee.
3 What would you *rather/prefer* to do this evening?
4 I think I'd prefer *go/to go* to the cinema.
5 I generally *prefer/rather* coffee to tea.

2 Study this pair of sentences. Both are correct, but what happens when *rather* is followed directly by a noun or pronoun?

a I'd rather go to the cinema.
b I'd rather we/all of us went to the cinema.

3 Work in pairs or groups. Look at these pictures of different types of restaurant.

- Imagine that you are going to spend the evening together in one of these places.

- Make sure that you ask each person in the group so that you can agree where to go.

- Use *prefer* and *rather* to ask about and state your preferences.

Sonya the Black Widow

At a chicken-wing eating competition in Philadelphia, USA, Bill Simmons, a 150kg truck driver, was confidently expecting to win the title for the fifth successive year. His optimism was in no way affected by the appearance of a 45kg, 36-year-old South Korean woman called Sonya Thomas. (1) _____ After ten minutes Bill had managed to consume 151 chicken wings. Sonya had eaten 154.

Competitive eating used to be an entirely male affair, but Sonya has taken on the men and beaten them. Two years on, and competitive eating has taken off in a big way in the States. Now there are around 150 contests a year with the most popular being televised. Sonya has won an estimated $100,000 in prize money and a nickname to go with it. 'I'm Sonya "The Black Widow" Thomas', she announces. Then she gives a high-pitched giggle and adds 'Kill the men'.

(2) _____ As usual she has eaten sparingly in the days before the competition, but she gets used to consuming vast quantities by drinking a gallon and a half of cola before every meal. 'Because the cola is gassy, it seems to push it out that little bit more and allows you to fit in more food.' An expanded stomach, everyone agrees, is key – and the reason why thin people appear to be at an advantage. (3) _____ With no spare flesh to impede her, Sonya believes she could keep on eating until she bursts.

When the countdown begins she leans over her plate in concentration. Then as soon as the compère shouts 'Go!', she begins forcing deep fried asparagus into her mouth. The crowd gasps in astonishment to see so much food disappear into such a tiny person. To this onlooker, it all seems like a form of mass suicide. (4) _____ She is used to running around serving the customers. Halfway through the competition the 12 competitors are still eating away. Deep fried asparagus falls from their lips, sticks to their cheeks and piles up in little heaps on the ground. It is without doubt the most disgusting thing I have ever seen.

(5) _____ There, her parents used to be so poor that they couldn't afford a fridge and Sonya would have to fight for food with her brothers and sisters. On moving to America she was so amazed by the produce on display, she was determined to take the opportunity to eat as much of it as possible. 'When I started eating competitively I didn't mind what I ate, I just liked all the different tastes. (6) _____

Reading: all mouth

1 **What are the people in the photograph doing? What are the rules of the competitions? Does it look like fun to you?**

2 **You are going to read about a woman who takes part in competitive eating competitions. Read the text quickly. What is surprising about her success? Does she deserve her nickname? How does she train?**

EXAM SPOTLIGHT

Gapped sentences

PAPER 1, PART 2

3 **Imagine you are talking to someone about how to answer this part of the Reading test. Read about how they answer it and decide what you would say to below:**
- 'I never waste my time reading the text all the way through.'
- 'I always trust my instinct and go for the sentence which feels right.'
- 'I start matching sentences to gaps straight away.'
- 'I always do the answers in order.'
- 'I don't bother looking for pronouns and references.'
- 'I don't try to identify the extra sentence. At the end it's obvious.'
- 'Never guess if you don't know.'

PAPER 1, PART 2

4 **GAPPED TEXT SENTENCES Read the article about Sonya again. Seven sentences have been removed from it. Choose from the sentences (A–H) the one which fits each gap (1–7). There is one extra sentence you do not need.**

A However, when she started eating his confidence turned to disbelief.

B If you're fat this will produce a kind of belt around your waist, thereby stopping your stomach expanding.

C I entered the qualifying rounds of a competition and ate 18 hot dogs in five minutes.

D In geographical and cultural terms, all this is about as far away as you can get from South Korea where Sonya was born and brought up.

E However, Sonya claims she is in good shape and that her job at a local fast-food restaurant gives her plenty of opportunity to stay fit.

F She raises one arm to acknowledge the cheers of the crowd.

G It is time that competitive eating was recognised as a serious sport alongside athletics or football.

H Today she has come to the small town of Stockton in California to take part in its deep-fried asparagus eating competition.

5 **What do you think of this kind of competition? What risks do you think the competitors are taking?**

A week later I did 25. Two weeks after that I was up to 37. All the time I was learning about technique; how to use your jaw strength, and also how to eat really fast, but not so fast your throat closes up'. 'Everyone stop eating,' shouts the master of ceremonies. The contestants wipe their mouths and the judges announce that Sonya has won. (7) _____

Sonya stretches out on the grass and considers her future. 'What I want to do is make as much money from this as possible,' she says. 'And then I can achieve my dream.'

'What is your dream?', I ask.

'My dream is that one day, not too far away in the future, I will own my own fast-food restaurant.'

_____

6 **Make nouns from the following words.**

1 optimistic (adjective) ➡ _____ (noun)

2 astonish (verb) ➡ _____ (noun)

3 concentrate (verb) ➡ _____ (noun)

4 appear (verb) ➡ _____ (noun)

Grammar: forms of *used to* and *would*

1 **Identify the forms of *used to* in sentences 1–3 below. Which sentence describes …?**

a a current habit _____

b a developing habit _____

c an old habit/something we no longer do _____

1 Her parents used to be so poor that they couldn't afford a fridge.

2 She is used to running around serving the customers.

3 … but she gets used to consuming vast quantities by drinking a gallon and a half of cola before every meal.

2 **Which sentence in exercise 1 uses *used to* …?**

1 as an auxiliary: _____

2 as an adjective: _____ and _____

3 **What happens to verbs which directly follow *used to*?**

4 **Study sentences 1–5 and tick those where *will* and *would* describe habits.**

1 One in ten people aged 16 to 24 will use at least ten ready meals a week. _____

2 Sonya would have to fight for food with her brothers and sisters. _____

3 Steffi said she would cook dinner tonight. _____

4 She would always take the seat at the back. _____

5 Would you like to try this cake? _____

GRAMMAR SPOTLIGHT

Used to or would?

We can use both *would* and *used to do* to describe discontinued past habits.

*We **used to/would** have a big meal on Sundays.*

But we can only use *used to* to talk about states.

*She **used to/would** have long red hair.*

Used to or the simple past?

If we say how long we did something, then we use the simple past, not *used to*.

We used to live in that house over there. =
We lived in that house for ten years
NOT *We used to live in that house for ten years.*

➡ Grammar Reference (Section 15) page 184

---

5 **Decide which sentences below need to be corrected. If necessary, write the corrected version beneath it.**

1 I would be really fat when I was younger.

_____

2 When his mother got home she would make a cup of tea and read the newspaper.

_____

3 That's the place where I used to going to school.

_____

4 Are you getting used to your new job?

_____

5 You're Jo, aren't you? I would know your mum. We used to work together for ten years. When you were young you would have blond, curly hair.

_____

6 After five years she finally got used to live in London.

_____

Speaking: talking about the past

1 Work in groups. Discuss these topics using forms of *used to* and *would*.

Describe:

- life in your town in your grandparents' time.
- your early childhood, and the people who were important to you then.
- a time in your life where you found it difficult to adapt to a changing situation.
- how eating habits have changed over the past two or three generations in your country.
- changes in transport in your town.

Listening: in the dark

1 Study the pictures on the right. What do you think is happening?

PAPER 4, PART 4

2 ∩ **9.2** MULTIPLE CHOICE Listen to the interview about a particular type of restaurant. For questions 1–7 choose the best answer (*A*, *B* or *C*).

1 What is the main purpose of *In the Dark*?
   A to raise money for charity
   B to improve understanding about the blind
   C to provide an unusual evening out

2 How successful has this restaurant concept been?
   A very
   B hardly
   C moderately

3 How are clients introduced to the dark?
   A They go straight through some curtains
   B gradually
   C along a brightly-lit corridor

4 What can you take into the dining room?
   A mobile phones
   B keys
   C watches

5 How does Roddy think he would behave in the restaurant?
   A He would be fine if he told himself not to panic.
   B He would only go if Katrina held his hand.
   C He couldn't stand it.

6 How did Katrina get on with the person sitting next to her?
   A Very well, after some initial embarrassment.
   B She never got to know him at all.
   C They recognised each other after the meal.

7 What did Katrina think of the food?
   A She'd go there again just for the food.
   B Her other senses compensated for her lack of sight.
   C It was hard to tell what she was eating.

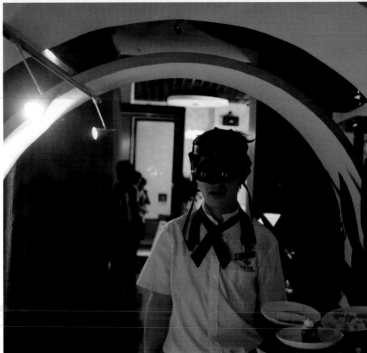

3 What do you think of the *In the Dark* concept? Would you try the restaurant?

4 If you were going to open an unusual restaurant, what would it be? Work in pairs or groups. Using the questions below as a guide, discuss your ideas, then tell the rest of the class.
   - What will the theme of the restaurant be?
   - Where will it be?
   - Who will it appeal to?
   - What will your specialty be?
   - What music or entertainment will you have?
   - Where will people eat?
   - What kind of atmosphere will you try to create?
   - How will you choose your waiters and waitresses?

Key word: *take*

1 Complete the definitions by matching a beginning (a–e) to an ending (1–5).

If we *take* ...

a *care of* someone or something,
b something *into account,*
c *advantage of* someone or something,
d *something for granted,*
e the *opportunity* to do something,

we ...

1 only notice it when it is no longer there.
2 exploit someone/a situation to our benefit (often unfairly).
3 include it in our consideration.
4 take a chance which presents itself.
5 look after them.

2 Work in pairs. Use the expressions from exercise 1 to add a comment on these situations?

1 When I lived at home, I never cooked a meal or ironed a shirt. My mum used to do everything. Now that I live on my own I really miss that!
2 Last year's holiday cost more than I had planned. I had forgotten to include the cost of petrol and motorway charges.
3 She isn't nice to her brother. She borrows money from him that she has no intention of paying back.
4 When I was in Paris on business I had an unexpected free afternoon so I visited the Louvre museum.
5 When I go away, my neighbour feeds my cat and waters the plants.

3 Work in pairs. Look at the pairs of sentences (1–3) below. Discuss the different meanings of the phrasal verbs in bold.

1a She **took off** her watch.
1b The idea has **taken off**.

2a They have been able to **take on** some blind members of staff.
2b Sonya hasn't been afraid to **take on** the men at their own game.

3a How's your new job? How are you **getting on**?
3b I couldn't **get on** the bus because it was so crowded.

SPOTLIGHT ON VOCABULARY

Phrasal verbs and their different meanings

Often the same phrasal verb can have entirely different meanings. Look at this example:

a *I can't come tomorrow. Can we **put** lunch **off** until next week?* = postpone/delay

b *The kitchen was so dirty it **put** me **off** my food.* = disgust

Use of English: key word transformations

PAPER 3, PART 4

1 KEY WORD TRANSFORMATIONS Complete the second sentence so that it has a similar meaning to the first one. Do not change the word given. You must use between two and five words only, including the word given.

1 In the old days customers smoked in restaurants all the time.

used

Customers always _____ in restaurants.

2 I'll never learn the art of eating with chopsticks.

get

I'll _____ eating with chopsticks.

3 I think I'd prefer us to stay in and watch TV this evening.

rather

I _____ and watched TV this evening.

4 Shall we cook or shall we order a takeaway?

rather

Would you _____ ordered a takeaway?

5 They considered her age before making their final decision.

account

They _____ before making their final decision.

6 We enjoyed ourselves, even though the food was fairly awful.

nevertheless

The food was fairly awful but _____ good time.

7 They turned us away from the restaurant even though we had booked.

fact

They turned us away _____ we had booked.

8 Don't assume that your parents will always be there for you.

for

Don't _____ granted.

Writing: an opinion essay

1 Work in pairs or groups. Read the short news item below. What do you think about the girl and the responsibility of her parents?

ISABELLE TAYLOR, an eight-year-old girl, has damaged her hands from sending up to 30 text messages every day. She said she would continue texting because otherwise her social life would be destroyed. Isabelle has had a mobile since the age of six.

2 Read this First Certificate exam question.

Exam question

A magazine has asked readers for their opinions on mobile phones. Write an essay giving your opinion about the advantages and disadvantages of mobile phones.

Now brainstorm the advantages and disadvantages of mobile phones. Create a list of the positive and negative points and write them in the table in order of their importance.

Advantages	Disadvantages

An opinion essay

PAPER 2, PART 2

In the writing test you may be asked to write an essay (composition) on a topic where you have to give your opinion about something and must balance two sides of an argument.

To answer it well you need:
- good content/ideas.
- the right range of expressions to put forward ideas.
- a clear and logical organisation of the essay.

Follow these steps:
1 Start by brainstorming ideas and creating a spidergram (see opposite).
2 Choose the two or three most important points for each side of the argument.
3 Create a linear plan.
4 Write the essay!

3 Read the essay below, written by one student, Melanie. How closely do the ideas in her essay match the list you drew up in exercise 2?

Mobile phones have had a massive impact on people's lives. They are excellent for keeping in touch and text messaging is a fairly effective way of communicating important information instantly. What's more, lives have been saved in emergencies because one was available.

Nevertheless, it is extremely annoying to hear them ringing in public places, or to be forced to listen to loud conversations. Furthermore, while they can save lives, accidents are caused by reckless drivers engaged in mobile phone conversations.

Despite these considerations, it is their impact on the young that worries me the most. Radio waves from mobiles can damage the brain, putting the young most at risk as they use them so much. Mobile use can become an obsession. Teenagers often generate huge bills, and even place themselves in possible danger with strangers contacted on chat lines.

To sum up, the mobile phone is undoubtedly a useful tool. It is a part of modern life we have to live with. The most important thing is that we remain in charge, and that we do not allow ourselves to be controlled by the phone.

4 Before writing her essay Melanie brainstormed her ideas. Look at her 'spidergram'. Which points did she keep, and which did she reject? What would you add to her spidergram if you were writing this essay?

Part of modern life
grandparents didn't have them
relied on phone
had to write letters

Bad things/drawbacks?
annoying!!!
restaurants/trains/in concerts!!
teachers hate them in class

MOBILE PHONES

Good things/advantages
business people

Dangers?
drivers & accidents
mobile phones – cook brain!!
mean people – chat lines
dangers of virtual friends – like Internet
psychological probs? – obsession

5 After putting her ideas into a spidergram, she wrote a plan. Is there anything you would add to her plan?

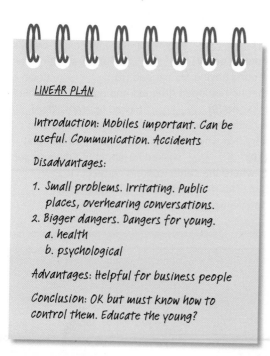

LINEAR PLAN

Introduction: Mobiles important. Can be useful. Communication. Accidents

Disadvantages:

1. Small problems. Irritating. Public places, overhearing conversations.
2. Bigger dangers. Dangers for young.
   a. health
   b. psychological

Advantages: Helpful for business people

Conclusion: OK but must know how to control them. Educate the young?

6 You are going to prepare to write the following exam question:

> **Exam question**
>
> Write an essay giving your opinion on this subject:
>
> 'Young people are eating a less healthy diet nowadays than in their grandparents' time.'

Work in pairs or groups. Before you write the essay discuss these questions together.
- How often do you or your family use ready meals?
- How often do you or your family cook from basic ingredients?
- How many times a month do you go to a fast food restaurant?
- Do you choose light/diet sodas?
- How often do you read the list of ingredients on the packaging?
- How often do you count calories?
- How are your eating habits different from your grandparents'?
- How much exercise did your grandparents get compared to young people nowadays?
- What choice of food was available when they were young?
- Have they changed their own eating habits over the years?

7 After discussing the questions, create a spidergram. Decide which points are important and which are less important. Are there any you won't include in your essay?

8 Now create a logical, linear plan for your essay.

9 With the help of the expressions in the Writing Guide on page 205, and using your plan, write your essay.

WRITING CHECKLIST

Opinion essay
Writing a essay is a process. Don't expect to write it as you go along. You need to prepare first.
Use this checklist to help you:

Have you ...?	Yes (✓)	No (✗)
• brainstormed your ideas	☐	☐
• been selective	☐	☐
• created a plan	☐	☐
• prioritised your points	☐	☐

Remember: Don't attempt this question if you have no point of view or if you don't know the key vocabulary for the topic.

➜ Writing Guide, page 205

Review and Use of English

1 Quickly read the text in exercise 2 below and choose a suitable title from this list.

   a The Western diet

   b Eat yourself healthy

   c How to lose weight

2 Complete the text with the words from the box. Study the clues after each gap – they tell you the type of word missing.

on	their	much	still	found	which
an	little	until	some	take	were

One of the healthiest diets in the world is enjoyed _____by_____ (*preposition*) the people of the south-eastern areas of the Mediterranean. **(1)** _____ (*conjunction*) quite recently the diet was simple and healthy – olive oil provided a third of **(2)** _____ (*possessive adjective*) energy intake and cereals, beans, vegetables and fruit, and to a lesser extent, cheese, milk, eggs and fish provided the rest. A **(3)** _____ (*quantifier*) red wine is drunk with every meal. There is **(4)** _____ (*indefinite article*) almost total absence of butter and red meat. It ignores the animal fats **(5)** _____ (*relative pronoun*) have led to the obesity epidemic in some other countries. There is also proof that it can lead to longer and **(6)** _____ (*adverb*) healthier lives. One study involving seven countries produced **(7)** _____ (*determiner*) extraordinary results. It focused **(8)** _____ (*particle of phrasal verb*) men from the Mediterranean island of Crete. Over many years these men **(9)** _____ (*auxiliary verb*) given regular health checks. The group had the lowest rates of cancer and heart attacks of any of the other subjects. Decades later they **(10)** _____ (*stem of phrasal verb*) out that around half of the men were **(11)** _____ (*adverb*) alive. In the remaining countries where there wasn't even one survivor left! Even though there may, of course, be genetic considerations to **(12)** _____ (*collocation phrase*) into account, changing to a Mediterranean style diet could probably extend our lives.

EXAM SPOTLIGHT

PAPER 3, PART 2

OPEN CLOZE In this part of the Use of English test you, have to complete a text by writing one word only for each of the gaps. (Most of these words are grammar words, rather than content words nouns or verbs.)

Use this list to help you:

- articles
- quantifiers
- prepositions
- auxiliaries
- adverbs
- verbs or particle of phrasal verbs

- possessive adjectives and pronouns
- reflexive pronouns
- conjunctions
- adjectives and adverbs and their dependent prepositions
- question words

3 **OPEN CLOZE** Read the text below. Read it through at least twice to gain a general understanding. Think of the word which best fits each gap. Use only **one** word in each gap.

A man has stumbled out of Australia's outback looking like a walking skeleton after surviving for **(1)** _____ than three months on raw frogs, lizards and leeches. Ricky Megee was found by farm workers in a shelter made **(2)** _____ of branches on a remote cattle farm on the edge of the vast Tanami Desert. He estimated that he had **(3)** _____ 60kg. He claimed **(4)** _____ he ate the leeches raw straight from a dam. The only thing he 'cooked' **(5)** _____ the frogs which he put on a piece of wire to dry in the sun **(6)** _____ they were nice and crispy. Details of how he got **(7)** _____ are unclear with some reports saying his car had **(8)** _____ down or that he had been drugged and dumped by a hitch hiker he **(9)** _____ picked up. Mr Clifford, a cattle station manager, said that Megee was very thin when he was found, and that he must **(10)** _____ walked for about ten days to get to where the cattle workers came **(11)** _____ him. The man was taken to hospital **(12)** _____ he was treated for six days.

10 Is it real?

Getting started

1 Discuss. Do people dowse for water in your country? Hold two sticks in your hands and walk. If the sticks cross, you have found water below the ground. There is no scientific explanation for why it works. Some people also dowse for ghosts!

2 Stand up and move around the class. Interview other students and write their names if you find someone who ...

has 'dowsed'. _____

knows someone who has seen a ghost. _____

believes we are not alone in the universe. _____

has dreamed they were flying. _____

often sees a situation they think they have seen before. _____

has had a dream which has come true. _____

believes they had another life in the past. _____

has felt scared being in a building on their own. _____

believes everything can be explained by science. _____

Listening: out of the blue

1 Discuss. Do you think the photo is real? What do you think it is? Have you or anyone you know ever seen something peculiar in the sky?

2 🎧 10.1 Listen to the police officer and write down as much information as you can about the appearance of …

- the boy.
- the object in the sky.

EXAM SPOTLIGHT

Sentence completion

PAPER 4, PART 2

Before listening:
- read all of the sentences.
- try to predict what the missing words (between one to three) might be.
- note that the words in the sentences are not always the same as in the listening BUT the missing words are from the listening.

While listening for the *first* time:
- write in the answers you can.
- leave an answer if you don't hear it and move on to the next question. (You'll have another chance to listen.)

While listening for the *second* time:
- check any answers from the first listening.
- try to fill any remaining gaps.
- don't leave any empty answers. Write something!

After listening:
- check your answers for spelling or any other mistakes.
- transfer your answers on to the answer sheet.

---

3 🎧 10.1 SENTENCE COMPLETION Listen again. For questions 1–10 below complete the sentences.

The police officer was supposed to have finished

(1) _____.

She thought the odd-looking boy was no more than

(2) _____.

The boy had been found wandering down a lane about ten miles

(3) _____.

She thought that someone would come for him

(4) _____.

She was surprised because the boy was

(5) _____.

The boy's badge was made from metal and was

(6) _____ in shape.

Later on she was on her way home in her police car when she thought a car was driving (7) _____ her.

The number of lights on the UFO grew and then they

(8) _____.

The base of the UFO was smooth and reflective like

(9) _____.

Then she saw the triangular shape for the

(10) _____ that day.

Vocabulary: describing objects

SPOTLIGHT ON VOCABULARY

Order of adjectives

1 Read these sentences from Tapescript 10.1 and match the **adjectives in bold** to the categories in the table below.

a Someone brought in an **odd-looking**, **small** boy.

b He had a **triangular**, **metal** badge on his jumper.

c It had a **smooth**, **round** base like a mirror.

d There was a **beautiful**, **orange** light.

OPINION	DIMENSION (SIZE)	AGE	TEXTURE	COLOUR	SHAPE	MATERIAL

NOTE: The table above gives a general rule but the order of the adjectives can vary.

➡ Grammar Reference (Section 1.2) page 165

2 Complete the sentences by placing the adjectives in italics into the most likely order.

1 We saw a *silver/thin/long/metal* object in the sky.

2 On the farm in winter, he would always wear a(n) *army/shapeless/ancient* overcoat that had belonged to his father and *gardening/green/rubber/dark* boots.

3 My uncle always used a(n) *iron/old/heavy* frying pan.

4 They brought in a *rectangular/wooden/mysterious/document/large* box.

5 Their own offices are in a(n) *modern/glass/tall/ugly* building.

6 She turned up in a *bright/sports/gorgeous/German/red* car.

3 What objects are being described here?

> It normally comes in a clear, round roll. It's useful stuff for sticking things together.

> You see them in the sky on windy days. They're sort of colourful, triangular shapes. You can also have square ones.

> It's made of leather and is used in all sorts of sports. It's usually round.

SPOTLIGHT ON VOCABULARY

Avoiding too many adjectives

We can avoid having too many adjectives before a noun by transferring information elsewhere.
Example:
We saw a long, thin, metal object in the sky. =
The silver object in the sky was made of metal and was sort of long and thin.

4 What changes can you make to sentences 2–6 in exercise 2 to avoid having too many adjectives before the noun? Use expressions such as *kind of, sort of,* and *made of.*

5 Turn these nouns into adjectives.

Example: *length (n) → long (adj)*

~~length~~	wood	width	depth	height	triangle
hardness	sphere	circle	softness	colour	metal

EXAM SPOTLIGHT

Individual 'long turn'

PAPER 5, PART 2
In this part of the Speaking test, you might need to describe something in a picture. If you don't know the word for something in the picture then use reference words such as *thing, stuff* or *it.*

6 Look at the photos and describe the objects using the phrases below. Do not say the name of the object. Can your partner guess which picture you are describing?

It's {
made of ...
kind of/sort of ...
a thing/stuff for ... + ... -ing (noun)
(normally) used for/in + ... -ing (noun)
useful for + ... -ing (noun)
used by (people) to/for ...
}

Reading: crop circles

1 Discuss. These are crop circles. How do you think they are made?

2 Read the article about crop circles.
- What are some of the reasons people have given for crop circles in the article?
- Do you have similar unexplained phenomena in your country?

3 Match the words in bold from the text to these definitions.

1 a plan (or trick) to deceive someone _____

2 group of people with shared interests _____

3 three-dimensional squares _____

4 the length across a circle _____

5 area with dead people (from long ago) _____

6 cause the start of something _____

7 complicated, with lots of small pieces _____

8 things that are real but also especially unusual and interesting _____

9 impossible to explain by science or known fact _____

10 rotate quickly, twisting and turning _____

4 MULTIPLE CHOICE For questions 1–8 choose the answer (*A*, *B*, *C* or *D*) which you think fits best according to the text.

1 This is the first time that a crop circle ...
 A has been found in England.
 B has appeared in Oxfordshire.
 C of this kind has appeared anywhere.
 D has been made in a corn field.

2 Every time crop circles appear ...
 A you only find them a long way into the countryside.
 B people see an unidentified flying object in the sky.
 C people discuss and argue where it has come from.
 D the majority of people say they are designed to deceive.

World's first 3-D crop circle found in field

The world's first three-dimensional crop circle has been discovered deep in the English countryside. This latest event has **sparked off** the start of the crop circle season with enthusiasts driving all over the countryside in search of these natural – or unnatural – **phenomena**. Along with the believers at this time of year come an equal number of sceptics and people who think they are created as jokes. So is this new crop circle another example of an artistic **hoax** or is it really part of the **paranormal**? Perhaps it's a message left by aliens in a spaceship, the footprint of a giant animal or even some sort of communication from another time?

The new circle was only spotted last week by a pilot in a field in the county of Oxfordshire. From the air it was difficult to miss, with it measuring over 100 metres in **diameter**. Within hours the news of the image had attracted local people, crop circle spotters and journalists from around the country. Steve Alexander, a crop circle photographer for more than 15 years, said 'We have not seen anything like it before. It is the first of its kind and is a very, very powerful thing to look at. The crop circle **community** is very excited about this event.'

In the past crop circles have come in all shapes and sizes. Traditionally, there is one large circle with patterns inside such as triangles or squares but the use of three-dimensional **cubes** in a corn circle has never been seen before. The first written recording of the crop circle phenomenon dates back to about 800AD. They began appearing in fields in France. The bishop of Lyon was convinced that local people were worshipping the

3 The new crop circle is special because ...
   A it has attracted more people than any previous crop circle.
   B it is only visible from the air.
   C it has more than two dimensions.
   D it's the largest circle ever found in a field.

4 Crop circles ...
   A appeared even before 800AD.
   B were created to protect people from evil.
   C only used to appear as triangles.
   D have appeared in many designs over the centuries.

5 In the past, some believed in a connection between crop circles and ...
   A the dead.
   B aliens.
   C airports.
   D farmers.

6 Nowadays we can be certain that crop circles appear ...
   A where you see strange lights.
   B in the morning.
   C near ancient sites.
   D in many different places.

7 More and more people in the village think that ...
   A a helicopter landed in the field.
   B the helicopter's motion created it.
   C the helicopter's blades cut the corn down.
   D the helicopter explains the lights in the night sky.

8 Steve thinks that local people ...
   A can't give a real explanation for it.
   B must have created it as a joke.
   C don't understand the purpose of crop circles.
   D don't understand how long it takes to make a corn circle.

5 **Discuss. Here are photographs from three hoaxes. Do you believe in the paranormal? Have you ever experienced unnatural phenomena?**

devil because strange circles regularly appeared in the crops and so he tried to put a stop to the practice.

However, they have continued to reappear throughout history. Early accounts describe how they always show up near to sites of historical importance such as **burial grounds** or places of worship. In the modern world some crop circle specialists say that this is still the case but that we no longer know where many ancient and important sites are. Others say that the appearance of similar circles made in snow and in sandy deserts suggest that the circles are not necessarily connected with the dead or the religious. Instead they would say the numerous worldwide sightings, including circles in Australia, Brazil and the USA, are the leftovers from alien spacecraft since many circles appear the morning after a UFO sighting or 'strange lights' have been seen at night in the sky.

Even though some people in the local village of Ashbury in Oxfordshire reported strange noises the night the crop circle appeared and one person out walking their dog said they saw lights in the sky above the field, most residents are already calling their 3-D circle a hoax. A popular theory also gaining support is that a helicopter from a nearby base flew close to the ground and the **swirling** air from its rotor-blades flattened the corn. But Steve Alexander says 'It is very difficult to say what its purpose is and how it got there but how could somebody create such an **intricate** design overnight? They would have seven hours of darkness to cut it in the wheat and such a formation would be impossible to create in such a small space of time.'

99

Listening: crop circles

EXAM SPOTLIGHT

Identifying the speaker's purpose

PAPER 4, PART 3

In part 3 of the Listening test, you listen to five different people. Then you match each speaker to an item in a list of six possible answers. The items may need you to listen for information such as:

- the speakers' relationship to other people.
- something which happened to them, perhaps in a specific place.
- topics which the speakers are interested in.
- the speakers' attitudes or opinions about something.

PAPER 4, PART 3

1   🎧 **10.2** MULTIPLE MATCHING **You will hear five different people commenting on a new crop circle. Choose from the list (A–F) what each person thinks. Use the letters only once. There is one extra letter which you do not need to use.**

Speaker 1: _____
Speaker 2: _____
Speaker 3: _____
Speaker 4: _____
Speaker 5: _____

A   is totally convinced aliens made it
B   thinks the circle looks nice
C   doesn't mention aliens or UFOs
D   believes local people made it
E   doesn't think people had enough time to make it
F   criticises newspaper reporters

Speaking: guessing and speculating

1   🎧 **10.2** **Listen again to the five people and write in the missing words from these expressions.**

1 It _____ _____ any number of things ...
2 Or _____ it was some ...
3 it _____ _____ _____ as a result of ...
4 I'm absolutely _____ that ...
5 In this case it would _____ _____ impossible for ...
6 They _____ have done it ...
7 It _____ have been something ...
8 In my _____ it's ...
9 I _____ it's probably ...
10 I'm not really _____. Maybe it ...

Key word: *seem*

1   **These five sentences are describing the first picture below. Replace the words in bold with these words.**

I'm unsure	appear	appear to be
I'm fairly certain	In my opinion	

1 The people in this picture **seem** to be celebrating something. _____
2 They all **seem** very happy. _____
3 **It seems to me that** they are all having a good time. _____
4 **I can't seem to tell** what kind of party, but it is probably. _____
5 **It seems very likely that** it's a celebration for the birth of a baby. _____

2   **Work in pairs. Take turns to talk about the second picture in the same way. Remember to use some of the expressions from the Speaking and Key word sections.**

Grammar: modal verbs for guessing, speculating and deducing

1 Study these pairs of sentences. Which is more certain? *a* or *b*?

1

   a I'll answer the phone. It could be my mother.

   b That must my mother. She said she'd call at five.

2

   a It can't be Jim. He's coming tomorrow.

   b It might not be Jim. He didn't say exactly when he's arriving.

3

   a Ruth could have sent this package but there was no return address.

   b Ruth must have sent this package because it's her address on the back.

4

   a It couldn't have been Tricia who rang because she's away.

   b It may not have been Tricia who rang. Trevor also wanted to speak to me.

2 Look at the pairs of sentences in exercise 1 again. Which sentences refer to past events?

GRAMMAR SPOTLIGHT

Verbs for speculating and deducing

For speculating, guessing or discussing possibilities ...
- about the present, use *could/might/may be.*
- about the past, use *could/might/may have* + past participle.

For making deductions which you are very certain of ...
- about the present, use *must be/can't be.*
- about the past, use *must/can't/couldn't have* + past participle.

→ Grammar Reference (Section 11) page 176

3 Work in pairs. Speculate and make deductions about these situations.

- You arrive home late at night to find a broken window.

- You arrive at the train station. There are hundreds of people waiting.

- You are driving. The road is blocked and police are standing on either side.

PAPER 3, PART 4

4 KEY WORD TRANSFORMATIONS Complete the second sentence so that it has a similar meaning to the first sentence, using the word given. Do not change the word given. You must use between two and five words only.

1 It could well be my wife on the phone.

   sure

   I'm fairly _____ my wife on the phone.

2 He should have been here by midday.

   supposed

   He _____ here by midday.

3 It must be Meg because Ania doesn't arrive here until tomorrow.

   can't

   It _____ Ania because she doesn't arrive until tomorrow.

4 She must be waiting for someone because she's late.

   likely

   It seems _____ for someone because she's late.

5 It can't be a hoax because the marks look so real.

   certain

   I _____ a hoax because the marks look so real.

6 Without doubt, the burglar used that window. The locks are broken.

   must

   The burglar _____ window as the locks are broken.

7 It wasn't a human because the footprint belongs to an animal.

   couldn't

   It _____ a human because the footprint belongs to an animal.

8 Maybe it was the wind but I don't think so.

   possibly

   It could _____ the wind, but I don't think so.

Writing: compulsory email

Informal exchange

1 Read these emails. What is the relationship between Michelle and Yvonne?

Hi Michelle,

Hope you're well. <u>Just to let you know</u> that <u>there's a sale until the end of the week at 'Shoeshine'</u>. It's that shop at the far end of High Street. Do you know the one? I picked up two pairs of shoes for work at half price. I couldn't resist a pair of high heels, too. <u>They're plastic, pink and the heels are 3cm high</u> – just right for our holiday in Ibiza next month!

Anyway, <u>you should</u> get down there before they sell out.

All the best,
Yvonne

Hi Yvonne,

<u>Thanks</u> for letting me know about the sale but I've got some good news and some bad news. <u>The good news is that</u> I've been offered a promotion. <u>The bad news is that</u> they want me to do three weeks' training next month so <u>I'm sorry but</u> I won't be able to go on holiday at that time.

<u>Is it OK</u> if we go the following month? Would that work for you?

Tell me what you think.
Michelle

Hi Michelle,

No problem. Don't worry. Congratulations on the new job!

<u>Why don't we</u> meet at the weekend and you can tell me all about it? <u>Would you like to</u> have dinner at my place? We can eat and talk about other possibilities for the holiday.

<u>See you soon,</u>
Yvonne

---

2 Here are some rules for writing formal letters. Which rules do the emails break?

GUIDELINES FOR WRITING FORMAL LETTERS

1. Start your letter with *Dear …*
2. Always use full sentences.
3. Start a new line or use separate paragraphs where necessary.
4. Avoid contracted forms such as *I'll*.
5. Do not use exclamation marks (!).
6. Avoid direct questions.
7. Spelling and punctuation must be accurate.
8. End your letter with *Yours sincerely* or *Best regards*.

3 Rewrite some of the rules in exercise 2 for writing less formal emails.

4 Match and write the underlined expressions in the emails to the functions a–l.

a Give reason for writing *Just to let you know that*

b Apologise _____

c Give good news _____

d Offer _____

e Recommend _____

f Suggest _____

g Give bad news _____

h Thank _____

i Request _____

j Say when and where _____

k Give details _____

l End email _____

5 Match more expressions below to the functions above. Write the letter a–l from exercise 4 next to the phrase.

1 I'm afraid … _____

2 How about …? _____

3 I'm so grateful that … _____

4 I'm emailing you to … _____

5 Can you help …? _____

6 Unfortunately … _____

7 You ought to go … _____

8 There are … _____

9 It starts at eight by the … _____

10 Look forward to seeing you. _____

11 I'm so happy because … _____

12 Can I help …? _____

6 Work in pairs. Practise writing each other very short emails, following the flowchart below. You will need pieces of paper to write on. Write your first email and swap it with your partner, then write the next email and swap again. Continue until the end of the flowchart.

Give details of something you have just bought / Recommend the shop to a friend

Thank your friend / Suggest you meet this weekend

Give bad news / Say sorry / Explain why you can't

Offer to cook dinner instead next week

Thank / Offer to bring something to eat

Request your friend brings something / Say when

Confirm / End email

8 You have just visited your English-speaking friend, Sara, and you receive an email from her. Read Sara's email and the notes you have made on the print out. Then write an email to Sara using all your notes.

From: Sara Pierron
Sent: 17th June
Subject: Visit

Thank her

Hi Margo

I'm so glad that you made it home OK. It was great to have you stay and I'm so glad you liked my country. You mentioned that you left a box at my flat which you'd bought at the local market. I haven't found it yet. What does it look like? My flatmate is away but she's back tomorrow – maybe she knows where it is.   *Give details*

Anyway, the good news is that I can get time off work and can come over next month to visit you! I'm really looking forward to touring round. I have three weeks so what should I see?   *Recommend somewhere*

Of course, I'd really like to meet up but maybe you're busy. Anyway, email me when you have time.

Reply soon.

Sara.   *Give bad news: you are away next month. Suggest she comes the month after.*

9 Use this checklist to check your answer or to comment on your partner's email.

WRITING CHECKLIST

Email

The writer	Yes (✓)	No (✗)
… uses fairly informal language (as if to a friend).	☐	☐
… thanks her friend.	☐	☐
… describes a box she bought at a local market.	☐	☐
… recommends somewhere to visit.	☐	☐
… explains that he/she will be away.	☐	☐
… suggests she comes the following month.	☐	☐

➜ Writing Guide, page 200

EXAM SPOTLIGHT

Compulsory letter or email

PAPER 2, PART 1

7 Check what you know about this part of the exam. Are the following statements true or false?

1 There is only one question to answer in part 1 of the writing exam. T / F
2 You don't have to answer it. T / F
3 You always have to respond to another piece of correspondence. T / F
4 You must respond to the handwritten notes. T / F

1 MULTIPLE-CHOICE CLOZE **Read the text below and decide which answer (*A*, *B*, *C* or *D*) best fits each gap.**

Telepathy does exist claims Cambridge scientist

Many people have had the experience of getting a telephone call from someone just as they were thinking about them. Now a new study suggests that might **(1)** _____ be down purely to coincidence. Scientist Dr Rupert Sheldrake says he has performed tests into 'telephone telepathy' which show 45 percent of the time people can correctly **(2)** _____ who is ringing them. This is much higher odds than if it was due to **(3)** _____ alone, he claimed. However his research has sparked **(4)** _____ controversy in the scientific **(5)** _____.

Dr Rupert Sheldrake receives funding to investigate unexplained **(6)** _____ from Trinity College in Cambridge. He **(7)** _____ to his critics, saying 'By far the most common kind of telepathy in the modern world occurs in connection with telephone calls – when you think of someone for no apparent reason and then they ring and you say 'what a **(8)** _____. I was just thinking about you.'

For his experiments, four volunteers were told they would get a call and were asked to predict which of the four was calling them before they picked **(9)** _____ the phone. Although only four people were used, they repeated the test more than 270 times. He found that they correctly **(10)** _____ the caller 45 percent of the time.

But scientists and sceptics of the **(11)** _____ have questioned the reliability of the work. Professor Peter Atkins, tutor in Physical Chemistry at the University of Oxford, said 'Work in this field is a complete waste **(12)** _____ time.'

1 A not	B also	C could	D never
2 A ask	B speculate	C guess	D wonder
3 A possibility	B opportunity	C risk	D chance
4 A off	B on	C of	D out
5 A group	B people	C locality	D community
6 A nature	B phenomena	C flying objects	D questions
7 A disagreed	B attacked	C responded	D speculated
8 A hilarious	B funny	C laughter	D coincidence
9 A up	B out	C on	D off
10 A looked up	B answered	C found	D predicted
11 A paranormal	B hoax	C abnormal	D unidentified
12 A in	B for	C of	D with

2 **Underline the correct forms (in *italics*) in these conversations.**

Conversation 1

A: I'll get it.

B: It **(1)** *will have been/will be* my mother on the phone. She's the only person who calls on Sunday evenings.

A: Hello? Oh hello, Mum. Samantha guessed it **(2)** *might be/might have been* you. I thought it **(3)** *might not be/might have been* my boss calling me. I have been expecting him to call this evening.

Conversation 2

A: There's the doorbell. It **(4)** *must be/must have been* Gill and Fred.

B: It **(5)** *can be/can't be* them. They're in Paris for the weekend.

A: Well, they **(6)** *must cancel/must have cancelled* the trip because I spoke to them this afternoon and they said they were coming round ...

Conversation 3

A: Someone left a message for you on your voicemail. They didn't give their name but it was an American accent.

B: That's strange. Larry is the only Amercian I know and it **(7)** *can't be/couldn't have been* him because he was with me all day.

A: Actually it was a woman. **(8)** *Might it be/Might it have been* his wife?

B: That **(9)** *seems/must be* unlikely. Larry isn't married!

3 **Complete the email below.**

> To: Sara Solly
> From: Margo Brennan
> Subject: My visit
>
> Dear Sara,
> Thanks **(1)** _____ letting me stay with you. I was **(2)** _____ grateful and I had a really great time. The box I left **(3)** _____ your house is silver, but made **(4)** _____ plastic. I think it has coloured triangular shapes **(5)** _____ the lid too.
> It's good news **(6)** _____ you're planning on visiting. Unfortunately, I have to go away next month for three weeks. **(7)** _____ don't you come the month after? I'll be living in a new flat in the centre of the old town **(8)** _____ then so it will be perfect for you to **(9)** _____ some sightseeing. Also, you ought to visit the national park **(10)** _____ you are here.
> Let **(11)** _____ know your plans. I look **(12)** _____ to seeing you!
>
> Margo

11　Shopping and money

MAIN MENU

Vocabulary:	shopping and consumerism; key word: *if*
Grammar:	conditionals; mixed conditionals/ *wish*
Speaking:	regret, advice and suggestions
Reading:	*Pocket money*
Listening:	*Money habits*
Writing:	an opinion essay

EXAM MENU

Reading:	multiple matching
Writing:	an essay
Use of English:	key word transformations; multiple-choice cloze
Listening:	multiple choice
Speaking:	individual 'long-turn'

Getting started

1　Do the quiz below to discover what kind of shopper you are and compare your answers with your partner.

ARE YOU AN INTELLIGENT SHOPPER?

Are these statements true for you?
Write 1, 2, 3, 4 or 5 (1 disagree, 2 disagree strongly, 3 neither agree or disagree, 4 agree, 5 agree strongly).

I always try to spend as little money as possible. ☐

I always stay within my budget when I go shopping. ☐

I usually want to try most new products and brands that I hear about. ☐

I often go from shop to shop comparing items before I make a final purchase. ☐

I always try and gather information about products and compare prices before I make a purchase. ☐

YOU SCORED 19 OR ABOVE
You are at the top of the class when it comes to shopping – you have a great eye for a bargain and always try the latest fashions and brands. You are a single-minded shopper and avoid buying just because something is on special offer, has a designer logo or was advertised on TV. As a clever consumer you make sure you're getting the best deal.

YOU SCORED BETWEEN 11 AND 18
You are a good shopper but there is definitely room for improvement. You understand the principles of intelligent shopping but don't always follow the rules. Whether it's clothes you bought on a whim but have never worn, or something which you saw down the road for £50 less, you need to learn to shop smartly and get as much information as possible before you splash out on the latest thing.

YOU SCORED 10 OR BELOW
Sales assistants love customers like you. You are a disaster when it comes to shopping – not only do you buy whatever you see, but the word bargain just isn't in your vocabulary. You wouldn't recognise the word discount if it hit you in the face. You need to set yourself a budget, then only buy things that you really need. Shop around and compare prices before buying from the first shop you enter.

Vocabulary: shopping and consumerism

1 Find three words from the text on page 105 which all mean 'a person or people who buy'.

2 Look at the words in orange at the bottom of page 105. Add them into sentences 1–7.

  1 Look at this! If you buy two of these today you get a third one free. What a _____!

  2 She always wears the latest in designer footwear. If it hasn't got the _____ of one of the most famous _____ she isn't interested.

  3 Normally I plan what I'm going to buy but yesterday I suddenly saw this and without thinking bought it on a _____. Now I'm not sure that I like it.

  4 We have a _____ so we know exactly how much we can spend each month and we can't go over it.

  5 This was on _____ _____ for one week only. It had 50 percent off so I bought it!

  6 He made a _____ with us that if we bought the car there and then, he'd give it a free service at the end of the first year.

  7 I can give you a ten percent _____ if you pay for it in cash.

3 Choose the correct word (in *italics*) in sentences 1–15.

  1 More people than ever before are *on/in* debt.

  2 I always try to stay *within/over* my weekly budget.

  3 Lending money *to/from* friends usually ends in tears.

  4 Can I pay *by/in* cheque, or would you rather I paid *on/in* cash?

  5 Excuse me, what's the *amount/price* of this shirt?

  6 Do you know what he *cost/paid* for his car?

  7 I'm *broken/broke*. Could you *borrow/lend* me some money until Friday?

  8 How much did it *pay/cost* to have your hair done?

  9 We couldn't *afford/pay* a new car, so we bought one second hand.

 10 He's so mean. He never *buys/pays* the drinks.

 11 The *price/cost* of living has gone up since the euro.

 12 Can you *pay for/pay* the taxi driver? I don't have any cash.

 13 He paid a high *price/cost* for his mistake.

 14 They're crazy to *cost/spend* so much on their new kitchen.

 15 They eventually agreed to *refund/retail* the money I had spent on the holiday.

Phrasal verbs

4 Join the beginnings of sentences (1–10) with the endings (a–j).

  1 I can't be bothered to *shop* …

  2 I had lost the receipt so they refused to *take* …

  3 They celebrated their engagement by *splashing* …

  4 You should *set* some money …

  5 When my brother left university he couldn't *pay* …

  6 When I saw what the bill *came* …

  7 If you can't afford to *pay* me ….

  8 Lots of elderly people find it hard to *get* …

  9 Kids these days aren't prepared to *save* …

 10 I'd like to *pay* …

  a *to,* I almost fainted.

  b *off* any of his student loan for three years.

  c the dress *back.*

  d this cheque *into* my account, please.

  e *around* for the best price.

  f *by* on a tiny pension.

  g *up* for something they want.

  h *aside* in case of emergencies.

  i *back* the money, you shouldn't have borrowed it.

  j *out on* an expensive meal.

I always like to set a bit of money aside for emergencies.

5 Work in pairs. Ask and answer these questions:
- Do you think it's a good idea to lend money to or borrow money from friends or family?
- Do you think it's important to set aside a bit of money every month? Why/Why not?

Listening: money habits

1 🎧 **11.1 Listen to people talking in eight different situations.**

 1 Which speakers are customers? Speakers _____, _____, _____, _____ and _____.

 2 Which are selling something? Speakers _____ and _____.

 3 Which speaker is giving advice? Speaker _____.

PAPER 4, PART 1

3 🎧 **11.1 MULTIPLE CHOICE Listen again and for questions 1–8 choose the best answer (*A, B* or *C*).**

 1 You hear a woman talking about her shopping habits. What is her approach to shopping?
   A She knows exactly what she wants before she leaves the house.
   B She'll only buy something she really likes.
   C She can't leave the house without buying.

 2 You hear a man talking about prices. How does he get the best bargains?
   A He looks for price information on the internet.
   B He always uses loyalty cards and never shops around.
   C He tends to buy online rather than in a shop.

 3 You hear a woman thinking of buying a second hand car. What does she decide to do?
   A to buy it
   B to look at some other models
   C to negotiate the price with the salesman

 4 You hear a sales assistant talking to some customers looking for furniture. Why can't he sell them the sofa and chairs they want?
   A They are all at another shop.
   B The manufacturer won't be producing any more until next year.
   C They don't have them in stock any longer.

 5 You hear a salesperson talking to some customers. What is she explaining?
   A the policy on damaged goods
   B the policy on refunds
   C the policy on faulty goods

 6 You hear a financial expert on the radio. What does he advise listeners to do?
   A Don't rush into starting a pension fund.
   B Only use your savings in a real emergency.
   C Keep setting some money aside.

 7 You hear a woman talking about her holiday. What does she regret?
   A the hotel
   B the day she booked it
   C the destination

 8 You hear a teenager describing his financial situation. What is he complaining about?
   A that his sister has a new bike
   B that his sister has lots of money
   C that his dad wants the money back

Grammar: conditionals

1 🎧 **11.2 Listen to the first four people again and complete these sentences. Write in the missing words.**

 1 **Woman:** If I suddenly _____ something I like, I either _____ it or _____ back the following week with the money I need.

 2 **Man:** If you _____ to the same shop every time, they'll often _____ you a loyalty card so you save money when you shop there.

 3 **Woman:** Maybe if he _____ the price, I _____ _____ interested.

 4 **Man:** If you _____ _____ in last week I _____ _____ _____ just what you were looking for.

2 Study the explanation of four types of conditional (zero, first, second and third) in Section 6 of the Grammar Reference, page 170. Match the four sentences in exercise 1 to the four types of conditional sentences.

Sentence 1: Conditional type _____

Sentence 2: Conditional type _____

Sentence 3: Conditional type _____

Sentence 4: Conditional type _____

3 Write the verb in the correct form.

Example:
If you sign up today, you automatically ~~got~~ the discount. *get*

1 If you _____ (book) online, you'd probably have the ticket by Monday.

2 Would you mind if I _____ (bring) a friend with me?

3 He'll pass the exam if he _____ (revise) for it.

4 If I _____ (know) Rachel was going, I would have gone too.

5 If we continue to argue like this, we _____ (not come) to an agreement.

6 I _____ (take) it if you had sold me another at half price.

7 If I _____ (get) the house I want, I'll paint it yellow.

8 If I _____ (not hear) from you by eight o'clock, I'll assume you're coming.

4 Work in pairs. Look at 1–5 below. Make sentences in the zero and first conditional. Decide what you think is very certain (*C*) and what is likely (*L*).

Example: *If you **heat** water to 100°C, it **boils**.*

1 heat water to 100C → it boils   *C (certain)*

2 eat too much sugar → get bad teeth _____

3 eat healthily → live a long life _____

4 do homework → get better at English _____

5 jump in the sea → get wet _____

5 Work in pairs. Look at the list of things we have or don't have in our everyday lives. What would life be like with or without them? Make sentences with the second conditional.

cars	mobile phones	computers	money
satellites in space	free air travel	tax	coffee

Example: *If we didn't have cars, we wouldn't be able to …*

6 Study the pairs of pictures showing events in the past. Make a sentence for each in the third conditional.

Reading: pocket money

1 Discuss. Can you remember the first time you received pocket money and how you spent it?

PAPER 1, PART 3

2 MULTIPLE MATCHING Read the text about a pocket money survey. For questions 1–15 choose which part of the world each one refers to (A–D). Each part of the world may be chosen more than once.

Where in the world …

1 do parents view giving pocket money as part of learning to be responsible with money? _____

2 do a lot of children receive an increase once a year? _____

3 are children increasingly making their own choices? _____

4 can you get more if you negotiate? _____

5 are toys and electronics the most popular purchase? _____

6 isn't pocket money spent straight away? _____

7 are there many different purchases competing for our money? _____

8 do boys have less money than girls? _____

9 might children not have the chance to spend it how they like? _____

10 don't children view material items as the most important thing in their lives? _____

11 do many children not receive pocket money? _____

12 do many children have a say in what their mother and father buy for the home? _____

13 does a rise in pocket money happen on a particular day? _____

14 is the most popular purchase the same as in India? _____

15 do many children earn money rather than being given it? _____

EXAM SPOTLIGHT

Multiple matching

PAPER 1, PART 3

3 Underline the correct word in this advice to make it good advice.

1 Quickly read all four *texts/questions* to get the main idea of each.

2 Read each question and underline the parts of the *texts/question* which you think answer the question.

4 Discuss. Should the money children earn from doing jobs and working be included as part of their regular pocket money?

POCKET MONEY

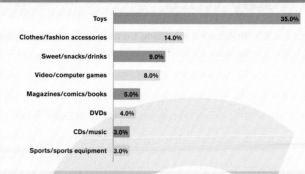

Top Categories for Spending Among European Children	
Toys	35.0%
Clothes/fashion accessories	14.0%
Sweet/snacks/drinks	9.0%
Video/computer games	8.0%
Magazines/comics/books	5.0%
DVDs	4.0%
CDs/music	3.0%
Sports/sports equipment	3.0%

Four different surveys into the spending habits of the young recently uncovered how attitudes to pocket money differ from country to continent.

(A) INDIA

This first survey shows that almost half the children (about 49%) in India now enjoy pocket money, averaging about 132 rupees per month. Along with this increase in economic independence, the child has emerged as having a greater influence over parents in household purchases and this increases as the child grows older. A higher percentage of older children also admitted buying items for the home and his/her own clothes. However, this independence need not be mistaken for growing disenchantment with family or home. Most children surveyed, rated parents to be their most valued possessions followed by toys and books at a distant second and third respectively.

(B) EUROPE

Children in Europe generally start receiving pocket money when they reach six years old, often coinciding with their entry into primary school. Six years old is the average age when a regular allowance begins in northern European countries (Belgium, Sweden, The Netherlands and Germany), and also in Spain. In the other southern countries surveyed (France, Italy, Greece and Portugal), the average rises to seven years of age. Parents in Northern Europe are more likely than other Europeans to buy kids the things they ask for. When given money for holidays and birthdays, most children (58%) choose to save it though the survey found that many don't manage to keep their money for very long – 44% say they end up spending it within two months. When they part with their pocket money, kids across Europe are most likely to purchase toys and the latest electronic

equipment. Clothing is next in importance, with sweets and electronic games also being important to them.

(C) THE UK

Teenagers in London are the pocket money winners, receiving an average of £11.71 per week, well above the UK average of £8.20, according to new research from the Halifax bank. Across the UK girls come out on top with 12% more per week than boys. The main factor in how money is allocated came down to age, but over three quarters of children get pocket money in return for doing jobs around the home. 31% clean the house, and 29% do the washing up. The basis for a raise in pocket money was varied but for many (39%) the increase usually occurred on a birthday. As to what the money is being spent on, nothing much has changed there from previous years – clothes, music, electronic games, mobile phones – but the biggest change has come

in methods of spending, with more than half the children surveyed regularly purchasing goods online.

(D) CHINA AND JAPAN

Children in Japan have less money in their pockets than their counterparts in China, according to a survey by Japanese scholars. Chinese parents, it seems, are more casual in giving money to their children, though the children there have less control over the money given to them. For example, during the Chinese New Year, gifts of money from relatives to children are usually spent by their parents on education fees and textbooks. In Japan students were found to have control over their own money while education fees were paid for by parents. Though Japanese parents are careful in giving money, they tend to give a fixed amount regularly and then don't say how it is to be spent, taking the view that children need to learn how to deal with money by themselves. In China the approach is to give money upon a child's request or wishes, but that the agreed amount is negotiated in return for parental influence over how it is eventually spent.

Key word: *if*

1 The word *if* is missing from these sentences. Write it in.

Example:
        if
*I asked Sam he wanted to join us but he said he was
too busy.*

1 I wonder they're ready yet.

2 What you tried doing it this way?

3 Do you mind she comes, too?

4 I wouldn't do that I were you.

5 I keep thinking only Molly had come too ... she would have loved it!

6 I'll do it but only he does, too.

2 What is the function of each of the expressions with *if*? Write the sentence number (from exercise 1) next to the function.

a requesting _____
b expressing a condition _____
c suggesting _____
d speculating _____
e reporting a question _____
f giving advice _____
g expressing regret _____

3 Work in pairs. Take turns to give a response or answers to 1–7. Try to use *if* in your answers where possible.

1 Report the most important question you ever asked in your life. Who did you ask? *I asked ...*

2 Speculate about what you might be doing in ten years' time. *I wonder ...*

3 Your partner wants to go out at the weekend. Make a suggestion.

4 Your partner wants to borrow your car. Agree but express a condition.

5 Your teacher has given you lots of homework but you are really busy. Request help from your partner.

6 Give your partner a piece of advice your parents or grandparents used to give you.

7 Express regret about one thing you did when you were a child.

4 🎧 11.3 The sentences below are similar to those in Listening 11.2. What does each speaker say differently? After listening turn to Tapescript 11.3 on page 219 to check.

1 There's a 28-day money-back guarantee on all our products if you bring it back within 28 days of purchase ... that's fine.

2 Oh, that's also if you have the receipt with it, of course.

3 There's short-term saving if you have an emergency.

4 If I had known, I wouldn't have bought it in the first place.

5 Sometimes there are alternatives to using *if*. Choose the correct alternative (*A, B* or *C*) which would also fit into each sentence.

1 We give your money back _____ you return it in good condition.
  A provided that   B in case   C unless

2 _____ you pay on time, I don't see a problem.
  A If only   B I wish   C As long as

3 _____ I seen him, I would have let him know.
  A Even if   B Had   C Should

4 _____ they arrive late, can you meet them?
  A Had   B Should   C No matter when

5 They're leaving at nine, _____ they've changed their minds since we spoke.
  A unless   B had   C only

6 Call to let me know. _____ I'll meet you at the shop.
  A Unless   B Otherwise   C Provided that

Grammar: mixed conditionals/*wish*

GRAMMAR SPOTLIGHT

Mixed conditionals

It is possible to combine conditional forms when one clause refers to the past and the other clause refers to the present or future:

If I had bought that lottery ticket, I would be rich by now.
If you don't want the job, you shouldn't have applied.

➜ Grammar Reference (Section 6.6) page 170

1 Complete these mixed conditionals by writing the verb in brackets in the correct form.

1 They would be on holiday by now, if the airport workers _____ (not/go) on strike.

2 You're supposed to _____ (inform) your boss two weeks ago if you want to take any holiday at Christmas.

3 Mark might still be driving that car if he _____ (not catch) by the police for speeding.

4 Had I _____ (study) harder at school, I might _____ (be) earning as much as my friends.

5 If they think they're going to get more pocket money then they _____ (be) wise to help around the house a bit more.

6 If Leah only _____ (start) learning Spanish last month, she really can't _____ (expect) to be advanced yet.

2 Read 1–6 below and answer the questions.

1 I wish I could afford it.

2 I wish I had the money for it.

3 I wish we hadn't bothered.

4 If only we hadn't gone on that holiday.

5 I wish you wouldn't spend all your money on toys.

6 I wish I could play the saxophone.

a Which sentences describe a situation in the present which is unlikely to change?

Sentences _____, _____ and _____.

b Which sentences refer to a situation in the past which the speaker regrets?

Sentences _____ and _____.

c Which sentence describes lack of ability?

Sentence _____.

In sentence 4, which words replace *wish*?

3 Work in pairs. Read the first sentence and say the second sentence so it has the same meaning.

1 I wish I'd saved my money rather than spent it.

If only ...

2 I wish I'd studied medicine when I was a student and become a doctor.

If I'd studied ... I would be ... now.

3 If you'd taken that job, we would have had more money.

I wish ... so that ...

4 I regret not being able to speak Spanish.

I wish ...

→ Grammar Reference (Section 18) page 185

Speaking: regret, advice and suggestions

1 Work in pairs. Look at the two pictures below. They show people in two different situations where their travel plans have gone wrong. Discuss:

- how you think the people in them feel.

- what advice you would give them for the next time they travel.

USEFUL EXPRESSIONS

They probably wish they'd ...
They shouldn't have ...
If only they'd ...
If I were them I'd ...
What if they ...?
Next time I think they should ...

Writing: an opinion essay

1 **Read the three essay introductions below. Which introduction (1, 2 or 3) ... ?**

   a creates a question to answer _____

   b explains the result of a situation _____

   c expresses what many people think _____

Exam question

1 Should people be allowed to borrow more money than they can afford?

Every day we hear about banks lending people more money than they earn and as a result they cannot pay off their loans. More people therefore are in debt in the modern world than ever before.

Exam question

2 Do you agree that young people should learn to earn money early on in life rather than being given pocket money?

From the moment we leave school to the time we retire, most of us will have to work in order to earn money during our lifetime. So the question is whether we should have to work before this time as children, or wait until we become adults.

Exam question

3 Some people believe we should only pay for the things we use. Do you agree?

Every month the government takes part of your salary to pay for things like health, roads, public services and the military. However, some people claim that a lot of this money is wasted unnecessarily and that it is unfair to pay for the things we don't use.

---

2 **Underline the useful expression in each of the three essay introductions, for each technique listed in exercise 1.**

3 **Look at the parts below taken from five middle paragraphs. Match the first half (1–5) to the second half (a–e). Write your answers below.**

   1 __*e*__   2 _____   3 _____   4 _____   5 _____

   1 On the one hand, borrowing money allows us to spend more and this helps the economy to grow.

   2 One argument for this is that they will grow up with a greater sense of responsibility.

   3 You could argue that if you prefer sport to the arts you shouldn't have to pay for the theatre or art galleries.

   4 While it is true that money might be spent on things we might disagree with,

   5 Even though I agree that parents should provide for their children,

   a on the whole everyone would agree that we need a good health service and the best standard of education we can afford.

   b However, if they spend too much time working, it may affect their school work and education.

   c one disadvantage is that children can become spoilt.

   d Nevertheless, taxes also give us the opportunity to experience things we wouldn't normally choose to do, like to visit the opera.

   e On the other hand, if lots of people get into bad debt, the long-term effect can be very damaging.

4 **Underline the useful expressions for introducing arguments (for and against) in the sentences in exercise 3.**

---

5 Imagine you are writing the following essay:

Exam question

Read about a school in America and give your opinion of the head of school's decision.

A school in America has come up with a new way to encourage pupils aged 16–18 to come to classes. It pays them $25 a month to attend lessons. The principal of the school defended the decision saying that at 16 many pupils would leave school and become unemployed. This way they stay at school and get better qualifications.

Think of arguments for and against this method of encouraging students to go to school. Then write the arguments into these sentences using the words given:

1 On the one hand _____
_____
_____.
However, on the other _____
_____.

2 Another argument for this is that _____
_____
_____.
Nevertheless, _____
_____
_____.

3 You could also argue that _____
_____.
However, one big disadvantage with the idea is that
_____
_____.

6 **Read these different conclusions to the essay. Which do you agree with?**

So, on balance, I believe that paying students is a waste of public money. The school should look at a number of alternative ways to encourage the pupils to keep on attending.

In my opinion, this is an interesting way of making students feel more responsible for both their education and what it means to earn money. I would propose this idea.

To sum up, I feel that students can be paid for learning but should also be expected to earn that money. This could be done by raising money for the school or helping the local community in some way, such as taking care of old people.

7 **Look back at exercise 1. Choose one of the three exam questions and write a 'for and against' essay. Write 120–180 words.**

WRITING CHECKLIST

Does your opinion essay ...

	Yes (✓)	No (✗)
• have an introduction?	☐	☐
• contain some middle paragraphs?	☐	☐
• use paragraphs and expressions to give arguments *for* and *against*?	☐	☐
• have a conclusion with a clear opinion?	☐	☐
• use between 120 and 180 words?	☐	☐

➡ Writing Guide, page 205

Review and Use of English

1 Each sentence contains one incorrect word. Underline it and write the correct word at the end.

1 Can you borrow me a little money until Monday? _____

2 How much does the bill come at? _____

3 Every month I set down ten percent to pay into a pension plan for when I get old. _____

4 When do you think you can pay me off what you owe? _____

5 There's a special budget on all shoes this week. Don't miss it. _____

6 Would you like to pay on cash or by credit card? _____

2 KEY WORD TRANSFORMATIONS Complete the second sentence so that it has a similar meaning to the first sentence. Do not change the word given. You must use between two and five words only, including the word given.

1 How much money did you borrow from the bank?
lend
How much money _____?

2 I regret all the money I spent on my new car.
wish
I _____ all that money on my new car.

3 If you change your mind, let me know.
should
_____ mind, let me know.

4 You can pay now if you have some proof of identity with you.
provided
You can pay now _____ proof of identity with you.

5 The final bill is €3,900.
comes
The _____ €3,900.

6 I didn't earn enough so now I'm poor.
wouldn't
If I'd earned _____ poor now.

7 If they don't change their minds, we're meeting at two o'clock.
unless
_____ minds, we're meeting at two o'clock.

8 Is it OK if Molly joins us too?
mind
_____ Molly joins us too?

3 MULTIPLE-CHOICE CLOZE Read the text below and decide which answer (*A*, *B*, *C* or *D*) best fits each gap.

Be smart while shopping online

Sitting in **(1)** _____ of a computer screen can certainly be faster and less stressful than looking for a **(2)** _____ space and fighting your way through crowds **(3)** _____ fellow shoppers. But is online shopping safer?

Many **(4)** _____ still seem to have some hesitation when it comes to online shopping, but authorities say it has in many ways become more secure than **(5)** _____ purchases at an actual store. After all, every time you use a credit card in a store you **(6)** _____ someone all your personal details and financial information.

Experts advise that online **(7)** _____ may now be better protected than traditional shoppers, especially if they follow a few useful **(8)** _____. First of all, use one credit card for all **(9)** _____ so if someone does use it illegally, only one card is affected.

Next, be careful that you are on the site of a real company. Some thieves have **(10)** _____ websites that look like the real thing just to get your information and money. The best way to check if a site is real is to **(11)** _____ for the "s", which stands for secure, in the "https" part of the website address bar at the top of your browser.

The final thing you can do to **(12)** _____ safe while shopping online is to always make sure the computer being used has a firewall and up-to-date antivirus software.

1	A front	B behind	C next	D beside
2	A car	B large	C parking	D blank
3	A in	B of	C along	D at
4	A police	B shop assistants	C clients	D consumers
5	A making	B paying	C giving	D doing
6	A pay	B write	C give	D copy
7	A websites	B addresses	C goods	D customers
8	A tips	B advice	C ideas	D discounts
9	A bargains	B offers	C purchases	D deliveries
10	A visited	B set up	C bought	D accessed
11	A look	B pay	C find	D click
12	A protect	B make	C have	D stay

12 Forces of nature

MAIN MENU

Vocabulary:	weather and disasters; key word: *way*
Grammar:	the definite article
Speaking:	criticising and complaining
Reading:	*Weather forecasts*
Listening:	*Natural disasters; Hurricanes*
Writing:	a discussion-type essay

EXAM MENU

Reading:	gapped text sentences
Writing:	an essay
Use of English:	multiple-choice cloze; open cloze
Listening:	sentence completion; multiple matching; multiple choice
Speaking:	two-way conversation

Getting started

1　When British people want to start a conversation with a stranger, they often begin with a comment about the weather. How do people start conversations in your country?

2　There are lots of expressions and idioms associated with the weather in English. Match questions and comments (1–7) with a response (a–g).

1　Do you think we should buy a new car?
2　How do you transfer photographs from this camera to a computer?
3　Is your grandmother feeling any better?
4　Why hasn't Dan found another job?
5　What were you and Melinda arguing about last night?
6　She made some lifelong friends while she was recovering from her car accident.
7　Thieves broke into her apartment *again* last weekend.

a　It just shows that *every cloud has a silver lining*.
b　Well, he left his old job *under a cloud*, maybe that's why.
c　And they say *lightning never strikes in the same place twice*.
d　No, I don't. We should *save some money for a rainy day*.
e　Not really, she still *feels under the weather*.
f　Don't ask me. I *haven't the foggiest idea*!
g　Nothing important, it was just *a storm in a teacup*.

3　Discuss the following questions:

1　How important is the weather in forming the national character and way of life?
2　How does the weather affect your mood?

Vocabulary: weather and disasters

1 Choose the correct word (in *italics*) in sentences 1–10.

1 The continental *climate/weather* has typically short cold winters and long hot summers.

2 London used to be famous for its thick *fog/mist*.

3 The weather *prediction/forecast* is good, so we can go ahead with the picnic.

4 Be careful how you drive. The roads are *frozen/icy*.

5 A light *gale/breeze* provides the ideal conditions for windsurfing.

6 It's horrible when it *drizzles/dribbles* all day. I'd rather it *poured/soaked* for an hour.

7 Can you hear the *lightning/thunder*? I think there's a *storm/tempest* coming.

8 The *snow/hail* was so strong that it damaged the paintwork on our car.

9 It's *sunny/shining*; let's go to the beach.

10 The *raining/rainy* season begins in May.

2 Match descriptions 1–8 to the words in the box.

earthquake	drought	famine	meteorite
tidal wave	tornado	flood	volcanic eruption

1 People could see the lava flowing down the mountainside towards the town below. _____

2 After eight days of constant rain the houses near the river were under a metre of water. _____

3 We could see it twisting and turning across the plain, lifting and dropping houses and cars as if they were children's toys. _____

4 First of all, the sea went out, then we saw a huge wall of water coming towards the beach and we ran for our lives. _____

5 We were having coffee when the whole building started to shake and our cups and saucers all rattled. It was terrifying. _____

6 The harvest has failed again and people will die from starvation unless something is done to help them quickly. _____

7 It is expected to pass by the earth only three million miles away – a near miss in scientific terms. _____

8 The sight in front of us is terrible. It hasn't rained here for three years; the earth is totally cracked and open. _____

3 Choose the correct word (in *italics*) in sentences 1–8.

1 A passerby *raised/rose* the alarm and called the fire brigade.

2 Millions of olive trees were *lost/disappeared* during the fire.

3 Sea temperatures have *raised/risen* because of greenhouse gases.

4 Comparatively few people *died/killed* in the last epidemic.

5 The island completely *lost/vanished* after the eruption.

6 More people are *killed/died* in domestic accidents than on the road.

7 This incident *rises/raises* some important issues.

8 Several new difficulties have *arisen/risen* as a result of the investigation.

→ Grammar Reference (Section 17.2) page 185

4 Is your region or country vulnerable to natural disasters? If so, what natural disasters has it suffered in the past?

Example: *In 1755, Lisbon was destroyed by an earthquake. Nowadays in Portugal, we have big problems with forest fires.*

Listening: natural disasters

1 🎧 12.1 MULTIPLE MATCHING You will hear five people talking about different events in the earth's history, and their scientific explanations. Choose from the list (A–F) the event each speaker talks about. There is one event you do not need to use.

Which speaker talks about ...?

A a theory which is probably wrong

Speaker _____

B a warning that wasn't given

Speaker _____

C how a region became less fertile

Speaker _____

D the dangers of nuclear accidents

Speaker _____

E people who failed to take notice of a warning

Speaker _____

F how an island was formed

Speaker _____

2 Put the events described in the listening passages in order from the most recent to the furthest in the past.

3 Imagine you could go back in time. Which of the events would you have most liked to witness (from a safe distance, of course)?

Speaking: criticising and complaining

1 Work in pairs. Read 1–4 below and discuss when you might hear them.
1 She **keeps on** taking my umbrella without asking!
2 **Why on earth** didn't you tell me about the storm warning?
3 You **should have closed** the sun roof in the car.
4 He**'s always complaining** about the weather, but he lives in a perfect climate.

2 Which sentences ...?
1 criticise someone for something they didn't do? _____; _____.
2 complain about annoying behaviour? _____; _____.

3 Which words in 1–4 would be stressed?

4 Turn to Tapescript 12.1 on page 219 and find examples of the forms used in 1–4.

5 Work in pairs. Javier and Peter are flatmates, classmates and friends. Decide what they would say to each other in the following situations.
1 Peter forgot to close the window when he went out. The neighbour's cat has come into the flat and destroyed the curtains.
2 When Javier comes back from the supermarket, Peter notices that they need coffee and orange juice and Javier didn't buy any.
3 Javier is annoyed because Peter always borrows his dictionary without asking him first.
4 Peter forgot to tell Javier that they were having an English vocabulary test at school. Javier has got a very bad mark in the test.

6 Work in pairs. One person is Javier and the other is Peter. Use the prompts below to have a conversation.

Javier	Peter
Ask to have a word with Peter.	
	Ask what the problem is.
Tell Peter the problem (the window/cat and the curtains) and criticise him for what has happened.	
	Apologise and defend yourself.
	Make a complaint about Javier (coffee and orange juice).
Respond – defending yourself. Criticise Peter for taking your dictionary.	
	Apologise. Remind Javier about the English test.
Make friends with Peter (nobody is perfect).	
	Make friends with Javier. Suggest watching TV, going out somewhere together, etc.

Reading: weather forecasts

1 Look at these different ways of predicting the weather. How do you think they work? Turn to Information File 12.1 on page 230 to find out.

2 Do you know any folk methods, or traditional sayings for predicting the weather? How accurate are they?

3 **GAPPED TEXT SENTENCES** You are going to read an article by a journalist who has the challenge of learning a different job or skill every month. Seven sentences have been removed from the article. Choose from the sentences (A–H) the one which fits each gap (1–7). There is one extra sentence which you do not need to use.

A Not exactly rocket science!

B As the song says, 'You don't need a weatherman to know which way the wind blows.'

C To begin with, we practised with those old-fashioned weather maps with shapes showing clouds and the sun and so on.

D I'd always treated the business of predicting the weather as a bit of a joke, and weather forecasters as figures of fun.

E Forecasting isn't just there to know if we should get the barbecue out; it has a deeply serious side too.

F Nevertheless, Francesca accepted our ignorance with good humour before swiftly demystifying the basics.

G I think it must have been a combination of the heat and the stress.

H Even as he stood there calling the poor man all the names he could think of, I recall thinking it was rather unfair.

After the excitement of being a stuntwoman, and a DJ to hundreds of clubbers in Marbella, my latest assignment, to present the weather on TV, came as a big disappointment. (1) _____ Childhood memories include my dad examining the wreckage of our garden fence after the worst storm in decades – an event that the country's most eminent weatherman had totally failed to predict. (2) _____ After all, even if Dad had known about the coming storm, he wouldn't have been able to do anything about it.

The night before I had to show up at the weather centre, I thought I'd jot down what I knew about predicting, or 'forecasting' the weather. My list was pathetically short. It amounted to a couple of traditional sayings of the 'red skies at night and shepherds' variety, and vague primary school

GRAMMAR SPOTLIGHT

Contrast and concession

Contrast

There are many different ways of making contrasts between two clauses. Think about what forms follow the words in italics below.

- *Even though/Although* forecasters get it right 95 percent of the time, it's the other five percent that people remember.
- *Despite* the magnets on the back they kept falling off.
- *Despite being* fully prepared, the first time I tried I completely dried up.
- *Despite the fact that* the studios are air-conditioned, the make-up and the lights make you feel really hot.

Concession

Look at these different ways of making concession between two apparently opposite ideas.

- The end result wasn't too embarrassing; *however*, I did look incredibly jerky and wooden.
- We started with a short quiz that showed just how little everyone knew. *Nevertheless*, Francesca accepted our ignorance with good humour before swiftly demystifying the basics.

➡ Grammar Reference (Section 6.7) page 171

4 Use words of concession or contrast from the Grammar Spotlight to link or join the pairs of sentences below.

1 The pine cone was open. It rained the rest of the day.
  _____

2 She knew nothing about the weather. She learned the basics quickly.
  _____

3 The weatherman had always had an excellent reputation. He lost it overnight.
  _____

GRAMMAR SPOTLIGHT

Though

In spoken English we may put *though* at the end of a sentence. This shows that there is a connection between what has just been said and what came directly before.

The weather was quite cold. It was sunny, though.

5 Discuss. What reputation do the weather forecasters have in your country?

---

memories to do with pine cones and seaweed. (3) _____ In the end, I gave up, hoping that people wouldn't be too appalled by my lack of knowledge. Francesca Cross, the head of the training centre and our course leader, proved unshockable. She had joined the weather centre having studied geography and statistics. At the centre she then learnt the secrets of forecasting. Eventually she moved over to presenting. There were half a dozen other people from local radio and TV stations. We started with a short quiz that showed just how little everyone knew. (4) _____ By the end of the morning I knew an isobar from an isotherm and could interpret one of those weather maps you find in newspapers.

The trouble with predicting Britain's weather, Francesca told us, is that we are on the edge of the Atlantic with consequently some of the most variable and unpredictable conditions on the planet. This explains the obsession the British have with the weather. Over the past few years, the extremes of weather we have witnessed have challenged the most experienced meteorologists and their sophisticated computer programmes. Even though forecasters get it right 95 percent of the time, it's the other five percent that people remember. (5) _____ Sea captains make life or death decisions based upon it. And insurance companies will seek advice before deciding whether to provide insurance cover for outdoor events like pop festivals.

and listened in to discussions where the professionals finalised their conclusions. In the afternoon, we concentrated on turning these findings into scripts the public would understand. Reading the forecast from a carefully prepared script wasn't too hard, but it was preparing for TV that proved the greatest challenge. (6) _____ They kept falling off despite the magnets on the back. Things have come a long way since then, and today's technology is incredibly advanced. Nowadays presenters use a 'blue screen system', which means that the presenter stands in front of a clear blue screen carrying a faint image that only the presenter is able to see. The images viewers see are back-projected onto it.

The climax of the course was giving a TV forecast in studio conditions with full make-up and lighting. Despite being fully prepared, the first time I tried I completely dried up. The second time I couldn't stop giggling. (7) _____ Although the studios are air-conditioned, the make-up and the lights make you feel really hot. The third time I managed to get all the way through without a hitch. The end result wasn't too embarrassing; however, I did look rather jerky and wooden. Professional presenters have to be incredibly well co-ordinated, pointing to different parts of the screen as they read their commentary from the Autocue. They may even have to cope with extra instructions through a hidden earpiece while they're speaking. All in all the experience left me with a new-found respect for the professionalism and cool of the people who present it live night after night, and the invisible

Listening: hurricanes

PAPER 4, PART 2

1 ⋂ **12.2** SENTENCE COMPLETION **You are going to listen to a radio interview about hurricanes with Dr Kate Jackson, a weather expert. Listen to part A of the interview and complete Kate's notes below.**

The floods caused by Hurricane Katrina covered an area the size of (1) _____.
Hurricanes form over the oceans in the (2) _____ either side of the equator. They can't form over the equator itself because the spin (the Earth's rotation) (3) _____.

Combined elements work together to create a (4) _____ which can result in a hurricane. Storms are called hurricanes when they (5) _____
120 kph; Katrina reached a speed of (6) _____.

A 'surge' is the sudden increase in the height of the level (7) _____ caused by the hurricane. The biggest recorded surge took place in (8) _____ a hundred years ago. Afterwards people found fish and (9) _____ on cliff-tops which were (10) _____ above sea level.

EXAM SPOTLIGHT

Activating your knowledge

2 Remember, before you listen make sure that you read the notes carefully so that you know what you will be listening for. Reading the notes will also help you activate whatever previous knowledge you may have about a topic. For instance, work in groups and brainstorm what you already know about global warming and hurricanes. Divide it into two columns.

What you know	What you would like to know

PAPER 4, PART 4

3 ⋂ **12.3** MULTIPLE CHOICE **Listen to part B of the interview. For questions 1–7, choose the best answer (A, B or C).**

1 How important does Kate think global warming is in the increase in hurricanes?
   A It is a key factor.
   B It has yet to be established.
   C Warm sea currents are far more important.

2 Kate says that over the past hundred years the temperature of the oceans …
   A has hardly changed.
   B rose, went down for a short period, then rose again.
   C has risen steadily and consistently.

3 Kate says that drops in temperature were probably caused by …
   A a temporary reduction in greenhouse gases.
   B an increase in volcanic activity.
   C pollution particles.

4 She is convinced that …
   A forests will be able to absorb rises in CO_2.
   B temperatures will eventually stabilise.
   C CO_2 is to blame for temperature rises.

5 How does the interviewer react to Kate's information about CO_2 levels?
   A He seems to think they present a threat to humanity.
   B He feels they are too small to be significant.
   C He is astonished that they are so high.

6 Which *aren't* the same as hurricanes?
   A typhoons
   B twisters
   C cyclones

7 What are the differences between hurricanes in the northern and southern hemispheres?
   A They rotate in opposite directions.
   B In the northern hemisphere they rotate like the hands of a watch.
   C In the southern hemisphere they turn anti-clockwise.

Key word: *way*

1 Read sentences 1–8. Rephrase the words in bold with an expression from the box, making any necessary changes.

change your ways	by the way
to my way of thinking	under way
to have one's way	show/tell someone the way
to come a long way	to keep out of someone's way

1 You should **avoid Simon** when he is in a bad mood.

2 Can you **tell me how to get** to the medical centre?

3 Meteorologists have **made a lot of progress** in forecasting the weather.

4 If **it were my decision,** everybody would have to travel by bicycle.

5 **I almost forgot**, we need to bring the plants indoors; there's going to be a frost.

6 He **is a much better person** since he married Linda.

7 **In my opinion,** there isn't enough evidence to support global warming.

8 The report is **in the process of being written** as we speak.

Grammar: the definite article

1 We use *the* to refer specifically to something. Match the examples (1–6) to the explanations (a–f).

1 a team of scientists has found evidence … **the** scientists believe

2 **the** British/**the** rich/**the** unemployed

3 **the** Atlantic/**the** Sun

4 **the** head of the weather centre

5 … **the** country's most eminent forecaster

6 **the** disappearance of the Maya perplexes scholars

a where there is only one of something

b for nationalities/classes of people

c for titles or places where *of* appears

d the subject under discussion

e when something/someone is mentioned for the second time

f with superlatives

➡ Grammar Reference (Section 3) page 167

2 Complete the passage below with *a*, *the* or ø (no article).

Bolts from the Blue

Roy Cleveland Sullivan, **(1)** _____ forest ranger from Waynesboro, Virginia, was known as **(2)** _____ 'Human Lightning Rod' because he was struck by **(3)** _____ lightning seven times in **(4)** _____ course of **(5)** _____ 36-year career. **(6)** _____ first strike, in 1942, caused **(7)** _____ loss of **(8)** _____ big toenail. Twenty-seven years later **(9)** _____ second bolt burned his eyebrows off. **(10)** _____ following year, in 1970, **(11)** _____ third bolt burnt his left shoulder. After Sullivan's hair was set on fire by **(12)** _____ fourth strike in 1972, he began carrying **(13)** _____ bucket of **(14)** _____ water around with him in his car. In August of **(15)** _____ following year, **(16)** _____ bolt came out of **(17)** _____ small cloud, hit him on **(18)** _____ head through the hat he was wearing and set fire to his hair again. Sullivan poured **(19)** _____ bucket of water over his head to cool himself down. He was struck on two further occasions before his death. Two of his Ranger hats, which are burned through **(20)** _____ top, are on display at **(21)** _____ local museum. This all shows that **(22)** _____ lightning *can* strike in **(23)** _____ same place more than once! Sullivan must have been one of **(24)** _____ unluckiest people around … or perhaps, the luckiest!

3 Find examples of *the* in the reading text above and say why it is used.

Writing: a discussion-type essay

1 **Work in pairs. Even if we think we know nothing about science, we may surprise ourselves. Talk about questions 1–4 below then share your answers with another pair.**

1 What are we drinking when we have H_2O with CO_2?
2 What are fossils? What is the problem with burning fossil fuels?
3 What is a greenhouse and what do we normally grow in one?
4 What do scientists mean when they talk about 'the greenhouse effect'?

2 **Discuss. How worried are people in your country about global warming?**

1 How much time do politicians and businesspeople spend discussing global warming?
2 What are some of the alternative sources of energy discussed in your country? Are they realistic?

3 **Read the title of an exam question and the essay opposite which has been written by an exam candidate. Decide if the statements are true or false.**

> **Exam question**
> Global warming is one of the greatest challenges facing the world today. Say how you would deal with this problem.

1 There is a lot of clear evidence of global warming.
T / F

2 The main reason for global warming is high levels of solar activity. T / F

3 Nuclear power offers a safe long term solution to emission problems. T / F

4 Electricity from dams and wind generators are greener ways of producing power. T / F

5 Brazil is a model for alternatives to fossil fuels. T / F

6 Plants used for biofuels compensate for emissions from flex-fuel vehicles. T / F

7 Public transport can help reduce emissions. T / F

8 Locally produced food is better for the environment. T / F

*Most people accept global warming as scientific fact; we need look no further than the melting polar ice caps, and ever more violent hurricanes. So what has caused **this rise in temperature**? The dramatic increase in greenhouse gases such as carbon dioxide (CO_2) into the atmosphere from the burning of fossil fuels is the most likely candidate. The challenge facing us is how to reduce **such emissions**. I would like to outline a few measures that governments and individuals can take. First of all, governments should commit themselves to reducing the level of greenhouse gas emissions. <u>Nevertheless</u>, they should avoid the temptation of nuclear energy **as its** associated risks are too great. **Instead**, governments should favour greener ways of energy production, **For instance**, China's 'Three Gorges' dam provides masses of hydro-electric power, while the Netherlands satisfy many of their energy needs from wind turbines. <u>In addition</u>, our leaders should make us less dependent on fossil fuels by copying Brazil's example. **There**, 'flex-fuel' vehicles can run on both petrol and alcohol from sugar cane. Admittedly, such vehicles produce CO_2 but growing plants absorb it, so biofuels are carbon-neutral. <u>Furthermore</u>, they provide a renewable and inexhaustible supply of energy. Finally, **they** should tax gas-guzzling vehicles and get them off the roads. So what can we do on a personal level? First, the biggest step is to end our love affair with our cars and switch to public transport. Or, at the very least, car-share with colleagues or classmates. <u>Next</u>, we should shop locally, and make sure that we eat locally produced food. And, <u>last but not least</u>, we should remember to turn off the lights – every little bit helps!*

4 **Work in pairs. Decide how you would divide the essay you have just read into three or four separate paragraphs.**

5 **Read the essay again and answer these questions.**

1 Which of the <u>underlined</u> words are ways of saying *but*; which are used to say *and*?

but _____

and _____

2 Which words and expressions you listed above are used to sequence ideas?

_____

_____

3 Focus on the words in **bold** in the composition. What, where or who do they refer to?

- this rise in temperature _____
- such emissions _____
- its _____
- instead _____
- for instance _____
- there _____
- they _____

6 **Find two examples of questions in the text on page 122. How do they help the writer?**

7 **Study the information below. What is likely to happen if this trend continues?**

AFRICAN ELEPHANT POPULATION:

1979 1.3 million
1989 600,000
2008 400,000
The biggest problem facing African elephants is poaching; i.e. illegal hunting. Poachers (the hunters) kill them for the ivory of their tusks. Most of the ivory is exported to countries where it is carved into valuable ornaments.

8 **Use the information in exercise 7, and the notes below to write an answer to the following question.**

Exam question

One of our best-loved animals, the African elephant, risks becoming extinct in the next 20 years. What can be done to save it?

Introduction:
Outline decline in elephant population. Worst affected countries Gabon, Kenya and Congo. Could be a modern-day mammoth. Root of problem is demand for ivory.
What to do?
Educate people about the desperate situation of the elephant. Destroy demand by educating public. Improve international co-operation. Ban international ivory trade. Suggest alternatives to ivory – resins look the same. Dealing with poachers: More police, stronger penalties. Establish secure park. Give poachers better things to do. Encourage farming. Pay them not to poach. Involve them in conservation.

WRITING CHECKLIST

Did you...?	Yes (✓)	No (✗)
• write between 120 and 180 words	☐	☐
• divide your composition into coherent paragraphs	☐	☐
• use linkers to move from one idea to the next	☐	☐
• use a variety of ways of introducing and ordering your main points	☐	☐
• use different ways of contrasting and balancing ideas	☐	☐
• use pronouns and other references to join the text together	☐	☐
• use one or two 'rhetorical questions' to move your discussion along	☐	☐

➡ Writing Guide, page 205

Review and Use of English

1 MULTIPLE-CHOICE CLOZE Read the text below and decide which answer (*A, B, C* or *D*) best fits each gap.

A legend which continues to fascinate us is that of the island of Atlantis which was lost, never to reappear. The disappearance of the island, wiped **(1)** _____ from one day to the next, would have mystified and terrified its neighbours. The story, passed down from the **(2)** _____ Egyptians, eventually reached the philosopher Plato (427–347BC) who **(3)** _____ of the catastrophic disappearance of an island empire, inhabited by wealthy and sophisticated people. Different locations have been **(4)** _____ as possible sites; the most **(5)** _____ candidate is the island of Santorini in the Aegean sea. Thera, as it was called in the Bronze **(6)** _____, was a developed Minoan civilisation originating in Crete. This civilisation would have **(7)** _____ probably controlled much of the eastern Mediterranean. In 1630BC a massive eruption and earthquake produced a tsunami which devastated the area. Part of the island **(8)** _____ sank beneath the sea as one plate of the earth's crust slid underneath another. Before the disaster Thera would have been a large circular island – which is exactly **(9)** _____ Plato tells us. There could have been **(10)** _____ hope for its population. Everyone must have **(11)** _____; it is impossible to imagine there being many survivors, if **(12)** _____ at all.

2 OPEN CLOZE Read the text below and think of the word which best fits each gap. Use only one word in each gap.

In evolutionary terms, the woolly mammoth became extinct yesterday, just 3,500 years ago in fact. A dwarf variety **(1)** _____ until 1500BC on Wrangel island in Russia, which was covered in its bones. Interestingly enough, the word mammoth comes from Russian, and **(2)** _____ borrowed from a Tartar language, 'maa' meaning 'earth'. Mammoth remains were dug from the earth, so people believed that it must **(3)** _____ lived underground! The woolly variety known to prehistoric man dates from about 700,000 years ago **(4)** _____ the Earth's temperatures fell. With its thick coat it was **(5)** _____ to cope with the extreme cold of the ice age. Quite **(6)** _____ it became extinct is open to question. Some experts claim over-hunting by man, caused **(7)** _____ disappearance but the most likely cause remains the dramatic end of the ice age. Rumours concerning mammoths hiding out **(8)** _____ ___ Alaska persisted until quite recently. One story from 1900 concerned a hunter who claimed he **(9)** _____ killed a mammoth and donated it to a museum – the story turned **(10)** _____ to be a hoax! Even so, they could **(11)** _____ making a comeback; there are some scientists who believe that they can take genetic material from frozen mammoths and inject it into the eggs of female Indian elephants. So **(12)** _____ knows, these magnificent creatures could roam the Earth again!

1 A off	B out	C down	D up
2 A historical	B old	C elderly	D ancient
3 A reported	B said	C told	D described
4 A risen	B arisen	C rose	D raised
5 A alike	B likelihood	C likely	D possibility
6 A Age	B Time	C Epoch	D Event
7 A most	B much	C almost	D highly
8 A still	B even	C yet	D but
9 A what	B which	C that	D why
10 A few	B hardly	C almost	D little
11 A killed	B dead	C died	D death
12 A none	B any	C one	D nobody

13 In the news

MAIN MENU

Vocabulary: news and newspapers; key words: *say and tell*

Grammar: reported speech; reporting verbs

Speaking: reporting; agreeing on what to watch

Reading: *The paparazzi*

Listening: a news report; *What's on TV?*

Writing: checking and editing

EXAM MENU

Reading: multiple choice
Writing: letter
Use of English: multiple-choice cloze; open cloze
Listening: sentence completion; multiple matching
Speaking: two-way conversation

Getting started

1 Where do you get your news? (Newspapers? TV or radio? The Internet?)
Do you believe everything you read or hear in the news? Why/Why not?

2 Consider these news sources. How much do you believe them? Score how much you trust the source. (1 = very rarely, 2 = usually, 3 = all the time).

The newsreader on the TV or radio	1	2	3
Your teacher	1	2	3
Text messages	1	2	3
Friends at school or where you work	1	2	3
The Internet and blogs	1	2	3
The daily newspaper	1	2	3

Now compare your answers with the rest of the class.

3 Work in small groups. You are in charge of a news programme on a local TV station and it is your job to select the three leading stories for the programme. Tonight you have the following seven news items to choose from. Discuss each one and choose the best three.

The weather will be windy and cold tomorrow.

A famous Hollywood actor has been stopped by local police for speeding.

A major supermarket has withdrawn jars of marmalade which may contain glass. One customer returned a jar with the glass and as a precaution the supermarket is advising customers to return the product.

Scientists have discovered that six-year-old children now prefer looking at a screen to a human face.

All ten passengers were unhurt as a private plane crash landed in a field next to a major motorway. The only injury was a scratch on the pilot's hand.

The next *James Bond* movie opens in cinemas across the country this weekend.

Wally, the whale at the city's aquarium, has recovered from a serious illness. Wally's keeper says the public's favourite whale will be on show again from next week.

Vocabulary: news and newspapers

1 Discuss. Look at this list of sections from a newspaper.

- Do newspapers in your country have all these sections?
- Do they include other information?
- What other sections might a newspaper include?

News	**Health**	**Sport**
Politics	**Horoscopes**	**Crossword**
Business	**Obituaries**	**TV listings**
Editorial	**Weather**	**Classified**
Science	**Showbiz**	**Personal**

2 Which section of the newspaper (from exercise 1) do you think these headlines come from? Which news item would you read first?

BANK BREAKS OFF TALKS WITH PARTNER

BRAZIL PULL AHEAD WITH GOAL IN FINAL MINUTE

POLITICIANS TRY TO COVER UP SCANDAL

RUMOURS OF PRESIDENT'S RESIGNATION LEAK OUT

NUMBERS ENTERING UNIVERSITY GO UP BY 3%

LEOS LIKELY TO FALL OUT WITH BOSS THIS WEEK

BRETT AND ANGELA ABOUT TO BREAK UP?

NON-GOVERNMENTAL ORGANISATIONS PULL OUT OF TALKS

Phrasal verbs

3 Match the underlined phrasal verbs in the headlines in exercise 2, to the synonyms in 1–8 below.

1 to go in front of someone _____
2 stop doing something suddenly _____
3 disagree and argue _____
4 withdraw _____
5 increase _____
6 hide the truth _____
7 slowly become known _____
8 separate _____

4 Use words from the box below to replace the words in bold, in these sentences.

editorial	front page news	blog	paparazzi
scoop	breaking news	item	celebrity
tabloids	censor	circulation	viewpoint

1 We have a **story that no one else has printed**. _____

2 The face of a **famous person** always sells more copies. _____

3 I have my own **online journal** where I write my thoughts and any news I've heard. _____

4 The **number of copies of this newspaper that we sell** is about 2 million a day. _____

5 This story will be **the most important news item** tomorrow. _____

6 They tried to **prevent us printing parts of** this article about his private life but we ignored them. _____

7 What's the biggest news **story** on TV today? _____

8 All newspapers have a particular **set of opinions** in order to sell to certain readers. _____

9 We interrupt this programme to bring you **news that is happening right now as we speak**. _____

10 I disagree with the **views of the chief journalist of the paper** today. _____

11 Newspapers can pay the **photographers who follow celebrities** $10,000 for a good picture. _____

12 There are two types of newspaper. There's the quality press with real news and then there's the **low quality** press with very entertaining stories! _____

SPOTLIGHT ON VOCABULARY

Spidergrams

Spidergrams are a good way to record new topic vocabulary or to revise vocabulary. They also let you add more words later.

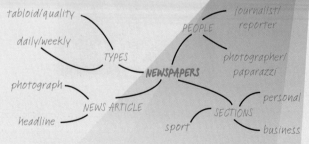

5 1 Add these words to the spidergram: *editor – editorial – national – local – correspondent*

2 Choose another vocabulary topic from a previous unit in this book and create a spidergram.

Listening: a news report

EXAM SPOTLIGHT

Sentence completion

PAPER 4, PART 2

1 Answer these questions about this part of the Listening exam.
1 Will the answers be in the same order as the sentences?
2 How many words do you write in each answer?
3 Are the words in the written notes always the same as those in the listening?

PAPER 4, PART 2

2 ⌂ 13.1 SENTENCE COMPLETION You will hear a journalist reporting on a problem in education. For questions 1–10 complete the sentences.

Critics say they are the worst results for more than **(1)** _____ years. An ex-**(2)** _____ said the situation is appalling. Last year's national tests show 11 and 14-year-olds made more **(3)** _____ errors last year than they did four years ago.

The most common errors were words such as 'change', 'known' and **(4)** _____. Mistakes were made because **(5)** _____ had missed out letters, put the wrong endings or used **(6)** _____. Basic punctuation mistakes include capital letters, **(7)** _____ and commas.

The **(8)** _____ for Education said she had sent schools a list of words all children should know by the end of their first year and by the age of 14.

The teachers' **(9)** _____ will give a statement later, but the new-style English lessons are popular with them. Each lesson begins with ten minutes of spelling. Maths teachers practise words like *geometrical* and sports teachers check pupils can spell *athlete* and **(10)** _____.

Grammar: reported speech

1 Read these extracts from Listening 13.1. Rewrite them into direct speech.
1 A new report on education says they are the worst results in over twenty years.
   'They are the worst results in over twenty years.'
2 One person told me that most errors had arisen because pupils had missed out letters ...
   '_____'

3 I asked the Minister for Education what she thought some of the reasons were ...
   '_____'
4 She said she'd sent schools a list of 600 words all children should know ...
   '_____'
5 The teachers' union said it would be commenting later ...
   '_____'

GRAMMAR SPOTLIGHT

Reporting spoken English

2 Write the sentence number (from exercise 1) in these rules.
a In sentences _____, _____, _____ and _____ the verb changes tense.
b The verb in sentence _____ stays the same because the fact still applies or is true.
c In sentence _____ we report the question as if it is a statement.

➜ Grammar Reference (Section 14) page 182

3 Study these pairs of sentences. Write in the missing words.
1 'I'm going out on Friday.'
   She said that she _____ out on Friday.
2 'Can you give me a hand?'
   They asked if I _____ them a hand.
3 'Don't lift that until I get home and can help you.'
   He told me not to lift it until he _____ me.
4 The spokesperson said they had seen the same results five years ago.
   'We _____ the same results five years ago.'
5 He asked me what I did for a living.
   'What _____ for a living?'

Speaking: reporting

1 ⌂ 13.1 Listen again to the report about education and make notes in order to complete each of the expressions below.

Have you heard about ...?

The report reveals that ...

One thing that surprised me was that ...

It's amazing that ...

It would be interesting to know more about ...

2 Think of a recent news story you know about. Tell your partner about it using some of the expressions above.

Reading: the paparazzi

1 Why do you think people like to read about famous people in magazines and newspapers?

2 Quickly read the article and answer the following.
1 What motivates someone to work as a 'paparazzi'?
2 What skills do you need?
3 Is it always an exciting job?

3 Match these words from the article to definitions 1–8.

scoop _____   fetch upward _____

mundane _____   ethics _____

sources _____   invading privacy _____

uncanny _____   scum _____

1 people who provide information to journalists
2 uninteresting or unexciting
3 set of beliefs about what is right and wrong
4 to get involved in a person's life without permission
5 people you think are very unpleasant (informal)
6 an exclusive story that no other newspaper has
7 strange
8 sell for more than (an amount of money)

4 Look at the highlighted words and expressions in the text and complete sentences 1–6 below.

1 Many people don't hunt to kill. They just do it for the

_____.

2 Wolves hunt in groups or as a '_____'.

3 We _____ when we won the lottery and made a million dollars.

4 She was furious when she saw stories of her private life _____ the front page of a tabloid newsapaper.

5 The hunters were _____ their _____ but the lion still managed to escape.

6 We _____ the escaped prisoner _____ in a building. We need more police to help capture him.

HOT ON THE TRAIL OF ANGELINA JOLIE

The name 'Paparazzo' comes from the name of an intrusive society photographer in Fellini's film *La Dolce Vita*. The character was called Paparazzo because the word means 'sparrow' in Italian and Fellini thought these society photographers were like the small hungry birds. Reporter Bud Bultman joins the paparazzi for a night and uncovers what makes someone join one of the most criticised professions of recent years.

We're racing down the streets of Beverly Hills after the Hollywood superstar actress Angelina Jolie. Her black Range Rover is just ahead of us. I'm in the middle of a pack of paparazzi in pursuit of the red-hot actress, and I'm starting to realise what drives these guys. It's the thrill of the chase, not to mention the huge amount of money they can make with an exclusive photo of a star.

But the life of the paparazzi isn't all fast cars and big pay cheques. Frank Griffin, who co-owns the paparazzi agency Bauer-Griffin and has allowed me to join Ben, one of his photographers hot on Jolie's trail for a few days, says they spend hours sitting around and wasting time and money. 'It's more mundane than anything else. It's sitting and waiting.' Griffin reminds me, 'Every day there's a $10,000 picture, and it's just the question of knowing where it is, and being there to take it.'

He believes it's all about good information. Bauer-Griffin keeps a database of more than 500 celebrity license plates and addresses, as well as the tail numbers of celebrities' private airplanes. They work much like detectives, making use of a network of well-placed, well-paid sources, ranging from parking attendants and hotel clerks to people inside

EXAM SPOTLIGHT

Strategies for unknown vocabulary

PAPER 1, PART 1
Remember:
• Sometimes you don't need to understand single words but it's important you understand the general sense in order to answer the question.
• Never leave a question unanswered. If you're not quite sure always make a guess. You might be right!

the celebrity industry.

Griffin takes all those bits of information and determines where celebrities are, and where they're going. I overheard him on the phone running down a list of stars and the hotel rooms where they're staying. He even had the inside scoop on Angelina's travel plans with her partner, Brad Pitt: 'Brad and Angelina did not fly into Nice today. I think they are going to fly into England the 24th.'

It's this uncanny ability of Griffin to piece all the parts of the jigsaw together that means his photographers are often responsible for pictures which can fetch upward of $250,000. Recently, *US Weekly* reportedly paid half-a-million dollars for photos of Brad and Angelina on a beach in Africa.

It's that same prospect of taking a big-money photo which means that Ben, along with a group of other paparazzi, are finally catching up with Angelina and following her into the parking lot of the Federal Building, just outside Beverly Hills. They have her cornered. Ben grabs his camera. I can feel the excitement of closing the net on our prey. 'Jolie's out! Jolie's out!' Ben shouts on his two-way radio. I see the actress walking toward the Federal Building with daughter, Zahara. Ben starts snapping away as she approaches.

At this moment, I'm not thinking, 'Wow, I'm seeing Angelina Jolie up close!' I'm not thinking about the ethics of tailing her, about whether the paparazzi go too far, or about whether we're invading Angelina Jolie's privacy. I'm thinking like the paparazzi: 'we're hitting the jackpot, scoring one of the hottest actresses on the planet.' And, I have to admit, I feel a bit of pride when I see those pictures splashed across newsstands a few days later.

With the paparazzi often hated and labelled as 'scum', I ask Griffin how he justifies what he does. He has a simple answer. He says 'If the only job you can do is street sweeping, then be at least the best street sweeper on the block. And that's what I've tried to do. There are obviously conflicts of conscience, and I really genuinely don't want to hurt people. But I try to be as professional as I can with my job.'

5 **Read the article again and choose the best answer for questions 1–8.**

1 The author of this article is …
   A a member of the paparazzi.
   B critical of the paparazzi.
   C researching the paparazzi.
   D secretly following the paparazzi.

2 What are the reasons he thinks the paparazzi enjoy their job?
   A the excitement and the money
   B the opportunity to meet famous celebrities
   C because it's like being a detective
   D they get to travel to exotic places

3 According to Griffin what is the truth about the job?
   A The majority of the work is dull and unexciting.
   B You spend most of your time with famous people.
   C You only work a few hours a day.
   D You have your own private aeroplane.

4 What does Griffin think is the secret to being successful?
   A watching celebrities' houses, cars and aeroplanes
   B not caring what people think of you
   C keeping good records and having lots of contacts
   D enjoying the chase

5 According to the article, why is Griffin successful?
   A He's good at taking photographs.
   B He is able to co-ordinate his network of people and information.
   C He goes to places where he knows celebrities will be.
   D He negotiates good prices for his pictures.

6 What is the subject of the metaphor that runs all the way through the text?
   A motor racing
   B shooting
   C tennis
   D hunting

7 How does the author feel about finally seeing the pictures of Jolie published?
   A a little guilty
   B very excited
   C rather pleased
   D slightly sad

8 According to the article, how does Griffin feel about what he does?
   A that criticism of him is unfair
   B that there's nothing wrong with doing a good job
   C that hurting people is just part of the job
   D that he feels guilty about what he does

6 **Discuss these questions:**

- Would you describe the Paparazzi as 'scum'?
- Do you think it's ethical to invade a celebrity's privacy?

Speaking: agreeing on what to watch

PAPER 5, PART 3

1 Work in pairs. Look at the pictures below showing what's on TV. What do you think is being reported? Imagine you live in a house with only one television. Discuss which programme you will watch.

Listening: what's on TV?

PAPER 4, PART 3

1 ∩ 13.2 You will hear someone changing TV channels. Number the TV screens (shown in the pictures) in the order the person watches them.

2 ∩ 13.2 MULTIPLE MATCHING Listen again. Choose from the list (A–F) what the speaker in each TV programme is saying. Use the letters only once. There is one extra letter which you do not need to use.

The speaker …

A reported gossip

B warned people about the future   Speaker 1: _____

C agreed with the situation   Speaker 2: _____

D criticised a political situation   Speaker 3: _____

E recommended more exercise and   Speaker 4: _____
  a healthier diet
                                            Speaker 5: _____
F explained a delay

Key words: *say and tell*

1 Choose the correct word (in *italics*) in sentences 1–4.

1 Please *say/tell* him I called.

2 The minister *said/told* they were dealing with it.

3 My parents *said/told* me to go to bed.

4 I *said/told* to him that it was a bad idea.

2 Write the correct form of **say** or **tell** in these common expressions.

1 To _____ you the truth, I don't have any money left.

2 So what are you _____? That you can't help me?

3 I'll _____ you what. Why don't I give you a lift?

4 So, you had a good time then?
You can _____ that again! It was brilliant.

5 Don't interrupt! Let her speak and then you can have your _____.

6 Only time will _____ if their relationship can survive all these problems.

Grammar: reporting verbs

1 What is the function of each of these sentences (1–8)? Write the number of the sentence against the correct function.

remind _____   recommend _____

advise _____   apologise for _____

invite _____   suggest _____

warn _____   criticise _____

1 Why don't we ask what she thinks?

2 There's a great new computer game you should buy.

3 This new law is ridiculous.

4 You both ought to be careful at that time of night.

5 If I were you, I'd accept his offer.

6 I'm really sorry for missing the party.

7 Don't forget to call me when you get there.

8 Would you like to come over for lunch?

GRAMMAR SPOTLIGHT

Suggest

Suggest can be followed by three different structures:

She suggested **asking him** what he thought.

She suggested **we ask him** what he thought.

She suggested **that we should ask (him)** what he thought.

You cannot use the *to* infinitive: ~~She suggested to ask her what she thought.~~

2 Try to report this sentence using the three ways above:

Why don't we tell the newspapers about it?

➡ Grammar Reference (Section 14) page 182

3 Complete these sentences from exercise 1. The first one has been done as an example.

1 She suggested *asking* her what she thought.

2 He recommended _____ the new computer game.

3 The spokesperson criticised _____.

4 His father warned _____.

5 She advised me _____.

6 Michael apologised _____ the party.

7 Mother reminded _____ her when I got there.

8 The neighbours invited _____ over for lunch.

4 You are a TV news reporter. There was a road accident earlier today. You interviewed three people for tonight's news programme. Read the notes you took earlier at the interviews and prepare them for your news report. Remember to use reporting verbs.

NOTES

Policeman: 'I think the driver was going too quickly and didn't see the lorry turning into his lane. In my opinion he should have slowed down when he approached the junction. The other point was that it was a foggy morning and we always say to drivers to put your lights on in this kind of weather'.

Pedestrian: 'I was just walking along when I heard a loud bang. It was definitely the lorry driver's fault. I don't think he was looking where he was going and didn't see the car coming up the road.'

Lorry driver: 'I'm really sorry about what's happened, but to be fair I don't think he had his lights on. He was wrong for not having them on. I didn't see him.'

5 Work in pairs. Take turns to read your news report to your partner. Compare your reports.

Writing: checking and editing

GRAMMAR SPOTLIGHT

Checking and editing your work

Follow these steps:

• Always check your writing for mistakes afterwards.
• Pay special attention to spelling and punctuation mistakes.
• It's often easier to find mistakes when you read what you have written a few hours later.
• It's even easier to find mistakes in someone else's writing so let other people read what you have written.

1 It's easy to make spelling and punctuation mistakes, even in your own language. Here are some signs from countries where English is the first language. What mistakes can you find in each one?

2 Here are some of the most commonly misspelled words in the English language. Do you think each word is spelt correctly or not? Tick the correct ones.

accommodation _____   business _____

separate _____   greatful _____

commitment _____   recieve _____

dependent _____   advertisement _____

embarassed _____   wich _____

goverment _____   comftable _____

3 Discuss. Do you know what each of these items of punctuation is called and when to use it?

: _____

; _____

! _____

' … ' _____

. _____

' _____

? _____

, _____

4 Sentences 1–8 are missing a punctuation item from exercise 3. Write them in.

1 Its your turn I think.

2 How long have you been here

3 The boy at the bus stop, who we'd seen earlier was now crying.

4 The rabbit said to Alice, I'm late, I'm late.

5 Please bring the following items with you to the exam pens, pencils and an identity card.

6 Jesse was late as usual it had always been the case since childhood.

7 My father shouted, 'Turn that music down '

8 I look forward to hearing from you

5 **Read this exam question.**

Exam question
Read the advert on your school noticeboard and write the letter.

New school newspaper!

We are planning to launch a new school newspaper and we need your ideas. What would you like to read about? Do you want to know how the football team did last Friday? Or perhaps read a review of the school Christmas play? Would you like quizzes and competitions? Let us know by writing us a letter with your views and post it in the special box in Room 221.

REVISION SPOTLIGHT

Checking your writing
Remember to use the last 5–10 minutes of the exam to check your writing.
Look back at a previous piece of writing you have done and identify your common mistakes.

6 **A teacher has marked the student's answer. Match the teacher's numbers on the essay to the feedback in red. Write the number next to the feedback.**

Dear Sir or Madam

i[1] am writing in response to your advertisement for the new school newspaper. I think it's a great idea[2] I never know what's happening[3] I'd like to read about things.[4]

I'm not very interesting[5] in football[6] maybe the back page could have information about all sports in the school. For example[7] the girl's hockey team what[8] won the championship last term.[9] My favourite activity after school is drama club so let's have information about that kind of thing. I think photos of students at these clubs are nice. It's nice[10] to see friends having fun. I don't really do crosswords but I think the students will like competitions, especially if there are prizes!

Finally, I think you should have a page in the newspaper for letters like this from students. This way people say what they think about the school.

I look forward to read[11] the newspaper when it comes out.

Best wishes,[12]
Paula Pilosi

.... capital letter

.... you need a conjunction

.... full stop

.... problem with the pronoun

.... new paragraph needed

.... gerund needed

.... incorrect ending

.... too informal

.... comma

.... avoid repeating words. Can you change one of these adjectives?

.... Is there a better adjective you can use?

.... Can you use a better word here?

Well done, Paula. You have lots of nice ideas in this letter and you've answered each part of the question. Make sure you check your work when you finish. There are a few mistakes and changes you could make which would improve it.

7 **Now rewrite and improve Paula's piece of writing.**

Review and Use of English

1 MULTIPLE-CHOICE CLOZE Read the text below and decide which answer (*A, B, C* or *D*) best fits each gap.

Newspaper circulation is on the **(1)** _____. However this isn't recent news. The problems go right back to the late 1940s when the number of **(2)** _____ was falling but at that time population growth maintained sales. But the 1990s saw fewer and fewer people developing the newspaper **(3)** _____. So where are they all going? It's impossible to say fully. Some people are getting all their news from cable television. With 24-hour news channels providing round-the-clock **(4)** _____, newspaper editors have had to shift their focus from new news to analysis of yesterday's news. We have **(5)** _____ whose role it is to comment on events and tell us what they (and therefore perhaps *we*) should think. **(6)** _____, while sales have gone down, newspaper width has progressively increased. There are more **(7)** _____ than ever: book reviews, TV guides, travel **(8)** _____, health and nutrition, comic books – there's no **(9)** _____ to what newspapers will now do to entice us. But it still hasn't **(10)** _____ readers back. And as for the young, they were never there in the first place. They went online. You can receive your news from free online news **(11)** _____. Blogs will let you discuss the news. Your mobile can even get the latest sports **(12)** _____. An automated email will fill you in on your favourite celebs. So why go looking for your news when it will find you wherever you are?

1	A fall	B decline	C decrease	D go down
2	A journalists	B people	C paparazzi	D readers
3	A addiction	B content	C habit	D headline
4	A updates	B downloads	C outlooks	D input
5	A politicians	B columnists	C celebrities	D photographers
6	A Due	B Furthermore	C Because	D Although
7	A adverts	B pages	C photos	D supplements
8	A places	B journeys	C tips	D agents
9	A finish	B end	C way	D stop
10	A brought	B held	C come	D carried
11	A places	B stands	C sites	D reporters
12	A results	B pages	C games	D figures

2 Correct each sentence. One word is either missing, incorrect or unnecessary.

1 She said that she is going last night but I didn't see her.

2 They told about the latest news – it's terrible.

3 He asked me I'd like to go with him.

4 Stacey said the weather will be hot yesterday.

5 I suggested that taking him with them.

6 My teacher reminded to me that my homework was late.

7 My aunt and uncle apologised for be late.

8 The journalist reported us that three people are missing – they still haven't found them.

9 The reporter wrote the incident in the local newspaper.

10 These days you can receiving your news online.

3 OPEN CLOZE Read the text below and think of the word which best fits each gap. Use only one word in each gap.

Blog reading explodes

There are those that do and those that **(1)** _____. Millions of us have one and many more **(2)** _____ still asking the question, 'What is a blog exactly?' Well, for those **(3)** _____ you still wondering, blogs, or web logs, are online spaces in **(4)** _____ people can publish their thoughts, opinions or spread news events in **(5)** _____ own words. However, reading blogs still remains far **(6)** _____ popular than writing them. And what we really want to read about is news, apparently.

The huge rise in the number of blogs **(7)** _____ given birth to a new desire for immediate news and information. Whatever **(8)** _____ event – a natural disaster, for example – local bloggers can post pictures and write their own observations with instant effect. Needless **(9)** _____ say, the traditional newspapers or TV channels just can't compete with this, **(10)** _____ journalists aren't happy. 'People reading blogs should be careful,' **(11)** _____ one journalist. 'After all, no one checks a blog's sources or edits the work. You simply can't believe everything you **(12)** _____.'

14 Fashion

Getting started

1 Work in pairs or groups. Look at the pictures and discuss the clothes and styles. When were they popular?

2 How far would you go to look good? Would you consider cosmetic surgery?

3 Work in groups and ask and answer these questions.

1 How long do you spend deciding what to wear ...?
• before school or work
• at the weekend

2 Who chooses your clothes?

3 Who buys them?

4 How long have you had the same hairstyle? How has it changed since you were young?

5 What is your favourite item of clothing?

6 What are your favourite designer brands?

7 Have you ever had an argument over your choice of clothes or hairstyle?

Vocabulary: fashion

1 Choose the correct word (in *italics*) in sentences 1–15.

1 A fashionable belt or scarf is the kind of *extra/accessory* which can completely transform an old outfit.

2 Have you noticed? Turn-ups on trousers are *making/doing* a comeback.

3 Oh dear, these patterns *clash/crash*; squares and stripes just don't *live/go* together.

4 She's *into/onto* weird diets like eating nothing but grapefruit for a month and then only brown rice for the next!

5 An old USSR hat is the kind of *fashion/cult* object people love to wear.

6 Be honest, don't you think I look *cold/cool* in these *designer/brand* sunglasses?

7 I think my grandmother tries too hard to look young and *trendy/stylish*. It's a bit embarrassing at her age!

8 Kids are refusing to wear the same *names/brands* as their parents.

9 Tattoos and piercings are silly *fads/fades* which cause lasting damage.

10 I believe a 'little black dress' is a *classic/classical* that really should be part of every woman's *wardrobe/cupboard*.

11 She has got a lot of *fashion/flair*. She knows how to make herself stand out from the crowd.

12 The *craze/crazy* for 'tamagotchis' didn't last long. Kids soon got tired of them.

13 My nephew used to be obsessed by *designer/logo* jeans.

14 I absolutely love your new *suite/suit*. Is it an Armani?

15 Change out of those old clothes and wash your hair. You look far too *scruffy/smart* to go for a job interview

2 Complete these sentences using words and expressions based around the word *fashion*.

1 Please don't worry about being fashion _____. Just be yourself.

2 Their offices may look old fashion _____, but inside they have the latest equipment.

3 Long hair simply went _____ _____ fashion in the 1980s. After that men started to have it short again, thank goodness!

Phrasal verbs

3 Complete the sentences by matching a beginning (1–7) to an ending (a–g).

1 There's no need to **dress up** later, …

2 You can **try** the dress **on** …

3 If you're hot, just …

4 You'd better **put on** something warm because …

5 What on earth does he **have on**; …

6 If these trousers are too big, …

7 I can't **do up** the buttons on this skirt; …

a he looks really strange!

b **take off** your jacket.

c can you **let** it **out** a bit?

d just come as you are.

e we'll **take** them **in** and **turn** them **up** for free.

f it's going to be cold later on.

g to check that it fits.

4 Which of the phrasal verbs in bold in exercise 3 above means to …?

1 make bigger _____
2 make smaller _____
3 make shorter _____
4 remove _____
5 cover oneself _____
6 wear your best clothes _____
7 wear _____
8 fasten _____

5 Work in groups. Who do you think is speaking to whom in each sentence in exercise 3? Think of a suitable response.

You'd better put on something warm as it's going to be cold later.

Listening: crazes

1 🎧 **14.1 MULTIPLE CHOICE You will hear people talking in eight different situations. Listen, and for questions 1–8, choose the best answer (A, B or C).**

1 You hear a father and daughter discussing how the father should dress. What does the father decide to do?
  A He changes the shirt and tie.
  B He puts on a different jacket.
  C He changes the suit.

2 You hear a radio phone-in programme. What is the speaker giving information about?
  A a miracle way of losing weight
  B taking care of sporting injuries
  C combining diet and exercise

3 Two people are waiting for a third. How do they feel about her?
  A They think she looks terrible.
  B They think she looks lovely.
  C They are jealous.

4 You hear a radio presenter talking about how students can manage their budgets. What does he say about clothes and fashion?
  A Buy top quality which will last.
  B Don't follow the crowd – be an individual.
  C You must have one or two expensive designer items in your wardrobe.

5 You hear a sociologist talking about a new phenomenon. What does it involve?
  A creating spontaneous crowds
  B circulating as many emails as possible
  C organising meetings of large numbers of people

6 You hear an elderly man talking about the objects which are special for each generation. What does he feel about this?
  A He thinks things were too expensive in the old days.
  B He thinks it is natural.
  C He doesn't understand the desire for retro fashions.

7 You hear a woman talking about fashion week. What does she think about it?
  A It's harmless.
  B It's immoral.
  C It's a waste of time.

8 An estate agent is showing some potential buyers a house. What does she say about it?
  A The house and area have a great future.
  B It is a modern family home.
  C It's in an excellent area with lots of facilities.

Grammar: *have something done*

→ Grammar Reference (Section 12.2.4) page 179

1 **Study sentences *a* and *b* below. In which sentence …**

1 did she lift her face herself? _____
2 did someone else do it? _____
a She had her face lifted.
b She lifted her face.

2 **Rewrite these sentences using the causative *have*. Begin each sentence with the word, or words, in bold.**

1 Marcello got the garage to spray his car in his team's colours.
  Marcello _____ .

2 A local firm built their new house in the mountains.
  They had _____ .

3 A professional photographer is going to take photos of their wedding.
  They are _____ .

4 A famous dressmaker from Milan is making Helen's wedding dress.
  Helen is _____ .

5 A dentist is going to whiten Kevin's teeth for the occasion.
  Kevin _____ .

6 The best hairdresser in town will be doing their hair on the big day.
  They _____ .

3 **Look at the list below and tick the things you usually *have done*. Write a paragraph including the things you ticked about what you *had done* last weekend.**

- wash curtains _____
- clean windows _____
- paint bedroom _____
- walk dog _____
- do the washing up _____
- cut my hair _____
- iron clothes _____
- fix bike _____
- repair computer _____
- whiten my teeth _____
- repair broken window _____
- fit new kitchen _____
- replace car tyre _____
- wash car _____

Reading: fashion victim

1 **Look at the the photographs. What do you think the text is about?**

2 **Read the first paragraph and check if you were right.**

3 **Quickly read the rest of the text and find out the importance of the following:**

   1 Lakshmi; Vishnu; Vered; Shri E.V.K.S. Elangovan

   2 Tirupati; Melrose Avenue

   3 £500; $120 million; 4,000; six months

PAPER 1, PART 1

4 **MULTIPLE CHOICE For questions 1–8, choose the answer (A, B, C or D) which you think fits best according to the text.**

   1 Western women have hair extensions ...
      A to show they are rich.
      B to copy the fashion of the rich and famous.
      C because they are ambitious.
      D because they are afraid of becoming bald.

   2 Women have their heads shaved at the temple ...
      A to sell it for their personal profit.
      B for medical reasons.
      C as a religious practice.
      D to raise money for its maintenance.

   3 The temple ...
      A costs more to maintain than any other religious site.
      B couldn't operate without the sale of pilgrims' hair.
      C is the most visited religious site in the world.
      D is deep in a valley.

   4 Lakshmi had her hair shaved off because she ...
      A wanted to earn some money for her family.
      B believed it would bring her family good fortune.
      C had to.
      D needed money to give to her future husband.

   5 Why is temple hair popular in LA?
      A It is both sacred and lovely.
      B Salons want to profit from the latest fashion in hair styles.
      C There are skinny blonde women who want it.
      D It provides excellent value for money.

   6 The article suggests that ...
      A the fashion is already beginning to fade.
      B temple hair lacks the versatility of acrylic.
      C for once the fashion originated in London.
      D one colour dominates customer choice.

   7 Women who sell their hair on the black market ...
      A may have received pressure to do so.
      B tend to come from larger towns and cities.
      C can then support their families for many months.
      D generally receive a fair deal from buyers.

8 Which word below most closely describes the writer's mood?
   A shame
   B disapproval
   C jealousy
   D admiration

In Northern India, thousands of women queue patiently to have their hair shaved off with a dry razor, leaving them completely bald. Within weeks, the hair will have been lightened and bonded on to the heads of rich Western women who want to imitate the latest red carpet fashion. For £500 you, too, can have real human hair bonded on to your own, thickening or lengthening it instantly. 'Temple hair' is hugely popular with top celebrities, but while top hair salons enjoy the profits made from selling human hair, does anyone dare to ask where it comes from, or how much women are being paid to donate their locks to fashion?

The shocking truth is that not a penny is given to the women who sacrifice their hair. In fact, they are not even told that soon it is going to be sold for profit. All the money goes to the temple itself. Perched on the hills of Tirupati, in India, the Hindu temple is the second richest religious site in the world after the Vatican city. Boasting up to 20 million pilgrims a year, the popular site costs $120 million a year to maintain. Money mainly comes from donations, but the most prevalent source of income, however, is from the sale of human hair.

Every day, up to 4,000 women visit the temple to take part in this religious rite. Lakshmi Srinivasan, a beautiful 21-year-old girl, lives nearby. From the age of 11, she sorted hair to export to the US. 'Indian women rub oils into their hair to keep it soft and beautiful. Also, they grow it very long. Our hair is a major source of pride and beauty.' Lakshmi, coming from a poor family, needed to work to feed her parents, as well as to save for a dowry so she could marry. But she had to make far greater sacrifices for their prosperity. 'When I was younger, I was made to have my own hair cut off at the temple,' she remembers. 'My parents believed that it would bring us some luck, so I could not say no.' Many poor families go to the temple to pray for good crops; for poor farmers, the sacrifice of hair to Vishnu adds to their chances of having a good harvest.

And in LA, where looks are everything, women will pay premium prices to get their hands on temple hair. LA's hottest shopping street, Melrose Avenue, is teeming with skinny blondes in designer clothes. The idea of 'temple hair', with all its spiritual connotations, has a special appeal in the city where religious fads are considered part and parcel of celebrity.

5 Discuss:

- What do you think about temple hair and the hair extension business?
- Do you think there should be any controls on this practice?
- If so, what controls?

We do have every colour,' explains Vered, the owner of one salon, 'but this is LA, so obviously blonde is the most popular. Most of the hair is used by people who want to be beautiful, plus spirituality is very "in" over here, so that adds to the whole experience of getting temple hair.' And where America leads, Britain is quick to follow. 'Indian hair really is the best quality, I find,' says a spokesman for Tyrone and Company, a London salon. 'It can be treated just like your own hair. It can be heated and curled, coloured and blow-dried, unlike acrylic.' The look is also far more expensive.

There are now more than 50 salons in London alone which deal in Indian temple hair, and business is booming. But as with anything in fashion, merchants are waiting to provide a cheaper version for the masses on the black market.

Shri E.V.K.S. Elangovan, an Indian trade minister, is worried. 'Aside from the temple hair, we have no idea where the rest comes from,' he says. 'In many cases we fear women are being exploited.' Preying on desperately poor women in Indian villages, these suppliers cajole them into selling their hair for next to nothing. The cost of a set of hair extensions in the West is enough to feed a family in India for six months. It is the salons and the hair distributors, however, who recover the profits.

EXAM SPOTLIGHT

PAPER 1, PART 1

6 In this part of the reading test there may be one 'global' question which asks about the writer's overall attitude. Look again at exercise 4. Which question from 1–8 do you think does this?

GRAMMAR SPOTLIGHT

Homophones

Homophones are words which sound the same but which usually have a different spelling.

Example: *flour, flower*

7 Which two pairs are homophones (sound the same)?

| 1 | a through | b threw | 3 | a site | b sight |
| 2 | a effect | b affect | 4 | a accept | b except |

8 Choose the correct word (in *italics*) in sentences 1–6.

1 She looks far too skinny. I wonder how much she *ways/weighs*.

2 The eagle *preys/prays* on rabbits, mice and even lambs.

3 Last year I went on a *lightning/lightening* business trip to New York.

4 We shouldn't condemn the *rites/rights* and ceremonies of other cultures.

5 If your T-shirt is stained you can always *die/dye* it a different colour.

6 She lost her *site/sight* when she was only 24.

Grammar: the passive

➡ Grammar Reference (Section 12.2) page 179

1 Study *a* and *b*. Which sentence is …

1 active? _____   2 passive? _____

a People who want to be beautiful use most of the temple hair.

b Most of the temple hair is used by people who want to be beautiful.

2 Which sentence in exercise 1 emphasises …

hair? _____   people? _____

3 Identify examples of the passive in the text.

4 Work in pairs. Decide if statements 1–3 are true (T) or false (F).

1 The passive always uses a past participle. T / F

2 The passive always uses a form of the verb 'to be'. T / F

3 We can transform every active sentence into the passive. T / F

5 Identify the tense or the form which has been <u>underlined</u>. Then rephrase the sentences beginning with the words in italics and using the passive voice. The first one has been done as an example.

1 <u>We only employ</u> adults in our factories.
   Form: *present simple*
   Only adults <u>are employed in our factories.</u>

2 <u>Young women are sewing</u> the labels onto designer clothes.
   Form: _____
   Labels _____

3 <u>They sold</u> 80 million pairs of trainers last year.
   Form: _____
   Eighty million _____

4 <u>They have taken</u> Japanese designs as their inspiration.
   Form: _____
   Japanese designs _____

5 <u>They are going to present</u> their new range of swimwear at the Olympic pool.
   Form: _____
   Their new range of swimwear _____

6 Our new puppy <u>was destroying</u> my favourite shoes.
   Form: _____
   My favourite shoes _____

7 <u>Moths had made</u> hundreds of holes in the clothes in the wardrobe.
   Form: _____
   Hundreds _____

8 <u>We will have finished</u> the costumes by next weekend.
   Form: _____
   The costumes _____

9 Governments <u>should take action</u> against this immoral trade.
   Form: _____
   Action _____

10 Someone <u>should have banned</u> the trade.
   Form: _____
   The trade _____

6 Complete sentences 1 and 2 below using *with* or *by*. Which preposition do we use with the agent, and which with the instrument?

1 He had his teeth straightened *with/by* a top dentist.

2 They shaved the women's heads *with/by* a dry razor.

7 The passive is often used to describe what happens without saying who does it. In pairs, describe from start to finish how temple hair becomes hair extensions.

Listening: school uniform

1 In Britain, most children have to wear a uniform to school. How common is this in your country? Do you think it is a good idea or a bad idea? Why?

2 ☐ 14.2 Three friends, Florence, Damien and Philip, are talking about school uniforms. Listen and decide who says what by writing *F* for Florence, *D* for Damien, and *P* for Philip after questions 1–7.

Who ...?

1 likes the way someone used to look ____

2 had to wear a strange-looking hat ____

3 thinks that a school uniform is convenient ____

4 thinks that children have the right to choose what they put on ____

5 thinks a uniform reduces social differences between pupils ____

6 claims that uniforms only look nice for a short period ____

7 didn't have a new uniform every year ____

3 ☐ 14.2 MULTIPLE CHOICE Listen again, and for questions 1–5 choose the best answer (*A, B* or *C*).

1 What happened when Florence wore the winter uniform?
   A She found it difficult to button up her coat.
   B People made fun of her.
   C She had to change her hairstyle.

2 What does Damien think about school uniform?
   A The problems it creates are bigger than those it solves.
   B It stops school kids from expressing themselves.
   C It is better than the alternative.

3 What happened at Philip's school during hot weather?
   A Everyone had to suffer.
   B Only the teachers were allowed to take off their jackets.
   C The children could take off their ties.

4 What does Florence believe about school uniform?
   A It teaches school children self-discipline.
   B It looks nice.
   C It soon starts to look scruffy.

5 What happened when Damien was a schoolboy?
   A His uniform was never the right size.
   B The arms of his jacket were never long enough.
   C He had a new uniform every other year.

Grammar: *make, let, allow* and *need*

1 Look at the difference in the use of *make* in sentences a and b below? In which sentence does it mean ...?

1 force/oblige _____

2 prepare _____

a She made him a sandwich for breakfast.

b She made him eat his breakfast.

2 Study the two pairs of sentences below. Write the number of the sentence in each pair that is active and the one that is passive.

Active sentence: Pair 1: _____   Pair 2: _____

Passive sentence: Pair 1: _____   Pair 2: _____

1a I hated that hat, but I was made to wear it.

1b They made me wear that hat.

2a The teachers didn't allow us to take off our jackets.

2b We weren't allowed to take off our jackets.

3 Work in pairs. Look at the pictures and talk about what *needs doing/needs to be done.*

4 Study the three sentences below. Where can you use *let* instead of *allow/ed*?

1 They *allowed* us to take off our jackets.

2 They didn't *allow* us to take off our ties.

3 We weren't *allowed to* take off our caps.

5 Work in groups. Tell the group about your childhood. Use a mixture of active and passive forms to discuss some of the following: bedtime, TV, music, hair, clothes, food, family, friends.

Example:

Carla: *When I was a kid I was made to practise the cello every evening.*

Nick: *Well, when I was a teenager I wasn't allowed to go out with my friends until the weekend.*

Speaking: challenging

1 ⌂ 14.1 Listen again, or turn to Tapescript 14.2 on page 222 and find continuations for these introductory phrases.

1 Yes, but ...

2 Don't you think ...?

3 I suppose so/not ...

4 What I mean is ...

5 All the same, ...

6 After all, ...

2 Match introductory phrases 1–6 above to definitions a–f below. Which introductory phrase is used to ...?

a give more detail/expand on something you've just said

_____

b disagree without saying 'No!' _____

c say 'Despite everything which has been said' _____

d challenge someone to agree with you _____

e say 'nevertheless' _____

f agree (reluctantly) with what someone has said _____

3 Work in groups. Your school has decided to organise a fashion show to raise money for charity. Students from the school will be the fashion designers and models. Look at the different possible themes, and decide which one the school should choose. Use some of the phrases from exercise 1.

- disco
- flamenco
- historical
- 60s/70s
- evening dress
- 1920s

PAPER 5, PART 4

4 Take turns to be the candidate and the examiner by asking and answering these questions.

a Don't you think that fashion is a waste of time, energy and money?

b Don't you think young people worry far too much about how they look and which brands and designer labels they wear?

Key word: *think*

1 Work in pairs. Replace the words in bold with phrasal verbs and expressions from the box.

thought up	think things through	think back to
to my way of thinking	thinking about	think so
do you think you could	don't you think we should	

1 **I'd like you to** give us your views.
2 **Wouldn't it be a good idea to** hear what she has to say?
3 We are **considering** their proposal.
4 Do you really **believe that**?
5 She has **imagined** another crazy scheme.
6 Your problem is that you never **analyse things carefully**.
7 When I **remember** the old days, things weren't any different.
8 **In my opinion**, we should ban the trade in human hair.

Writing: a descriptive essay

1 In part 2 of the Writing test, you may have the choice to write an essay which includes a description of people or places. Read the four short descriptions on page 143 and match them to the pictures (a–d).

2 Work in pairs. What general impression do each of the four texts give? Discuss which ones feel happy, or optimistic, and which ones feel sad, or pessimistic.

3 Go through the four texts again and find words which describe people. Write the words in the table under the category headings shown.

age	height/build	hair	skin

Giving a full description
Two adjectives can be put together using *and*.

Example: *small and cramped*

If we want to add other elements to the description we can add *with* and another noun phrase.
Example:

adjective + *and* + adjective + *with* + noun phrase

It was small and cramped with nasty wallpaper and faded floral curtains.

4 Find further examples of this pattern in the texts in exercise 1.

a

b

c

d

1 After our long walk we entered the bar which was bright and welcoming. There was a fire crackling in the fireplace and a kind-looking woman in her early forties was standing alone behind the bar. She was smallish and plump with untidy blonde hair and when she smiled at us dimples appeared in her cheeks. It was pleasant, warm and cosy after the freezing temperatures outside.

2 I opened the door and entered what would be my room for the first year of student life. It was small and cramped with nasty wallpaper and faded floral curtains. The floor was covered in old cracked lino which was sticky underfoot. The smell of cooked cabbage was so strong you could almost taste it. Seth must have read my thoughts. 'Don't worry,' he said, as cheerful as ever, 'we'll soon brighten it up with some of your posters, and the lamps your mum lent you.' At the mention of Mum, I immediately felt desperately lonely and homesick.

3 The house stood alone at the end of a long winding lane. It had roses climbing up the walls and looked like everyone's idea of what a country cottage should be. As we got out of the car the sweet smell of honeysuckle hit us. A wrinkled elderly lady with steel-grey hair was standing on the path leading to her door. A pretty little girl with freckles and red hair tied in pigtails stared at us as she pulled up the flowers in the flower bed next to her.

4 The door opened before we had had time to knock and a skinny young woman dressed in a black leather jacket covered with chains and skulls appeared. The woman, who was in her twenties, had messy, dyed hair and unhealthy pale skin covered in piercings. Behind her loomed a tall man, presumably her boyfriend, who had a tattoo of a black and red spider's web over his neck. She glared at us and through lips covered in black lipstick snapped aggressively, 'What do you want? We were just going out.'

PAPER 2, PART 2

5 Write an answer to this exam story question.

Exam question

Your school has organised a creative writing competition. Write a story of a memorable event in your life, or in the life of a fictional character, which includes a description of people and places. Begin your story with:
'I'll never forget the time we …'

GRAMMAR SPOTLIGHT

Connotation

'Connotation' is where words have an additional, emotive meaning. For example, the literal meaning of *skinny* is *thinner than thin*. However, *skinny* has the additional, negative connotation of being, in the view of the speaker or writer, unattractively thin.

6 Look up these words in a good English dictionary and try to think of a more neutral word for each one.

Example: skinny = very thin.

cosy	snap	cramped	elderly	glare
lonely	messy	plump	pretty	stare

7 Each of the words in the box has a certain connotation. Decide which ones you can add to the categories below. Some words could belong to more than one category:
- affectionate/sympathetic: *elderly,*
- welcoming/comforting:
- negative/unattractive:
- menacing/aggressive:
- small and uncomfortable:

8 Sometimes in a text we may want to convey meanings which relate to our senses. Look at the four short texts on this page again and find words which refer to smell, sight, taste, touch and hearing.

- smell _____
- sight _____
- taste _____
- touch _____
- hearing _____

WRITING CHECKLIST

Did you …?	Yes (✓)	No (✗)
• position your description (say when and where it happened)	☐	☐
• use a variety of narrative tenses	☐	☐
• give a full physical description of the person or place	☐	☐
• use adjectives and verbs which carry connotation	☐	☐
• say how people felt	☐	☐
• introduce some direct speech	☐	☐

➡ Writing Guide, page 202

Review and Use of English

1 WORD FORMATION
Use the word given in capitals at the end of some of the lines to form a word that fits in the gap in the same line.

EXAM SPOTLIGHT

PAPER 3, PART 3

In this part of the Use of English test remember to read the passage all the way through without thinking about the gaps. Try to get an overall impression of what the passage is about.

The world is a terrible place. While many millions live in misery and families hardly know how to satisfy the **(1)** _____ of their children, other people will go to ridiculous **(2)** _____ to follow the latest trend and starve themselves to look thin. It is an insult to millions of poor people that in rich countries it is **(3)** _____ to wear jeans which have been deliberately aged and torn, while millions of others have no **(4)** _____ other than to dress in rags. The gap between the rich and poor is **(5)** _____ all the time. Moreover the **(6)** _____ of cotton farmers by powerful importers of this raw material means they get a fraction of the price of a pair of **(7)** _____ denims. Franco-Italian fashion producers Rica-Lewis have made the **(8)** _____ brave decision to use more expensive fair-trade cotton in some ranges thus lifting farmers out of **(9)** _____ and providing **(10)** _____ to workers in other developing countries.

HUNGRY

LONG

FASHION

CHOOSE

WIDE
EXPLOIT

DESIGN

ETHIC

POOR
EMPLOY

2 KEY WORD TRANSFORMATIONS
Complete the second sentence so that it has a similar meaning to the first sentence, using the word given.

1 Her parents would not let Sue have a nose ring.

allowed

Sue _____ a nose ring by her parents.

2 I used a professional to decorate the kitchen.

by

The _____ a professional.

3 When Tim joined the army he had to have a haircut.

made

Tim _____ a haircut when he joined the army.

4 Fashion magazines are encouraging young women to be unhealthily skinny.

by

Young women are encouraged to be _____ fashion magazines.

5 My Dad finds this new fashion quite shocking.

is

My Dad _____ by this new fashion.

6 They used a laser to remove Jo's tattoo.

removed

Jo _____ with a laser.

7 It's time the dog had a bath.

needs

The dog _____ a bath.

8 You are going to hurt yourself if you do that.

get

You _____ if you do that.

3 OPEN CLOZE
Read the text below and think of the word which best fits each gap. Use only one word in each gap.

Flash mobbing is the latest craze to hit Europe from the United States. Seemingly spontaneous crowds are created by calling people via the Internet to do something unexpected, **(1)** _____ lying down on the floor for a period, and then disappearing as quickly as they arrived. Europe's first flash mob took **(2)** _____ in Rome when people went to a shop and asked staff **(3)** _____ books that did not exist. The latest New York flash mob caused consternation in a toy store **(4)** _____ flash mobsters gathered recently. Participants **(5)** _____ told to stare at the store's giant animatronic dinosaur for three minutes then fall to their knees and react to **(6)** _____ roars by moaning **(7)** _____ four minutes. But panicked staff quickly shut off the dinosaur and called the police **(8)** _____ a minute into the mass-moaning. **(9)** _____ June flash mobs have sprung up in around 40 locations and one seems to be taking place **(10)** _____ in the world every few days. But some hope **(11)** _____ craze could die out as **(12)** _____ as it started thanks to the over-interested media and overreaction by the police.

15 New traditions

Getting started

1 **Work in pairs. Describe the two paintings in as much detail as you can. Use expressions from the Useful Expressions box at the bottom of the page.**

2 **Imagine the story behind each painting and talk to your partner about them.**

USEFUL EXPRESSIONS

- In the foreground (front of the picture) …
- In the background (back of the picture) …
- The one on the left is/shows/has got … whereas the one on the right is/shows/has got

3 **Work in pairs. Student A turn to Information File 15.1 on page 230 and learn about the first painting. Student B turn to Information File 15.2 on page 231 and learn about the second painting. Find out from each other …**

- the name of your partner's picture.
- the name of the person who painted it and when it was painted.
- the story behind the picture.

4 **What similarities are there between the stories? Which painting do you prefer?**

5 **Work in pairs. Imagine that you are a guide in an art gallery. Based on what you have learnt, describe the paintings to a group of visitors and tell them something about the inspiration behind them.**

Listening: statues

1 **Look at the photograph of a 'human statue'.**

- Have you ever seen a 'human statue' performance like this before?

- How successful is the performance?

- How do you think it feels to do this all day?

PAPER 4, PART 3

2 ⌒ **15.1** MULTIPLE MATCHING **Choose from the list (A–F) the model or statue each person talks about. Use the letters only once. There is one extra description you do not need to use.**

A an extraordinary war memorial

B an old TV series

C someone who joined an unusual army

D experts recognising a fake statue

E a technique used by a brilliant artist

F a way children raise money

Speaker 1: _____

Speaker 2: _____

Speaker 3: _____

Speaker 4: _____

Speaker 5: _____

3 **What materials do the speakers mention?**

_____

_____

_____

4 ⌒ **15.1 Listen again, and decide if the following statements are true or false.**

1 Wendel entered the museum in disguise. T / F

2 The warriors have just had their 1000th birthday. T / F

3 Wendel stayed still as the guards removed him. T / F

4 Guy Fawkes was a kind of terrorist. T / F

5 Children buy their Guys from toyshops. T / F

6 Children expect more than a penny. T / F

7 Stalingrad used to be called Volgograd. T / F

8 The statue is in the centre of Volgograd. T / F

9 It was the most moving thing the speaker saw on his trip. T / F

10 The show isn't on British TV any more. T / F

11 The puppets were easily recognisable. T / F

12 She thinks it was fair to make fun of the monarchy. T / F

13 Our first impression is often the right impression. T / F

14 Instinct comes from long experience. T / F

15 The museum escaped being tricked. T / F

5 **Work in pairs. Tell your partner about your favourite historical site, memorial, statue or building. Why do you like it?**

Vocabulary: culture and heritage

1 Choose the correct word (in *italics*) in questions 1–18.

1 There are some wonderful paintings at her *exhibition/ expedition*.

2 This street is home to several expensive art *museums/ galleries* and antique shops.

3 This peaceful-looking bay was once the *site/sight* of a terrible sea battle.

4 It is a *habit/tradition* for people to exchange presents at this time of year.

5 These castles and forests are part of our national *heritage/ heirloom*.

6 At the top of the steps there is a *monumental/statue* of the emperor on his horse.

7 I am fascinated by *old-fashioned/ancient* history.

8 The fall of the Berlin Wall was an emotional and *historical/ historic* occasion.

9 In the centre of the village there is a war *memorial/ souvenir* with the names of the soldiers who gave their lives.

10 The study of the Japanese tea *ceremony/event* can often take many years.

11 The boat-race between Oxford and Cambridge takes *part/ place* each spring.

12 He is one of the most *notorious/famous* murderers of the last century.

13 It is a wonderful *landscape/portrait* of a country scene.

14 An ancient *customer/custom* is to collect wild flowers for Mother's Day.

15 The Battle of the Bridge is a famous *festival/first of all* held in Pisa each year.

16 The statue the museum bought turned out to be a *priceless/ worthless* fake.

17 A good guide book with quality colour photographs is always a/an *invaluable/worthwhile* companion.

18 During the *middle-aged/middle ages*, it was a/an *infamous/ well-known* prison where some terrible events took place.

2 Work in pairs. Create sentences with the incorrect word choices from exercise 1.

Reading: genuine fakes

1 Work in groups. You are going to read an article about John Myatt, an artist with a difference. Look at the title. Brainstorm what you think the article will be about.

2 Read the article quickly and check if your predictions were correct.

EXAM SPOTLIGHT

Gapped text sentences

PAPER 1, PART 2
In this part of the Reading test, you match sentences to gaps in the text. There is an extra sentence you don't need to use. Follow these steps:
- The first time you read the text, only read the gapped text to get an overall idea of meaning.
- Never try to match sentences to gaps as you go along, the first time you read the text.
- Only read the extra sentences after you have read the text for overall meaning.
- Try to identify the unnecessary sentence.
- Exploit reference words such as pronouns to help you match the sentences.
- Mark your answers on a separate sheet.
- Don't fill in the exam answer sheet until you have answered all the questions.

3 GAPPED TEXT SENTENCES Now read the article again more carefully. Seven sentences have been removed from the article. Choose from the sentences A–H the one which fills each gap 1–7. Remember, there is one extra sentence which you don't need to use.

A It said that Myatt had made up his mind to end their partnership.

B Ironically, Myatt has been copied too.

C But whenever he tried to produce portraits or landscapes the results were invariably dull.

D This was followed by a commission from a member of the prosecution team.

E An eminent auction house had offered Drewe double the sum for the painting.

F Myatt has turned his back on a life of crime.

G He immerses himself in books and tries to hypnotise himself with examples of the artist's work.

H He also produced the paperwork which supplied each work with a convincing history.

4 Work in groups. Discuss the following questions.

1 Do you think Myatt was a real criminal or a victim?

2 Many of Myatt's fakes are hanging in museums or other collections. Should Myatt tell everyone which ones he painted?

3 Myatt's accomplice, Drewe, got a far longer prison sentence than Myatt. Why do you think was the case?

GENUINE

The artist John Myatt was responsible for one of the biggest art frauds of the last century and paid for it by spending time in prison. Over eight years he turned out more than 200 works by surrealists, cubists and impressionists. He passed them off as originals with the aid of an accomplice. This person, John Drewe, handled the business side, dealing with auction houses and museums. **1** _____ Provenance, knowing who has owned a work before, and in which catalogues it has appeared, is essential in proving the authenticity of a work of art.

Myatt didn't set out to become a forger. As a student he had high hopes of establishing his own style. **2** _____ Instead, he taught evening classes and sold the occasional fake to friends and colleagues. Eventually he decided to put an advertisement in the satirical magazine *Private Eye*, offering copies of 19th and 20th century paintings from £150. Myatt soon started getting commissions from Drewe who passed himself off as an atomic scientist and art lover. At first, he produced a Matisse and some Dutch-style portraits, but then Drewe asked him to produce a painting in the style of a German cubist. He then received a call from Drewe asking him how he would like £12,500 in a brown envelope. **3** _____ Hardly had Drewe made the offer than Myatt accepted it. He had been going through family trouble and he was looking after his two children on his own. He wanted a job he could do from home, and the money was as much as he made in a year from his teaching.

FAKES

Before he tries to paint anything in the style of an artist, he tries to find out as much as he can about the artist and their life. **4** _____ Even so, he is amazed that his paintings managed to take in so many experts. Drewe, in the meantime, dedicated himself to creating false provenances. Not only did he collect old receipts from galleries but he also forged museum records. In the end, the whole thing collapsed when Drewe's wife went to the police. When they turned up at Myatt's house he at first denied everything. Then officers made an important discovery: an un-posted letter to Drewe. **5** _____ No sooner did the officers show him the letter than he made a full confession.

Myatt survived prison by doing portraits of fellow inmates, earning himself the nickname 'Picasso'. When he was released he said the last thing he wanted to do was pick up another paintbrush. Soon after he left jail, he got a phone call which made him change his mind. It was from the policeman who had arrested him, asking for a portrait of his family. **6** _____ Myatt was soon back painting fakes in earnest. This time they are being sold from prestigious art galleries and no longer does he try to pass them off as the real thing. Even though he still takes off those painters he once forged – complete with the copied artist's signature – the back of each canvas carries a computer chip and the words 'genuine fake' written in indelible ink.

7 _____ Michael Douglas is playing him in a Hollywood movie based on the painter's life.

Grammar: inversion

➜ Grammar Reference (Section 10) page 175

1 Match sentences 1–4 with sentences of a similar meaning a–d.

1 *Hardly* had Drewe made the offer *than* Myatt accepted it.

2 *Not only* did he collect old receipts from galleries *but he also* forged museum records.

3 *No sooner* did the officers show him the letter *than* he made a full confession.

4 *No longer* does he try to pass them off as the real thing.

a He forged museum records and collected receipts from galleries.

b He doesn't try to pass them off as the real thing any more.

c Drewe made the offer and Myatt almost immediately accepted it.

d As soon as they showed him the letter he made a full confession.

2 What do you notice about the word order of 1–4 above? Which sentences carry more emphasis: 1–4, or a–d?

3 Rephrase sentences 1–5 below beginning with the words in bold.

1 He produced work by impressionists and surrealists. **not only**

2 Soon after he left jail, he got an important phone call. **hardly/no sooner**

3 The officer who arrested him asked for a portrait and so did a member of the prosecuting counsel. **not only**

4 He doesn't pretend that his paintings are works of art by famous artists any more. **no longer**

5 The moment Myatt recognised his letter to Drewe he realised the game was over. **hardly/no sooner**

6 He reads everything about the artist and tries to hypnotise himself with their work. **not only**

4 Work in pairs. Write comments on these situations using an inversion from exercise 3.

1 I closed the door to my flat and immediately realised I had left my keys inside.

2 They ate everything in the fridge. Even the cat food!

3 They used to employ 13-year-old children, but now they only employ adults.

Vocabulary

Phrasal verbs

1 Use the context provided by the article on pages 148–149 to match the phrasal verbs in the box to definitions 1–9.

turn out	find out	take off	go through	look after
take in	set out	pass off	turn up	

1 take care of _____

2 begin with the intention of doing something _____

3 produce _____

4 arrive (unexpectedly) _____

5 trick/deceive _____

6 discover _____

7 present something false as the 'real thing' _____

8 experience something difficult _____

9 imitate someone _____

2 What different meanings are represented by the phrasal verbs in the following sentences?

1a She **took** us **in** with her lies. We all really believed her.

1b When her parents died her aunt **took** her **in**.

1c It took me a minute **to take in** the news.

2a The factory **turns out** a car every ten months.

2b We eventually discovered what had happened to the parcel: it **turned out** it had been delivered to the wrong address.

2c They **turned** everyone **out** of the nightclub.

3a He **turned up** at my house at three o'clock in the morning.

3b Can you **turn** the volume **up**? I can't hear a thing.

3c These jeans are too long. Could you **turn** them **up** for me?

GRAMMAR SPOTLIGHT

Different meanings of phrasal verbs
Remember: A phrasal verb of the same form may have very different meanings.
take off The plane **took off.** (Type 1) – *leave the ground*
She was **taking** her teacher **off** when he suddenly came back into the classroom. (Type 2) – *imitate someone*
It was hot in the office so he **took off** his jacket and tie. (Type 2) – *remove clothing*

When you record a phrasal verb in your notebook, make sure that you put it in a context so that its meaning is apparent, and be sure to note its type.

Listening: living traditions

1 Look at the photo and read about Kelly Foster and her unusual hobby. Does it remind you of any similar organisations in your country?

In England, between 1642 and 1649, there was a civil war between King Charles I of England and his supporters, and the supporters of Parliament led by Oliver Cromwell. The king's supporters were known as 'Cavaliers' while the Parliamentary forces were called 'Roundheads'. The war ended with the victory of the Parliamentary forces and the king's execution. Kelly Foster is a member of a society which re-lives some of the main battles of the civil war. She is talking to Betty Johnson on a women's radio programme.

2 Discuss. What questions do you think the interviewer will ask Kelly?

PAPER 4, PART 4

3 🎧 15.2 MULTIPLE CHOICE You will hear part A of an interview with a woman who relives the battles of the English Civil War. For questions 1–7, choose the best answer (*A, B* or *C*).

1 Why did Kelly become involved in the re-enactment society?
  A she was a bit lonely
  B Some friends encouraged her to join.
  C It was part of her job.

2 Why did Kelly wait before making a decision to join?
  A She couldn't make a full commitment.
  B She thought the people might be strange.
  C She was shy.

3   What made Kelly join her 'regiment'?
    A   She had a love of history.
    B   There wasn't a roundhead regiment in the area.
    C   There was a strong connection to her town.

4   Why are the 'Roundheads' considered less appealing than
    the 'Cavaliers'
    A   The Cavaliers are more fun.
    B   The Cavaliers had better uniforms.
    C   The Cavaliers are too serious.

5   What happens during battles?
    A   The outcome is decided on the day itself.
    B   The result of the battle is agreed beforehand.
    C   Spectators already know which side will win.

6   How many soldiers does each side have?
    A   over a thousand
    B   a couple of hundred
    C   tens of thousands

7   Where do the society's events take place?
    A   in the same place as the original conflict
    B   on specially constructed stages and scenes
    C   wherever they can find a sympathetic farmer

PAPER 4, PART 2

4   🎧 15.3 SENTENCE COMPLETION **Listen to part B of the
    interview and complete the notes.**

Before she became a 'soldier' Kelly was a
(1) _____.
She changed role because the soldiers have
(2) _____. Women who want to play soldiers
have to (3) _____ as a man.

Women's military roles.
use a sword
fire a gun
join the cavalry
be a (4) _____

Difficulties:
Women can't easily handle the spears called
(5) _____. (They are (6) _____
long and very heavy.)

Dangers:
Small injuries. Be careful of (7) _____ standing
on your feet!

Other activities:
The social activities are (8) _____.
There are big meals (9) (_____) and
dances.
Every year there is a trip to London in memory of the king's (10)
_____ in 1649.

Key word: *mind*

1   **Complete the sentences with words and expressions based
    on *mind*.**

    1   _____ your head! The door is very low.
    2   I wish he would make a final decision; he keeps on
        _____ mind.
    3   Sorry, I forgot to go. It totally _____ mind.
    4   Her mum's crazy. She's completely _____ mind.
    5   It's time to make a decision. You need to _____
        your mind.
    6   Most people feel more comfortable with _____-
        _____ people who share the same opinions and
        attitudes.
    7   I haven't paid the phone bill; they have sent me a
        _____.

2   **Expand the prompts to form sentences using *mind*.**

    1   I hope/you/mind/my/mention/this/but/you/wear/
        different-coloured socks!

        _____

    2   Do/mind/you/window/close? It's terribly cold in here.

        _____

Speaking: adverbs in conversation

1   **Read the information about *basically*, *actually* and *anyway*
    and find how they are used in Tapescript 15.3 on page 224.**

    •   We use *basically* to introduce the most important
        information in an explanation.

        A: What does your job involve?
        B: Well, *basically* I am in charge of student registrations.

    •   We use *actually* to politely contradict.

        A: You're French, aren't you?
        B: Well, *actually* I'm Swiss.

    •   We use *anyway* to finish saying something without giving
        all the details, or to change the topic.

        *I tried everywhere for a copy of the book. Anyway,
        I eventually found one in a second-hand bookshop.*

2   **Work in pairs.**

    •   Make statements you know your partner will contradict using
        actually.

    •   Tell each other the essential reason why you are studying
        English using *basically*.

    •   Tell each other how you managed to do something difficult,
        without giving all the details, using *anyway*.

Reading: festivals

1 For questions 1–15 choose from the festivals (A–D).
The festival can be chosen more than once.

Which festival ...?

1 gives parents an excuse to spoil their children

2 is the earliest in the year

3 is a reminder of a nation's warlike past

4 predicted how much food there would be

5 has a dancing competition

6 has an international element

7 remembers a man of moral courage

8 includes a famous race

9 burns money for luck

10 pays respect to a leader

11 has a more private and public side

12 includes a cure for illness or bad luck

13 gathers people from different parts of its region

14 gives the opportunity to remember dead relatives

15 uses precious family objects

B

N'cwala is a ceremony which celebrates the harvest in the eastern province of Ngoni in Zambia. It is held each February and follows the tradition of offering the supreme chief the first produce of the year. The supreme chief drinks the blood of a cow and the women prepare a huge beef stew. Local chiefs and their finest dancers travel to the village of Mutenguleni to take part in the ceremony. The dancers perform a warlike dance in front of the supreme, or paramount, chief who elects one group as the best warrior dancers. The dancers are dressed in animal skin and headdresses, and each carries a shield and stick. During the performance Naoni women sing and clap to raise their men's morale for the coming battle.

C

Hong Kong's Dragon Boat festival, also known as 'Poet's Day' takes place in early June. It owes the name 'Poet's Day' to a distinguished poet and wise man who threw himself into the river to protest against corruption. In vain, fishermen tried to save him and he drowned. The Chinese believe his ghost returned and advised people that the best way to keep evil spirits away was to make parcels of rice in silk. Nowadays, people eat rice dumplings wrapped in leaves in his memory. The boat festival itself is a celebrated event with participants from all over the world. Each boat carries a large crew who paddles as fast as they can. Each boat is decorated with a carved dragon's head. Dragons are important symbols in China and are associated with luck and good fortune.

A

Hina Matsuri, which means 'little doll' in Japanese, takes place on the 3rd of March each year. These dolls are exquisite works of art and dressed in the most beautiful traditional costumes. They are often family heirlooms and handed down from generation to generation. In the week leading up to the festival the family gives the dolls pride of place in their home. On the day itself family and friends come to admire the dolls and eat traditional rice cakes called mochi which are carefully wrapped in cherry blossom. Afterwards, the dolls are put away for the next year. In addition, there is also a more public side to the event. A traditional belief is that misfortune or illness can be transferred to a doll. Dolls are taken to temples, and there may be hundreds of them. From there they are taken down to the sea by priests who say prayers and then send the dolls out to sea.

D

Vietnam's Trung Thu festival isn't on exactly the same date every year as it has to fall on the fifteenth day of the eighth lunar month. In the olden days, farmers and astrologers would observe the moon closely on this day as they believed its colour foretold how good the coming harvest was going to be. Nowadays, this ancient festival celebrates the beauty of the moon, and gives parents the chance to spoil their children. Children wear masks (pigs, demons or the moon are the most popular), and buy star-shaped lanterns with candles inside. People eat 'moon cakes' in the shape of fish or flowers. As well as providing an excuse to give their kids a treat, the festival is also an opportunity to remember one's ancestors. People say prayers and burn sweet-smelling incense, and bundles of fake money in memory of the dead person! The good luck represented by the money is carried heavenwards.

Writing: an article

1 Last year Lourdes visited relatives in Mexico. She was there at the same time as a famous festival. Study the photograph. What do you think the festival celebrates?

2 Lourdes has been asked to write an article about her visit. Complete it by choosing between the words in bold.

When I visited my mother's relatives in Mexico I happened to be there for the *Day of the Dead* festival. As its name suggests, this festival commemorates our departed loved ones. **(1) At first/Firstly** I thought it would be sad and even a bit scary, but in fact it was a joyful occasion. The celebration has its origins with the ancient Aztecs, who had rituals to celebrate their ancestors. **(2) Once upon a time/First of all**, it lasted the entire month of August. **(3) Afterwards/Nowadays**, it corresponds to 'All Saints' Day' on the first of November. In the days leading up to it, families clean and tidy up the graves. **(4) Once/While** they have finished they create an altar. They decorate the altar with brightly coloured flowers and sweets shaped like skulls and crosses. Sometimes they leave the departed person's favourite food, and glasses of tequila! No description would be complete without mentioning *Catrina* – the 'lady of the dead' – a key character you see everywhere. **(5) Before/On** going to the cemetery we put on our best clothes. **(6) First of all/At first** we said some prayers, **(7) after that/after** we lit the candles to guide people's souls to earth. It was a really moving and memorable event. **(8) After/Afterwards**, an uncle recited some satirical poetry about the dead person, I was slightly shocked, but apparently this is a tradition. **(9) Eventually/Lastly** it was time to leave and we made our way back home. **(10) In the end/At last** I felt that the candlelit cemetery was one of the most beautiful places I have ever visited. It left me with some wonderful memories and, perhaps this may surprise you, *no* nightmares!

3 Complete the table about the *Day of the Dead*.

Festival	Day of the Dead
name and origins • when it takes place • what it celebrates • its purpose • its origins • what it is like nowadays	
preparations • costumes • special food/drink	
characters	
bizarre/interesting facts	
what happens during the festival • beginning • middle • end	

4 Underline the words and expressions that show the writer's attitude and feelings.

PAPER 2, PART 2

5 You have been asked to write a short article for an international students' magazine about a festival in your country. Work in groups. Using the table in exercise 3 as a guide, brainstorm ideas about a local festival. When you are ready, write the article.

WRITING CHECKLIST

Did you ...?	Yes (✓)	No (✗)
• describe the name, origins and history of the event	☐	☐
• talk about the preparations leading up to it	☐	☐
• include two or three interesting or bizarre facts	☐	☐
• describe how the event unfolds	☐	☐
• use different ways of sequencing	☐	☐
• say how the event made you and other spectators feel	☐	☐

➔ Writing Guide, page 204

Review and Use of English

1 WORD FORMATION
Use the word given in capitals at the end of some of the lines to form a word that fits in the gap in the same line.

The Picture of Dorian Gray by Oscar Wilde is a fantastic story written and set in the 1890s. The hero, Dorian Gray, is a handsome young man from an aristocratic family. A **(1)** _____ artist friend, Basil Hallward, gets a hesitant Dorian to sit for his portrait. Seeing the final portrait upsets Dorian because he knows that while he grows old the picture will always stay young. **(2)** _____, he decides to keep the portrait hidden away, refusing to let anyone else to look at it. Until now Dorian has retained a certain innocence but this changes with the bad influence of the **(3)** _____ Lord Henry Wooton. Dorian becomes cruel and **(4)** _____. He meets a pretty young actress, Sybil Vane, who kills herself when Dorian ends their **(5)** _____. When Dorian next looks at his portrait he notices that this cruelty has been **(6)** _____ transmitted to his portrait. Time goes by: even though ugly rumours circulate about Dorian and his notorious behaviour he retains his **(7)** _____ good looks. Whenever he looks at his portrait it has become progressively more repulsive. Eventually he decides to show it to Basil who is horrified at the transformation. He urges Dorian to pray for **(8)** _____ but instead Dorian kills him. At last Dorian decides to destroy the portrait with a knife. No sooner does he cut the canvas than his servants hear a terrible scream and make a terrible **(9)** _____. When they come into the room they discover their master's portrait as handsome and **(10)** _____ as it was originally painted. By it lies a wrinkled and ugly old man. It is only when they examine his rings that they find out who the creature is.

PERSUADE *(1)*

AFTER *(2)*

FAMOUS *(3)*
HEART *(4)*

RELATION *(5)*

MYSTERY *(6)*

REMARK *(7)*

FORGIVE *(8)*

DISCOVER *(9)*
YOUTH *(10)*

2 KEY WORD TRANSFORMATIONS
For questions 1–8 complete the second sentence so that it has a similar meaning to the first sentence. Do not change the word given. You must use between two and five words, including the word given.

1 You need to make a decision about the costume.

   mind

   It's time you _____ about the costume.

2 The festival happens each November.

   place

   The festival _____ November each year.

3 She speaks Chinese and Japanese.

   does

   Not _____ but she also speaks Japanese.

4 Could you open the door; it's terribly smoky in here.

   mind

   It's terribly smoky in here; _____ the door?

5 She managed to trick us with her lies.

   taking

   She succeeded _____ with her lies.

6 The moment we turned it on it broke down.

   did

   No _____ it on than it broke down.

7 Carlos likes to contribute to class discussions.

   part

   Carlos enjoys _____ in class discussions.

8 He always arrives late for class.

   on

   He keeps _____ up late for class.

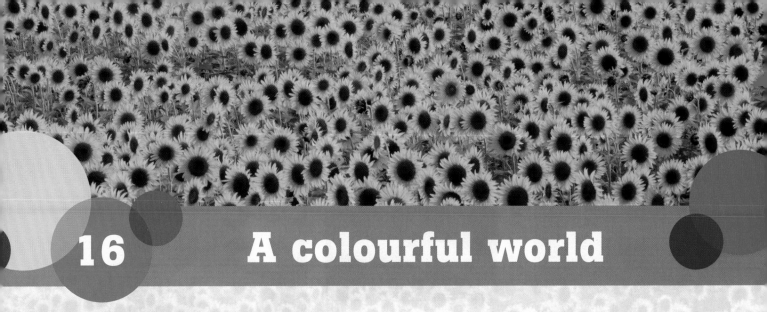

16   A colourful world

Getting started

1   **What kind of shape and colour are you? Choose your favourite coloured shape below.**

Now turn to Information File 16.1 on page 231 to find out what it says about your character.

2   **Work in pairs. Discuss with your partner:**

- What colours are the clothes you are wearing today? Do you think they reflect your character?

- What colour is your classroom? Do you think it is a good colour for learning?

- Describe your favourite room at home to your partner. Why do you like it? What colour is it? What do you think it says about you?

Listening: design and colour psychology

1 Work in pairs and discuss these questions. Look at the rooms above.

- Do you think the colour of a room can affect your mood and feelings?

- Which of these rooms would you like to spend time in?

- How would the colours in each make you feel?

2 🎧 **16.1 Listen to a TV interviewer talking to a home design expert. Make notes about the colours in this table. What positive or negative emotions are associated with the colours? Which rooms are they good/not good for?**

Colour	It's good for ... because ...
Red	
Purple	
Pink	
Blue	
Yellow	
Brown	
Black	

PAPER 4, PART 4

3 🎧 **16.1 MULTIPLE CHOICE Listen again to the TV interview. For questions 1–7, choose the best answer (A, B or C).**

1 What is the first thing many of us think about when we decorate?
   A the layout of the room
   B the contents of the room
   C the colour scheme of the room

2 What does Laurence say colour tells a visitor?
   A the mood we are in
   B the sort of person we are
   C whether they will like you

3 What does Laurence think about the choice of colours these days?
   A there aren't enough of them
   B that people still tend to prefer white or pale colours
   C people find it hard to choose

4 What don't people often think of when they choose a paint colour?
   A whether everything in the room will match
   B whether they will be able to relax with it
   C that some colours are no longer fashionable

5 How do interior designers appear to know what to do?
   A through following strict rules of design
   B through doing courses
   C through natural talent and experience

6 What kind of colours do you need for rooms facing north?
   A dark
   B pale
   C bright

7 In order to learn more, Laurence recommends that people ...
   A experiment with colour and do what feels right.
   B hire a decorator.
   C always follow the rules of colour.

Vocabulary: colour and decoration

1 **Choose the correct word (in *italics*) in sentences 1–7.**

1 It's *a bit run down/well-cared for,* with paint falling off the walls and holes in the floor. Are you sure you want to buy it?

2 The kitchen in this London house is *north/south*-facing which means you get plenty of sun during the day.

3 You get more space living in a *suburban/terraced* house but I'd miss living in the city centre.

4 I love *pale/strong* colours like red and bright orange. I can't see the point of painting a room if you don't notice the colour.

5 My grandmother's house is one of those old-fashioned cottages with a *cosy/impersonal* sitting room and a fireplace.

6 That's a *cheerful/dreary-looking* room. Don't you find the dark colours a bit depressing?

7 The walls in this room are rather *bare/cluttered*. We could put some pictures up to make it feel more homely.

2 **Categorise the italicised words in exercise 1 in this table.**

Colour description	Style/appearance	Type/position
pale	a bit run down	suburban

3 **Add two more adjectives for talking about houses to each category. Compare your ideas with a partner.**

Phrasal verbs

4 **Each of these words has the same meaning as a multi-word verb in sentences 1–8. Write it at the end of the sentence.**

select	not care for (appearance)	transform
redecorate	make light and cheerful	combine
continue	be (more) visible	match

1 The dining room is looking a bit dreary and gloomy. Let's **do** it **up** a bit with something more bright and cheerful.

_____

2 This old farmhouse is a bit run down because the previous owners **let** it **go** but with a bit of paint, it'll be fine.

_____

3 That's a great job you're doing on that bathroom floor. **Keep up** the good work! _____

4 You need red and yellow and if you **mix** them **up** well you should get a nice bright orange for the lounge that will **go with** the sofa. _____

5 Can you come with me on Saturday to **pick out** which wallpaper we're having for the hallway? _____

6 The portrait over the fireplace would probably **stand out** more if the walls weren't such a strong colour.

_____

7 Do you ever watch that TV show where they take some old shed or barn and somehow they **turn** it **into** the most amazing house? _____

8 A lemon colour would probably **brighten up** the kitchen.

_____

5 **Work in pairs. You have just bought this apartment. The previous owners didn't take care of it and so it's rather neglected with dreary wallpaper. Discuss each room in turn and decide on the colour scheme.**

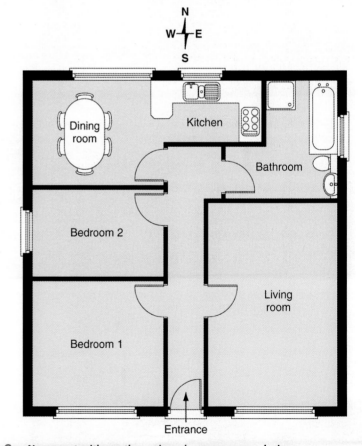

6 **Now meet with another pair and compare your designs. Explain the reasons for your choices of colour.**

Reading: a dream island

1 **Discuss.** Where would you have your dream home? What would it look like?

2 **Read the text about Reishee Sowa and answer the following:**

- What two places does he mention living in?

- What problems and difficulties has he had to overcome?

- What are the advantages of this kind of house? Would you like to live here?

REISHEE SOWA: A MAN AND HIS ISLAND DREAM

It looks like an exotic island, it feels like an island, it has the beautiful vegetation of a tropical island – but it just happens to be made of plastic bottles.

Who would have known and, more importantly, who would have thought it possible? A man named Reishee Sowa, that's who. This island is his inspiration, his baby, his dream. With the help of friends he met along the way and a lot of hard work, his dream has become a reality. It is an amazing sight. You see a house on the island and you think how lucky that person is to be able to live out there.

Reishee always had a passion for a better world, a desire to create a self-sufficient paradise. The dream ended up being made with all recycled materials. Everything from plastic bottles to wood and bags of leaves go into making up his island, house and yard. This island took approximately 250,000 bottles to make.

Reishee, originally from England, is a musician and an artist, and as it turns out, a visionary. He spent so much time talking of his dream that his family finally pushed him to just go out and do it. It took Reishee six years to create this island. For the first year he lived on it in a tent – then he built his first house and it fell apart in a storm so he tried again, and once again it fell apart in a storm. Never a quitter, as you might have guessed, he built a third time. 'Things all seem to come in threes for me', Reishee says 'this is actually my third try at an island and my house fell twice before I got it right.' Now his little house stands strong and it is complete with guest room and a deck on top where he still pursues his love of painting. The plants, once very small, have grown and matured over time, as has his cat population. He now lives with eight cats and a dog. They show up and don't want to leave.

Were there challenges building here in Puerto Aventuras? 'Oh yes,' replies Reishee. 'You see not even the president is allowed his own island in Mexico – but technically I don't have an island, I have a ship – I can move it after all. The local people have been very understanding and helpful.'

'If there's a storm or a large wave most of the wave goes under the island. Only about 10% comes on top. The part of the wave going under actually makes it flip down again and stay level.

'We are being faced with a population explosion and maybe building islands is the answer. This island is an example of something that could be built worldwide. You could be totally self-sufficient with it. All is as natural as possible. I catch rain water for showers, the toilet naturally composts, and you can grow your own produce,' adds Reishee.

His desire is for a simple life and to share his environmentally friendly, planet-saving ideas with others. The door is always open for you on Reishee's little tropical paradise. What does the future hold for Reishee and his island? 'Wave powered flippers and sails, and a journey through the Panama Canal,' says a very enthusiastic Reishee.

Want to find a way to become involved? Reishee will gladly accept donations of old plywood, solar panels to run a fridge, money for solar panels or anything else that will make the island more beautiful and more self-sufficient.

3 MULTIPLE CHOICE **For questions 1–8, choose the answer (A, B, C or D) which you think fits best according to the text.**

1 What wouldn't you know when you first look at the island?
   A that someone made it
   B that someone lives there
   C that you'd be able to grow vegetation on it
   D that it is an island

2 When she first sees the island, how does the writer feel?
   A frustrated
   B a little envious
   C amused
   D cynical and critical

3 Reishee always imagined living in a place where …
   A he didn't have to rely on resources or energy from anyone else.
   B he never saw anyone else.
   C he would live on the sea.
   D he could move the house without moving home.

4 Reishee eventually built the island because his family …
   A suggested the idea to him.
   B locked him out of the house.
   C encouraged him to do it.
   D needed somewhere to live.

5 The writer regards Reishee as someone who …
   A is mad.
   B is stubborn.
   C likes his own company.
   D never gives up.

6 Why isn't his island illegal?
   A because no one can see it from the mainland
   B It is illegal but the local people don't mind.
   C because it doesn't have to remain in one place all the time
   D because it's environmentally friendly

7 Reishee thinks that the island demonstrates how humans can …
   A live together in the world.
   B survive on their own.
   C survive anywhere in the world.
   D all live on islands.

8 Anyone reading the article is welcome to …
   A build their own island.
   B give Reishee some money to help maintain the island.
   C join Reishee on the island.
   D give Reishee useful items for the island.

Grammar: cleft sentences

GRAMMAR SPOTLIGHT

Cleft sentences

Use cleft sentences to change the emphasis in a sentence. For example, look at all the ways you can change this sentence: *Reishee built an island from plastic bottles.*

(1) Emphasising *who*: *Reishee **is that man who** built an island from plastic bottles.* / ***It was** Reishee **who** built an island from plastic bottles.*

(2) Emphasising *what*: *Plastic bottles **are what** he built an island from.* / ***What** Reishee built an island from **are** plastic bottles.*

(3) Emphasising the verb: ***What he did was to** build the island from plastic bottles.*

(4) Emphasising the whole sentence: ***What happened next was that** Reishee built an island from plastic bottles.*

(5) Emphasising time: ***It wasn't until his family pushed him to do it that** Reishee built an island from plastic bottles.*

➡ Grammar Reference (Section 4) page 168

1 **Transform these sentences into cleft sentences using the word in bold.**

1 I didn't break the vase. Michael did it! **who**
   It wasn't me. It was _____ the vase.

2 You know Rachel. She ran a marathon for charity last year. **woman**
   Rachel _____ who ran a marathon for charity last year.

3 He cheated in the exam in order to pass. **did**
   What _____ cheat in the exam in order to pass.

4 The storm came next and destroyed the second island. **happened**
   What _____ that the storm came and destroyed the second island.

5 I met his father and then I understood the situation. **until**
   It _____ met his father that I understood the situation.

2 **Work in pairs. Make cleft sentences about the reading on page 158 by completing these sentences.**

1 What Reishee always dreamed of doing was to …

2 It was his family who …

3 It wasn't until he built the house a third time that …

4 A simple life is what …

5 Building more islands is what Reishee thinks …

Use of English: multiple-choice cloze

1 Work in pairs. These days many people are trying to find ways to make their homes environmentally friendly and save money on bills. In what ways are people doing this in your country?

2 MULTIPLE-CHOICE CLOZE **Read the text and decide which answer (A, B, C or D) best fits each gap.**

Eco-friendly Living

Too many of (1) _____ go home at night so unaware of how much energy we waste. OK, so we might turn (2) _____ the standby button on the TV these days or use energy-saving light bulbs but how many of us (3) _____ change our house to make it eco-friendly? Matthew Bennett would. In fact he thought it was such a good idea that he totally rebuilt it, making his four-bedroom home into (4) _____ of the most eco-friendly in any Canadian urban area.

From the street the house looks (5) _____ a typical home in the middle of a suburban neighbourhood. (6) _____ from the wind turbine perched on the roof you wouldn't really know it was any different. But hidden below the ground underneath his basement there is a 50,000-litre tank (7) _____ catches enough rain to supply all of his water. Any water from washing machines, showers and other household (8) _____ is recycled through filters and ponds and (9) _____ re-used on a small orchard because instead of grass, plants and flowers he (10) _____ planted trees.

The biggest benefit for Mr Bennett is (11) _____ he has virtually no water or energy bills. The wind turbine, (12) _____ panels and small biodiesel generator provide nearly 100 percent of his household requirements.

1	A them	B us	C all	D people
2	A of	B on	C away	D off
3	A would	B can	C try	D must
4	A all	B one	C many	D first
5	A at	B than	C as	D like
6	A Apart	B However	C Although	D Along
7	A it	B when	C which	D what
8	A appliances	B technology	C goods	D furniture
9	A first	B then	C addition	D to
10	A hadn't	B was	C has	D had
11	A why	B also	C that	D so
12	A solar	B sun	C wood	D bright

3 Which of the energy-saving techniques in the photos in exercise 1 does the text mention? What other techniques is Mr Bennett using in his house? Do you think that one day all houses will be like this?

Grammar: *so/such/too/enough*

1 **Look at the three sentences from the text and put the words in bold in the four sentences.**

- **Too** many of us go home at night **so** unaware of how much energy we waste.
- In fact he thought it was **such** a good idea that he totally rebuilt it
- The tank catches **enough** rain to supply all of his water.

Too/enough

1 _____ has a negative meaning.

2 _____ has a positive meaning.

So/such

3 _____ appears before an adjective or an adverb.

4 _____ appears before an adjective + noun.

➡ Grammar Reference (Section16) page 184

2 **Choose the correct word (in *italics*) in sentences 1–6.**

1 *Too much/Enough* money is being wasted each year on energy.

2 I think that living on an island is *so/such* a good idea!

3 I find that I learn English *so/such* easily.

4 The colour of the walls in our classroom is *so/such* dull.

5 There isn't *so/enough* time to study for the First Certificate exam!

6 There are always *so/enough* many things to do at the weekend that I don't have time to relax.

3 **Complete the second sentence so that it means the same as the first sentence in 1–4 below. Use *too*, *enough*, *so* or *such*.**

1 We need more houses for the world's population.

   There aren't _____ houses for the world's population.

2 The children had a really interesting time at the museum.

   The children had _____ an interesting time at the museum.

3 This room isn't bright enough for a kitchen.

   This room is _____ dull for a kitchen.

4 It's incredibly hot today!

   It's _____ hot today!

Writing: an email

You have received an email from your English-speaking friend who is decorating her new apartment. She wants some advice. Read her print-out of the email and the notes you have made about the rooms. Write an email to her (120 – 150 words).

From: Rowen
Date: 6th June
Subject My new apartment!

Hi!
Guess what! You know that apartment I told you about on the phone — well, I've bought it! *[Congratulate her]*

They accepted my offer and I managed to get a good price but it does need a lot of work. The room that needs the most time is the kitchen *[Ask if it looks north or south]* — it's really dreary.

Anyway, I know how stylish your house looks now so I wondered if you had any advice on doing it up. For example, the living room only has one window and seems VERY dark. I suppose I'll only be in there in the evening so maybe it doesn't matter. *[Suggest warm colour]*

The bathroom is in good condition so I'll probably leave that but the bedrooms need furniture. I remember when you bought your house you found some websites selling cheap furniture. Can you recommend some sites? *[Yes, give details]*

I was wondering if you have any time to come and visit. I'd love to show you round and discuss some ideas. How about next weekend? *[No, because.../Say when]*

The email ...	Yes (✓)	No (✗)
• includes all the information in the handwritten notes.	☐	☐
• is written in an appropriate style.	☐	☐
• uses paragraphs (at least three).	☐	☐

➡ Writing Guide, page 200

Speaking: paper 5

The Speaking test

PAPER 5

1 **Here are some sentences taken from a First Certificate Speaking test. For each one decide *which part* of the four parts of the exam it comes from and *who* said it – the interlocutor (*I*) or a candidate (*C*).**

Use the flowchart, showing the four parts of the Speaking test, to help you decide.

Part _1_ First of all we'd like to know something about you. (I)

Part _2_ In the first picture you can see four people skiing … (C)

Part ___ I'm from Colombia. ( )

Part ___ I would prefer to spend my free time skiing as in this picture … ( )

Part ___ And what do you like about living in Colombia? ( )

Part ___ Now, I'd like you to talk about something together for about three minutes. ( )

Part ___ Maybe you could have a dinner in the evening and then later have a little party. ( )

Part ___ Do you prefer spending time at home or do you like to go out in your free time? ( )

Part ___ As many people can work from home with computers, do you think more of us will move away from cities in the future?

Part ___ In this part of the test, I'm going to give each of you two photographs. ( )

Part ___ I'd like you to compare the photographs … ( )

Part ___ What do you think is important when choosing where to live? ( )

Part ___ That's right. And the last activity we can choose might be the firework display. ( )

Part ___ I'd like you to imagine that your local town is 500 years old and is planning events to celebrate the anniversary. ( )

Part ___ Well, I think at the moment with all the opportunities and technical advances it is very easy to work away from the office. ( )

Part ___ Can you tell me about a day that you've enjoyed recently? ( )

FLOWCHART

Part 1
Conversation between the interlocutor and each candidate
(3 minutes)

Part 2
Each candidate talks about two pictures.
(4 minutes)

Part 3
The two candidates collaborate to complete a task by discussing visual prompts.
(3 minutes)

Part 4
The interlocutor and the two candidates discuss questions about topics related to part 3.
(4 minutes)

(Sometimes there are three candidates in the FCE Speaking test so the time for each part increases: **Part 1: 5 minutes, Part 2: 6 minutes, Part 3: 4 minutes, Part 4: 5 minutes**).

2 🎧 **16.2 Now listen to a Speaking test with two students from Colombia and Switzerland. As you listen, check your answers in exercise 1 and refer to the visual prompts from parts 2 and 3 of the Speaking test on the opposite page and on page 190.**

When we speak it's easy to make mistakes – especially in the exam! When you practise for the Speaking exam, record yourself. Afterwards, write down any of your common mistakes and correct them.

3   🎧 16.3 **Look at the checklist of advice below for each part of the Speaking test. Listen to the interview again and score how well the two students followed the advice.**
Key to scoring:
1 = They did this very well.
2 = They did this quite well.
3 = They need to improve this part of the exam.

In part 1 …	Score		
• talk about general topics.	1	2	3
• make sure you answer the examiner's questions clearly.	1	2	3
In part 2 …			
• briefly describe each photograph.	1	2	3
• compare and contrast the two photographs.	1	2	3
• answer the question with the two photographs.	1	2	3
• clearly answer the examiner's supplementary question.	1	2	3
In part 3 …			
• discuss the pros and cons for each suggestion.	1	2	3
• compare and contrast some of the suggestions.	1	2	3
• ask for your partner's opinion.	1	2	3
• show you are listening to your partner.	1	2	3
• discuss and give a final answer to the question or questions with the suggestions.	1	2	3
In part 4 …			
• answer the examiner's questions.	1	2	3
• give opinions.	1	2	3

4   **Work in groups of three and practise the Speaking test using the materials in Speaking File 1 on pages 187–190.**
   • **One of you is the interlocutor (examiner) and will ask the questions provided.**
   • **The other two are the candidates. Try to follow the correct timings for each part of the test (see the Exam Spotlight above on page 162).**
   • **Afterwards, change roles and use Speaking Files 2 and 3 on pages 191–195.**

1 Choose the correct word (in *italics*) in sentences 1–9.

1 For sale – a beautiful house in a perfect *city centre/urban* setting only ten minutes from the countryside.

2 We bought this run *down/out* old barn which we're going to convert into a house.

3 Can you go down to the *cellar/attic* and get me the brush?

4 This is a south-*facing/looking* property with views of the hills.

5 Do you need any more *appliances/furniture* for the kitchen other than this washing machine?

6 That's *so/such* a fantastic way to save the environment.

7 Let's *do/show* it up with some bright colour.

8 That blue is rather *dreary/pale*. How about using something stronger so it really makes a difference to the room?

9 The apple trees in the *orchard/forest* haven't done very well this year.

2 Complete sentences 1–8 using the correct form of the words in the box.

cheer	design	generate	power
green	environment	home	neighbour

1 Most _____ have an instinct for what colours go well together.

2 People say that flying isn't very _____ friendly because of the CO_2 emissions.

3 I live in a nice _____. Everyone around me is very friendly.

4 The _____ for the electricity is run off biofuels.

5 The traditional fireplace gives the whole room a very cosy _____ feel.

6 I think maybe you should choose the yellow or pink paint because it's brighter and more _____ than the blue or purple.

7 Yesterday I bought a gorgeous new dress. It's a kind of an _____-brown colour.

8 My swimming pool is solar-_____ by the sun shining on these panels so it's cheap to run and is always warm.

3 OPEN CLOZE **Read the text below and think of the word which best fits each gap. Use only one word in each gap.**

PROTESTERS TAKE TO THE TREES

In an attempt to prevent developers **(1)** _____ building 630 homes on a woodland site, 20 protesters have set up home **(2)** _____ some of the 250 trees by building three 12-metre-high tree houses. However, **(3)** _____ owner of the small forest, Bill Thwaites, **(4)** _____ already said he will try to move protesters as quickly **(5)** _____ possible from the area. Mr Thwaites also said he would **(6)** _____ legal action to remove the campaigners and is seeking advice. One campaigner determined to look **(7)** _____ the trees by living there said '**(8)** _____ makes us all really angry is that fact that it's all about money. These companies build lots of big houses and they **(9)** _____ millions. Meanwhile, local people can't afford to buy anything to live in. We love our green space and countryside more than money. The police say **(10)** _____ we have got to move from our tree homes but we want to demonstrate just to show **(11)** _____ strongly we feel,' he added. The tree protestors welcome anyone **(12)** _____ wishes to join them in the trees.

EXAM SPOTLIGHT

Ways of revising vocabulary

How do you remember and revise vocabulary?
Do you use any of these techniques?

• Draw a spidergram to group words (see Unit 13, page 126).

• Take a word and write it in different forms; e.g. *compete – competitive – competitor – competition.*

• Make sets of small cards. On each card write the word on one side and a definition on the other side. Test yourself by reading the definition and guessing the word.

• Work with a partner. Say a word and your partner has to say a sentence with the word in.

• Choose ten words and write your own gap fill test to give to your partner.

• With phrasal verbs, choose a verb (e.g. *take, give, put*) and think of as many particles you can add (e.g. *up, out, in*). Say a sentence with each combination.

Grammar Reference

Index

1 Adjectives

We use adjectives to classify or describe the qualities of something or someone. We use adjectives:

1 After the verb *'to be'*:
   He is old.
   Form: *to be* + adjective
2 After 'linking' verbs such as *look, seem, become* and *feel*:
   Are you OK, you look tired. No, I feel fine.
   Form: verb + adjective
3 Before nouns and pronouns:
   Her new coat is beautiful.
   Form: adjective + noun

Remember:

i) Adjectives do not change according to the number or gender of the thing they describe:
   There were some ~~youngs~~ young boys in the street.
ii) Adjectives come **after** *the* to describe a class or group of people:
   The rich, the unemployed, the homeless
iii) Colour adjectives come **before** the noun:
   She was wearing a red dress, not a ~~dress red~~.
iv) Some adjectives such as *asleep, alive, afraid* can only be used **after** a linking verb:
   *The boy who was hiding in the cellar **looked afraid**.*
   There was an ~~afraid~~ boy hiding in the cellar = There was a frightened boy hiding in the cellar.

Which one of the following sentences is correct? Correct the rest.
1 There were four greens cars in front of their house.
2 That watch looks like expensive.
3 You look a lovely today.
4 He was feeling sad yesterday.
5 The government should look after the poors.
6 There was an asleep baby lying in its pram.

1.1 Participial adjectives

Many adjectives are formed from the present particle (*-ing* form) and past participles (*-ed* form) of verbs.
For example: to interest = interested, interesting.
1 Adjectives ending in *-ing* tell us a characteristic or quality of the person or thing being described. They also have an active sense. They show the effect someone or something has on someone or something else:
   It's an interesting book = It makes me feel interested.
2 Adjectives ending in *-ed* have a passive sense and describe what has happened to the person or thing it describes. They describe states and feelings:
   *The grammar class was **boring*** = The class actively had that effect.
   *Nikki was **bored*** = That's what happened to Nikki.

Choose the correct form of adjective in the sentences below.
1 We were ***worrying/worried*** about the news from Canada.
2 Am I ***boring/bored,*** Maria? People don't listen to my stories anymore.
3 What's the most ***embarrassing/embarrassed*** experience you've ever had?
4 We are ***exhausting/exhausted,*** baby Oliver kept us awake all night.
5 I've never eaten anything quite so ***disgusted/disgusting***.
6 I enjoy watching Sumo wrestling, I think it's a ***fascinated/fascinating*** sport.

1.2 Adjective order

1 When we use two or more adjectives before a noun then we generally follow this order: **opinion – dimension – age – texture – colour – shape – origin – purpose**
2 If we want to use more than two adjectives we will usually try to place some of them after the noun:
   She had short curly dark hair.
   Better: *Her dark hair was short and curly.*
   He carried a worn old leather briefcase.
   Better: *He carried a worn old briefcase made of leather.*
3 Opinion adjectives, where we give our point of view usually come before adjectives which give more factual information. Examples of opinion adjectives are *beautiful, lovely, nice, pretty, awful, ugly, horrible.*
   She wore a beautiful blue dress, made of silk.

Which one of these sentences shows a correct order of adjectives? Correct the others by putting the adjectives in the right order.
1 She put a ***plastic black long*** snake on her teacher's chair.
2 He was a given a/n ***diver's expensive Swiss*** watch for his eighteenth birthday.
3 She was wearing a ***shiny Japanese lovely*** dressing-gown ***silk.***
4 He has bought a ***wonderful new graphite tennis*** raquet.
5 They have a ***grey big fat gorgeous*** cat ***Siamese.***
6 Last night I watched a ***Swedish new fascinating*** documentary on TV.

1.3 Gradable and non-gradable adjectives

1 Gradable adjectives:
a) Many adjectives and adverbs describe qualities which are gradable. In other words, they can have more or less of the quality in question. We can modify, or grade ordinary adjectives using: *a little, fairly, slightly, rather, quite, very, extremely*, etc.

> *We were fairly tired after a long day of shopping.*

b) However we **can't** use *absolutely, completely, totally*, or *utterly* to modify gradable adjectives:

> *I was ~~absolutely angry~~ when I heard the news.*

2 Non-gradable adjectives:
a) Non-gradable adjectives describe qualities that are already at their limit. e.g. *exhausted*.
b) We can modify them to emphasise the degree of completeness with *absolutely, completely, totally*, or *utterly*:

> *We were exhausted after a long day's shopping.*

c) We **can't** use *a little, fairly, slightly, rather, quite, very, extremely*, etc. with non-gradable adjectives:

> *We were ~~a little exhausted~~ after a long day of shopping.*

3 Gradable adjectives like *tired* or *angry* may have one or more non-gradable counterparts:

> *good = marvellous, wonderful, fantastic ...*

Gradable

Modifiers	Adjectives	Example
A little, fairly, slightly, rather, quite, very, extremely	Tired, hungry, bad, angry, pretty, embarrassed, disappointed	I was very angry when I heard the news.

Non-gradable

Modifiers	Adjectives	Example
Absolutely, completely, utterly, totally	Terrible, awful, dreadful, exhausted, furious, gorgeous, starving, mortified, devastated	We were utterly exhausted after a long day's shopping.

Complete the responses to these exchanges using non-gradable adjectives.

1 A: Were you pleased with your results?
 B: Pleased? I was completely _____.
2 A: You must have been angry when you heard the news.
 B: Angry? I was totally _____.
3 A: She looked lovely in her wedding dress.
 B: Lovely? She looked absolutely _____.
4 A: I heard that the play was bad.
 B: Bad? It was utterly _____.
5 A: Were you tired and hungry after the walk?
 B: Tired and hungry? We were absolutely _____ and _____.
6 A: Were they disappointed to lose the match?
 B: Disappointed? They were utterly _____.

2 Adverbs

2.1 Adverbs of frequency

1 We use adverbs of frequency to say how often we do something:

> *I sometimes go to the cinema at the weekend.*

These are some of the most common adverbs of frequency:

> *never – seldom – rarely – hardly ever – occasionally – sometimes – often – usually – always*

2 Word order: adverbs of frequency follow 'to be':

> *She ~~never is~~ on time. She is never on time.*

Otherwise, they usually come before the main verb, and between modal auxiliaries and the main verb:

> *We occasionally eat out.*
> *We don't usually watch TV.*
> *Customers will often arrive just before we close.*

Notice that we can replace *sometimes* or *occasionally* with expressions such as *from time to time, once in a while, every so often*. These either come at the beginning or the end of a sentence:

> *Once in while we go to the cinema.*
> or *We go to the cinema once in a while.*

> **Remember:**
>
> i) We can use *always* with the present or past continuous to show annoyance or disapproval:
> *She's **always** borrowing my dictionary without asking me.* (I wish she would stop.)
> ii) When we want to emphasise something, we may begin the sentences with an adjective of 'negative force' e.g. *never, seldom*. (See Section 10 **Inversion** for more information on this.)

Put the parts of the sentences in italics into the correct order.
1 We **always take nearly** the train between Brussels and Paris.
2 Tess and Jerry go to **cinema time the to time from**.
3 Why don't we go to a restaurant? We **seem these eat hardly to days out**.
4 I'm really fed up, **clothes he borrowing is my always** without asking.
5 They used **on to tennis mornings always play Sunday** but since the baby **time ever they hardly have**.
6 Since I moved to Chicago **I see my while only a once parents in**.

2.2 Adverbs of manner

Adverbs of manner are used to describe how an action is performed:

> *She plays the piano beautifully.*

We generally form them by adding *-ly* to adjectives:

> *Slow* → *slowly*.

We transform adjectives ending in *-y* with *-ily* in the adverb:

> *Angry* → *angrily*.

2.3 Irregular adverbs

Adjective	Adverb
fast	fast
hard	hard
good	well

e.g. *She is a good singer, she sings well.*
(For comparative adverbs see Section 5 **Making comparisons**.)

Complete the sentences by transforming the adjectives into adverbs. Make any other necessary changes.
1 He's a very good chess player.

He plays chess _____.
2 Greta is a very hard worker.

Greta works _____.
3 The way April sang that piece was beautiful.

April sang that piece _____.
4 Be careful how you handle that vase.

Handle that vase _____.
5 I'm happy to do that for you.

I'll _____.
6 He is an extremely persuasive speaker.

He speaks _____.

2.4 Introductory adverbs

Many adverbs can be used at the beginning of sentences to comment on what comes next.

Basically/essentially students have to sit down and learn their irregular verbs. (= *this is my main point.*)

Obviously, I need to improve my computer skills. (= *it's obvious that...*)

Unfortunately/sadly, Hamish failed the entrance exam for medical school. (= *I regret to give you this news.*)

Hopefully everything will be ready for the next time you come. (= *if there are no problems.*)

2.5 Meaning shifts from adjectives to adverbs

Changes of meaning between adjectives and adverbs. Adverbs generally retain the meaning of the adjectives from which they are drawn. However, sometimes there is an important change of meaning.

Late = *not on time; lately* = *recently.*
Short = *not tall; shortly* = *soon.*
Hardly is an adverb meaning *almost not*, or *only a little*.
His handwriting was so messy I could hardly read what he had written.

Replace the words in **bold** with a one-word adverb.
1 Oh dear, the dog is **only just** breathing, I hope she's OK.
2 I haven't seen Malcolm **for a while,** has he gone on holiday?
3 **If everything goes according to plan** we'll be at your place by six o'clock.

4 **It's a pity but** we won't be able to fix your car.
5 Would you mind waiting, I'll be with you **in just a couple of minutes**.
6 **There's no question about it,** we have to have the roof mended.
7 Well, **what I want to say is** you should eat five pieces of fruit a day.

3 Articles

Articles precede and modify nouns.
a/an = indefinite articles
the = definite article

3.1 Indefinite article use

We use the indefinite article *a/an* in front of singular countable [C] nouns, when we use them in a general sense:
*They gave us **a** table for two.*

3.2 Definite article use

We use the definite article *the* with all types of noun, for things which are specific:
1 When we want to refer to a particular thing:
Where's the key? (The specific key that opens this door.)
2 When mentioning something for the second time:
They gave us a table for two. Unfortunately the table was right next to the door.
3 With superlatives:
It's the best film I've ever seen.
4 With things which are unique:
The world, the earth, the universe.
5 With some geographical names:
The Himalayas, the Channel.
6 With some names of organisations and titles, particularly those with 'of' or the idea of 'of':
The Head Teacher, the International Olympic Committee, the President (of France).
7 With adjectives to describe a class or group of people:
The unemployed, the elderly.
8 For places and amenities known to everyone:
I need to post this letter, I'm going to the post office. They took her to the hospital.
9 When referring to something specific:
I love wild animals, but the animals I saw at the zoo seemed tired and depressed. (Plural countable noun.)
I hardly drink coffee, but the coffee you gave me this morning was exceptional. (Uncountable noun.)
It was a terrible secret. She found the knowledge too hard to bear.
The money he earned over the summer allowed him to go on holiday.
10 With ordinal numbers:
The next meeting is planned for the ninth of January.
11 With musical instruments:
She plays the violin and the flute.

3.3 Zero article Ø

We **don't** use articles:
1 With plural countable nouns used in in a general sense:
   I love animals.
2 With uncountable, and abstract nouns:
   Money makes the world go around.
   Knowledge is power.

Complete the sentences with *a*, *the* or Ø (no article).

1 _____ two biggest problems we face are _____ global warming and _____ pollution.

2 She bought _____ violin for her daughter who said she wanted to learn _____ guitar.

3 There's no doubt about it, _____ rich are getting richer and _____ poor are getting poorer. _____ government should do something about this and help _____ homeless and _____ unemployed.

4 _____ famous author once said that _____ past was _____ foreign country.

5 Last month I bought _____ pair of trousers for £80 then _____ minutes later I saw exactly _____ same ones for £50!

6 They say _____ little knowledge is _____ dangerous thing. I discovered _____ truth of this when I tried to fix _____ car. In _____ end I had to call _____ mechanic from _____ nearest garage to repair it.

7 _____ cost of _____ materials like _____ oil, _____ copper and _____ rubber keeps going up. _____ last time I filled up my car I almost fainted when I saw _____ price on _____ pump.

8 _____ money can't buy you _____ happiness or _____ love, but I'd rather be _____ miserable rich person than _____ miserable poor one.

9 She is _____ third woman to be _____ minister of _____ education.

10 _____ fear of _____ snakes is much more common than you might think.

4 Cleft sentences

Cleft sentences let us focus on what is important in a sentence. They are particularly common in spoken English and can add extra emphasis.
1 Sentences *a–c* all carry a similar message, although the emphasis of *b* and *c* is the year of the fire, rather than the fire itself:
   a The Great Fire of London took place in 1666.
   b **It was** in 1666 that the Great Fire of London took place.
   c **What** happened in 1666 **was** the Great Fire of London.

Notice that cleft sentences often begin with *what* and *it* and need the introduction of the verb *to be*.
2 a You should look for last-minute flights on the Internet.
   b **What** you should do is look for last minute flights on the Internet.
3 a She took all of the money from her boyfriend's account.
   b **What** she did was take all of the money from her boyfriend's account.
4 a The thing that worries me is ...
   b **What** worries me is that ...

Rephrase these sentences.
1 Her last concert began at nine o'clock in the evening.
   It was _____.
2 They took the legs off the piano and carried it through the window.
   What they did _____.
3 She slipped on the ice and broke her arm.
   What happened _____.
4 I think you ought to try a dating agency.
   What you _____.
5 I find loud music in restaurants annoying.
   What annoys _____.
6 They broke into our car while they were at the beach.
   What happened was _____.

5 Making comparisons

5.1 Comparatives

We form comparative adjectives by adding *-er* to one syllable adjectives. For example:
   soft → *softer*, *cheap* → *cheaper*, *sweet* → *sweeter*, *short* → *shorter*.

Remember:

Spelling

i) One-syllable adjectives:
- If a one-syllable adjective ends in a single vowel letter followed by a single consonant letter, the consonant letter is doubled

  thin ➔ *thinner, big* ➔ *bigger, sad* ➔ *sadder, slim* ➔ *slimmer, fat* ➔ *fatter*
- If an adjective ends in *-e*, this is removed when adding *-er*

  wide ➔ *wider, rude* ➔ *ruder, brave* ➔ *braver*
- If an adjective ends in a consonant followed by *-y*, *-y* is replaced by *-i* when adding *-er*

  dry ➔ *drier, coy* ➔ *coyer*

ii) Two-syllable adjectives:
- Two-syllable adjectives ending in *-ed, -ing, -ful,* or *-less* always form the comparative with *more or less*

  worried ➔ *more worried, boring* ➔ *more boring, careful* ➔ *more careful, useless* ➔ *more useless.*
- However with two-syllable adjectives ending in *-y*, we use *-ier* instead of *more*

  pretty ➔ *prettier, happy* ➔ *happier, healthy* ➔ *healthier.*
- With some other two-syllable adjectives we can either precede them with *more* **or** add *-er* to the adjective

  clever ➔ *cleverer/more clever, quiet* ➔ *quieter/more quiet, polite* ➔ *politer/more polite.*

iii) Three-syllable adjectives:
- Three-syllable adjectives take *more or less*

  ~~*expensiver*~~ – *more expensive, dangerous* ➔ *more dangerous, difficult* ➔ *less difficult.*
- The only exceptions are some three syllable words which have been formed using the prefix *un-*

  unhappy ➔ ~~*more unhappy*~~ *unhappier, unpleasant* ➔ ~~*more unpleasant*~~ *unpleasanter.*

Notice: *As* may be used to compare the way two things are similar or different:

Form: *as + adjective + as*

*She is **as old as** her husband.*

*This one isn't **as valuable/well-made as** the other one.*

It is used as a substitute for the superlative (see below).

There isn't a more expensive hotel in the town. (It's the most expensive hotel in town.)

It is also used when we want to show that actions and results are connected in a progressive way.

The older he gets the more stubborn he becomes.

5.2 Superlatives

Most superlatives are formed by adding *-est* to adjectives which are short (one or two syllables); and using *the most/ least* before longer adjectives (three or more syllables).

She's **my youngest** student and also **the most** intelligent.

We use the superlative:

1 To express the greatest degree of comparison.

*I think that Use of English is **the most difficult** part of the exam.*

Form: *to be + superlative*

2 To describe experiences or events.

*It's **the most frightening** ride I have ever been on.*

Form: superlative + present perfect

5.3 Comparative adverbs

We use comparative adverbs when we want to contrast how actions are performed.

1 If we want to make adverbs comparative we use *more* or *less*:

She has been working more conscientiously this term.

2 We don't use *-er* or *-est*.

There are important exceptions, as explained below.

Adjective	Comparative adverb	Superlative	Adverb
good/well	better	best	well
bad	worse	worst	badly
hard	harder	hardest	hard
fast	faster	fastest	fast

1 Complete the sentences using a comparative or superlative form of the word provided.

1 It was a wonderful meal, in fact it was _____ (*delicious*) I had ever eaten.

2 Last term her English was excellent and she was the _____ (*good*) in the class, but this term it's the _____ (*bad*), I wonder what has happened.

3 Gordon is much _____ (*happy*) than Harry and Russell, but Gerald is the _____ (*successful*) and _____ (*rich*) of all of them.

4 Why is it that people who live the _____ (*close*) to their work always arrive late?

5 I feel much _____ (*good*) this morning so I'll go to school.

6 The exam wasn't as _____ (*easy*) I had imagined.

7 His brother doesn't speak _____ (*good*) than him.

8 Cristiano plays football more _____ (*beautiful*) than any other player.

9 Felicia swims _____ (*fast*) than Samantha but not _____ (*quick*) as Ana.

10 Nobody works as _____ (*hard*) Xu, he has learned all the irregular verbs even the _____ (*hard*).

2 Continue and complete the second sentence so that it has a similar meaning to the one above it.

1 I have never felt so tired.

This _____ ever felt.

2 Nobody knew him better than Amanda.

Nobody knew him as _____ Amanda.

3 I have never had such a bad flight.

It was the _____ ever had.

4 Her car goes faster than mine.

My car doesn't _____ hers.

5 Do you have a more recent version of this song?

Is this the _____ version of this song?

6 Each book I read adds to my understanding.

The more I _____ I understand.

6 Conditionals

Conditional sentences typically contain two clauses – a condition clause and a result clause. They allow us to talk about possible and impossible/unreal situations and their consequences.

6.1 Zero conditional

We use the zero conditional ...
1 To describe a straightforward cause and effect
   If you open that door, it makes a terrible noise.
2 To write a scientific truth
   If you mix oil and water the oil floats.

6.2 First conditional

Form: *If + present simple/will + infinitive (without 'to')*
We use the first conditional:
1 When we believe that something is likely (more probable) to happen, than not as the result of a future action:
   *If I **have** the money, **I will buy** the car.*
2 For promises or threats:
   ***If** you pass your exam* (condition), *I'll buy everyone a coffee* (result).
   ***If** you don't do your homework, I'll have to phone your Mum and Dad.*
3 We use *when* and *as soon as* when the first action is sure to happen:
   *When/as soon as I **get** the results **I'll call** you.*

6.3 Second conditional

Form: *If + past simple/would/could/might + infinitive (without 'to')*
We use the second conditional ...
1 When we think that the outcome of a future event is not very likely to happen:
   *If the students **were** more serious, they would have a better chance in the exam.*
2 For unreal or imaginary situations in the present or the future:
   *If I **ran** Cambridge Examinations, I'd **make the exam easier** (but I'm just a candidate).*
3 For polite requests:
   Would you mind if I borrowed these DVDs?

Remember:
Can, could may, might, should and *ought to* can replace *would* in second conditional sentences.

6.4 Third conditional

Form: *If + past perfect → would/could/might + have + past participle*
We use the third conditional to describe imaginary or 'unreal' situations in the past and to express regrets:
   ***If** I had known he would be upset, I wouldn't have said anything* (but I *did* say something and he *was* upset).

(See Section 18 **Wish** for more information on expressing regrets.)

6.5 Alternatives to *'if'*

1 *Unless* and *otherwise*
   We use *unless* meaning 'if ... not' in the condition clause and *otherwise* before the likely result:
   *You will lose marks **unless** you improve your spelling.*
   *We'd better hurry up. **Otherwise** we'll miss the start of the film.*
2 *As long as/provided/on condition that*
   We use *provided/as long as/on the condition that* when we want to make the condition stricter:
   *I'll lend you my dictionary **provided/as long as/on the condition that** you promise to bring it back.*
3 Inversion:
   ***If** I had known he would be upset, I wouldn't have said anything.*
   ***Had I known** he would be upset, I wouldn't have said anything.*
(See Section 11 **Inversion** for more on this.)

6.6 Mixed conditional

The mixed conditional combines the third conditional in the condition clause with the second conditional in the result clause. We use it to describe a past action which has a consequence in the present:
   If I hadn't eaten that seafood, I wouldn't feel so awful now.

1 Change the verbs in brackets to form conditional sentences.
   1 I (take) _____ her to the station if she (do) _____ my French homework!
   2 I know it's just a dream, but what (you do) _____ if we (win) _____ the lottery?
   3 If (you say) _____ that again, I (tell) _____ your father.
   4 She was lucky. If she (not miss) _____ the flight she (not be) _____ with us today.
   5 I don't believe he'll ever stop, but if he (give up) _____ smoking his health (improve) _____.
   6 When our guests (arrive) _____, Lucy, (you call me) _____ immediately?
   7 (you give) _____ him the money if you (know) _____ how he was going to spend it?
   8 If I (be) _____ in charge I (make) _____ some big changes, but I'm just a temporary worker.
   9 If Hannah (know) _____ the truth about Duncan she (think twice) _____ before marrying him.
   10 I'm so stupid, if I (remember) _____ lock up my bike, it (not be stolen) _____.

2 Rephrase these sentences using the words in **bold**.
1 We'll miss the beginning of the film if you don't hurry up. **unless**

_____

2 If you leave your car there you'll get a parking ticket. **you'd better not/otherwise**

_____

3 You can borrow my car on condition that you fill it up afterwards. **provided**

_____

4 I'll tell your sister what you did unless you give me a sweet. **if**

_____

5 Unless you promise to take care of it I won't lend you my iPod. **I'll/as long as**

_____

6 If he doesn't drive more carefully he'll have an accident. **unless**

_____

6.7 Contrasting ideas

1 Consequence:
   He felt ill. He stayed at home.
   In the first pair of sentences there is not a contrast between the two ideas. After all, if we feel ill it is logical to stay at home. We can join these ideas with _so_:
   = He felt ill **so** he stayed at home.
2 Contrast:
   He felt ill. He went to school.
   In this second pair, there is a contrast between the ideas
   a We can show the contrast between these ideas with _but_:
      = He felt ill **but** he went to school.
   b We can show the contrast between these ideas with _however/nevertheless_:
      = He felt ill, however/nevertheless, he went to school.
   Notice: like _but_, _however_ and _nevertheless_ come after the original proposition, and introduce the contrast, that is, **between** the contrasting ideas.
3 Other ways of expressing contrast:
   a although/even though
      Although he felt ill he went to school.
      Even though he felt ill he went to school/He went to school even though he felt ill
   b _in spite of/despite_ + **gerund**
      In spite of/despite feeling ill/the fact he felt ill He went to school.
   c _in spite of/despite_ + **noun**
      In spite of/Despite of his illness he went to school.
   d _Despite the fact_ (_that_) + **tense**
      Despite the fact that he felt ill, he went to school.
   Notice: These ways of expressing contrast introduce the original proposition, not the contrast.
   ~~Even though he was unhappy he was rich.~~ Even though he was rich he was unhappy.

1 Decide if the following sentences are correct or incorrect.
   1 It was a perfect day although we had a wonderful time.
      Correct [   ] Incorrect [   ]
   2 Nevertheless we were late, we managed to see the film.
      Correct [   ] Incorrect [   ]
   3 He managed to pass his exams even though he hadn't studied.
      Correct [   ] Incorrect [   ]
   4 Even though she went to bed she was tired.
      Correct [   ] Incorrect [   ]
   5 Despite it was a long journey we enjoyed the trip.
      Correct [   ] Incorrect [   ]
2 Beginning with the word in **bold**, put the rest of the sentence in the right order.
   1 **Even** – she – came – minister – poor – though – from – a – family – she – became – prime.
   2 **In** – tired – of – the – time – didn't – spite – we – feel.
   3 **The** – was – rough – managed – sea – the – port – sailors – nevertheless – reach – the – to.
   4 **We** – a – raining – had – lovely – evening – fact – that – the – despite – it – was.
3 Rephrase the sentences using the words in brackets.
   1 She has lots of money but she never spends it. (despite)
   2 He refused to wear a coat. It was cold. (nevertheless)
   3 She had hurt her foot but she still won the race. (fact)
   4 He felt tired but he still drove through the night. (even)

7 Countable and uncountable nouns and their determiners

7.1 Countable nouns

A countable noun is a clearly separate unit which can be easily counted. When there is more than one, they can be made plural: _tables, chairs, students, cats, ideas, thoughts, people, children._

7.2 Uncountable nouns

Uncountable nouns are things or notions which cannot be counted (or only counted with difficulty) or abstract nouns and notions. They include liquids, mass, abstract nouns and things such as _water, oil, butter, sand, information, happiness, hair, spaghetti._

Remember:

In some languages uncountable nouns such as _hair, information, news_ and _advice_ are countable.

7.3 Determiners

Determiners are used before nouns to express quantity. Which one we choose depends on whether the noun it introduces is countable (C) or uncountable (U).
We can make uncountable nouns appear countable by putting the name of a container, a quantity/weight/its length, or _a piece of_ before it:
   A bottle of water, a jar of instant coffee, a slice of cake, a tin of soup, a packet of biscuits, 200 grams of butter, a grain of sand, a piece of information, etc.

7.4 Determiners with countable and uncountable nouns

1 We use *all*:
  a Before **plural** countable nouns [C] and uncountable nouns [U] to express the idea of 'all the ones':
    All the students left early. [C]
2 We use *every*:
  a Before **single** countable nouns and uncountable nouns to express the idea of 'every one' (we drop the use of *a/the*):
    Every student left early. [C]
3 We use *some*:
  a Before plural countable nouns and uncountable nouns:
    She met some interesting people while she was on holiday. [C]
    I asked for ~~an information~~.
    I asked for some information about language courses. [U]
  b In requests and offers, particularly when we expect the answer to be 'yes':
    *Could you give me **some** advice about which wallpaper to choose?* [U]
    *Would you pass me **some** more coffee, please?* [U]
4 We use *any*
  a Before plural countable nouns and uncountable nouns to express the idea of 'all or nothing':
    Any child can use this computer programme. = all children. [C]
    You can come and see me any time. = there is no limit. [U]
    Oh dear, there isn't any sugar left. = none at all. [U]

Remember:
i) We place *not* **before** *any* to express the idea of *no*.
We use *not any/no* before plural countable nouns and uncountable nouns:
There weren't any students in the classroom/There were no students in the classroom. [C]

ii) We place *hardly* **before** *any* to express the idea of 'not a lot':
*There were **hardly any** customers in the shop.* [C]

iii) We place *have* **before** *any* to ask about the existence or availability of something:
*Do we **have any** milk?* [U]

iv) *Some/any/no + one/body/where/thing*:
Add *some/any/no* **before** *one/body/where/thing* to create indefinite pronouns.
These follow the same rules of form as *some* and *any*:
There is someone outside.
Really! I can't see anyone/anybody.
There was nowhere to park.
We couldn't find anywhere to park.

Complete the sentences with *a*, *some* or *any*.
1 Would you like _____ cup of tea and _____ biscuit, or perhaps _____ piece of cake?
2 You don't need to ask, you can sit _____ where you want.
3 We've got _____ eggs and _____ cheese, but we don't seem to have _____ milk.
4 Could I have _____ more tea, please, and is there _____ more cake?
5 Ring me _____ time you need _____ advice, here's _____ card with my number.
6 I can't get _____ reply, there isn't _____ one there after five o'clock.
7 Oh dear, there aren't _____ rubbish-bags, can you get _____ more the next time you go shopping.
8 She won't do _____ thing without first checking with her boss.
9 Do you fancy _____ coffee? There's _____ new jar in the cupboard.
10 There isn't _____ thing _____ one can say or do – it's hopeless!

4 *Much* and *many*; *a lot of* and *lots of*:
  a We use *many* with countable nouns, and *much* with uncountable nouns:
    Many students leave their revision to the last minute.
    The changes to the exam have encouraged much discussion.
  b However, *a lot of/lots of* are used with both countable and uncountable nouns. We tend to use them instead of *much* and *many* in positive statements:
    ***A lot of/lots of** students use bi-lingual dictionaries.*
    *Harry wasted **a lot of/lots of** time trying to mend the Play Station.*

Remember:
i) *Lots of, loads of, plenty of* are considered to be less formal than *a lot of*:
*Don't worry about me, I've got **lots/loads/plenty** of friends.*
ii) *Much* and *many* are generally reserved for negative statements and questions:
*How **much** time do we have before we need to leave?*
*We don't have **much** money left.*
*How **many** people have you invited?*
*We weren't expecting so **many** people at the open day.*

5 *Few* and *a few/little* and *a little*

We use *few/a few* with countable nouns and *little/a little* with uncountable nouns. *A few* and *a little* mean 'some', while *few* and *little* mean 'not much/many', or 'less than normal or what we would usually expect:*

A few (= *some*) students know how to pronounce 'th' properly.

Few (= *not very many*) students carry on to take the Proficiency exam.

There's a little *(= some)* bit of coffee left, who would like to finish it?

There's little (= *not much*) point in trying to learn anything now.

6 *Several*

Several is used with countable plural nouns. It has a similar meaning to *a few* (i.e. three or four):

There were several people waiting in the doctor's surgery.

7 *A great (large) number (amount) of/great (good) deal of*

a We use *a great/large number of* with plural countable nouns:

A great number of tourists were affected by the strike.
Not: *A great deal of tourists*...

b We use *a great/good deal of* with uncountable nouns to mean 'many' or 'much':

The strike caused a great deal of inconvenience.
Not: *The strike caused a large number of inconvenience.*

Choose the correct word to complete the sentences

1 How *many/much* butter and how *many/much* raisins do we need for this recipe?
2 It doesn't matter how *much/many* times you tell her, she never remembers.
3 Her ex-boyfriend is giving her a great *number/deal* of trouble.
4 There's *little/a little* advantage in changing Internet service providers.
5 The police found the fingerprints of *few/several* different suspects.
6 Were there *much/lots* of people at the procession on Sunday?
7 Not really, there weren't *much/many* at all. Just *a few/few* regulars.
8 She's lucky she has got *a lots of/loads* of money and a big house.
9 She has got very *little/few* friends, she stays in her room watching TV all day.
10 Our advertisement received a great *deal/number* of replies.
11 There doesn't seem to be *many/much* choice, let's try the other place.
12 I called him *loads/several* of times but only got his answering machine.

8 Future

There are different ways of expressing the future. The form we use depends on the circumstances and how we view the future event.

1 We use the **present continuous** to talk about future personal arrangements and plans, especially when we mention the time and place:

We're leaving for Athens on Saturday.

2 We use the **present simple** when we refer to timetables or programmes:

The next train to Brusssels departs in fifteen minutes.

3 We use **be going to**:

a to talk about things we have already decided to do.

I'm going to take part in the Erasmus programme next year.

b to make predictions based on what we can see right now.

Oh my goodness, look at that child. She's going to fall off her bike and hurt herself.

8.1 The future simple (*will*)

We use *will* (the future simple):

1 For facts and predictions:

Anika will be three years old on Friday.
Next season will be a good one for our team's supporters.

2 For decisions made at the time of speaking.

Don't take the bus, I'll drive you home.

3 To predict what is about to happen, or has just happened.

There's someone at the door.
That will be the post woman (she always comes at this time).
You're right, she's carrying a parcel.
That will be the books I ordered. (They always come by mail and I ordered them last week.)

Remember:

We can also use *should* to make predictions based on experience and expected behaviour.

What time do we get to Amersham?
Well, we should be there at six o'clock (that's the time the train usually arrives there).

8.2 Future continuous

We use the future continuous (*will be + -ing*) to talk about actions which will be in progress at a time in the future.

A: *Hi, Jen, it's me. Just to say I'll be arriving at 17.15. Can you pick me up?*
B: *Sure, I'll be waiting outside the station.*

8.3 Future perfect

We use the future perfect to express the idea that something will happen before a specific time in the future:

We'll have taken our exam by July.
Don't worry about us, we'll have already eaten.

8.4 Future perfect continuous

We use the future perfect continuous to describe activities which began before a point in the future and which are still in progress at that point in time:

> *By next September, she'll have been studying German for two years.*
> *In six months' time we'll have been living in this house for ten years.*

8.5 *Was going to* (the future in the past)

1 *Was going to* is used talk about something that, in the past, was thought would happen in the future:

> *Don't blame me, I didn't know he was going to react so badly to to the news.*
> *We were going to go camping, but then it rained so we decided against it.*

2 *To be* + infinitive
We use the verb ***to be* + infinitive** to make announcements:

> *The student exchange programme is to begin in the autumn.*

8.6 Adjectives with a future meaning

Bound/likely due + infinitive are adjectives with an implicit future meaning.

1 We use *bound to* when we are sure that a future event will happen:

> *The plane is bound to land late because of the fog.*

2 We use *likely to* when we think it is highly probable that something will happen:

> *She is likely to be disappointed with her results.*

3 We use *due to* when something which has been planned is expected to happen:

> *The reception is due to begin at six o'clock this evening.*

1 Read the situations carefully and complete the sentences with ***will*** or ***going to***.

1 You look nice, what's the special occasion?
   Thanks. I _____ (visit) my boyfriend's parents.
2 Come back to my place for dinner.
   That's kind, I _____ (bring) some wine.
3 Have you made up your mind about your studies next year?
   Yes, I've finally decided. I _____ (study) hotel management.
4 I'm in the bath! Can you pick up the phone?
   Sure, I _____ (answer) it.
5 Have you heard? Max Bremner _____ (play) for Chelsea next season.
6 Is that the time! Where can I get a taxi?
   Don't worry. I _____ (give you) a lift.

2 Complete the conversation by choosing between the words in ***italics***.
Jenny: (1) ***Are you doing/Do you do*** anything nice next weekend?
Katie: Yes, actually, (2) ***I'm going/I go*** to Bordeaux with Vincent.

Jenny: Lucky you! How (3) ***are you getting/do you get*** there?
Katie: Well, we (4) ***will take/are going to take*** the plane. There's a flight that (5) ***leaves/will leave*** at eight. It (6) ***is taking/is going to take*** just over an hour.
Jenny: Marvellous. Who (7) ***looks after/is going to look after*** your dog, Toffee?
Katie: Now there's a problem, Maryse (8) ***was going to/would*** look after the dog but now she says she can't.
Jenny: Don't worry, (9) ***I'll/going to*** take care of her if you like. When (10) ***will you come/are you coming*** back?
Katie: We (11) ***should/due*** be back on Sunday evening, by nine o'clock. I (12) ***am going to/will*** pick her up then.
Jenny: No, don't bother. You (13) ***are feeling/are going to be*** tired after your trip. (14) ***I'll drop/I'm going to drop*** her off at your place on my way to work.
Katie: That's really kind, (15) ***I'm waiting/I'll be waiting*** for you outside. I will ***have taken/be taking*** her for a walk before you pick her up.

9 Gerund and infinitive

9.1 The gerund

The gerund is the noun form of the verb. We form it by adding *-ing* to the verb. Be careful not to confuse the gerund with the present participle:

> ***Smoking*** *is bad for you* = gerund.
> *He is **smoking** his pipe* = present participle.

We use the gerund:

1 After verbs such as *involve, avoid, consider, mind* and *risk*:

> *Do you **mind telling** me what you are doing in my room?*

2 After many verbs which express likes and dislikes, such as *hate, love, loathe, enjoy*:

> *I **love cooking** but I **loathe doing** the washing up.*

3 As a subject or object:

> ***Eating*** *is not permitted on the premises.*

4 After prepositions, phrasal verbs and expressions ending in a preposition:

> *He burned the letter **after reading** it.*
> *She **took up studying** Ancient Greek in her spare time.*
> *I'm **tired of listening** to your excuses.*

Remember:

i) *Despite,* and *in spite of* are prepositions/prepositional phrases. As such they are followed by the gerund or another noun:

> *She played tennis **despite feeling** tired.*
> *She played tennis **despite her tiredness**.*

Form: *used to + doing /look forward to + doing*

ii) Although *to* is part of the 'full infinitive', it can also be a preposition and be followed by the gerund:

> *I'm used to ~~get up~~ **getting up** early in the morning.*
> (*used to* = adjective made from the past participle.)
> *I'm looking forward to ~~see~~ **seeing** the latest film with Julia Roberts.*

iii) We can follow *need* with the gerund to lend it a passive sense:

> *These windows need cleaning = Someone needs to clean these windows.*

9.2 The infinitive

1 We use the bare infinitive (infinitive without *to*):
   a After modal verbs:
     We should listen to what she says.
   b After *make* and *let*:
     *They **made me wear** school uniform.*
     *They wouldn't **let me play.***
2 We use the full infinitive (with *to*):
   a To express a reason or purpose:
     *He enrolled in evening classes **to improve** his German
     (to achieve an outcome).*
     *She took off her shoes **so as not to** wake up the baby
     (to avoid an outcome).*
   b After certain verbs such as *appear, manage, seem, want,
     would like,* and *prefer.*
   c With the 'lexical future': *intend, plan, decide:*
     We intend, plan, decide to stay there for three nights.
   d With some verbs which have two objects: *encourage,
     request, advise, recommend, tell,* and *ask:*
     *His mother **encouraged** him **to apply** for the course.*

9.3 Gerund or infinitive

Some verbs take both the infinitive or the gerund with little
change in meaning e.g. *like, try.* Others have an important
change in meaning e.g. *stop, remember,* and *hate.*
1 A small change in meaning:
   *I **like to go** to the dentist every six months. (It's a
   habit.)*
   *I **like going** for long country walks. (It gives me
   pleasure.)*
   *I **tried to open** the door. (This was my aim.)*
   *I **tried turning** the key in the lock and **pushing** it. (This
   is how I tried to do it.)*
2 An important change in meaning:
   *We **stopped to look** at the map. (We stopped in order to
   look at the map.)*
   *We **stopped looking** at the map and continued our
   journey. (We finished studying the map, afterwards, we
   continued.)*
   *I **remembered to pay** the bill. (I remembered I had to
   pay it, so I did.)*
   *I **remembered leaving** my bag on the bus. (I left my bag
   on the bus, later on I remembered.)*
   *We **hated telling** him the awful news. (We told him even
   though it was a painful and difficult task.)*
   *I **hate to tell** you this. (I am about to tell you
   something you won't like.)*
   *I **meant** to post the letter but I forgot. (I intended to
   post the letter.)*
   *When we discovered the problem **it meant starting** from
   the beginning. (It involved starting from the beginning.)*

1 Choose the correct form to complete the sentence.
   1 We tried **to open/opening** the door but it was locked
     from the other side.
   2 I didn't enjoy **to play/playing** rugby when I was at
     school.
   3 I hate **to tell/telling** you this but smoke is coming out
     of the engine.

4 Would you mind **to check/checking** this form I have
   filled in?
5 Are you looking forward **to go/going** to college next
   year?
6 I know it's difficult, but have you tried **to tell/telling**
   her the truth?
7 Mildred likes **to keep/keeping** empty egg-boxes, it's a
   strange habit of hers.
8 The child stopped **to cry/crying** when we gave him an
   ice-cream.
9 Greg keeps on **to phone/phoning** Sarah – it's really
   annoying.
10 Did you remember **to post/posting** that letter I gave you
   this morning?
11 Would you like to **come round/coming round** for dinner
   tonight?
12 That's not true, I don't remember **to say/saying** that!
13 She didn't mean **to upset/upsetting** him by what she
   said.
14 They were tired after **to climb/climbing** the hill, so they
   stopped **to have/having** a rest.
15 Could you remind me **to take/taking** the car to the
   garage?
16 We got so lost, it meant **to go back/going** back the way
   we had come.

2 Complete the second sentence so that it has a similar
  meaning to the one above. Use the 'key word' in capital
  letters.

   1 I forgot to take my passport. **REMEMBER**
     I _____.
   2 Remind me to record that programme. **FORGET**
     Don't let _____.
   3 I can't wait to go to Canada next summer. **FORWARD**
     I'm _____ next summer.
   4 Do you think you could close the window, please? **MIND**
     Would _____?
   5 He was overweight so he went on a diet. **ORDER**
     He went on a diet _____ weight.
   6 How about going to a restaurant tonight? **LIKE**
     Would _____ to a restaurant tonight?
   7 Even though he didn't have a ticket he travelled to
     Athens to watch the match. **SPITE**
     He travelled to Athens to see the match
     _____ a ticket.

10 Inversion

Sometimes, we may invert the verb and subject of a phrase.
1 Inversion is used with *so* and *neither* in short answers to
  agree with something someone has just said.
     A: *I really enjoyed the play.*
     B: *So did I.* Not: ~~So I did.~~

Notice: you use *so* for answering a positive structure.
   I don't have any money left/I haven't got any money left.
   Neither do I or *I don't either.*
   Neither have I or *I haven't either.*

You use *neither* to provide a short answer with a negative
structure.

2 Inversion is used with adverbs of negative force to express surprise or emphasis. This use is common in more formal or literary writing:

Not only did they steal the kitchen equipment but also the food from the fridge/the food from the fridge too.
Hardly had I opened the door than I noticed a strange smell.
No sooner had they left the flat than Mary rang to say she couldn't come.
Never/Rarely/Seldom had we witnessed such a terrible scene.

3 With the third conditional:

If we had known about his past, we wouldn't have gone to the police.
Had we known about his past, we wouldn't have gone to the police.

1 Match the statements with short replies which agree with what has been said.

1 I laughed all the way through the film ____.	a Neither can I ____.
2 We don't often eat out ____.	b So are we ____.
3 I am going to Italy this summer ____.	c I did too ____.
4 We didn't mean to upset her ____.	d So had we ____.
5 I can't ski very well ____.	e We didn't either ____.
6 They had planned to leave after lunch ____.	f Neither do we ____.

2 Beginning with the word in brackets, rephrase the sentences.

1 The moment he finished one job his boss gave him another. (Hardly)
2 The second I got the exam results I phoned my parents. (No)
3 I have never seen such an untidy bedroom! (Never)
4 She speaks Italian, Chinese and Japanese too. (Not)
5 I would have told him if I'd seen him. (Had)

11 Modals

Modal auxiliary verbs such as *can*, *must*, and *will* allow us to express concepts such as 'ability' and 'obligation'. We also use them to allow us to perform a wide range of functional tasks, such as making requests or speculating. The context in which modal verbs appear is important as each modal has a number of different uses.

Some modals **do not** have a future or past form.

We can't use two modals together.

11.1 *Can* (infinitive *to be able*)

We use *can*:
1 To talk about abilities:
   She can skate beautifully.
2 To ask for permission:
   Can I borrow your dictionary?
3 For requests:
   Can you lend me £10?

11.2 *Could*

As well as being the past form of *can* we use *could*
1 To discuss alternatives and options:
   We could invite everyone to a restaurant, or else we could have a picnic on the beach.
2 To make more polite requests:
   Could you bring me the bill, please?
   Could you speak a little more slowly, please?
3 for speculating, guessing and discussing possibilities:
   The weather could be better tomorrow (it's possible.)
4 *Could* or *was able to*:
   We use *could* to talk about general past abilities.
   He could run for miles and miles when he was younger.

   However, if we want to say we succeeded in doing something on a particular occasion, or after a lot of difficulty we use *be able to*:
   I drove around for forty minutes, finally I was able to find somewhere to park.

11.3 *Must*

We use *must*:
1 For orders we give to ourselves:
   I must pay the phone bill, otherwise they will cut me off.
2 To prohibit something (used in mainly written rules and regulations):
   You mustn't speak on your mobile while you're driving.

3 For a strong recommendation:
   You must see the new James Bond film, it's wonderful.
4 For making intelligent guesses and deductions:
   She must be Melanie's twin sister. They are almost identical.
5 For deductions in the past we use *must have been/can't have been*:
   He must have been disappointed not to pass. His teacher can't have been pleased either.

For negative deductions we use *can't be*, not ~~*mustn't be*~~.
My parents want me to revise all weekend – they can't be serious! (Not: ~~They mustn't be serious.~~)

11.4 *Have to*

We use *have to*:
1 To talk about our duties or obligations:
   I have to deal with phone calls and enquiries and give advice to students.
2 To show that something isn't obligatory or necessary:
   You don't have to bring a dictionary to school, we have one in every classroom.

11.5 *May*

We use *may*:
1 To talk about possibility:
   It may rain this afternoon.
2 To ask for permission:
   May I use your phone?

Remember:
May I is generally considered more polite than *Can I*.

11.6 *Might*

We use *might*:
1 To express a more remote possibility than *may*, and to speculate:
   It might be difficult to get a baby-sitter.
2 As a very polite or formal way of asking for permission, or making a request:
   Might I say something here?
   Might I borrow your phone book for a minute?

11.7 *Will*

We use *will*:
1 For making predictions and talking about the future. (See Section 8 **Future** for more information.):
2 When we make offers or decisions as we speak:
   Leave the washing up, I'll do it later.
   Q: *Can someone answer the door?*
   A: *I'll go.*
3 To talk about habitual actions:
   Most days, I'll normally take the 7:42 train to Marylebone.
4 To make requests or give orders:
   Will you drop me off in front of the bus station, please?

Remember:
Shall can sometimes be used instead of *will*.
In formal, or more old-fashioned English, when the subject of the modal is *I* or *we*, we can use *shall*, although this is quite rare.
   I shall give you my decision in the morning.
Shall is more commonly used with *I* and *we* for offers, or to ask for suggestions.
   Shall I answer the phone?
   What shall we do tonight?
   Shall we go to the cinema?

11.8 *Would*

We use *would*:
1 To make polite requests:
   Would you look after my bag for a few minutes?
2 In conditional sentences. (See Section 6 **Conditionals**.):
3 In reported speech as the reported form of *will*:
   He said he would help me, but he didn't.
4 To talk about past habits:
   When we were young we would sit on that old bench near the entrance to the park. (See Section 15 **Will, would and *used to*** for more information.)

11.9 *Should* and *ought to*

We use *should* and *ought to*:
1 To give advice
   You should/ought to be more careful about what you say in front of her, she repeats everything.
2 To say what we think is morally right:
   Rich countries should help developing countries.
3 To criticise a past action:
   You should have made sure that the tickets were in the bag.
   You shouldn't have been so greedy.
   We tend not to use *oughtn't to/oughtn't to have* as it is too hard to say.
4 To make predictions based on previous experience, or what is expected:
   Don't panic, there should be another bus in a couple of minutes.

11.10 *Need*

1 We use *need* to say when something is necessary or unnecessary:
   We need to enrol everyone for the exam before the deadline.
2 We use *needn't/don't need* to say that something is not necessary:
   You needn't buy/don't need to buy uniforms and equipment, everything is included in the fees.

1 Choose the correct modal verb.
   1 According to the law, you **have to/must** pay your taxes by January 1st.
   2 You **needn't have bought/didn't need to buy** this. We already have one. Take it back.
   3 A: I need someone to help me with this.
      B: I have nothing to do. I **'ll/'d** help you.
   4 They **must/might** be late. Julie rang earlier and said it's possible because Ray has to work late.
   5 A: What **shall/will** we do tonight?
      B: We could go to the cinema.
      A: Good idea.
   6 You **would/ought to** invite them too or they'll be insulted.
   7 **Are you able to/could you** give me the bill, please?

2 Rewrite the first sentence using the words in the second sentence.
   1 **Do you** always say the first thing that pops into your head?

   _____ you think before you speak?
   2 You **should go** tonight.
      You _____ to go tonight.
   3 Your father **must have** been angry about your exam results.
      Your father _____ happy about your exam results.
   4 We were **able to** find somewhere to park.
      We _____ find a place to park.
   5 There's no **need to** help.
      You don't _____ to help.
   6 **Maybe** they left earlier.
      They might _____ .

12 Narrative tenses

12.1 Past tenses

1 Past simple
   We use the past simple:
   a To talk about single past actions or a clear sequence of past actions.

   b To talk about past states:
      I taught in that school for thirteen years.
2 Past continuous
   We use the past continuous:
   a To describe past actions which were in progress at a given time or period in the past.
   b At the beginning of a narrative we use the past continuous to set the scene:
      The lawyers were looking through their papers preparing their arguments for the trial to come. The defendant's wife was anxiously twisting a handkerchief between her fingers.
   c To show an action was in progress when another action took place:
      We were watching TV when we heard a loud bang from the street below.
   d To show that different actions were in progress at the same time:
      While we were lying on the beach someone was going through our things in the hotel room.

3 Past perfect
   We use the past perfect to show that an action happened earlier than a later action:
      By the time we got there, the film had already started.

4 Past perfect continuous
   We use the past perfect continuous:
   a To show that an action had started and was still in progress when another action took place:
      We had been standing there for ages when the night bus finally turned up.
   b To describe repeated actions up to a point in the past:
      I had been ringing her all morning but I couldn't get a reply.

Complete the story by changing the verbs in brackets into a suitable narrative tense.

A few months (1) _____ (go by) since the disaster at the beach so Olivier (2) _____ (decide) to try his luck with Isabelle again. He (3) _____ (try) to ring her, but each time she (4) _____ (hear) his voice she (5) _____ (hang up). This time; however, Olivier (6) _____ (have) a secret weapon! He (7) _____ (receive) an invitation to a smart party in a country château, and many stars (8) _____ (going to) be there. Isabelle (9) _____ (not able) to resist. This time Olivier (10) _____ (borrow) his mother's new BMW Isabelle (11) _____ (wear) a silk evening dress and pearls – she (12) _____ (never look) so wonderful.They (13) _____ (drive) through the forest to the château, when suddenly a wild boar (14) _____ (appear). Olivier (15) _____ (can not) avoid it and the car (16) _____ (go into) it with a tremendous bang – killing the creature! Fortunately the boar (17) _____ (not do) too much damage, but Olivier (18) _____ (know) his mother would never believe what (19) _____ (happen) without seeing the evidence. With Isabelle's help, they (20) _____ (push) it into the back. Unfortunately while they (21) _____ (do) this, Isabelle's necklace (22) _____ (break) so they (23) _____ (have to) spend ten minutes picking up the pearls. Once they (24) _____ (finish) they (25) _____ (be) were ready to continue on their journey when they (26) _____ (hear) a loud cry from the back – the boar (27) _____ (wake up)! They (28) _____ (jump) out of the car and (29) _____ (watch) in horror as the angry creature (30) _____ (destroy) the interior. When the police (31) _____ (arrive) they (32) _____ (have to) fire fifty shots into the car to kill it. Needless to say, they never (33) _____ (go) to the party!

12.2 Passive voice

The active voice emphasises the actions performed by people or things. The passive voice focuses on what happens to people or things as the result of the actions they experience.

Active:
  Debbie ate all the cakes. = we are more interested in what Debbie did.

Passive:
  All the cakes were eaten by Debbie. = we are more interested in the cakes and what happened to them.

In the first sentence, Debbie is the subject of the sentence and the cakes the object. In the second sentence, the cakes are the subject and Debbie the agent (i.e. the performer of the action); there is no object.

We use the passive:

1 When the agent (the person who performed the action) is assumed, unimportant, or unknown:
  *The poor old gentleman **was taken** directly to hospital* (probably by ambulance, but this isn't important.)
  *My bag **has been** stolen* (by an unknown person.)
2 When the action, event, and process is seen as more important than the agent. This is often the case in formal or scientific writing:
  *The formula **was checked** carefully.*
3 To put new information later in the sentence:
  *Pride and Prejudice **was written** by Jane Austen.*

Remember:
The passive voice is *not* a tense.
It **always** includes a form of the verb 'to be' and a past participle. The main changes are:

Present simple: *She eats the cake/s.*
  The cake/s is/are eaten.
Present continuous: *She is eating the cake/s.*
  The cake/s is/are being eaten.
Simple past: *She ate the cake/s.*
  The cake/s was/were eaten.
Past continuous: *She was eating the cake/s.*
  The cake/s was/were being eaten.
Present perfect: *She has eaten the cake/s.*
  The cake/s has/have been eaten.
Past perfect: *She had eaten the cake/s.*
  The cake/s had been eaten.
***Going to** future:* *She is going to eat the cake/s.*
  The cake/s is/are going to be eaten.
Modals in present: *She can/should/will eat the cakes.*
  The cake/s can/should/will be eaten.
Future perfect: *She will have eaten the cake/s.*
  The cake/s will have been eaten.

4 The causative *have* (*have something done*)
  We use *the causative have*
  a To talk about services others perform for us:
    She had her teeth whitened by a famous dentist.
  Form: *have + something + past participle*
    She didn't whiten them herself, the dentist did it for her.
  b To describe unfortunate incidents and accidents:
    She had her handbag stolen from under the seat in the cinema.

Remember:
The present and past perfect continuous do not have a passive form (except for rare examples).

5. Intransitive verbs do not have a passive form
   a *Get*
   Get can be used in a similar way to *the causative have*:
   We got (had) our car repaired at that garage.
   Get is also used with adjectives like *married* and *hurt*:
   Luckily nobody got hurt in the crash.
   Get also has a passive sense:
   I thought we had bought too much food, but in the end all of it got eaten.

> **Remember:**
>
> *Let* does not have a passive form. We use *allowed to* in the passive:
> *She doesn't **let** us talk on the phone. We **aren't allowed** to talk on the phone.*

   b *Need*
   Need can be used with a passive sense.
   We use need when something has to be done without saying who should do it:
   We need to freeze the vegetables (active sense.)
   The vegetables need freezing (passive sense – gerund.)
   The vegetables need to be frozen (passive infinitive.)

6. Passive with *say, know* and *believe*
   We use reporting verbs such as *say, know* and *believe* in the passive when we want to report widely-held views, or opinions which are common knowledge. It is also used to distance the speaker from the information, which is why it is commonly used in news broadcasts:
   *The victim **was known to have** a large number of enemies in the underworld.*
   *Chinese silk **is said to be** the best in the world.*
   *He **was believed to have** a fortune in gold hidden in his house.*

7. Agent or instrument?
   With an instrument we use *with* rather than *by*:
   The cakes were eaten by Debbie. by = the agent.
   They broke into his desk with/by means of a paper knife. with = the instrument.

Continue the second sentence so that it has a similar meaning to the one above it.

1. Architects have turned the building into luxury apartments.
   The building _____ by architects.
2. The mayor is going to open the new leisure centre.
   The new leisure centre _____ the mayor.
3. Someone should show Sally what to do.
   Sally should _____ what to do.
4. A journalist was writing the story as we waited.
   The story _____ as we waited.
5. A photographer is going to take my photograph tomorrow.
   Tomorrow, I'm _____.
6. We need to hide Melanie's present before she sees it.
   Melanie's present needs to _____.
7. Thieves broke into their apartment while they were on holiday.
   They had their _____ while they were on holiday.

8. We used a large screwdriver to open the car window.
   The car window _____ large screwdriver.
9. A lot of people say *Le Cheval Blanc* is the best restaurant in the region.
   Le Cheval Blanc is _____ in the region.
10. His parents didn't let him watch the match.
    He wasn't _____ watch the match.

12.3 Phrasal verbs

Phrasal verbs consist of the verb and one or two prepositional or adverbial particles. When combined in this way their meaning can be idiomatic.

Compare:
   *He **turned up** the street* (this just tells us where he turned, he could have turned down the street).
   *He **turned up** three hours late* (= He arrived three hours late. Here *up* is part of the phrasal verb *turn up*, meaning to arrive).

There are four principal types of phrasal verb. To fully appreciate the differences, we need to understand the differences between transitive and intransitive verbs (see Section 17).

Type 1: intransitive no object e.g. *get on; to progress/ have a relationship:*
   How are you getting on?
Intransitive phrasal verbs do not have an object. We can follow them with an adverbial or prepositional phrase:
   How are you getting on with your new flatmate?

Type 2: transitive separable e.g. *let down*:
Transitive separable phrasal verbs have to take an object. If an object pronoun is used it **must** come between the verb and the particle. The pronoun can't come after the particle:
   He let Sally/her down.
   (Not: *He let down Sally/her.*)

Type 3: transitive inseparable e.g. *break into*:
The direct object and object pronoun cannot come between the verb and the particle. They must always follow the particle:
   They broke into my flat while I was on holiday.
   (Not: *They broke my flat into while I was on holiday.*)

Type 4: three-part transitive (phrasal prepositional) e.g. *look forward to*:
Here, the object always comes after the phrasal verb. Three part phrasal verbs are always inseparable:
   I'm really looking forward to seeing Ian again.
   (Not: *I'm looking forward really to seeing Ian again.*)

> **Remember:**
>
> The same phrasal verb can have a different meaning and a different grammar.
>   *She turned up late* = She arrived late. (Type 1 intransitive.)
>   *His trousers were too long so he turned them up.* = He altered the trousers. (Type 2 transitive separable.)

Decide if these sentences with phrasal verbs are correct or incorrect.

1 She finally found out the truth about her real parents.
Correct Incorrect

2 We got into the car and set off.
Correct Incorrect

3 She can't turn up it at this time, class starts at half past eight.
Correct Incorrect

4 Cigarettes were given up as a New Year's resolution.
Correct Incorrect

5 Can you look after while I go to the shops?
Correct Incorrect

6 I have always looked up to my father.
Correct Incorrect

7 Don't worry about the lights, I switched off them before we left.
Correct Incorrect

8 Guess what! I bumped her mother into at the supermarket.
Correct Incorrect

9 Sorry I am late, the bus had been broken down.
Correct Incorrect

10 They are really looking their holiday forward to.
Correct Incorrect

11 My car was broken into while I was at the cinema.
Correct Incorrect

12 Her illness was got over in five days.
Correct Incorrect

12.4 Present tenses

1 Present simple
We use the present simple:
a To talk about facts, routines and with adverbs of frequency:
> *She comes from the north of Brazil.*
> *I go to English classes three times a week.*
> *We usually order a pizza on Friday nights.*
> *They often take on extra staff at Christmas.*
b with verbs which deal with:
> likes and dislikes: *like, love, prefer, hate, detest, dislike*
> - which deal with states: *be, seem, looks*
> - with verbs of cognition: *think, know, understand, believe, remember, mean*
> - with verbs of perception: *see, taste, hear, smell*
> - with verbs of possession: *own, belong*
> - other verbs: *need, want, cost.*

Remember:
Some of these verbs can also be dynamic, with a change in meaning:
> To be (stative) = natural state.
> To be (active) = to act/behave.
Dynamic verbs can be used in the present continuous to show the temporary nature of the action:
> *What do you think about global warning? What's your general opinion* (stative sense.)
> *Is everything OK? What are you thinking about?* (right now – dynamic sense).
> *She is lazy* (it is her natural state).
> *She is being lazy* (at the moment).
> *She is smelling the flowers. The flowers smell nice. The flowers ~~are smelling nice.~~*
> *She is tasting the soup. The soup tastes good. The soup ~~is tasting good.~~*

2 Present continuous
We use the present continuous:
a To talk about activities which are in progress:
> Q: *Hey, what are you doing in my room?*
> A: *I'm looking for the CD I lent you.*
b To talk about ongoing activities. In other words, activities that began in the past, are going on now and into the future:
> *Justine studies at Bordeaux University; at the moment she is spending a term in Oxford.*
c To talk about trends or a changing situation:
> *Unemployment is still going up by 1% a month.*
d To express a future meaning (See Section 8 **Future**):
e With *always* to add expression:
> *She's always taking my things.* (to express annoyance):

3 Present perfect simple
We use the present perfect simple:
a To talk about something which started in the past and continues into the present:
> *We have lived in this house for thirty years.*
b To talk about past events when no specific time is given or suggested:
> *Have you ever eaten oysters?*
> *Mandy has been to Argentina.*
c To talk about recent events where the result is still visible:
> *Your sitting room looks different. Have you painted it?*
d With adverbs such as *yet, just* and *already* (especially in British English):
> *Have you written your composition yet?*
e To talk about quantities, a number of repeated, completed actions:
> *She has done more than fifty parachute jumps.*

4 Present perfect continuous
We use the present perfect continuous:
a To talk about continuous activities which started in the past and continue into the present (with an emphasis placed on the duration of the activity):
> *Your father has been working in the garden since eight o'clock this morning.*
b To talk about repeated actions up to the present:
> *I've been trying to call the box-office all day, but I just can't get through.*

c To emphasise an activity rather than a quantity/result:
   She has been writing short stories for ten years
   (activity), *she has written more than fifty* (result).
d To talk about a recent activity where a result is still
   visible:
      Q: *Why are you all red?*
      A: *I've been sunbathing.*

Remember:

Rather is not a verb. Not: ~~I rather the cinema than the
theatre~~ but *I prefer the cinema to the theatre.* = *I'd (would)
rather go to the theatre than the cinema.*
If we want to include a noun or pronoun within the
sentence then we have to use the simple past:
   I'd rather go to the cinema.
   I'd rather we went to the cinema. (See **Time**).

Choose the correct form.
1 They regularly **leave/are leaving** this early in the
   morning.
2 A: Where is she? We need to go.
   B: She **be/is being** difficult. She won't come out of her
   room.
3 A: What **do you do/are you doing** here?
   B: I work in the production department.
4 The price of oil **actually falls/is actually falling** around
   the world at the moment.
5 A: How's the cheese?
   B: It **tastes/is tasting** good!
6 They **are working/have worked** here for over ten years.
7 She's **been revising/revised** for over three hours. It's
   time she took a break.
8 The phone **hasn't stopped/been stopping** ringing
   all day.
9 This room looks nice. Have you **redecorated/been
   redecorating** it?
10 This room is looking nice. How long have you **painted/
   been painting** it?

13 Relative clauses

Relative clauses give us more information about the subject
or object of a sentence. They link two ideas within the same
sentence and can be defining, or non-defining.

13.1 Defining relative clauses

1 Use defining relative clauses to complete sentences with
   essential information.
   Defining relative clauses often begin with the pronouns:
   Who/that ➔ for people
      There's the man who/that helped me.
   Which/that ➔ for objects and animals
      This is the computer that/which broke down.
   Where ➔ for place
      This is the restaurant where we first met.
   Whose ➔ for possession
      That's the stupid woman whose dog bit me.
   When ➔ for time
      *Do you remember the time when Mary and Jack came to
      stay?*

Whom (In more formal written or spoken English *whom* is
used as the object pronoun)
   Here is the man whom we told you about
Why for reason
   He gave the reason why he couldn't come.

2 In writing and more formal speech we may use
prepositions with a pronoun:
   on which = when e.g. *This is the day on which we got
   married.*
   in which = where
   for which = why
   to whom = who... to

Remember:

In defining relative clauses, *who*, *which* and *that* can be left
out when they refer to the object of the verb in the relative
clause.
   Do you want to watch the DVD **(which/that)** *I got for my
   birthday?*
   The person **(who/that)** *I spoke to yesterday said it would
   be free.*
   Sam bought the jeans **(which/that)** *she'd seen last week.*

13.2 Non-defining relative clauses

Non-defining relative clauses give extra information
which is not absolutely essential for the main meaning of
the sentence. In written English we separate them from
the main clause by commas. In speech, the speaker will
generally pause an instant before continuing with the extra
information:
   *The Colossus of Rhodes, which/that stood by the harbour,
   was destroyed by an earthquake.*

Notice: We can't use *that* in non-defining relative clauses.
   *Vincent, ~~that~~ who had never eaten mangoes before,
   developed dark red patches all over his body.*

Correct the pronouns in each sentence.
1 Jurga is the man whose gave me my first job.
2 This is my lodger, that I was telling you about.
3 India, where is the place I first visited in 1980, is a
   country I'd like to return to.
4 Christmas is a time in some countries that family and
   friends get together.
5 The reason when I didn't call you was because my phone
   battery ran out of charge.
6 My only sister, that lives in Toronto, is coming to visit next
   month.
7 The church on which we got married is no longer here.
8 My car, which I left at home had a flat tire yesterday.

14 Reported speech and reporting verbs

We use reported speech to say what someone else has said.
We usually take one step further back in the past when we
report. This is called 'backshift'.
   Jenny: *I am going to see Barry* ➔ *Jenny said she was going
   to see Barry.*

Form: present continuous + past continuous

1 Use *say* and *tell* to **report statements**

    Steve: I've got a headache, Malcolm.   Steve said that he had a headache.

    Steve said to Malcolm that he had a headache.   Steve told Malcolm/him (that) he had a headache.

    Not: *Steve told to Malcolm/him that he had a headache* *Steve said Malcolm.*

    Form: verb (+ *that*) + clause

2 *Tell* is generally used to **report instructions and orders**

    Mum: Tidy up your bedroom, Felix. ➔ Felix's Mum told him to tidy up his room.

    Form: verb + object + infinitive with *to*

3 Reported questions

    a *Wh-* questions: Use *ask* and *want to know* to **report *wh-* questions**

    Katia: Where does Günther live, Rita? ➔ Katia asked (Rita) where Günther lived.

    Katia wanted to know where Günther lived. (We don't know who Katia asked.)

    Form: The *wh-* word is followed by a statement word order (subject followed by verb)

    b *Yes/No* questions: Use *if* and *whether* to report *yes/no* questions

    Katia: Do you know where Gunther lives? ➔ *Katia wanted to know if/whether we knew where Gunther lived.*

    Form: verb + *if/whether* + word order is the same as reported statements

4 Advice and suggestions.

    Terry: Let's go for a bike ride.

    Terry suggested going for a bike ride.

    Terry suggested that we go for a bike ride (less formal).

    Terry suggested our going for a bike ride (more formal).

    Terry suggested that we should go for a bike ride.

    Form: suggest + *-ing*; suggest + *that* + past simple; suggest + *that* + (*should*) + infinitive without *to*

    a *You ought to go on a diet.*

    Dr Morris advised Henry to go on a diet. (Used to advise someone to do something.)

    b *'Let's buy a drink', she said.*

    She suggested buying a drink.

    She suggested that we buy a drink.

    She suggested that we should buy a drink.

Remember:

Some reporting verbs contain the sentiment of the original statement. It is important that the correct forms and word pattern follow the reporting verbs in question.

Form: verb + *to* + infinitive (*offer, refuse, threaten, promise, agree*)

verb + object + *to* + infinitive (*convince, persuade, tell, advise, encourage, remind, warn*)

verb + gerund (*suggest, propose, recommend, deny, admit, mention*)

Cindy: I'm sorry about breaking the vase. ➔ Cindy **apologised** for breaking the vase.

Paul: Don't touch that switch, Ben. ➔ Paul **warned** Ben not to touch the switch.

Steffi: Don't forget to keep the receipt, Martyn.   Steffi **reminded** Martyn to keep the receipt.

Rees: I think you should see a doctor, Milton.   Rees **advised/encouraged** Milton to see a doctor

Katie: You must go and see Borat, it's hilarious.

    Katie **recommended** seeing Borat.

or   Katie **recommended** that we see Borat.

John: You were stupid to leave your car unlocked, Martha.

John **criticised** Martha for leaving her car unlocked.

5 Changes to place and time

Remember that using reported speech may involve making changes to references to place and time.

    Now ➔ then

    Today ➔ that day

    Before ➔ earlier

    The day before yesterday ➔ two days earlier

    This evening ➔ that evening

    Last night ➔ the previous night/the night before

    The next day ➔ the following day

1 Correct the sentences.

  1 Paul said me to call this number.

  2 Melinda told she felt tired.

  3 Marissa told to Kevin to be careful.

  4 He told to me the story.

  5 She asked what time did the train leave?

  6 Howard wanted to know from where we had bought the flowers.

2 Use the reporting verb you are given to change the sentences from direct to reported speech. Make any other necessary changes to the words in **bold**.

  1 Lionel: You really should apply for the job, Romain.

    Lionel encouraged _____.

  2 Sam: I wouldn't walk round **this** part of town after dark, Derek.

    Sam warned _____.

  3 Joan: Let's visit the ruins **tomorrow**.

    Joan suggested that _____.

  4 Lori: I'm sorry I was late **the day before yesterday**, Kim.

    Lori apologised to _____.

  5 Patrick: Don't forget to collect **my** prescription from the chemist's, Charlene.

    Patrick reminded Charlene _____.

  6 Paul: I didn't call you **last night**, Sarah, because I couldn't find your new number.

    Paul explained to Sarah why _____.

  7 Doctor: You should try to go to bed earlier, Mr Rossi.

    The doctor advised _____.

  8 Penny: You shouldn't have brought the subject up, Nick.

    Penny criticised _____.

15 *Will/would* and *used to*

1 *Will* is used to talk about expected behaviour:
  The cat scratched me when I tried to pick him up.
  Ah yes, he will do that with strangers. (He has done this with other people.)

2 *Would* is used to describe past habits and repeated actions:
  When mother came home from working in the shop all day long she would sit in the armchair and put her aching legs up.
  Would **can't** be used to talk about past states:
  He ~~would be~~ fat when he was a child.

3 *Used to* is used:
  a As an auxiliary:
  Used to + base form can be used to describe both discontinued past habits and states:
    She used to be skinny when she was a teenager (= a state).
    I used to play tennis every Saturday morning (= a habit).
  Form: *used to* + base form

Remember:

If we give precise information about how long a state or habit lasted then we use the simple past.
  Not: *I used to smoke ~~for ten years~~*; but: *I smoked for ten years.*
  Q: *Do you smoke Martin?*
  A: *Not any more, but I used to.* (Notice the short reply)

  b As an adjective:
  We use '*be used to* + gerund' or '*get used to* + gerund' to express the idea of being, or becoming accustomed to/ familiar with something.
  Sally is used to getting up early. (She is accustomed to getting up early, it's not a problem for her.)
  Form: *be used to* + gerund
  When Sam went to university he missed his family a lot, but now things are better, he is getting used to living away from home. (He is developing the habit of being away from home.)
  Form: *get used to* + gerund

Complete these sentences with *will*, *would*, *was* or *used to*.

1 Nigel _____ do that when he's tired, I'm afraid.
2 We _____ always walk this way home when we were children.
3 She _____ have black hair didn't she?
4 They _____ always be late – even when they were children.

16 *So* and *such*; *too* and *enough*

1 Use *so* and *such* clauses to show a relationship of cause and effect between clauses. *So* and *such* appear in the cause clause:
  The lesson was boring.   I fell asleep at my desk.
  Cause   effect
  The lesson was so boring that I fell asleep at my desk.
  Form: *so* + adjective
  It was such a boring lesson that I fell asleep at my desk.
  Form: *such* + (adjective) + noun
  A less usual variation is:
  It was so boring a lesson that I fell asleep at my desk.
  Form: *so* + adjective + *a* (indefinite article)

2 Use *too* and *enough* to show that too much or too little of something prevented something else from happening. *Too* and *enough* provide an explanation for what happened or didn't happen:
  Julian wanted to join the army. He was only 15 years old.
  = He was too young to join the army.
  Form: *too* + adjective + infinitive
  He wasn't old enough to join the army.
  Form: *not* + adjective + *enough* + infinitive

Remember:

We put *enough* **before** nouns, but **after** adjectives.
She didn't have enough money to rent a flat.
Form: *enough* + noun
She wasn't rich enough to rent a flat.
Form: adjective + *enough*

1 Beginning with the word/s in **bold**, put the sentences into the right order.
  1 **She** – have – finish – enough – didn't – time – exam – the – to.
  2 **The film** – was – all – made – me – that – so – laugh – it – day – funny.
  3 **They** – too – holiday – children – were – poor – take – to – their – on.
  4 **He cried** – because – day – he – sad – all – so – was.
  5 **Rupert was** – such – that – a – in – mood – to – refused – bad – me – he – to – speak.
  6 **Unfortunately** – to – fit – Lucy – enough – in – wasn't – final – play – the.

2 Continue the second sentence so that it has a similar meaning to the one above.
  1 We were so tired after the journey that we went straight to bed.
    It was _____.
  2 She is too young to travel on her own.
    She isn't _____.
  3 His exam results were such a disappointment for his parents.
    His parents _____.
  4 There isn't enough space for an extra suitcase.
    The suitcase _____.

17 Transitive and intransitive verbs

17.1 Intransitive verbs

Intransitive verbs (I) only concern the subject (the person who performs the action) and the verb (the action). There is no direct object. Examples of intransitive verbs are *arrive, go, come, sleep, watch, move, vanish* and *disappear*:

The bus came.
The boat disappeared.

We can introduce another person or thing with an adverbial phrase or a prepositional phrase:

Melinda finally arrived twenty minutes late.
The boat disappeared in the storm.

Form: subject + verb

17.2 Transitive verbs

Transitive verbs (T) concern or affect another person or thing (the object) as well as the subject.

1 They cannot stand alone and must take an object.
Transitive verbs include *see, do, make,* and *own.*

I found. = incomplete.
I found her watch. = complete.

Form: subject + verb + object

2 Transitive verbs, unlike intransitive verbs can be made passive:

Her watch was found under the sofa.

3 Many transitive verbs can be used intransitively:

Q: *What did you do this morning, children?*
A: *We played.* (I)
A: *We played tennis.* (T)

Remember:
Do not confuse intransitive verbs and their transitive equivalents.
die (I) kill (T); rise (I) raise (T); vanish/disappear (I) lose (T)

Are these sentences correct or incorrect? Write I or T.
1 She slept.
2 I own.
3 We played golf.
4 We play.
5 Three hundred people died.
6 Three hundred people were died.
7 Magically, the wizard vanished.
8 What have you found?

18 *Wish*

We use *wish*:
1 To express our hopes for what we want to happen or not to happen in the future:

I wish I knew the answer. (= but I don't).

Form: subject + simple past

I wish I could speak Arabic. (= but I can't).

Form: subject + wish + *could/was able to* + infinitive (without *to*)

2 For present/future situations you would like to change we use *would*:

I wish he would stop whistling, (but I don't think he will).

Form: *wish + would* + infinitive (without *to*)

3 For regrets about things which happened entirely in the past and which we are unable to change we use *wish + past perfect*:

I wish I hadn't said anything.

Form: *wish + past perfect (had + past participle)*

Remember:
To express regrets, wishes and lost opportunities in the past we can substitute *if only* for *wish*:
If only I hadn't said anything.

Match the two halves of the sentences.

1 I wish I could ____.	a would stop interrupting.
2 I wish I was able ____.	b German
3 I wish he ____.	c to speak Chinese.
4 I wish I had visited ____.	d I spoke German and Chinese
5 I wish I spoke ____.	e speak Chinese.
6 If only ____.	f Germany last year.

19 Verb groups: irregular verbs

Irregular verbs can be organised into sub-groups which behave in a similar ways.

19.1 No pattern

Some verbs, including some of the most common, do not follow a pattern.

be	was/were	
do	did	done
eat	ate	eaten
go	went	gone/been
see	saw	seen
win	won	won

19.2 Past simple and past participle (the same)

We can make sub-groups of similar verbs.

Ending in *-ought* or *-aught*

catch	caught	caught
bring	brought	brought
buy	bought	bought
seek	sought	sought
think	thought	thought

Ending in *-eep, -ept*

keep	kept	kept
sleep	slept	slept

Ending in *t* or *d*

get	got	got/gotten (US)
learn	learnt	learnt
mean	meant	meant
meet	met	met
sit	sat	sat
find	found	found
have	had	had
hear	heard	heard
hold	held	held
make	made	made
stand	stood	stood
understand	understood	understood
lend	lent	lent
send	sent	sent
spend	spent	spent
sell	sold	sold
tell	told	told
pay	paid	paid
say	said	said

Past participle in *-en*

beat	beat	beaten
break	broke	broken
choose	chose	chosen
fall	fell	fallen
forget	forgot	forgotten
freeze	froze	frozen
give	gave	given
hide	hid	hidden
rise	rose	risen
speak	spoke	spoken
take	took	taken
write	wrote	written

19.3 Other patterns

Present and past participle the same

become	became	become
come	came	come
run	ran	run

Change from *-i* to *-a* to *-u*

begin	began	begun
ring	rang	rung
swim	swam	swum

Change from *-ear* to *-ore* to *-orn*

bear	bore	born
wear	wore	worn

Change from *-ow* or *-y* to *-ew* to *-own* or *-awn*

fly	flew	flown
grow	grew	grown
know	knew	known
draw	drew	drawn

No change

cost	cost	cost
cut	cut	cut
forecast	forecast	forecast
hit	hit	hit
put	put	put
read	read	read

Speaking Exam Files

Notes for using the speaking files:

There are three speaking files. Speaking File 1 is the same material used by candidates in the exam recording in Unit 16. Speaking Files 2 and 3 provide further opportunities to prepare for the exam.
When using the Speaking Files, work in groups of three. One student is the examiner and asks the questions provided and reads out the directions to accompany the sets of visual material. The other two students are Candidate A and Candidate B. Each candidate must answer the examiner's questions and follow the directions, referring to the visual material in the speaking file.

Speaking Exam File One

Part One

- Good morning/afternoon/evening. My name's ... and your name is?
- First of all we'd like to know something about you.
- Where are you from?
- What do you like about living in ...?
- Do you prefer spending time at home or do you like to go out in your free time?
- Do you like to do cooking in your spare time?
- What's your favourite food?
- Do you prefer to spend time on your own or with other people?
- Can you tell me about a day that you've enjoyed recently?
- Who are the most important people in your life?

Part Two

In the next part of the test, I'm going to give each of you two photographs. I'd like you to talk about your photographs on your own for a minute, and also to answer a short question about your partner's photographs. [Candidate B], it's your turn first. Here are your photographs. They show people living in different types of homes. I'd like you to compare the photographs and say why people choose to live in these types of homes.

Candidate A speaks for one minute.

- Would you like to live in either of these homes [Candidate B]?

Now here are your photographs [Candidate B]. They show people spending free time in the countryside. I'd like you to compare the photographs and say which you think is the best way to enjoy the countryside, and why.

- Thank you. Now which kind of activity would you prefer to do in the countryside, [Candidate A]?

Candidate A answers.

Part Three

Now I'd like you to talk about something together for about three minutes. I'd like you to imagine that your local town is five hundred years old, and everybody is planning events to celebrate the anniversary. First, talk to each other about how successful these suggestions might be for the events. Then decide which two might appeal to the most people within the town.

Candidates A and B speak for three minutes.

Part Four

- Do you celebrate events in your town?
- What do you think is important when choosing where you're going to live?
- As many people can work from home with computers do you think more of us will move away from cities in the future?
- Would you prefer to work from home or go out to work?

Candidate A

Why do you think people choose these types of homes?

Candidate B

Which activity is the best way to enjoy the countryside?

- How successful might these suggestions be?
- Which two will attract the most people?

Speaking Exam File Two

Part One

- Good morning/afternoon/evening. My name's ... and your name is?
- First of all we'd like to know something about you.
- Where are you from?
- What do you like about living in ...?
- How do you spend your free time?
- What sort of holidays do you and your family go on?
- Can you tell me about your best holiday ever?
- How do you find out news where you live? On TV or newspapers?
- How important is TV to you?
- Do you think Internet will replace television in the future?

Part Two

In the next part of the test, I'm going to give each of you two photographs. I'd like you to talk about your photographs on your own for a minute, and also to answer a short question about your partner's photographs. [Candidate A], it's your turn first, here are your photographs. They show people with different paintings. I'd like you to compare the photographs and say why you think visual art is important to the different groups of people.

Candidate A speaks for one minute.

- Do you think paintings are an important part of life, [Candidate B]?

Candidate B answers.

Now here are your photographs, [Candidate B]. They show people involved in two different sports. I'd like you to compare the photographs and say why you think people choose these kinds of sport.

Candidate B speaks for one minute.

- Which kind of sport would you prefer to do, [Candidate A]?

Candidate A answers.

Part Three

Now I'd like you to talk about something together for about three minutes. I'd like you to imagine that some friends of yours have recently formed a jazz group which plays music for all ages of people. They are playing at an outdoor summer event in their local village. They need an image for their posters. First, talk to each other about how successful these suggestions might be. Then decide which one would attract the most people.

Candidates A and B speak for three minutes.

Part Four

- What kind of music do you enjoy listening to?
- Do you ever attend live music where you live?
- What kinds of traditional music do people play or listen to in your country?
- As more and more music is recorded and available via the computer, do you think we will stop listening to live music in the future?

Candidate A

Why do you think paintings and visual art are important to the different groups of people?

Candidate B

Why do you think people choose these kinds of sport?

Candidates A and B

- How successful might these suggestions be?
- Which two will attract the most people?

Speaking Exam File Three

Part One

- Good morning/afternoon/evening. My name's ... and your name is?
- First of all we'd like to know something about you.
- Where are you from?
- What do you like about living in ...?
- Who are the most important people in your life?
- Tell me about your best friend.
- Why is learning English important for you?
- When do you think children should start learning other languages?
- What do you think makes a lesson enjoyable and effective?
- Tell me about your favourite learning experience at school.

Part Two

In the next part of the test, I'm going to give each of you two photographs. I'd like you to talk about your photographs on your own for a minute, and also to answer a short question about your partner's photographs. [Candidate A], it's your turn first, here are your photographs. They show people communicating in different ways. I'd like you to compare the photographs and say how these forms of communication might be important to these people.

Candidate A speaks for one minute.

- Do you like communicating by telephone or do you prefer face-to-face communication, [Candidate B]?

Candidate B answers.

Now here are your photographs, [Candidate B]. They show different buildings being constructed. I'd like you to compare the photographs and say what you think these buildings might be used for?

Candidate B speaks for one minute.

- Thank you. How much do you think buildings affect our environment [Candidate A]?

Candidate A answers.

Part Three

Now I'd like you to talk about something together for about three minutes. I'd like you to imagine that your local school has recently been given some money by an ex-pupil to help improve its facilities for the pupils and build something for people in the local community to use in the evening. First, talk to each other about how useful these suggestions might be. Then decide together which suggestion would both pupils and local people most benefit from.

Candidates A and B speak for three minutes.

Part Four

- What kind of recreational facilities are available where you live?
- How important do you think sport is for people?
- Do you think people are eating healthier food than they used to?
- In the future, do you think people will spend more or less time exercising?
- Young people usually prefer to spend their free time in different places to older people. Why do you think this is?

Candidate A

How are these forms of communication important to these people?

Candidate B

What do you think these buildings might be used for?

Candidates A and B

- Which of these suggestions might be useful?
- Which would both pupils and local people most benefit from?

Writing Guide

A formal/semi-formal letter/email

Dear Sir or Madam,

I'm writing in response to your advertisement for 'The Journey of a Lifetime' in the June edition of the Student Gazette newspaper.

I have just finished my studies at school and have a place at university. Before I start my degree in Business Studies and then pursue a career, I would like to take a gap year in order to increase my experience of the world.

My interests include mountain biking and sailing. This year at school I was involved in raising money for a local children's charity and I was also responsible for helping to organise the school drama festival.

I enjoy meeting people and I feel being involved in one of your gap year projects could help me to improve my communication and teamwork skills.

I would be grateful if you could send me information about your organisation and details of how to apply.

Yours faithfully,
Becky Raven.

Formal expressions

Opening salutation	Closing salutation
Dear Sir or Madam	Yours faithfully
Dear Mr Rylands	Yours sincerely/Best regards
Dear Martin	Best wishes

Reason for writing

I am writing	to ... (request/complain about/inform ...)
	in response to ...
	in connection to ...

Referring to previous contact
Thank you for your letter/email ...

| With regard | |
| Further | to your letter dated ... |

Give good/bad news
I would be delighted to ...
We would be happy to ...
Unfortunately ...

Refer to future contact
I look forward to hearing from you.

| If you | have any further questions | |
| | require any further information, | please do not hesitate to contact me. |

Extra Writing Practice

Write an answer to this question. Write your answer in 120–180 words in an appropriate style.

You have seen an advertisement on your school notice board to have a pen friend in the United Kingdom with the chance to stay in England for a week in the summer. In return your pen friend would also visit you. Write a letter to introduce yourself for the first time. Begin your letter *Dear Pen Friend...*

A less formal letter/email

Hi Maria

I'm really sorry about last week. I was really ill so I had to cancel my own party. Anyway, this is just to let you know that I'm now having my birthday party next Saturday. So the good news is that I can invite you again! Would you like to come?

I can't hire the local hall so it will be at my house. It starts at 7 and there'll be about 20 people there. You can get to my house on the number 60 bus. Ask the driver to stop on Insley Road. We're at number 76.

By the way thanks for the birthday present you sent. The shirt was a great fit! I'll wear it at the party. Look forward to seeing you on Saturday.

Best wishes

Ritchie.

Less formal or informal expressions

Give reason for writing
Just to let you know that ...
I'm emailing you to ...

Apologise
I really sorry but ...
I'm afraid that ...

Offer/Request
Would you like to ...?
Can I ...?/Could you ...?
Would you mind if ...?

Recommend and suggest
You should/ought to ...
Why don't you ...?
How about ...?

Give good news/bad news
I'm so happy because ...
The good/bad news is that ...
Unfortunately ...

Say when and where/Give details
There is/are ...
It's at/starts at ...
You can get there by ...

Thank
Thanks for ...
I'm really grateful for ...

End
Look forward to seeing you./See you soon.
Bye for now.
All the best/Best wishes.

Extra Writing Practice

Imagine you are Maria in the email from Ritchie above. Write your reply in 120–150 words in an appropriate style.

- Apologise that you cannot come to the party.
- Explain why not.
- Suggest meeting for lunch/Say when/Recommend somewhere.

A review

<table>
<tr>
<td>Introduce your subject for review.</td>
<td>My favourite film of the last few months was 'Quantum of Solace'. It's the latest James Bond film but it's very different from previous films.</td>
<td></td>
</tr>
<tr>
<td></td>
<td>The first thing you notice about the film is that Bond is younger and even more aggressive than usual. The female character is also a spy and more than the usual 'Bond girl'. In addition, it's worth seeing because it's much more realistic.</td>
<td>Review some of the positive points.</td>
</tr>
<tr>
<td>Mention some weaker points.</td>
<td>One problem with the film is that it happens in lots of locations and the plot is a bit too complicated. It also needs to be about 15 minutes shorter. Nevertheless, the scenes in the desert have lots of action and the criminal characters are particularly evil and interesting.</td>
<td></td>
</tr>
<tr>
<td></td>
<td>So overall I'd recommend the film as it's a new kind of Bond movie and not the usual predictable mix of fancy cars and stupid gadgets. It's certainly a good choice if you want to watch a DVD next Friday night.</td>
<td>Conclude with your overall opinion.</td>
</tr>
</table>

Useful expressions

Introducing your review
The aim/purpose of this review is to ...
My favourite ... is ...
The first thing you notice is ...

Describing positive feature
One thing I really like about it is ...
It's worth seeing because ...
A really good part is when ...

Describing weaknesses
One problem is ...
It isn't very ...
One thing that could be improved is ...
It also needs more ...

Final comments
Overall, I (strongly) recommend ...
It's certainly a good ...
(Nevertheless) it's much better than ...

Extra Writing Practice

You recently saw this notice in an English-language magazine called *Cinema World.*

Tell us about your favourite film of the year!

What was your favourite film of the last few months? Write us a review of the film you saw (120–180 words.) Include information on the characters and the style of the film and explain why you liked it so much. The best reviews will be published next month.

A short story

Carl's family had an important reason for leaving the house at two in the morning, and so everyone had gone to bed early. In fact Carl had been so excited about flying for the first time he could hardly sleep. When he managed to, he dreamt his saw his mother, the twins and himself all running down the airport runway chasing the plane as it took off. He was screaming, 'Wait! Wait!' Suddenly, he woke to a voice saying, 'Wake up Carl. Get dressed! We're late!'

After a one-hour journey down the motorway they finally arrived at the airport. 'Your flight is boarding now,' said the person at check-in. 'If you run you might catch it.' As they ran through the airport and reached the gate the plane was moving off. Carl shouted to his family, 'Quick, follow me!' He raced ahead out onto the runway. 'Wait! Wait!' he shouted.

Just then, he woke. Carl's alarm clock was ringing and his mother smiled at him. 'It's time to get up Carl. We don't want to miss the plane.'

Useful expressions

Background and atmosphere
It was raining with flashes of lightning outside …
The house was quiet and I sat all alone …
It all began on a day when I had been …
We were very tired and had been travelling all day …

Contrasting time and events
After …
As soon as I …
By the time …

At the same time …
While I was … -*ing*, they were …
Meanwhile …
A second later …

The climax/ending
Just then …
In the end …
Eventually …
Finally, I realised …
That was the last time I'd ever …

Extra Writing Practice

Your teacher has asked you to write a story (120–180 words) for an international magazine. The story must begin with the following words: *Rachel's family had an important reason for waking up early that morning and her mother had set the alarm clock for 5 a.m.*

A report

Always include a title to explain the purpose. You could also say who the report is for.

To: The Principal of the School
From: Class 5
Subject: Ideas for the school 'eco-week'

The aim of this report is to present Class 5's ideas for events at the school during 'eco-week'.

Sub-headings are a good idea and help the reader.

State the purpose of the report.

Poster competition
Our first idea is to run a poster competition. Each student could design a poster about the environment. For example, it might show how to recycle or suggest switching the standby switch off on the TV.

Give examples to help explain.

No cars
We could ask all students to walk or cycle to school during the week. The only problem would be that some students live too far from the school. However, they could ask their parents to share car journeys with others and save petrol.

Contrast and add information where necessary.

Display
Our final plan is to have a display in the main hall of all the objects you can recycle. For example, we could show how plastic bottles can be made into coats.

To sum up, everyone was very enthusiastic about the 'eco-week'. Next we would like to advertise the events during the week by sending a letter to all teachers to give to their students.

Don't forget to summarise. You might also want to say what needs to happen as a result of the report.

Useful expressions

Introducing the report/Stating the purpose
The following reports outlines ...
The aim of this report is to ...
The report is based on ...

Introducing ideas
The first/Another idea is to ...
One possibility is to ...
Our final idea/plan/suggestion is to ...

Proposing and suggesting
We should/could ...
We would like to ...
If possible, we ...
It might be a good idea to ...
One suggestion is to ...

Giving reasons/Recommending
As result of ... we think ...
This is a good idea because ...
We recommend this because ...

Contrasting and alternatives
On the one hand ... on the other ...
One problem is .../However ...
In contrast ...

Generalising
In general ...
On the whole ...

Concluding and summing up
In conclusion ...
To sum up ...
Our final recommendation is that ...

Extra Writing Practice

Write an answer to this question. Write your answer in 120–180 words in an appropriate style.

There is a problem with parking at your place of work (or study). There is not enough room for cars. You recently attended a meeting with a group of people to discuss ways to solve the problem.

Write a report on the meeting. Describe the best ideas and propose a solution.

An article

Give it a title.

THREE WAYS TO SAVE ENERGY AROUND THE HOME

In a time when the world is trying to save its natural resources, it's easy for many of us to help by using less energy in our houses.

Introduce the subject by restating the question.

Use clear paragraphs for each part of your article.

Take, for example, standby switches on TVs. Many people don't realise that when you aren't watching it, you might still be using electricity. All you have to do is switch it off at the plug when you go to bed and you've already reduced your electricity bill.

A second way to use less energy is to fit special light bulbs which last longer than normal light bulbs and use less energy. They cost a little more but in the long run, they save you money.

Finally, put a sweater on! When it gets cold, many people turn up the heating. But if they just put a sweater on they would quickly get warmer without using fuel.

Don't forget a conclusion. Sometimes you can include a message to the reader.

So next time you are about to switch it on or turn it up, ask yourself if you really need to and save yourself some money at the same time!

Extra Writing Practice

Write an answer to this question.

We are looking for an article (120–180 words) that suggests three ways to improve the local community. Explain why this is an important issue and suggest three ideas to help. The winning article will receive a £50 book token!

An opinion essay

Read the student's answer to the following exam question.

> Write an article and give your opinion on the following statement: 'It's important that young people should learn to earn money early on in life rather than being given pocket money.'

From the moment we leave school to the time we retire, most of us will have to work in order to earn money during our life. So the question is whether we should have to work before this time as children or wait until we become adults.

In my opinion, children should have to earn pocket money. By that I don't mean that they should have full-time jobs but that there are plenty of things they can do around the house such as the washing-up or gardening.

In addition to helping at home, working for money gives children a greater sense of responsibility. What's more, parents who simply give children money are not preparing them for the adult world. You could also argue that when children earn their money, when they buy something it will mean so much more.

So, to sum up, I believe that children learn from the experience of earning money and find out that nothing in life is for free.

Useful expressions

Introduction
Some people claim/believe/say …
It is sometimes said that …
The question is …
We often read/hear that …

Stating your opinion
In my opinion, …
As I see it, …
From my point of view …

Making extra points
What's more …
In addition …
Furthermore …

Introducing a contradictory point
Although/Even though …
Despite + noun/gerund/
    Despite the fact that …
However …

Contrasting views for and against
On the one hand/side … on the other
While it's true that …
You could also argue that …
Nevertheless, …/
    However, …
One advantage/
    Another disadvantage is that …
Even though …

Concluding
On balance …
I feel/believe that …
In my opinion …
Summarising …
To sum up, … in conclusion, …

Extra Writing Practice
Write an essay (120–180 words) giving your opinion on the following statement: 'Young people are spending too much time in front of screens (TV, computer) and have stopped learning what "real life" looks like.'

A 'for and against' essay

There are two ways to structure a 'for and against' essay. You can either contrast an argument for and against in each paragraph OR give all the arguments for in one paragraph and then all the arguments against in the next paragraph. Notice how these two answers for the same FCE question are structured:

> Some people believe that learning a language is one of the most useful subjects at school and should be compulsory for all pupils. State the arguments for and against this view.

Version 1

For many children, school is the obvious place to learn another language. However, there are so many other important subjects such as mathematics or history that not all pupils have enough time to study everything.

Restate the question in the introduction.

Contrast an argument for and against in each paragraph.

One argument for making language lessons compulsory is that more and more professions need people with language skills. So schools need to prepare children for their future careers. On the other hand not everyone will have an 'international job' so it might never be useful to them.

It's also true that learning a language introduces you to other cultures and helps your understanding of other people. Nevertheless, many other subjects such as geography also provide knowledge of the world.

Some people also argue that learning a language helps young children become more intelligent and helps them learn other subjects. However, if you teach children another language too early, it may also confuse them.

Conclude with your own overall opinion.

So, to sum up, I believe that learning another language at school is important for a child and will give them an advantage later in life as well as being more enjoyable than many other subjects.

Version 2

Restate the question in the introduction.

For many children, school is the obvious place to learn another language. However, there are so many other important subjects such as mathematics or history that not all pupils have enough time to study everything.

One argument for making language lessons compulsory is that a child's future profession may need language skills. Another reason is that learning a language introduces you to other cultures and helps your understanding of other people. Thirdly, some people believe that it helps young children become more intelligent.

Use paragraph two to state two to three arguments for.

Use paragraph three to state two to three arguments against.

On the other hand we also have to remember that not everyone will have an 'international job' so language learning might never be useful to them. In addition to that, there are many other subjects such as geography which also provide knowledge of the world. Finally, some people believe that it may not be good for children to learn another language too early in life.

Conclude with your own overall opinion.

So, on balance, I believe that learning another language at school is important for a child and will give them an advantage later in life as well as being more enjoyable than many other subjects.

Useful expressions

Giving arguments for
On the one hand …
You could argue that …
While it is true that …
I agree that …

Giving arguments against
On the other hand …
An argument against this is …
However …
One disadvantage is that …
Nevertheless …

General expressions
Another reason for/against …
First, … secondly, … thirdly …
In addition …
Finally …

Conclude
So, on balance, I believe that …
In my opinion, …
To sum up, I feel that …

Extra Writing Practice

Write an essay (120–180 words) stating the arguments for and against this view.

Some people believe that many children spend too much time on the Internet and playing computer games.

Tapescript

Listening 1.1

Examiner: First of all I'd like to know something about you. Where are you from?

Candidate: I'm from Greece. I'm living in Piraeus. It's near Athens.

Examiner: And how long have you lived there?

Candidate: I am living there all my life. But at the moment I also look for a place at university. So maybe I'll move away. I don't know exactly.

Examiner: What do you like about living in Piraeus?

Candidate: Oh I enjoy to go to the beach and it's very easy to visit some of the islands by boat. My family has a boat so we often go sailing.

Examiner: Do you prefer spending time on your own or with other people?

Candidate: I think with my friends but I think it's important to be on your own also.

Examiner: What's the most exciting thing you've ever done?

Candidate: Oh, that's a difficult question ... hmmm ... I suppose when I been visiting London was fun. Every year my school visited a school in England and we have met English school children. So that's fun ...

Listening 1.2

One

B: What's the problem?

A: I don't know how long I can put up with her.

B: She seems OK to me.

A: Do you think so?

B: Well, she's very friendly. The other staff get on with her. And she's got some good ideas. She wants to move the office around but that's fine. It doesn't work the way things are at present.

A: You don't think she's a bit bossy? I mean, all these changes. She's only been here a week!

Two

A: I ran into Michelle's boyfriend, Nigel, the other day.

B: Really?

A: I didn't know he lives down the road from me. He was at the bus stop. How well do *you* know him?

B: Not very. I've met him a couple of times. I heard she wants to break up with him again.

A: Oh, that's a pity.

B: Don't worry. They always fall out over something then she leaves him and then a week later they get back together again!

Three

I've been watching this TV show for a few weeks now. It was one of those shows where people are really angry all the time and talk about their problems at home. It's stupid really but good fun to watch. So, anyway, this morning there was this mother and father who still look after their three children but these children are all in their thirties! Anyway, the mother and father were saying the 'kids' never do anything around the house and constantly let them down. Unbelievable! I couldn't understand why they just didn't ask them to go and find their own place!

Four

Yes, it's true. You know how he told his brother he would stand by him whatever happened? Well, not last night he didn't! He just walked out and said he didn't want to see him ever again. I can't wait to see what happens next week!

Listening 2.1

Speaker 1: Actually, a friend from university who had gone straight into their graduate training program originally told me that they were looking for people. But at the time I was working for a charity and I really wanted to finish the project I was working on. It was unpaid but I was getting good experience. Anyway, a few months later I noticed in the newspaper they were looking for someone so I called my friend again. She said I had a good chance of getting the position so I applied.

Speaker 2: I grew up on a farm so it's always been in my family. We had dogs and cats and of course lots of animals. The vets used to come out when there was a problem so I knew what they did so it made sense I did something related to the countryside. I suppose my parents had hoped I'd follow in their footsteps but farmers work hard and the money isn't anything like as much as a vet can earn. So I guess that was what convinced me in the end.

Speaker 3: I normally hate people asking me questions but at my last interview I was quite calm for a change. Actually I didn't really want the job that much but I thought I'd go along for the practice. There were two people interviewing and they were both very nice and asked me lots of questions about my other work and why I wanted to leave my current job. It turned out one of the interviewers knew my boss but he was OK about it. Advertising and marketing is a small world and everyone knows everybody else. In the end I was short-listed and finally they offered me the job so I took it.

Speaker 4: A lot of people think being a journalist is quite a glamorous profession. They think we must all be meeting celebrities and interviewing world leaders every day of the week! Actually *I* deal with stuff from all the towns and villages in the area most of the time, like finding out which village team won the football or going to council meetings at the town hall. It really can be quite dull. It would be nice to report on something more interesting for a change!

Listening 3.7

Kasia: Right, well, let me see. They aren't exactly sports, but they are the kind of thing you can see at a festival or a children's party, you know, somewhere like that. Both photos look as though they were taken in the States. The people look American to me. Anyway, in the first one there's a sort of wall, the kind you put air in... and a person stuck on the wall! It looks strange. I think I understand ... he has a suit with that sticky stuff, maybe. It is a game to see how high you can jump. It must be fun to do that, to jump up and see how high you can go! The second picture is different, because it is a kind of competition between two children, I think. They are dressed in ... big ... suits ... costumes. It is like that Japanese sport, the one those big, very fat men play. I don't like it really. I wouldn't find it fun. I don't think it is nice to encourage children to fight like that, even if it *is* meant to be fun.

Listening 4.1

Speaker One: Well, I suppose we first noticed when I was about four. My mum and dad took me to the circus. I had really been **looking forward to** it. There were going to be lion-tamers, clowns and, best of all, horses. My parents knew that I was slightly allergic to dust, but they didn't want to **let me down** so off we went. Anyway, shortly after the show started, in came the horses, you know with riders and acrobats, they came into the ring and started galloping around. And within a couple of minutes my eyes had gone red and I had started sneezing badly. When I started having trouble breathing, mum got really anxious about me and we had to go. So it was then that we discovered that although I was crazy about horses, they couldn't stand me!

Speaker Two: People **look down on** scorpions, but human beings have no need to feel superior. We are likely to become extinct, you know to **die out**, well before the scorpion. Scorpions have hardly changed in the past 350 million years. You can find them everywhere except Antarctica – so they are hardly an endangered species. Their habitat can be under rocks and in rainforests. You can even **come across** them between the bark of trees, so **watch out!** They can **live off** one meal for up to a year and their favourite snack is another scorpion! It has such strong pincers that it doesn't need to use its sting that often. It breaks its victim into little pieces and then spits its digestive juices onto the bits. Then, when these are nice and soft it'll suck them up. Bon appetit!

Speaker Three: I've never been very keen on guinea pigs – I mean they don't do much, do they? Anyway, we finally agreed to get a pair on condition that the girls looked after them, although I was usually the one who **ended up** taking care of them. I got really fed up with doing it. But then one morning, a few months after we'd had them, I went into the garage and one of them had **passed away**. Now you can imagine what a drama that was, we had to have a funeral for it – we buried it in a shoe box I remember and the girls were terribly upset. And then we had to **go through** the same thing a couple of months later for the other one. Never again!

Speaker Four: The study of ants or bees can really give us an insight into the collective intelligence they use to complete tasks. Many species can achieve a common goal without a leader. Each insect simply reacts to its immediate environment. Together they can achieve enormous results. Just think of beehives and ant heaps! Scientists who have **carried out** research into insect behaviour have realised that they can teach us some valuable lessons. They've **come up with** programmes which imitate this behaviour, which can, in turn, be used to understand big problems like traffic jams, and how to control crowds and so on.

Speaker Five: So this cat, Sid, had six, yes *six* different owners, and *six* different names! None of the owners was aware of anyone else. And in each place he lived he was given something to eat every night. That's why this story is called 'Six Dinner Sid'. Sid **took everyone in**; each person believed he or she was his one and only owner. Just look at how fat he got! But one day he got a cough and all of those people took him to the vet. In the end the vet said to himself, '**Hold on,** I've seen this fat fellow with a cough already today.' So he phoned around to all the owners and they each **found out** that they weren't the only one to think they 'owned' him! So, they started taking turns to give him a dinner once a week ... one owner for each day! But, Sid was a six-dinner-a-day cat, so he moved to a new street and started again with six new owners!

Listening 4.2

Rebecca: Charlotte, did you see that article, the one about the owners who spend a fortune on their dogs?

Charlotte: Mm, yes. They look so lovely don't they, all clean and beautiful, their owners must be so proud of them.

Terry: Come on, Charlotte. Alright, so they look nice, but in my opinion they could spend their money far better ... you know ... in a much more sensible way.

Rebecca: I hear what you're saying, Terry. I know, for instance that there are a lot of kids out there who don't have anything to eat, but that doesn't mean that you can't give love to a pet either.

Charlotte: Yeah, I agree with you Rebecca. But, we don't know what else the owners do, do we? I mean they could be helping the homeless *too* for all we know.

Terry: I suppose so, but as far as I'm concerned it just goes completely against decent behaviour to spend so much on dogs – I'm sorry, Charlotte, but that's the way I feel.

Charlotte: I can see where you're coming from, but they aren't doing anything wrong as such, are they? It's not as if they were being cruel to animals or anything.

Rebecca: Mm, but I suppose Terry is right, Charlotte, it is rather unhealthy to be so obsessed with a pet, don't you think? And I'm not even sure that they are treating the dogs that kindly. As *I* see it dogs just want to be dogs and run around and enjoy themselves. I'm sure if they could speak they'd say how awful it was having to be dressed up and shown off all the time.

Charlotte: I see your point, but as far as I'm concerned it's up to the owners to choose. And if taking care of a pet is what pleases them, who are we to argue?

Listening 4.3

Interlocutor: Right, thank you. In the second part of the test, I'm going to give each of you two different pairs of photographs. I'd like you to talk about your photographs on your own for about a minute, and also to answer a short question about your partner's photographs. OK. So we'll start with you first, Beate. Here are your photographs. They show people and dogs interacting in different ways. What is the relationship between the animals and the humans in each picture?

Listening 4.4

Beate: Well, let me see. Both photographs show people working together with dogs. In the photo on the left there is a man ... hmm ... it *looks* like a policeman ... who is with a young-looking dog; it looks like a German shepherd, I think. Whereas in the second photo, the one on the right, there are a lot of dogs, huskies I think, and these dogs are pulling a sledge. It looks as though they are going to be in a race, or maybe they have as the dogs look a little bit tired. The person in the sledge looks happy so maybe they have won. Anyway, going back to the first picture, I think that the man is trying to train the dog, you know, to be a police dog. Perhaps he is teaching it how to jump over things, and fences, yes? I think it takes a long time to train a dog to do this. The dogs in the other picture of course they must already be trained, but all they have to do is run and follow their leader. I imagine that this kind of dog is much wilder than the one in the first picture.

Listening 4.5

Interlocutor: Thank you, Beate. So, Walter, which of the dogs do you think is happier?

Walter: Which is happier? Well, I guess the ... huskies, they are in the open air and they can run and act more like dogs together, with other dogs like in nature, while the police dog ... I don't know if I would be satisfied with its life because it is going to be a bit like a slave for a human being, isn't it, and it will be lonely without other dogs.

Interlocutor: Thank you, Walter. Now I'd like you to look at this pair of photographs because now it's your turn to give a description.

Listening 4.6

Part A

Interviewer: The distinction between human beings and other animals is an artificial one isn't it? We live and breathe and take care of our young in a similar way, don't we?

Professor: Mm, well, yes, you're right, biologically there is little difference between us – and chimpanzees – but there are a number of key distinctions which separate us from other mammals. There is language; then there is

intelligence: the ability to think about things, if you like. Animals are driven by their instincts and how they react to sensation. And another important distinction is our capacity for self-awareness.

Interviewer: Self-awareness?

Professor: Mm, yes. You know if we see ourselves in the mirror, we know that it is us we are looking at.

Interviewer: But how can you know whether an animal is self-aware?

Professor: Quite simply by placing it in front of a mirror and seeing how it reacts. Hardly any animals are capable of recognising themselves, but there are a few exceptions to this. A small number of creatures including chimps, dolphins and elephants can do this.

Interviewer: Elephants! Really!

Professor: Yes, after some research at a zoo in New York, we can now add elephants to this group. Three elephants which were given the mirror test behaved in a way which showed that they understood the animal in the reflection was them.

Interviewer: So how did they react, then?

Professor: Well, they did several things like putting their trunks in their mouths and watching themselves in the mirror which show they're interested in themselves. One of the three, Happy, I think it was, tried to remove a spot she was ashamed of, you know a mark which the researchers had put on her face.

Interviewer: Oh I see. And what about cats and dogs? Many people believe that they have an almost human intelligence too.

Professor: Mm, yes. But I'm afraid dogs and cats show no self-awareness at all. They are incapable of recognising themselves. People who pretend otherwise are just fooling themselves.

Listening 4.7

Part B

Interviewer: If that's the case, how come dogs have such close relationships with human beings. They couldn't do that if they weren't self-aware, could they?

Professor: Well actually, this has nothing to do with self-awareness, basically it is all because dogs are brilliant at reading human expressions and gestures, and interpreting them. They are much better at this even than chimpanzees who are our closest relatives.

Interviewer: There is scientific proof of this, is there? Has anyone looked into this area?

Professor: Yes. There has been a great deal of research so scientists have gathered a large amount of evidence. There's another simple experiment where there are two cups, one has food underneath it, and the other is empty. Well, with dogs, if someone touches the cup, or even just glances at it, then a dog will pick up the signal and choose the one with the food every time. Chimps, would you believe, simply guess.

Interviewer: I see, and how did this come about ... the dog's ability to do this?

Professor: Good question. The most likely explanation is that it is a result of evolution. In domesticated dogs, you know, dogs which have been tamed and in human contact generation after generation, well, this ability to recognise human emotions and gestures has evolved.

Interviewer: So it wouldn't be developed in wild dogs, then?

Professor: Absolutely not. No ... wolves and so on, they're different from domesticated dogs.

Interviewer: Hold on, though, how can we be sure of that? You know ... that this ability to recognise human emotions is as a result of evolution?

Professor: Well, in another piece of research one scientist did the two cup experiment on a breed of dog called the New Guinea singing dog.

Interviewer: New Guinea singing dog? Weird.

Professor: It's called that because it's famous for its funny bark. When it howls it sounds like a cross between a wolf and a whale.

Interviewer: Bizarre.

Professor: Anyway. What is special about this breed is that once upon a time, many generations ago, it had been domesticated, you know tamed and trained how to live with humans. But then it returned to the wild and had no more human contact. This made it ideal to test the evolution theory.

Interviewer: So what happened when they carried out the experiment? How much importance does evolution really have?

Professor: Well, to cut a long story short, when they performed the cup test with these dogs, none of them were able to pick the cup with the food under it. They couldn't read human expressions or gestures any more. Any ability which had once evolved had been lost.

Interviewer: Fascinating.

Listening 5.1

One I spent most of my time travelling around on a horse with my servant trying to rescue young ladies from dragons, and fighting giants. People said I was crazy.

Two I just wanted to be left alone but a horrible priest fell in love with me. I was rescued by a hunchback. He was a nice guy but so intense. He used to ring the bells at the cathedral, you know.

Three Well I came up with this great idea to trick the enemy. We got into Troy inside a wooden horse, and that was the end of the war. It took me another ten years to find my way home and I had lots of adventures and had to fight a giant.

Four I wasn't born as such – my dad, he wanted a son so badly that he made me from pieces of wood. I became just like any other little boy, but each time I told a lie (and I used to lie a *lot*) – my nose grew, and kept on growing.

Listening 5.2

Part A

Lorolei: So, Jacinta, how did you get into adapting books for the cinema?

Jacinta: Well, by accident really. I started off editing scripts for radio plays, then I had the chance to join a team writing for a TV series – a soap opera if you like. Then one day I was asked if I'd be interested in adapting a book by Thomas Hardy for the radio, and one thing led to another.

Lorolei: So tell me, how do you begin adapting a book, or a piece of literature for the screen? What do you need to know before you begin?

Jacinta: Well, there are two main things really. First of all what the story is, you know, if is a long novel with hundreds of chapters, or a short story or play. And the second thing is the medium – is it going to be for the big screen, you know a movie for the cinema, or for TV?

Lorolei: And I know you've done both ... adapt for both TV and the cinema ... but which do you prefer?

Jacinta: Well, it may seem strange, but all things considered, I'd rather adapt a classic, say a novel by Dickens, for the small screen.

Lorolei: Why is that, then?

Jacinta: Well, even though the budget is smaller, you have more time to do justice to the original. For instance, instead of two hours to tell your tale you may have, six, ten, or even twelve one-hour episodes. In a long serial you can take it at a slower pace, and focus much more on the development of the personalities of the characters. Another thing is you can include some of the smaller characters and sub-plots which you would just have to cut for a film.

Lorolei: Is it just a question of time, or is there anything else?

Jacinta: Well, the other thing of course is that for most films, if you are making something for the cinema, you know for the big screen, which has to appeal to a large audience, you have to introduce an element of spectacle.

Lorolei: Spectacle?

Jacinta: Yes, you know, breathtaking scenery, battle scenes, chariot races – the sort of thing which is going to fill the cinema screen. Something to make the audience say 'Wow!' I don't know if you've seen the recent big screen adaptation of *Pride and Prejudice*.

Lorolei: The one with Keira Knightley as the heroine, Elizabeth Bennett?

Jacinta: Yes, that's the one. Well, essentially the novel itself is a domestic drama, not the subject of a typical big budget movie. But the director made a really big thing of the big formal dances, the balls. And of course it looked magnificent and the attention to period detail was fabulous, you could only really appreciate it at a big cinema, but, of course, it took up a lot of time which could have been dedicated to other aspects of the story. I prefer the adaptation the BBC did a few years ago, but that's probably because I've got a thing for Colin Firth, the actor who played the hero, Mr Darcy.

Lorolei: I know what you mean! So, how free do you feel to change the story?

Jacinta: Well, I know some people take enormous liberties when they are adapting a book – you know they'll mess around with the plot or change the ending. Personally, I try to be as faithful to the original book as I can. In my view, if you want to do your own thing, that's fine, but then you should create something original.

Listening 5.3

Part B

Lorolei: But can film, and here I'm talking about TV as well as the cinema, can it ever be superior to the written word?

Jacinta: Mm ... yes. It is much more economical in terms of time ... you know ... setting the scene and so on. With just a couple of seconds of camera work, you can set a scene which, in a classic novel, would take pages and pages of description. If you choose the right location, go to where the book was set with the right scenery, the effect is immediate.

Lorolei: So a picture is worth a thousand words. And is there anything that film or TV can't do?

Jacinta: Oh yes, lots. For me the biggest thing is the narrator, you know the storyteller's voice, if you like. Although it's easy to use dialogue straight from the page it's very difficult to do that with the narrator's voice, unless, that is, you are going to have voice-overs every few minutes.

Lorolei: Can you give me an example of that?

Jacinta: Well, the one which immediately comes to mind is *Vanity Fair*. Now *Vanity Fair* is a story about a young woman called Becky Sharp who will do anything to rise in society.

Lorolei: Yes, she's the ultimate social climber.

Jacinta: Absolutely – she is a terrible, heartless, ruthless young woman. Now in the original book by Thackeray, the narrator is always looking down on the action, you know making comments on what's going on. This, in my opinion, is what makes the book. But recently, when *Vanity Fair* was turned into a blockbuster, well this was missing. OK, it was wonderful to look at. There were some fabulous scenes and the costumes were breathtaking. Yet, the thing is, *despite* having a huge budget, *despite* its cast of stars, there was something missing from the film, which made it rather empty, in my view.

Lorolei: And that 'thing' which was missing was the narrator's voice.

Jacinta: Exactly.

Listening 6.1

One

Harry: Hi, Sophie. Nice to see you. You're going to university this autumn, aren't you?

Sophie: Hi, Uncle Harry. Well, actually I've decided not to go this year. I'm going to take a gap year and travel around the States. I'm planning to get a job as a nanny or waitress or something like that. Apparently even if you just turn up you can find something quite quickly. Otherwise, I might try and join a voluntary organisation ... you know ... do some work in Africa. Don't say anything to Mum and Dad though, will you, Uncle Harry? I haven't told them yet!

Two

Mark: Hello. This is Mark Wilson. I'm afraid I'm not able to take your call right now, but please leave a message after the beep.

Juan: Mark, hi it's Juan. Just to say that I'm setting off at three o'clock. The journey takes about three and a half to four hours which means I should get to the exhibition centre at around seven. Hope that's not too late. Anyway, will you, or somebody else from the office be able to come and help me unload the van? There's a lot of stuff and I won't be able to do it on my own. Can you call me back on my mobile?

Three

Sharon: I hate the whole thing of organised holidays and excursions. I'm really into couch surfing. That's where you meet someone on the Internet who will then put you up for a couple of days on their sofa and show you around. It's great, honest, for a short trip somewhere ... who cares if it's a bit uncomfortable? I've just come back from Prague where I spent two nights on this guy's sofa. He showed me around places you'd never find in a guide book. It was brilliant. I've had some fascinating and unexpected experiences on my travels. You should give couch surfing a try, I'll mail you the website details.

Four

Blanka: Now, listen please ... Professor Heron's flight takes off at three and lands at four fifteen; I'm going to meet him with Marika. A taxi is due to pick us up at the airport and drop us off at his hotel. Marika will help Professor Heron check in and make sure he knows the arrangements. Now, he'll be tired after the journey so he's bound to need some time to himself. If we plan to meet at around eight he'll have had time to freshen up and relax. We'll take him to the conference centre and show him where he's giving his talks. Remember, he likes everything to be perfectly organised so it's very, very important that *everything* goes smoothly. Afterwards we'll take him out for dinner at the new restaurant at the Hilton.

Five

Seb: Listen, everyone. Kate will be waiting at the station. She'll call as soon as Mum has left the station to say that she's on her way home. She's likely to be feeling a bit sad. Now, the lights are going to be off, and I want everyone to hide in the kitchen with the food and drink. The kids can go behind the sofa – *not a sound*, OK ... so when Mum opens the door and walks into the sitting room, everyone will shout 'Happy retirement!' She really deserves it after twenty five years of commuting backwards and forwards to London.

Six

Kim: It's not a hotel, it's a building site! And we have to cross a main road to get to the beach. Someone is going to get hurt, I can see it happening. I wouldn't come here again if they were *giving* holidays away.

David: Well don't blame me. I didn't know it was going to be like this. It was supposed to be a package holiday in a *luxury* resort!

Kim: Well, you should have chosen a holiday from a *real* brochure, from a *proper* travel agent – not a so-called last minute bargain off the Internet. Next time we go away *I'm in charge!*

Seven

Dagmara: This evening we could go and visit the old town. We're very proud of our heritage here. There are some lovely squares and monuments and I could show you around a bit. What do you think? Later on we can meet up with some of the others from head office and eat out in a nice restaurant in the old town.

Roy: That sounds brilliant. I'd like to do a bit of sightseeing and maybe get a couple of souvenirs ... you know ... the kids always expect to me to buy them something when I'm away!

Eight

Waiter: Welcome signora. Are you ready to order?

Gemma: Yes, I think so. I'd like to try some of the local specialities. I'll begin with the artichokes and parma ham.

Waiter: Yes madam, and for your main course?

Gemma: Can you tell me what the special is?

Waiter: Ah yes, it's baby cow, cooked in the milk of the mother.

Gemma: Mm, no thanks. That's enough to turn you into a vegetarian. I think I'll have the spaghetti bolognese, if that's OK.

Listening 6.2

One To present yourself and register at a hotel or airport.

Two To give somebody somewhere to sleep for the night.

Three To choose.

Four To entertain another person by taking them to, say, a bar or restaurant.

Five To leave on a trip or a journey.

Six To have a wash and change your clothes after a journey.

Seven To move from place to place.

Eight To take someone in your car and let them out at the destination.

Nine To arrive or present yourself somewhere; often late or without warning.

Ten To have a meal in a restaurant.

Eleven To give someone a guided tour of somewhere.

Twelve To have a rendezvous.

Thirteen To collect someone in your car.

Fourteen To give something free of charge.

Fifteen To take a break.

Sixteen To delay something until a later date.

Listening 6.3

One Tell each other about your plans for next weekend or your next major holiday.

Two You want to know the time of the next coach from Oxford to Cambridge. You would also like to know the journey time.

Three Make some predictions about the results of the next elections or your country's performance in the world cup or Olympic Games.

Four A neighbour has telephoned to find out if your friend has had her baby. Promise to phone the moment you have some news.

Five You are phoning a friend to tell him or her about your travel plans. You are planning to leave your home in half an hour. Even though the traffic is heavy, you believe that you can be there by five o'clock if everything goes to plan.

Six You are in a job interview. One of the interviewers asks how you see yourself in five years' time. Make some predictions about your position in five years, and some of your achievements between now and then.

Seven You have just left the cinema. The film was awful and the people you are with are criticising you for having suggested it. Defend yourself!

Eight The roads are icy and you're starting to get worried, you expected your friend, Marina, to arrive half an hour ago. What do you say to yourself?

Listening 6.4

Tess: It's time we decided about our travel arrangements. I mean, if we leave it too late the prices will have rocketed.

Loïc: We'd better make up our minds then. I suppose we could take the tunnel and then drive all the way down.

Tess: What do you think, Marco?

Marco: It's a long way and the motorway charges will be high.

Loïc: Mm, I know what you mean, and we shouldn't forget the petrol.

Tess: We could fly, you know, take one of these low cost flights and then we could always hire a car if we need one when we get there. We should be able to afford that.

Loïc: But wouldn't that end up just as expensive as driving?

Marco: Yes, but driving down could be part of the holiday, couldn't it? I don't mind spending a few days stopping off at different places.

Tess: OK, but personally I'd rather we got there as quickly as possible. We only have two weeks, I don't really want to spend a lot of time just getting there.

Loïc: I was just about to say the say the same thing. I just want to lie on a beach and relax.

Tess: I've got to say too I am a bit nervous about driving. I've never driven on the continent before.

Loïc: That doesn't bother me. I don't mind doing the driving.

Marco: And I could share it with you.

Tess: Not the way you drive, Marco! I tell you what, why don't I take the plane and meet you down there!

Loïc: Very funny. Hold on, I've just had an idea There is another option. What if we took the ferry from Portsmouth, across to Britanny? It would make the journey at the other end a lot shorter.

Marco: And if we took a night crossing, it would give us a night's sleep and then we could get down there by the middle of the afternoon. We'll have gained an extra day.

Tess: The ferry. Mm, I like that idea. But before I look at prices, does anyone suffer from seasickness?!

Listening 7.1

Interviewer: We all remember watching those old black and white science fiction films at the cinema with androids and robots. As soon as you saw a robot you expected to see them go crazy and then they started attacking people. In reality there has never been a real case of robots attacking humans and robots have been used in manufacturing, especially car production, for years. And now robots are becoming part of our home life. In Japan for example, scientists are working on robots to be companions for elderly people. You might also have seen robot toys which children can control with their voices. Well, some manufacturers are looking at ways for such toys to look after children while their parents are at work. So, should we be worried? Do we risk having our day-to-day life controlled by machines that think for themselves? To discuss these questions I have Noel Witfield with me in the studio today. He's a professor of electronic engineering and is also a specialist in robot ethics. Professor Witfield, first of all, isn't all this talk of robots in the house a bit scary? Don't you think most people would prefer to communicate with a real person?

Professor: That's possibly true but you mentioned the work being done in Japan for example. The Japanese have succeeded in developing household robots for some time because they have an aging population. If they don't have robots, there won't be the people to take care of the elderly. Also I don't agree with your comment that we don't want to talk to machines. After all, we spend hours a day on our mobile phones and computers. But in fact a human being isn't designed to look at a screen all day. I'm actually better-suited to communicate with a computer which has a humanlike appearance – which is of course what a robot is. A computer with a face.

Interviewer: But we've also heard a lot about scientists who've managed to make robots with intelligence.

Professor: Well there I do think there's a potential problem with this and we need to look at this.

Interviewer: In what way?

Professor: Well, when we talk about intelligence, we're really talking about the fact that robots in the future will be able to make their own decisions. In the past robots have always been controlled by humans but we are giving them the abilities to make decisions and have some free will.

Interviewer: So do you think we should stop moving in this direction?

Professor: No, I wouldn't say stop it altogether but I would like to see a real public debate take place on how this will affect society in the future. And there's also the issue of safety and reliability. After all, some of the major work that is being done into robots is for military purposes. Governments should consider using robots ethically.

Listening 7.2

One We all remember watching those old black and white science fiction films at the cinema with androids and robots.

Two As soon as you saw a robot you expected to see them go crazy.

Three Do we risk having our day-to-day life controlled by machines that think for themselves?

Four Don't you think most people would prefer to communicate with a real person?

Five The Japanese have succeeded in developing household robots for some time.

Six A human being isn't designed to look at a screen all day ...

Seven But we've also heard a lot about scientists who've managed to make robots with intelligence.

Eight I would like to see a real public debate take place on how this will affect society.

Nine Governments should consider using robots ethically.

Listening 7.3

Because it's so easy to use the Internet these days, virtually anyone can think to themselves 'let's set up a website'. Maybe you want a home page for friends to look at, or how about advertising your local club? Perhaps you could even start an e-business and become a dot com millionaire. Before you begin, make sure you know why you want a website and what it's going to be for. It's also important to choose a good name early on and get an address for the web page. It should be a name that's easy to remember and the best ones are generally those which say what the site does or which get your attention.

Take the site www.milliondollarhomepage.com. Alex Tew, the student who came up with it, chose a name that said what it was about and it was also interesting because most people want to know about anything that mentions money. Another reason people visit sites is because they want information. So I strongly recommend that you include links to other sites. These need to be up-to-date and useful.

You might think that links to other sites will send people away but in fact if you can help users they will keep coming back to yours. Also, don't forget that links can take the form of words that you click on or they can be icons which are more visual and make the site colourful.

People also often ask me about things like having pictures and music. That's OK but it's also worth remembering that the more features and effects you have, the harder it will be to find what you want and it may take a long time to load the site. Visitors will get bored if they have to wait every time they click on another page. It's a good idea to give a contact email so you can get feedback from visitors to the site.

Listening 8.1

Speaker One I really don't know what we would have done if he hadn't arrived. We'd been driving round the same part of the city for at least an hour and I must have asked about five different people where to go. And it was all rather dark and scary. I even drove the wrong way down a one way street! *That* was when, suddenly, out of *nowhere* this policeman stopped us! Well, once I'd explained that I was completely lost he told us the way and we were able to ...

Speaker Two Have you seen that poster they're showing everyone? It has a man's face – he has a beard but he still looks like any number of other people. Anyway there were about three police officers asking people in the High Street if they saw anything strange outside the local supermarket last Thursday night at 8 o'clock. I suppose they spoke to *me* because I always walk past at that time of night, and, well, actually, when I started to think back it occured to me that I *had* seen a couple of suspicous people in that street that goes down the side of the shops, who perhaps ...

Speaker Three Believe me! I wouldn't want to be the *actual* attacker. I mean, the way they spoke to me was *really* scary! I even *felt* like a criminal by the time I left the police station. Even once they'd realised my name was spelt differently and I've never even *known* anyone called Rita, I still *never* got an apology I couldn't believe it. I mean you'd think that if ...

Speaker Four The shopping bags were both sitting there and they were identical. I'd just grabbed them and put them in the trolley and I'd only gone halfway across the car park before a security guard was running and using his radio. The next thing I know is the police arrive to question me. I think they realised I'd just made a mistake and taken the wrong ones but that security guard was determined to get me! He really fancied himself as one of those detectives you see on TV! You know the ones ...

Speaker Five It was just my luck, wasn't it? I mean, I normally go through that area quite carefully because I know they wait there. But, well, I was in a rush that day to pick up Lionel from work and I wasn't thinking. Within seconds I saw the lights flashing and they'd pulled me over. The young man was very nice about it but it didn't stop him from giving me a fine! It just wasn't my day ...

Listening 8.2

Presenter: Today, we've got Connie Wicher on the phone and Connie has rung in to let listeners know about her new idea to recycle things in your home. Is that right, Connie?

Connie: That's right Geoff, though it isn't really *my* idea. It's part of something called Freecycling.

Presenter: OK. So tell us about it, Connie.

Connie: Well, the Freecycle Network, or 'Freecycling', began in 2003. There was a group of people who wanted to save the landscape around their town from having more landfills and being used for dumping trash – which you guys would call rubbish. So they set about finding ways of helping the town reduce its waste.

Presenter: I see, but didn't it cost them money to do something like that?

Connie: Well, no, it was absolutely free. It wasn't a government thing or anything like that ... just a bunch of people getting together and doing something about all the stuff being thrown away. It's all done in people's spare time.

Presenter: It sounds great. Now, people listening will be wondering how this is different to recycling.

Connie: It isn't *quite* the same as recycling because everything is just reused rather than taking it away for recycling. So, for example, if I have a fridge I don't want, I advertise to my local freecycling community and someone can have it for nothing. It's as simple as that.

Presenter: OK – I see. I had a look at the website earlier, Connie, and there are over *three* thousand of these communities around the world! That's a *lot* of people.

Connie: Yes ... I think the most recent number is three thousand, seven hundred and nineteen, with close to three million members in places all over the world, in countries including the USA and Germany ... all sharing their unwanted things.

Presenter: Wow! So tell our listeners how they can become freecyclers.

Connie: Just go the website www.freecycle.com and find your local group. You click 'join' and then you get an email telling you what to do. If you can't find a freecycler nearby then you can start your own in your local area.

Presenter: And what can people give away?

Connie: Literally anything. Chairs, fax machines, pianos. You name it! I gave away a door last week.

Presenter: Right. So pretty much everything, then!

Connie: Sure, as long as it's legal and free, you can freecycle it.

Presenter: Well thanks, Connie. And if you want to get in touch here's the website again. It's www.freecycle.com ...

Listening 9.1

Speaker One I used to go there a lot, but the last time I ordered a steak, it was hardly cooked at all. Anyway, when I asked one of the staff if I could, you know, have it cooked a bit more he said that I'd asked for it rare – you know as though it was *my* fault. I told him it was more like *raw* than rare. Of course he took his revenge – when he brought it back it was so well-done I could hardly cut it. I won't be going *there* again.

Speaker Two It's often a problem when I go out because I'm not used to eating hot, spicy food. I prefer, you know, plain home cooking – if it's *too* spicy, well, it upsets my stomach. A Chinese takeaway, you know, sweet and sour, that's OK, but on the whole I'd rather have something plain and bland ... you know ... quite unadventurous. So, as I was telling you ... we went to this Indian restaurant and I ordered the mildest curry on the menu but it was still far too hot for me. I couldn't eat it!

Speaker Three Well, I don't like to give away my secrets, but it's quite simple really. I prefer to use low fat cream for this. So what you do is ... when the pasta is cooked, you mix in the egg and cream mix – it'll cook on its own without going back on the heat. Stir in the chopped up bacon pieces ... like so. And *then* sprinkle on some fresh basil to decorate it. Food has got to *look* good too – tasty *and* tasteful – that's what I always say. We eat with our eyes as much as with our mouths! If you don't have basil you can use parsley – *only* use the leaves though because the rest is bitter.

Speaker Four Well in those days they would work in the fields harvesting the corn by hand, and then they'd come in for a simple meal at lunchtime. It was a tradition that the farmer and workers ate *together*. The farmer used to sit here at the end of this long table. Meals were quick because they had to get back to work. Usually, there would be soup and bread and cheese. Anyway, once the farmer closed up his knife, well, that was the end of the meal. Everybody had to get up and get back to work – even if they hadn't finished eating! There were no arguments about that back then.

Speaker Five To begin with the waiter brought us a tasty salad, with locally produced cheese. Then there was fish and a fabulous stew. There was a different wine for each course – dry white with the fish, red with the meat. I drank lots of water. I always drink still – sparkling makes me too full. Finally, there was a delicious dessert with a sweet white wine. At the end I felt like, you know, one of those snakes which can swallow a whole sheep! All the same, I could get used to eating like that!

Listening 9.2

Roddy: So here in the studio we have Katrina, our food and restaurant critic. Now Katrina, what have you been up to since we last spoke?

Katrina: Well, I have had the most extraordinary eating out experience at a restaurant called In the Dark.

Roddy: In the Dark?

Katrina: Yes, it's precisely that – you eat in a pitch-dark restaurant where you can't see a thing.

Roddy: Well, OK, but what's the point of that?

Katrina: Well, first of all I should say it is run for the blind.

Roddy: Oh really? It's a kind of charity then is it?

Katrina: Mm, more than that the idea is to give us, that is sighted people – those of us who can see, the sensation of what it must be like to be blind. It also provides work for blind people who are taken on as staff and some of the money it is true is donated to charities for the blind

Roddy: So mainly it raises awareness among sighted people and provides jobs. And is it popular, as a concept I mean?

Katrina: Oh yes, it has really taken off – there are restaurants like it in major European cities, from Paris to Moscow. Anyway, the next thing is, once you've ordered your food from the menu and your drinks, blind serving staff lead you down the corridor towards the dining room. They took really good care of us.

Roddy: What, straight into the dark? That's scary.

Katrina: Not really, they let you get used to it bit by bit. There are a few red lights and then it gets darker and darker and you go through heavy drapes, you know ... thick curtains ... into the dining area where they help you sit down.

Roddy: How do they get it to be so dark – I mean in most situations a bit of light normally manages to penetrate the room, doesn't it?

Katrina: Mm, that's true. You have to leave things like matches and cigarette lighters with your stuff, and you aren't even allowed to take a mobile phone in with you, 'cos that could act as a source of light. Oh and another thing – you have to take off your watches as well ... those which have a face which glows in the dark

Roddy: I've got to say, I wouldn't be able to cope with it at all. I'm claustrophobic and I panic if I can't see anything. I always have to have a light on somewhere.

Katrina: So you wouldn't come with me? Not even if I held your hand?

Roddy: Not even. And what about the meal, how did you get on with that?

Katrina: Well, the practical aspects were quite difficult. You have to grope for everything – your knife and fork and so on, and your wine glass. So I found myself knocking into my neighbours and drinking his wine.

Roddy: Oh no!

Katrina: Yeah, but he took his revenge by pouring wine over my arm – so in the end we were even! At first everyone was nervous and giggly at the beginning but pouring wine over each other is a real ice-breaker. After that we got on really well. He had a lovely voice, although I never got to see his face.

Roddy: Shame. And how easy was it to eat?

Katrina: Well, let's say that good table manners go out of the window too. But you can take advantage of the dark to eat with your fingers.

Roddy: Gross! And how did you know what you were eating, then?

Katrina: Well, we had opted for the surprise menu so we had no idea what would be landing on our plates. I think we had meat.

Roddy: You think!

Katrina: Well, OK we could tell it was meat, but not what type. The same goes for most of the vegetables.

Roddy: So would you recommend it?

Katrina: Well the food wasn't bad, but it was the overall experience, of course, which is memorable. So basically, yeah, I'd recommend it – I would. But if you do go, make sure you don't wear your best clothes.

Roddy: And what else did you get out of it – apart from, of course, an evening out?

Katrina: Well, it made me much more aware of what it must be like to be blind. Like most of us I've always taken my eyesight for granted – it made me realise how hard it must be to get by without one of your major senses.

Listening 10.1

It was ten o'clock and I was supposed to have finished for the night. But then someone brought in an odd-looking, small boy. He couldn't have been much more than nine or ten. They said he'd been wandering down a lane about ten miles south of town. But he couldn't say a word – in *any* language. Anyway, we made him a bed in one of the cells at the station. Maybe someone would show up in the morning looking for him. He seemed surprisingly calm – not worried at all. There was nothing on him to say where he was from. The only thing that was strange was a triangular, blue metal badge on his jacket. It was a deep blue colour. It must have been special to him cos when I reached out to touch it he got kind of angry. I tried asking him about it but he didn't answer. His eyes just got big and more angry.

Anyway, I had kids of my own waiting at home so had to leave him with the other officers. Anyway, while I was driving home I was on the road out of town when I had to stop. I thought it was a car coming towards me. I flashed my car lights because his lights were so bright. But they weren't two lights like a ordinary car. First of all there was a beautiful orange light. Then it grew and became three, four, and then they changed colour!

I thought 'what is going on here?' so I switched my police lights on. I thought it's someone making fun of me. Then the lights rose above me and I could see it. It had a smooth round base like a mirror. I could see the lights changing colour on it and then realised it was the blue and red lights on the top of my car. Then suddenly it flew off and all I remember is a metal disc with a triangular shape across it. That was the second time I'd seen that blue triangle that day.

Listening 10.2

Speaker One It could be any number of things. We had some strong wind last night. It was blowing *really* hard and a tree fell down in my garden so it could have blown the corn over. Or maybe it was some kids playing around. We often get teenagers coming down from the city in the summer and they sleep out so they could quite easily have done it. I also read that helicopters can make shapes like this so it might have been as a result of some kind of flying machine. There's a military air force base about fifty miles away. Who knows? Perhaps a plane or something flew over last night.

Speaker Two I'm absolutely certain that aliens did it. I mean, there have been lots of UFO sightings round here. A friend of mine saw lights in the sky only last week. This triangle of lights flew past his house, it was sort of metal he said and movng really quite quickly. Anyway, he saw them land in the distance. So it seems to me that any spaceship would leave a mark on the ground like that.

Speaker Three Some crop circles are probably hoaxes and for fun but in this case it would have been impossible for someone to make something this complex in the middle of the night. They couldn't have done it all in seven hours! The farmer said he'd been to the field in the evening and saw nothing and then the next morning it appeared. It must have been something more mysterious. I know that some people have seen UFOs around here.

Speaker Four I can't believe all the fuss over this. In my opinion it's a complete hoax. For one thing, people are saying it's aliens. Well, aliens wouldn't come here and even if they did, why spend their time making circles in the corn? Surely they have better things to do! I *think* it's probably someone creating a story. It seems like the sort of thing a newspaper would set up because we have loads of journalists visiting the village all of a sudden. In my opinion they should all go home – leave us alone.

Speaker Five I can't seem to make my mind up on this. The fact is it's there and it is very clever, very beautiful in a way. Whoever did it was very artistic. I have heard that there are groups of people who travel round the country making these circles. They do it as a kind of hobby. But I live nearby and I didn't hear anything so ... I'm not really sure. Maybe it *was* aliens after all.

Listening 11.1

Speaker One Well, I'd say that I'm fairly good at staying within my budget. I mean I won't just buy stuff for the sake of it – like on a whim or anything. I go out with a certain amount of money in my purse and I won't go over that amount. Most of my friends have credit cards but they're always in debt so I just carry cash. That way if I suddenly see something I like, I either buy it or come back the following week with the money I need. And then if it's gone, it's gone but usually you find it still there.

Speaker Two I'm a bit of a bargain hunter. If I see something on special offer, I'll buy it but I'll never pay full price for anything. I don't go from shop to shop but what I will do is look it up on the Internet and compare prices of things. There are some great websites that will actually show you how much you can save depending on where you go. And besides, if you go to the same shop every time, they'll often give you a loyalty card so you save money when you shop there. And that's on top of any discounts.

Speaker Three I just can't make my mind up. It looks in good working order. It only has about thirty thousand kilometres on it and he says the last owner was an old couple who only drove it at weekends but he probably says that about every one in the showroom. I don't know. It's not like I've even looked at any others. Maybe if he reduced the price, I would be interested. After all it's only two years old. It seems like a good deal. Let's see what he says.

Speaker Four Well it's funny you're asking for that 'cause if you had come in last week I would have had just what you were looking for. It was a green sofa and chairs that would have matched your wallpaper. I'd order you another but I'm pretty sure it was the last in that line. They said they'll be sending us the new catalogue for next year in the next couple of days and then I can tell you. Otherwise, all we have is what you can see here. Though one thing I can do is ring our other branch and see if they have any left in stock. Don't go away. I'll give them a call right now.

Speaker Five You don't have to decide now. If you want to take it home and see how it looks once you get it home, that's fine. There's a 28-day money-back guarantee on all our products so long as you bring it back within 28 days of purchase, that's fine. Oh, that's also provided that you have the receipt with it of course. So you could take it today with absolutely no obligation. All we ask is that you return it in the same condition as you bought it. You'd be amazed to see what some people bring back ...

Speaker Six At the end of the day I think the main thing to remember is that whether you earn a lot or a little, it's really important to make sure you've got some left over for a rainy day. So there are three ways you can do this. There's short-term saving in case you have an emergency. Then there's medium-term saving which means money that you might need to use in about five or ten years time. And finally, there are long-term things like pensions and the rule on that is you start paying into it as soon as you can. The younger the better, in fact.

Speaker Seven You know, I really wish we hadn't bothered. For one thing it's caused so much stress worrying about how much it's all going to cost and then they've changed the hotel twice. It isn't the one in the brochure anymore so I hope it's decent. Of course, I didn't want to go in the first place but Graham was with me and we went into the travel agent and the next thing I know, he's writing the cheque.

Speaker Eight I wish I could afford it but I can't borrow any more from my mum and dad. I already owe them money for my new bike. In fact it's a bit unfair because my sister got a bike for her birthday and so she has some money she's saving. But for me, my dad wants to know when I'm going to pay him back. Had I known, I wouldn't have bought it in the first place.

Listening 11.2

One ... If I suddenly see something I like, I either buy it or come back the following week with the money I need.

Two ... If you go to the same shop every time, they'll often give you a loyalty card so you save money when you shop there.

Three ... Maybe if he reduced the price, I would be interested.

Four ... If you had come in last week I would have had just what you were looking for.

Listening 11.3

One ... There's a 28-day money-back guarantee on all our products so long as you bring it back within 28 days of purchase, that's fine.

Two ... Oh, that's also provided that you have the receipt with it of course.

Three ... There's short-term saving in case you have an emergency.

Three ... Had I known, I wouldn't have bought it in the first place.

Listening 12.1

One A fascinating new theory suggests that Britain was once connected to the rest of Europe, by hills which rose above what is now the English channel. Then, 300,000 years ago, a violent flood swept them away and the link disappeared. Within 24 hours the hills had vanished and Britain became an island. This explains why Britain remained uninhabited for such a long time. Even though men had been present they had left for warmer climates. Once this new barrier appeared, it most probably prevented Neanderthal man from returning to the island.

Two While people say that weather forecasters are always getting it wrong the *opposite* is true. Yet it only takes one serious mistake for reputations to be affected as shown by Britain's most infamous weather forecast. Britain had been preparing itself for storms, but on the evening of October 15th 1987, even though someone telephoned the television station saying she'd heard there would be a hurricane during the night, the country's most eminent weatherman, Michael Fish, said that the expected gales would *not* reach disastrous speeds. When, during the night, many parts of the country were *devastated* by incredibly high winds, everyone pointed the finger at poor Mr Fish, accusing him of failing to make the public aware of what was about to happen. It was the country's worst storm since the Great Storm of 1703.

Three One of the biggest mysteries is the disappearance of the dinosaurs. For many decades scientists believed that they died out gradually due to climate change. Then the meteorite theory changed all that. A meteorite crashed into what is now the Gulf of Mexico and caused an immediate climate change, catastrophic to the dinosaurs which simply vanished. However, in the last few years geologists have raised objections to this theory – claiming that the meteorite occurred well before the dinosaurs came on the scene, so that it can't have been the cause of their extinction.

Four People are terrified of nuclear war, but the energy produced from a volcanic eruption can be even more catastrophic. Normally there is plenty of warning and in 1902 Mount Pelée, on the island of Martinique, had been showing signs that it was about to explode. Why on earth didn't people leave the island you might ask. The answer is depressingly simple, even though the authorities should have evacuated the island's capital St Pierre, they chose to ignore the signs because an election was going to be held. 28,000 people were killed in the eruption, there were just two survivors: a shoemaker and a prisoner.

Five In Roman times the southern part of the Mediterranean was known as the granary of the Empire. If the harvest failed it led to shortages and famine elsewhere. Once the Romans left north Africa the land was taken over by nomads who let their goats eat all the vegetation. Over-feeding led to the gradual desertification of the region. Despite the obvious damage this caused, they kept on allowing them to eat everything in sight until hardly anything green was left. All the same, this doesn't fully explain the increase in the desert. Climate change and long periods of drought are probably as much to blame. And once fertile land is lost it is difficult to reverse the process.

Listening 12.2

Part A

Interviewer: Hurricanes have been more and more in the news ever since the destruction caused by Katrina in 2005. You'll remember that Katrina devastated the south east of the United States. Flooding covered an area the size of the UK. With me today is weather expert Dr Kate Jackson who is going tell us about hurricanes. So, Kate, perhaps we could begin by asking what causes them.

Kate: Certainly, Jamie. It's all rather technical but I'll try my best. Let's start with where they appear, shall we? Basically they form over the oceans in the warm zones we find either side of the equator.

Interviewer: OK. Why not over the equator itself?

Kate: Because over the equator the spin, the rotation of the Earth, isn't great enough. It's the rotation of the Earth which helps to generate the wind, you see.

Interviewer: Mm, I think so. Anyway, go on.

Kate: Well, what happens is that water vapour evaporates and forms clouds.

Interviewer: Just like for ordinary rain.

Kate: Exactly, except the wind, combined with the rise and fall of temperature sets up a kind of chain reaction, which eventually creates a hurricane.

Interviewer: So when does a strong wind turn into a hurricane?

Kate: Well, officially when it reaches a speed of 120 kph, but some of those we've seen recently have been much more powerful. Katrina got up to 280 kph!

Interviewer: Wow, I understand that the wind caused a lot of destruction, but the southern states were flooded too, weren't they?

Kate: Indeed, they were. This is due to the surge – the increase in the height of the level of the sea caused by the hurricane. And, before you ask, the highest recorded surge happened 100 years ago in Australia. People found fish and even dolphins on the top of cliffs. Oh and by the way, these cliff-tops were 15 metres above the usual level of the sea.

Interviewer: Wow. Unbelievable. And what has been the most disastrous hurricane on record?

Kate: Economically, it was Katrina, but in terms of loss of life the worst so far was in Bangladesh in 1970. Half a million people died. Isn't that dreadful? With Katrina around 1800 lives were lost.

Listening 12.3

Part B

Interviewer: One thousand eight hundred. How terrible. But what is the reason for the increased number of hurricanes these days? Is it tied up with global warming?

Kate: To my way of thinking all the evidence points to that, but it is almost impossible to be 100 percent certain. There are other factors too. For instance, each three or four years there's a warm water current called El Niño which appears in the eastern Pacific – El Niño is linked with increased hurricane activity.

Interviewer: OK – but going back to temperature levels, I know some people claim that the temperature of the oceans goes up and down naturally.

Kate: Mm, yes, there is some truth in that. In the early 1900s sea temperatures started to rise. But then they went down again only to rise again, and continue to rise from the 1970s.

Interviewer: So people who claim that rises and falls in temperature are natural have got a point?

Kate: Perhaps, but other scientists, myself included, think that atmospheric pollution was responsible for keeping temperatures down.

Interviewer: Atmospheric pollution?

Kate: Yes. Particles from factories actually helped to block out sunlight. But now, there is no question that world temperatures are rising all the time mostly because of CO_2 emissions. Burning fuels like coal and oil, the so-called 'fossil fuels' releases the carbon stored in them into the atmosphere.

Interviewer: Yes, I see that. So, how much CO_2 is actually in the atmosphere, then?

Kate: Well, there is 0.03 of a percent. That's one part in 3300.

Interviewer: But that's absolutely minuscule. How can that possibly have any impact – I can't see what all the fuss is about?

Kate: Well, all I can say is that while it may seem very slight, just a tiny increase can have devastating consequences. If I had my way, I'd ban any car with a large engine.

Interviewer: Mm ... if you say so. Right ... and a couple of quick questions. First one. What is the difference between a hurricane and a typhoon?

Kate: Scientifically, none at all. They are just the names which have been used in different regions. Typhoon means, I think, 'big wind' in Japanese. We can also call them cyclones too. We shouldn't confuse them with tornadoes or twisters because *they* happen over land.

Interviewer: Right, like in the mid-west in the United States. And is there a difference between hurricanes or typhoons in the northern and southern hemispheres?

Kate: Yes, they rotate differently. It's all rather complicated, but basically a hurricane in the northern hemisphere rotates anti-clockwise, and one in the southern hemisphere goes the other way round.

Interviewer: I see. OK, well, thanks for being with us today. And now for a weather update ...

Listening 13.1

Newswoman: Have you heard about a new report on education which says these are the worst results in over 20 years and one ex-headmaster said the situation is appalling? That's the verdict on the spelling ability of school children in Great Britain after the results of last year's national tests were released. The report reveals that pupils who were tested, aged 11 and 14, made more spelling errors last year than they did four years ago. Some of the most common errors among half of the 11-year-olds were words such as 'change' and 'known', which were often spelled C-H-A-N-G and N-O-W-N'. In addition, the word 'technique' caused problems for the majority of the 600,000 pupils taking the test! Well, we have Michael Bryant our education correspondent in the studio with us today. Michael, what are people saying about this report?

Michael: Well, one person who actually marked the tests told me that the report reveals that most errors had arisen because pupils had missed out letters, put the incorrect endings on words or used the wrong vowels altogether. The slip in spelling standards among 11 and 14-year-olds also comes as researchers found a decline in the ability to use basic punctuation correctly such as capital letters, full stops and commas.

Newswoman: One thing that surprised me was that the government has been telling us that it has spent more money on education than any previous government. Given the results of the survey it's amazing that this can be the case. It would be interesting to know more about how the government has responded to all this criticism.

Michael: Well, I asked the Minister for Education what she thought some of the reasons were and she responded to the findings by suggesting that teachers may be at fault. She said she'd sent schools a list of 600 words all children should know in their first year at secondary school, at age 11, and another list of 700 words that pupils should have mastered by 14.

Newswoman: Really? And how have teachers reacted?

Michael: Well, the teachers' union said it would be commenting later in the day once it had studied the report in more detail. In the past the union has welcomed government initiatives including the new-style English lessons which were introduced in schools last term and where teachers begin each lesson with ten minutes of spelling. The idea is that every department plays a role. For example maths teachers are meant to drill pupils in words connected with maths like 'geometrical', and sports teachers ensure pupils can spell 'athlete' and 'muscles', but the problem is that ...

Listening 13.2

Channel 1

Interviewer: And if things weren't bad enough for the Prime Minister, today he came under fire again for his education policy. Heads of schools and teachers' associations issued a joint statement speaking out against what they see as a lack of interest and understanding in the future generations of the country. In the studio with me today is Michael Woods, chairman of the headmasters' association who supported this statement. Mr Woods, good morning. What is the basis for this statement against the Prime Minister?

Woods: Well, it's quite simple. Year after year, this government has promised they would deliver on education but instead all we've seen is a cut in funding in both schools and resources.

Channel 2

Woman: Scientists at NASA are still looking for somewhere to land the space shuttle which is currently in orbit here, over Australia. The shuttle had been scheduled to land two days ago but poor weather conditions have prevented a safe landing. Freezing fog and heavy rain have caused the agency to look for an alternative or wait for the weather to clear. A spokesperson for NASA said the astronauts aboard the shuttle are all in good health. He added that the shuttle is able to remain in orbit for another ten days.

Channel 3

Woman: I don't think anyone would argue that the economy has done well this year but the outlook for next year is less predictable and the government needs to think its strategy through very carefully. I'd predict a slow down in house prices and I'd also expect inflation to rise by about half a percent. The consumer will need to be a little more careful in the next 12 months and really start to watch their borrowing. Anyone with large credit card bills should pay them off as soon as possible otherwise they could really get caught out.

Channel 4

Woman/Man: This is a great week for you Leos, with good news at work – maybe a pay rise or a promotion. Romance might be coming your way. It's a good week to take up a sport or something healthy. Maybe you've been eating a little too much and it would be a good idea to go jogging or perhaps eat a little less. You get on well with the star sign Libra at this time of year, so spend some free time with them. Perhaps you should take a trip to the cinema and relax a little. You've been working hard and I think you need to reward yourself.

Channel 5

Woman: Well, the news coming from Hollywood is that they might be thinking of taking their friendship further. Rumours that Mel and Christina, who met on the set of their recent film, are to get married seem to be spreading across Los Angeles. We haven't been able to get an official response from the publicity office of either star but one close friend of the couple said they wouldn't be surprised and described the couple as 'very close in recent weeks'. This news comes very soon after Mel's much publicised break up with his second wife.

Listening 14.1

One

Daughter: Come on, Dad, you can't possibly wear that old-fashioned suit – it's *so* 70s.

Father: What do you mean? I've had this for years ... I'm proud I can still get into it.

Daughter: Yeah, but it looks as though you've just come out of an old TV programme. It's just so weird. Two buttons are out, three are in.

Father: Two buttons, three buttons – I couldn't care less, I'm not into fashion. Anyway if I wait long enough two buttons will make a comeback.

Daughter: OK, but do you think you could change the shirt and tie? They don't go together at all. Those green stripes clash horribly with the pink.

Father: Do you really think so? Alright, if that makes you feel better, I will.

Two

Doctor: Yes, I perfectly understand, Hannah. In my opinion, the best way of losing weight is to follow a sensible balanced diet. Avoid fads like avoiding all carbohydrates or eliminating all fat from your diet. There are *no* miracle solutions. Take up some form of light exercise and then build up so that your body is getting a good workout for 20 minutes or so at least three times a week. Make sure you don't overdo it or you could get hurt, you know, tear a muscle or something like that. So avoid sports to start with which involve sharp violent movements like football or even tennis.

Three

Melissa: Well, finally, here comes Lulu.

Raymond: And about time too. And oh my goodness! Look at her! She looks like an orange.

Melissa: Yes, and just look at that permanent smile.

Raymond: Mmm, she has had her face lifted at least three times. But gravity always wins in the end.

Melissa: And she should think about getting her eyes done, those bags look awful.

Lulu: Sorry I'm late. I've just been to the tanning salon.

Raymond: Don't worry, darling. We were just saying how gorgeous you look.

Four

You're on a tight budget; you don't have to wear expensive brands or designer labels to be stylish. Let the real you come through and develop your own look. Accessories such as scarves and brooches can give you that something extra with a bit of flair.

Five

One of the latest crazes is flashmobbing. This is where a large group of young people up to a couple of hundred, descend on a place they have agreed and decided on. They do something unexpected for a couple of minutes and then leave as quickly as they came. The meeting point is decided on the Internet. They gather and then they get a set of instructions to follow. Then they'll do things like invade a sofa shop and sit on the sofas for five minutes, or go to a bookshop and ask for a non-existent book.

Six

Well, when I think back to when I was a kid, you know when everyone smoked, there was nothing cooler than one of those petrol lighters ... Zippos, that's it ... a Zippo lighter. Anyway, I guess what I'm trying to say is that each generation has its own set of cult objects – it's normal. My lighter was a lot cheaper than an iPod, that's for sure. But these new objects, some *do* become classics in the end. And do you know, the other day in the shopping centre, I saw this place which was selling flying jackets – you know the type of thing airmen wore in the Second World War, with the fur collar and everything!? You can't get more retro than that, can you?

Seven

Well, here we go again. I know a lot of people will complain about it, because there are people living in poverty and dying of hunger but people need to dream a little too, don't you think? To my way of thinking, there are of a lot of other things which are far more unethical – like the arms trade for instance. Fashion week doesn't hurt anyone. If anything it brightens up people's lives and makes them happier – and that can't be bad, can it?

Eight

Well, it certainly is a little bit behind the times, but it's a wonderful renovation project. And if a few things need doing to it then it will be a good investment. True, the kitchen and bathroom need to be modernised but it has great potential. And it's an up-and-coming area; there are a few new and trendy restaurants starting to appear and I would say that in a couple of years this area will be as fashionable as Hampstead or Islington.

Listening 14.2

Philip: Is that you in that photograph, Florence?

Florence: Mm, yes, it is, Philip. It was the first time I'd worn my new school uniform. I was so proud of myself.

Damien: You look so cute with your hair in pigtails!

Florence: That's sweet of you, Damien. I'm in the summer uniform there. I've got a straw hat, see. But in the winter we had a coat with lots of buttons and a funny-looking hat. It was like a nightcap ... you know, red with a long bit hanging down.

Philip: Oh no! You poor thing!

Florence: Yeah, people used to tease us ... they called us 'Santa's little helpers'! It was complete misery. I don't know who thought the uniform up. I hated that hat, but we were made to wear it.

Damien: I know how you feel. We had to wear our school cap on the way to *and* from school. Things are a lot less strict nowadays!

Philip: I'm glad to hear it. I loathed wearing a uniform.

Damien: I didn't exactly like it either, but the great thing about a uniform is it's so easy. What I mean is you just get up and put it on.

Philip: Yes, but don't you think that kids should be allowed to wear what they want? After all it's a way of expressing themselves.

Damien: You say that, Philip, but kids end up putting on a kind of uniform of their own – you know designer jeans and trainers. Don't you think that leads to a lot of unhealthy competitive dressing? *You* know ... who is wearing the most *fashionable* brands, and so on.

Florence: Not to mention all the hours which are wasted gelling their hair to make it spiky or worrying about looking cool.

Philip: I suppose so, but I don't care what you say, that's still better than school uniform! You know, in the summer, we weren't allowed to take off our jackets! Our teachers didn't even let us take off our ties. It was torture.

Florence: I agree with you Philip. I don't see the point of making people uncomfortable. All the same, in a uniform at least everyone is the same. What I mean is there are no differences between the kids and it makes everyone look equal. It looks smart too.

Philip: Well, you say that, and at the beginning of the year it's true, but it soon gets scruffy – and when they grow they have a jacket which is far too small for them.

Damien: Philip has got a point. He's thought it through. When I was at school the uniform was really expensive so my family couldn't afford to let me have a new one every year. So my trousers always needed taking up for the first four months of the school year because they were too long, the next four months it was OK but then for the last four months of the year they were too short and needed to be let down. In the end they looked awful!

Florence: All the same, I still think uniform is a good idea as it is much less trouble for parents.

Damien: I agree. After all, parents have enough stress as it is. Having their children complaining about not having *exactly* the perfect clothing for school and saying their friends have got better clothes than them is just more stress for them!

Philip: Maybe.

Listening 15.1

Speaker One And finally, guards at the terracotta army museum in Xi'an, China couldn't believe their eyes when they saw a man jump into the pit and disguise himself as one of the warriors. German art student, Paul Wendel, who was studying in China, decided to join the warriors he admired. These remarkable ancient terracotta soldiers are over 2200 years old, and an important part of China's heritage. They were created to accompany their emperor in the afterlife. Wendel pretended he was one of them and stood as still as he could until the guards lifted him away. Apparently he stayed frozen in his pose as the guards lifted him out.

Speaker Two In Britain, November the 5th is 'Bonfire Night'. It celebrates the discovery of a plot to kill King James the first, by blowing up the Houses of Parliament. Before Bonfire Night there's a tradition that children make a 'Guy' – a life-size doll of Guy Fawkes the infamous conspirator. They'll take some old clothes and fill them up with newspaper. Then they'll make a head and draw a face on it, and perhaps stick on a beard. A few days before bonfire night, they'll display the Guy outside supermarkets and train stations saying 'A Penny for the Guy'. Of course, nowadays what they mean is 'at least 50p!' Then they'll use this money to buy fireworks or sweets for the celebrations on the 5th.

Speaker Three I enjoyed visiting well-known sights such as Red Square in Moscow and going to the Hermitage museum in St Petersburg, but, to tell you the truth the thing that most moved me was a short visit I made to Volgograd and seeing an absolutely awesome statue that some people call 'Mother Russia'. Volgograd used to be called Stalingrad and was the site of the terrible siege and historic battle which proved to be the turning point of the war. Anyway, the statue, which is made of concrete, stands outside Volgograd, overlooking the city. It is, for sure, the tallest statue in Europe and is a memorial which commemorates the struggle and sacrifices made by the people of Stalingrad and the Red Army.

Speaker Four One of my favourite TV shows used to be with those rubber puppets. They were real works of art – you could immediately see who they were supposed to be. I used to like the way they made fun of politicians or famous or notorious personalities from show business and so on. And the actors who took them off, sounded like the real thing. I don't know why they don't show it any more – I suppose they thought it was old-fashioned. The one thing I didn't appreciate, though, was the way they mocked the royal family – I mean, that's totally unfair, I think.

Speaker Five Sometimes we should rely on our first impressions. For instance, the Getty Museum spent $10m on a fake statue which was supposed to come from ancient Greece. Now, everything about it seemed perfect, and museum officials managed to talk themselves into thinking it was real, but other experts knew the second that they looked at it that the statue was a fake. Years of examining hundreds of examples of the real thing simply told them that the Getty museum had been taken in by a clever imitation.

Listening 15.2

Part A

Betty: So would you mind telling us how you got into these, the re-enactments?

Kelly: Well, basically it was a way of getting to know people. I moved from London to this small town where I didn't know anyone. I hesitated a bit at first, 'cos I thought, you know, that there would be lots of weirdoes, but I finally made up my mind to join and have been involved ever since.

Betty: Right, so basically you joined to make new friends, it wasn't because you were interested in history or anything like that?

Kelly: Actually, I wasn't that keen on history when I was at school. Mind you, since joining the society I have discovered a real love for history and our heritage.

Betty: And which side are you on?

Kelly: Well, I'm in a Royalist regiment, one which supports the king. You see, in the *real* war, in the 17th century ... there was a local gentleman who established a regiment loyal to the king in my town. So the regiment I am in is a tribute to the original one. Anyway, I've always preferred the Cavaliers.

Betty: Me too. They had long hair, and lovely clothes and hats with feathers and all the rest. The Roundheads must have been a miserable-looking crowd, I think, in the brown and black they always wore! You can't imagine them having a good time, can you? So tell me, what happens in these re-enactments?

Kelly: Well, basically, we form a little army with other royalist regiments then we re-enact battles and other historic events against Roundhead regiments – of course the outcome of the battle is decided at the planning stage, so we just act the story out like a play on a large scale. We do try to keep the suspense going as much as possible for the spectators.

Betty: Goodness. So how many people can be involved?

Kelly: Well, sometimes there can be several hundred participants on each side, not counting the thousands of people who come along to watch.

Betty: And do you do this on a stage or somewhere like that?

Kelly: No, not at all. We travel to the original battlefields and camp there for the weekend of the re-enactment battle. We may have to travel hundreds of miles. There is usually a farmer who will let us park or put our tents up on his land.

Listening 15.3

Part B

Betty: I hope you don't mind my mentioning this, fighting isn't a very lady-like activity is it?

Kelly: Well, there are more lady-like roles. At first I was one of the women-folk. I was a cook. But when I realised that the soldiers were having more fun I changed my mind and became a soldier too! Although this does mean dressing up as a man – there weren't women soldiers in those days as such.

Betty: So there's nothing to stop women from playing a full part in the fighting?

Kelly: No, anyone can wave a sword around. But I can't manage the pikes, those very long spears – well, they're five metres long and impossible for most of the women to handle! But there's nothing to stop a girl being a musketeer either, you know, firing a gun, or even joining the cavalry. Oh, and it almost slipped my mind, girls can be drummers too.

Betty: But isn't it dangerous? I mean taking part in a battle, even if it's a pretend one?

Kelly: No, not really, although people sometimes have small injuries. You have to mind where you stand – it hurts if a horse steps on your foot – it *really* hurts.

Betty: What was your first battle like?

Kelly: Great fun, although I did say to myself, 'you must be out of your mind, girl'. The noise and the smell of gunpowder are unimaginable.

Betty: Mm, goodness knows what the real thing must have been like. And what do you do other than this?

Kelly: Well, the social life is absolutely fantastic. You meet like-minded people from all walks of life and there are banquets ... you know ... *big* meals ... for all the regiment. And dances! Every year we go to London to commemorate the execution of King Charles in 1649. There's a parade to where his head was cut off at the Mansion House.

Listening 16.1

Presenter: Good morning and this week on 'Home help' we're looking at colour in the home. Now for many of us when we think of decorating the first thing we think about is things like curtains, paintings and furniture and quite often the colour of the walls comes after but in fact colour should be the starting point. And joining us this week is the design expert Laurence Cooper-Stafford to tell us why.

Laurence: Good morning.

Presenter: So Laurence, tell us why colour is so important.

Laurence: Basically it makes a statement about who we are to anyone coming into the house. It also says what the purpose of a room is.

Presenter: How do you mean?

Laurence: Well, I don't think people realise how much colour can affect our mood or how comfortable a visitor might feel.

Presenter: I see. So, imagine I've bought a new house and I'm getting ready to make it a home. Where do I start with colour?

Laurence: Well, one of the most exciting things about decorating any room is that moment when you first take the lid off the tin and start to paint. And the days when the choice was either white or something neutral are well over. These days people almost can't decide what colour to use because of the *huge* range available nowadays. But what happens as a result is that people cover their walls and then they realise it won't match the shade of their furniture or they find that bright red in the bedroom actually stops them from sleeping. So planning all your colours is crucial.

Presenter: But how do you know? I mean, most of us will find it quite difficult to imagine how it will look.

Laurence: It's true that interior designers often seem to have a built-in instinct for what goes with what but actually a great deal of their skill comes from years of working with different colours and learning to follow some basic principles.

Presenter: I see. Like what for example?

Laurence: Well, for example red looks great in dining rooms because it makes people feel social and stimulates an appetite. On the other hand you wouldn't use it in a nursery or baby's room.

Presenter: What colour would you use?

Laurence: Pink is restful though boys may find this a bit 'girlie' so blue is probably a better choice. They also say it prevents nightmares.

Presenter: Isn't blue a cold colour though? Not very welcoming.

Laurence: True but you can find warm tones of blue. Actually bedrooms are somewhere where purple can also work well. Downstairs you might choose yellows or something bright for the kitchen. These types of colours also help make north-facing rooms more cheerful. Brown is another very practical colour for kitchens or living rooms where you spend a lot of time during the day.

Presenter: And I guess black is a real no-no.

Laurence: In moderation black's OK. It can create a sense of drama if that's what you're looking for. But often it's the sort of thing you might see in a teenager's bedroom. But having said all that about rules and principles people should also rely on their own instincts and playing around with colour is one of the best ways of learning ...

Listening 16.2

I = Interlocutor
J = Julian
A = Adrian

I: So good morning, my name's John Hughes, and this is my colleague, Richard Webb. He'll be listening to us today. And your name is?

J: Julian

A: And I'm Adrian.

I: OK, thank you. Can I have your mark-sheets first of all? Thanks. OK first of all we'd like to know something about you. So, Julian where are you from?

J: I'm from Colombia. Medellin, naturally.

I: And you?

A: And I come from Switzerland.

I: And what do you like about living in Colombia?

J: Well, Colombia is a great country. I think the most I like of living in Colombia is the people ... the people and the weather of course. Actually, real nice weather.

I: And what about Switzerland?

A: I live in a small village, near the Lake of Constance, so I like the lake there, and it is quiet in my village but with also some cities not too far away, so we have both nature and cities, and that's what I like most.

I: So, Julian do you prefer spending time at home or do you like to go out in your free time?

J: I prefer to go out with my friends to see people, talk, speak with other people, other things. And I don't know ... actually, it's nice to be at home too, watching TV and just relaxing.

I: Do you like to do cooking in your spare time?

J: Mm, sometimes it's nice. For example, I like to cook breakfast. It's nice. Eggs, that kind of food.

I: And what's your favourite food?

J: My favourite food, maybe Chinese food and Mexican food – I like a lot Mexican food and Chinese food.

I: And Adrian, do you prefer to spend time on your own or with other people?

A: I need both. Sometimes I like to be alone at home, for example, doing something on my computer or read a book, or read a newspaper, watch a movie. And then on the other hand I need my friends. I like to do sports and play volleyball or go out with my friends.

I: Can you tell me about a day that you've enjoyed recently?

A: Yes, for example, there was this weekend here in London. My girlfriend visited me and we had a really great day in London. We did some sightseeing, went to a musical as well ... yes, I really enjoyed this day.

I: Who are the most important people in your life?

A: There are maybe three categories, I would say my family, my parents and my brothers and sisters. Then my girlfriend, of course, and I would say two of my friends.

I: OK, good. In the next part of the test, I'm going to give each of you two photographs. I'd like you to talk about your photographs on your own for a minute, and also to answer a short question about your partner's photographs. Julian, it's your turn first, here are your photographs. They show people living in different types of homes. I'd like you to compare the photographs and say why you think people choose to live in these types of homes, alright?

J: Perfect. Well, at first we can see ... three people joined together. It's a urban landscape. They are on a ship in a river. And the second photograph we can see, like a family, maybe five people, with their own beds or maybe animals for food, and it's very isolate landscape, but it's in the countryside. They seem like they take their own food for example for the animals they have there. Maybe they choose to live there, for example for the first photograph, they choose to live in there because they have their friends near to them, and maybe they like the city. And the second photograph, maybe they all just need is their family.

I: Would you like to live in either of these homes, Adrian?

A: Not really, to be honest. I'd prefer ... a proper house ... bigger as well.

I: Thank you. Now here are your photographs, OK, they show people spending free time in the countryside. I'd like you to compare the photographs and say which you think is the best way to enjoy the countryside, and why.

A: Yes, on the first picture you can see four people skiing, I guess it's winter, and they are skiing in the forest, whereas on the picture below, there are some, some friends around a fire. Maybe it's a late summer day. One boy is playing the guitar, and maybe the others around him are singing. I would prefer to spend my free time with sports, for example skiing as on this picture, and because I like to have some activity, and to have some activity with my friends together, and yeah, that's the main reason why I'd prefer to spend my free time with sport ... I like the second picture as well, because sometimes it is nice to be on a lake, and to sit around a fire and talk to friends.

I: Thank you. Now which kind of activity would you prefer to do in the countryside, Julian?

J: I'd prefer being, for example, singing with my friends, and playing maybe guitar and some instruments and near to the fire wood, all around, all joined together, I'd prefer that kind of activity, maybe with a barbecue.

I: Now I'd like you to talk about something together for about three minutes. I'd like you to imagine that your local town is five hundred years old and is planning events to celebrate the anniversary. First, talk to each other about how successful these suggestions might be for the events. And then decide which two might appeal to the most people within the town, alright?

J: In the first stage, or the first activity, it's a puppet show and it would be nice, but only for children, I think.

A: Yes, exactly, it might be something for children or families. The second picture seems like a concert. The woman is playing the violin there. And I think it would be very nice especially if you maybe have an artist from the local town or area.

J: A famous artist from the local town.

A: Yeah, maybe.

J: The third one, we can see maybe, it's a kind of food festival, maybe with typical food of the local city. It could be nice because they can put join people together. They can enjoy the special typical food of the region.

A: Maybe you could combine the third picture as you described with the fourth picture where there is a party or a disco. People are dancing there. Maybe you could have a dinner in the beginning of the evening then later make a little party and listen to music. Maybe dance.

J: It would be a nice mix. Or in the fifth stage, or fifth activity would be a photographic exhibition. It would be nice, for example, for a child that doesn't know the old buildings of the city. Maybe they want to see how was the city before they were born so it would be nice, for example, as a cultural activity.

A: Yeah I like this point and this exhibition. I think it's a good idea. Then we have free rides around the town with horses and it could be a good ideas for families and children to see the whole city. Maybe you have to abandon cars from the city during this day. I don't really like this idea because you can see the city by your own and you don't necessarily need a horse to do this.

J: That's right, that's right. And the last activity we can choose is … maybe a fireworks display. It would be nice as a finish a good finish for the activity for the day. So, I don't know. Maybe we can choose we can mix the food festival.

A: Yeah, together with the dancing, clubbing …

J: … Dancing, maybe that two activities at the end of the day, afternoon and night.

A: Yes, yes.

J: And in the morning the photographic exhibition, with the history of the town yes.

A: Yeah, I think a photographic exhibition, and then the dancing and food festival would be nice.

J: Yeah, I agree.

I: OK thank you. Have you ever been to these kind of events in your town, Julian?

J: Yeah, actually in my city, in Medellin, there are a lot of festivals. For example we have one week in August, it's a *feria della flores*. There's fireworks all days. There are all the clubs open from Monday to Sunday all days. There are food festivals … typical food festival. This kind of maybe puppets shows, so I've been in that kind of festivals and that kind of activities.

I: What about in your town, Adrian?

A: We have a fire work every year basically and in a city near where I live, so we celebrate like the end of the summer there. There's every year a huge firework, and there a lot of people there. When I was a child for example I like to go to puppet theatres and also to play by myself to invent new theatres.

I: What do you think is important, Adrian when choosing where you're going to live?

A: I think for me it is important that, my work is not too far away, so maybe within one hour by public transport. Then there has to be a good infrastructure so good public transport system, some sports' facilities. Maybe a lake and a forest so the nature is important as well for me and, yes as I've said an infrastructure is quite important and maybe you have to consider as well taxes and cost of living there.

I: Do you agree, Julian?

J: Well, I agree for example, if I had my family near to my home for example I think it's very important to have job opportunities, nice job opportunities. Of course we have to think about all that things that Adrian said before so I agree with Adrian.

I: As many people can work from home with computers do you think more of us will move away from cities in the future?

J: Well, I think in this moment with all the opportunities and all the tech advances that we can see it's very easy to work away from the office. Internet and network can give us all that kind of facilities, so it would be nice if we can work away from the office 'cos the office may, can, maybe be I don't stressful, I mean stressful. It would be nice to work in a relaxing environment.

I: Would you prefer to work from home, Adrian?

A: Sometimes, maybe, but I think I'd prefer to have a work on a separate place than where I live because I think it's important to work outside my home and when I've finished or have finished my work then I'd like to be at home and don't think about my work so for me this separation is quite important

I: OK, thank you very much. That's the end of the examination.

Useful Expressions

Part One

Good morning/afternoon/evening.
My name's .../I'm ...
I'm from ...
At the moment I'm studying/working for
...
In the future I would like to...
I like .../I prefer ... because
One thing I like doing is ...
I suppose my favourite ... is ...
One important ...

Part Two

Both photographs show ...
In the background/foreground
In the one on the left ... whereas in the
   second photo ...
The photo on the right shows ...
It is a bit like ...
It looks as though/like/as if ...
Perhaps/Maybe
There is .../There are ...
They are similar to the type you can see
   at ...
I think .../In my opinion ...

Parts Three and Four

**(Any of the following expressions
arranged alphabetically below could be
useful in these parts of the exam. Note
that many have also appeared in units in
this book.)**

Acknowledging what the other person says (Unit 4)

I hear/understand what you're saying
   but ...
I take your point, but...
I understand/respect your point of
   view but ...
That's true but ...
What you're saying is true but ...

Agreeing and disagreeing (Unit 4)

Absolutely ...
I (quite/totally) agree/disagree ...
I (completely/totally) agree/disagree ...
You're right.
I see what you mean but ...
Yes, but ...
I can't agree with you because ...
The problem with that is ...

Challenging (Unit 14)

All the same ...
But don't you think ...?
I suppose so but ...
What I mean is ...
Yes, but ...

Comparing (Unit 2)

How do you think it compares to ...?
I don't think it's anything like as ... as
Is it much different from ...?
It looks fairly similar to ...
This seems like ... a better/the best idea
X is (much) better than Y ...

Criticising and complaining (Unit 12)

He's always (verb + -ing)
She keeps on ...
Why on earth ...?

Discussing options (Unit 6)

One option is to ...
If we did X, it would/we could ...
Is there anything else we could do?
We could ...
We'd better ...
What if we ...?

Expressing ability (Unit 3)

They can/could/were able to
We managed to ...
We succeeded in (...-ing)

Expressing preferences (Unit 9)

I prefer to ...
I'd rather ...
My preference would be ...

Giving opinions (Unit 4)

As far as I'm concerned ...
As I see it ...
From my point of view ...
I think/believe ... (that)
In my opinion ...
What do you think?
How do you feel about that?

Giving someone else's point of view (Unit 4)

One view is that ...
Another view is ...

Guessing and speculating (Unit 10)

I can't seem to tell
I think it's probably ...
I'm absolutely certain of that.
I'm really not sure.
It could be any number of things.
It could be as a result of
It could have been ...
It seems like ...
It seems likely that ...
Maybe it was ...

Recommending and suggesting (Unit 3 and unit 7)

Don't forget that ...
How about ...?
I strongly recommend ...
I'd like to suggest that ... should
It should be ...
It's a good idea to ...
It's also important
It's also worth...
Let's ...
Make sure that you ...

Regret and advice (Unit 11)

If I were them, I'd ...
If only they'd ...
Next time I think they should ...
They probably wish they'd ...
They shouldn't have ...

Sequencing (Unit 3)

First of all/Secondly/To begin with
Next/then/after that
Finally

Showing you are listening (Unit 8)

I see, but ...
I see.
OK. So ...
Right.
Sounds great.

Information File

Unit 3 File 3.2 (page 25)

Never been Olympic sports: darts, chess, tenpin bowling
Used to be Olympic sports: croquet, tug of war
The rest are Olympic sports: snowboarding, beach volleyball and synchronised swimming are the most recent additions.

Unit 5 File 5.1 (page 45)

1 Pinocchio, Don Quixote, Alice in Wonderland, Sherlock Holmes, Romeo and Juliet, Esmerelda, Aladdin, and Odysseus (Ulysses).

Unit 7 File 7.1 (page 65)

World's worst ten inventions

1 Weapons
2 Mobile phones
3 Cigarettes
4 Cars
5 Computers
6 TV
7 Nuclear energy
8 Plastic bags
9 Fast food
10 Car alarms

Unit 7 File 7.2 (page 70)

Student A

It was three o'clock one Icelandic morning and Rebekka Guoleifsdottir couldn't sleep. So she picked up her camera and drove to a lake outside her town. Standing in the lake with water up to her knees for an hour, she took picture after picture. Her final favourite image did not appear on an advertising billboard or in a gallery or magazine but on the world wide web and her own homepage. Visitors who log on to her site just click on the photo they want and buy it online. She's recently been asked by the car maker *Toyota* to take photos. 'The web changes opportunities for all kinds of artists, like musicians,' said Guoleifsdottir. 'It's so much easier to get your stuff out there. Iceland is a small community of 300,000 people and it's hard to get recognised, but this way you can reach out everywhere.'

Unit 8 File 8.1 (page 75)

Bank robbery - ten years in prison
Computer hacking – probation for one year
Speeding – attend a talk by the police on how to drive safely
Shoplifting – do community service for 40 hours
Dropping litter – pay a fine of €100
Mugging - an 18-month prison sentence

Unit 8 File 8.2 (page 79)

[*adapted from: The Week 22 July 2006 p14*]

A prisoner, who wanted to wish his girlfriend a happy birthday, escaped from a jail in Montenegro. Dragan Boskovic, 26, escaped over a wall, which was over ten feet high, and went straight to his girlfriend's house where he spent the evening. He finally explained his reasons to the police, to whom he turned himself in two hours later: 'I promised my girlfriend that I would say happy birthday, which I hadn't been able to do on the prison phone. I had no other option but to get the message to her personally.'

Unit 12 File 12.1 (page 118)

'Red sky at night shepherd's delight. Red sky in the morning, shepherd's warning'.
This means that if the sky is red in the evening, the following day will be fine and the shepherd can leave his sheep on high ground. If, however, it's red in the morning, then the weather is going to be bad and the shepherd should move the sheep to lower, more sheltered ground.
'If a pine cone stays open, the weather will be fine; if it closes then rain is on the way'.
'If seaweed stays wet it is going to rain, there is humidity in the air'.
Spring is on the way when a creature called a 'groundhog' (also known as the 'woodchuck', 'land beaver', or 'whistlepig') wakes up after hibernation (sleeping through the winter).

Unit 15 File 15.1 (page 145)

Student A
Title: *The Lady of Shalott* (painted 1888)
Artist: John William Waterhouse (1849-1917)
Tate Gallery London
The painting shows a scene from the poem *The Lady of Shalott* by Alfred Tennyson. The Lady of Shalott was a prisoner in a tower and under a curse which said she would die if she left her prison. She could only look at the outside world through its reflection in a mirror. She created a tapestry which copied what she saw. Sadly for her, she was in love with Sir Lancelot, one of King Arthur's bravest knights. So, despite the curse, she left the tower and took a boat to Camelot to find Lancelot. On the way there she died.

Unit 7 File 7.3 (page 70)

After three years of odd jobs like stacking shelves in a supermarket and setting up websites, it took a 21-year-old student a few minutes to come up with an idea which has made him more than one million dollars in four months. Alex Tew lay on his bed one night wondering how he could pay for his three-year degree course at University. The first thing he wrote on his notepad was, 'How can I become a millionaire?' Twenty minutes later, the Million Dollar Homepage idea was born. The idea was that Tew would sell pixels, the dots which make up a computer screen, as advertising space for a dollar a pixel. Anyone could buy pixels and post their logo so users would have a link to their website. Four months and 2,000 customers later Tew is about to sell the last 1,000 pixels having made a million.

Unit 15 File 15.2 (page 145)

Student B
Title: *Dante and Beatrice* (painted 1883)
Artist: Henry Holiday (1839-1927)
Walker Art Gallery, Liverpool England.
The painting is set in Florence. It was inspired by the story of the Italian poet Dante's love for Beatrice - dressed in white. Dante is madly in love with Beatrice but she pretends not to see him as she passes by. Beatrice's friend Donna Vanna - dressed in red - looks at Dante for his reaction. Dante and Beatrice never met again but he continued to love her and dedicated his life to poetry. The artist, Henry Holiday, went to Florence so his representation could be as historically accurate as possible.

Unit 16 File 16.1 (page 155)

Find out what your choice of coloured shape says about you!

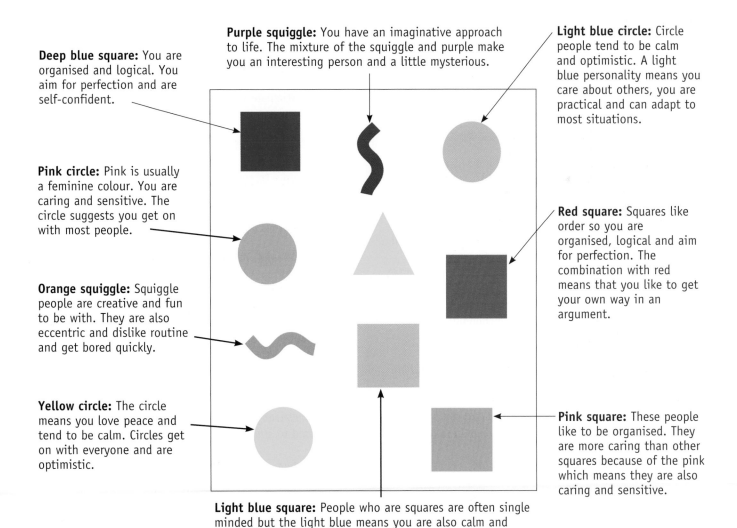

Deep blue square: You are organised and logical. You aim for perfection and are self-confident.

Pink circle: Pink is usually a feminine colour. You are caring and sensitive. The circle suggests you get on with most people.

Orange squiggle: Squiggle people are creative and fun to be with. They are also eccentric and dislike routine and get bored quickly.

Yellow circle: The circle means you love peace and tend to be calm. Circles get on with everyone and are optimistic.

Purple squiggle: You have an imaginative approach to life. The mixture of the squiggle and purple make you an interesting person and a little mysterious.

Light blue circle: Circle people tend to be calm and optimistic. A light blue personality means you care about others, you are practical and can adapt to most situations.

Red square: Squares like order so you are organised, logical and aim for perfection. The combination with red means that you like to get your own way in an argument.

Pink square: These people like to be organised. They are more caring than other squares because of the pink which means they are also caring and sensitive.

Light blue square: People who are squares are often single minded but the light blue means you are also calm and flexible. You are able to compromise and work with others.

Phrasal verbs

These pages list the phrasal verbs in *Spotlight on FCE*. Each verb has a short definition and a page reference so that you can see it in context. Different meanings have different page numbers. The position of *sbdy* (somebody), or *sthng* (something) show whether a verb is separable or inseparable e.g. *show sbdy around; look after sbdy*. For fuller grammatical information go to Section 12.3 of the Grammar Reference.

apply for *sthng* – officially request (often in writing) (17)

back *sthng* up – make a copy of a computer file (70)
break down – break/stop functioning (94)
break *sthng* off – end abruptly (126)
break into *sthng* – enter a building by force (76)
break up with *sbdy* – separate/end a romantic relationship (10)
brighten *sthng* up – make somewhere brighter and more attractive (143)
bring *sthng* back – return something to *sbdy* somewhere (110)
burn *sthng* down – destroy a building by fire (66)

carry *sthng* out – perform/execute (37)
catch *sbdy/sthng* up – move quickly to arrive at *sbdy* who is ahead of you (129)
check in – register at a hotel (57)
clean *sthng* out – make somewhere clean and tidy (43)
click on *sthng* – open a computer programme using a mouse (70)
come across *sthng* – discover by chance (37)
come round – regain consciousness (52)
come to – the total of a bill or account (106)
come up with *sthng* – have an idea/suggestion (28)
cope with *sthng* – manage a difficult or challenging situation (119)
cover *sthng* up – stop the truth from becoming known (126)

deal with *sbdy/sthng* – handle/take responsibility for (17)
do *sthng* up – re-paint/renovate a room/building (157)
do *sthng* up – fasten (136)
dress up – wear your best clothes (39)
drop *sbdy* off – quickly let someone out of a car somewhere (57)

fall out with *sbdy* – argue/end friendship (10)
fill *sbdy/sthng* in – supply information/complete a form (134)
fill up – completely fill a car with petrol (44)

get along/on with *sbdy* – have a good relationship (10)
get back (together) with *sbdy* – re-establish a romantic relationship (10)
get into *sthng* – become involved in an activity (List 5.2)

get into *sthng* – succeed in entering/joining (60)
get on – enter a bus or train (91)
get out of – leave a vehicle e.g. car (143)
get up – stand (34)
get/run away – escape (48)
give *sthng* away – tell a secret (List 9.1)
give *sthng* up – stop doing something/renounce (24)
go along with *sbdy/sthng* – agree/accept (10)
go down – decrease, opposite of go up (120)
go for *sthng* – make a choice (85)
go on – happen (List 10.1)
go out – leave (143)
go through *sthng* – endure a difficult period (148)
go/walk away – leave (49)
grow up – go from being a child to an adult (U1 tapescript)

hack into *sthng* – illegally access computer files (70)
hand *sthng* down – pass an object from generation to generation (152)
hand *sthng* back – return something to someone (49)
have *sthng* on – wear (136)
help *sbdy* out – give help or assistance (List 3.1)

join in – participate (30)
jot *sthng* down – write a note or a list (118)

keep on – continue doing something, often against *sbdy's* wishes (26)
keep *sthng* up – to continue doing *sthng* (157)
keep up with *sbdy/sthng* – maintain the same speed as *sthng/sbdy* else (61)
knock *sthng* over – overturn (List 3.1)

lay *sbdy* off – send workers away when there is not enough work (17)
leak out – let the truth or a secret be known (126)
let *sbdy* down – disappoint (10)
let *sthng* go – stop caring about something's appearance (157)
let *sthng* out – make clothing bigger/looser around body (136)
lie down – position your body flat on the floor or bed (35)
log into *sthng* – enter/register on a computer (70)
look after *sbdy* – take care of (10)
look for *sbdy/sthng* – try to find (17)
look forward to *sthng* – wait with pleasurable anticipation (13)
look into *sthng* – investigate (41)
look up to *sbdy* – respect/admire (10)

make *sthng* up – invent/create (158)
make up with *sbdy* – make peace/resolve an argument (10)
meet up with *sbdy* – meet informally (57)

pass away – die (37)

pass out – faint/lose consciousness (52)

pass *sthng* off – to pretend that *sbdy/sthng* is true or genuine (148)

pay *sbdy* back – repay the money you owe (106)

pay *sthng* off – repay a loan in its entirety (106)

phone *sbdy* back – return a telephone call (57)

pick *sbdy* up – meet/collect someone from somewhere (57)

pick *sthng* out – choose/select (157)

pick *sthng* up – take in your hand (149)

pick *sthng* up – find/retrieve something (67)

plug *sthng* in – connect an appliance with a cable (70)

put *sthng* on – cover oneself/one's body (136)

pull ahead – move in front of something (126)

pull out – withdraw/retreat (126)

pull *sthng* up – take a plant and its roots from the earth (143)

put *sbdy* off – break *sbdy* else's concentration (List 3.1)

put *sbdy* up – give someone a bed for the night (57)

put *sthng* away – arrange something in its proper place (152)

put *sthng* up – erect (e.g. a tent) (List 15.2)

put *sthng* on – present a show (60)

put up with *sthng/sbdy* – endure/suffer (10)

run into *sbdy* – meet by chance (10)

save up – gradually save money until you have enough to buy *sthng* (106)

set *sthng* aside – keep money for an emergency (106)

sell out – sell everything so there is nothing left (102)

send *sthng* off – dispatch (17)

set off – leave on a journey (57)

set out – begin/begin with the intention of doing *sthng* (148)

set *sthng* up – programme/organise (29) establish (61)

shop around – search for the best price for something (106)

show *sbdy* around – act as a guide for a visitor (57)

spark *sthng* off – ignite/start (98)

spell *sthng* out – give each letter separately (30)

splash out on *sthng* – spend a lot of money/more than you can afford on something (105)

spring up – appear unexpectedly (144)

stand by *sbdy* – loyally support (10)

stand out – be visible (157)

sum *sthng* up – make a conclusion (92)

take off suddenly – become successful (34)

take *sbdy* on – employ (17)

take *sbdy* out – invite someone for a meal (57)

take *sbdy* in – give *sbdy* in need a home/hospitality (150)

take *sbdy* in – trick or deceive (149)

take *sthng* in – absorb/understand news or information (150)

take *sthng* in – make clothing smaller/tighter around body (136)

take off – leave the ground (57)

take *sthng* off – remove clothing (136)

take *sbdy/sthng* off – imitate the way *sbdy* sounds, looks or behaves (149)

take *sthng* over – take control (List 12.1)

take *sthng* back – return something to from where it came (82)

talk about *sthng* – discuss (10)

tear *sthng* apart – destroy while searching for something (84)

think back – try to remember what happened (List 8.1)

think *sthng* through – consider a problem logically (142)

think up – imagine/create (142)

throw *sthng* away – dispose of something no longer needed (80)

travel around – tour/visit different places (57)

try *sthng* on – wear an item of clothes to see if it fits/suits you (136)

try *sthng* out – test/experiment with something (67)

turn *sthng* out – produce (148)

turn *sbdy* out – make somebody leave somewhere (150)

turn *sthng* down – refuse (17)

turn *sthng* off – stop the supply of *sthng* (160)

turn up – arrive, often unexpectedly (52)

turn *sthng* up – reduce the length of clothing (136)

turn *sthng* into – transform (119)

wipe *sbdy/sthng* out – annihilate/totally destroy (e.g. by war or disease) (124)

Wordlist

Unit 1

acquaint/acquaintance
assist/help
boyfriend
break up with
close/closeness
close relationship
cousins
difficult/difficulties
fall out
fiancé(e)
friendly/friendship
friendly relationship
get back together
get on with
go along with
go out with
gossip
half brother
hit it off
inform/tell
let down
look after
look up to
make up
mother-in-law
offspring
person/personal/personality
put up with
ran into
receive/get
relation/relationship
relatives
request/ask for
require/want
research/researcher
siblings
sisters-in-law
spouse
stand by
stepsister
strong relationship
strong/strength
take after
twin
unavailable/busy
verify/check

Unit 2

able/abilities
actor/actress
advertisement
apply (for)
artist
assess/assessment
assistant
chance
convenient
cook/chef
deal with

doctor
electrician
employer/employment/employee
experience
experiment
find out
flexitime
form
formation
hand in notice
journalist
lay off (staff)
letter
look for
manager
musician
notice
opportunity
organise/organisation
overtime
painter
possibility
qualifications
qualities
recruit/recruitment
redundant
refer/referee/references
resign
sack
salary
select/selection
send off
success/successful
suitable
teacher
training
turn down (a job)
wages
waiter/waitress
writer

Unit 3

archery
bat
beach volleyball
chess
compete/competition/competitive
contest/contestant
court
croquet
darts
difficult/difficulty
fan
friend/friendship
game
golf
hobby
hooligan
hope/hopeless
intelligent/intelligence
karate

pastime
pitch
puck
racquet or racket
rival/rivalry
sailing
satisfy/satisfaction
shuttlecock
snowboarding
soccer
spectator
supporter
synchronised swimming
tenpin bowling
tennis
tug of war
use/useless
win/winner
wrestling

Unit 4

appear/appearance
attack/attacker
breed
cage
carry out
come across
come up with
dead/deadly
die out
die/death
endangered
except/exception
extinction
extreme/extremely
find out
go through
habitat
harm/harmless
imagine/imaginary
instinct
invent/invention
let down
live on
look after
look down on
look for
look forward to
look into
lucky/luckily
mammal
mystery/mysterious
pass away
pet
pleasant/unpleasant
poison/poisonous
prey
react/reaction
real/reality
regular/irregular
relation/relationship

success/unsuccessful
take in
tame
terrify/terrified/terrifying
train
watch out
wild

Unit 5

angry
chapter
character
classic
delighted
devastated
dialogue
disappointed
embarrassed
episode
exhausted
fact
fiction
frightened
furious
gasp
gaze
ghastly
giggle
glance
glare
gorgeous
gulp
hero
heroine
legend
limp
location
lovely
mortified
myth
narrator
novel/novelist
playwright
pleased
plot
ridiculous
scene
scenery
script
serial/serialise
series
set in
shoot
sigh
sip
slurp
snigger
stagger
stare
stroll
stupid
terrified
tired
villain
yawn

Unit 6

anguished
attendance
brochure
celebration
check in
check out
cheer on
commuter
crossing
domination
drop off
endless
excursion
ferry
flea market
flight
gruelling
guide book
indigenous
irresistible
itinerary
journey
jovial
legend/legendary
meet up with
myriad
package holiday
pageant
pastures
phone back
pick up
popularity
put up
reminder
resort
set off
show around
sightseeing
souvenir
spectacle/spectacular
spoilt/unspoilt
stillness
take off
take out
timetable
tour
tourist/tourism
travel around
travel/traveller
trip
tunnel
turn up
unrivalled
voyage
waxed
waned
wilderness

Unit 7

attachment
back up
brain-child
breakthrough
burdens
came up with

carbon copy
click on
come across
device
experiments
funding
hack into
homepage
imagination
inbox
inventors
keyboard
license
links
log into
made out of
mouse
obsession
online
patent
pick up
pioneers
plug in
prototype
remote control
revolution
salary
screen
set up
setbacks
subject
tests
try out
world wide web

Unit 8

accuse
annoy
arrest
arson/arsonist
blackmail/blackmailer
blame
burglary/burglar
capture
community service
detective
drug dealing/drug dealer
fine (noun)
force
forgery/forger
get away
get away with
get into
get out
get up to
hacking/hacker
judge
jury
kidnapping/kidnapper
legal/illegal
mugging/mugger
police officer
prison/prisoner/imprison
probation
prosecution
punish/punishment
release

robbery/robber
shoplifting/shoplifter
smuggling/smuggler
speeding
steal
theft/thief
understand
vandalism/vandals

Unit 9

bitter
bland
boil
bowl
chop
cook
course
diet
dry (wine)
fast food
fry
frying pan
get on (progress)
grate
greedy
grill
ingredients
mild
mix
peel
put off (postpone; feel disgust)
rare (meat)
raw
receipt
recipe
roast
slice
sour
sparkling
spicy
sprinkle
still
stir
sweet
take advantage of
take care of someone
take off (remove; imitate)
take on (employ; challenge)
take something for granted
take something into account
take the opportunity
tasteful
tasty
well-done

Unit 10

ancient
army
beautiful
bright
burial grounds
circle/circular
clear
colourful/colour
community

cubes
dark
deep/depth
diameter
document
frying
gardening
ghost
glass
gorgeous
green
hard
heavy
high/height
hoax
intricate
iron
kind of
large
leather
light
long/length
made of
metal/metallic
modern
mysterious
odd-looking
orange
paranormal
phenomena
plastic
rectangle/rectangular
rough
round
rubber
shapeless
silver
small
smooth/smoothness
soft/softness
sort of
sparked off
spherical/sphere
sports
sticky
swirling
tall
thin
triangular/triangle
ugly
universe
wide/width
wooden/wood

Unit 11

afford
bargain
borrow from
brands
budget
come to
cost
customers
deal
discount
get by

in debt
lend to
pay (a cheque) into (an account)
pay by
pay off (a loan)
pocket money
price
refund
repay
save up
set aside
shop around
special offer
spend
splash out on
stay within
take something back
whim

Unit 12

breeze
climate
dribble
drizzly
drought
earthquake
famine
flood
fog
forecast
frozen
gale
hail
icy
lightning
meteorite
mist
raining
rainy
shining
snow
storm
stormy
sunny
tempest
thunder
tidal wave
tornado
volcanic eruption
weather

Unit 13

bias
blog
break off
break up
breaking news
business
celebrity
censor/censorship
circulation
close the net on
corner (v)
correspondent
cover up

crossword
editor/editorial
fall out
front page
go up
headline
health
hit the jackpot
horoscope
item
journalist
leak out
local
national
news
obituary
pack
paparazzi
photograph/photographer
politics
prey
pull ahead
pull out
quality newspaper
reporter
science
scoop
showbiz
splash across
sport
tabloid
thrill of the chase
TV listings
weather

Unit 14

accessory
bare
brand
cap
clash
classic
classical
cool
cosy
cramped
craze
cult
designer
dimples
do up
dress up
elderly
fad
fade
faded
fashion/fashionable
flair
freckles
hang up
have on
hungry/hunger
let out
long/length
loom
messy

miserable/misery
pigtails
plump
poverty
put on
retro
scruffy
skinny
smart
stylish
suit
suite
take in
take off
think about
think back
think through
think up
trendy
try on
turn up
uniform
wallpaper
wardrobe
wrinkled

Unit 15

ancient
auction
ceremony
custom
event
exhibition
expedition
fake
famous
festival
find out
gallery
go through
habit
heartless
heirloom
heritage
historical
historic
infamous
invaluable
landscape
middle aged
middle ages
monument
museum
notorious
pass off
persuade/persuasive
pike
portrait
priceless
set out
sight
site
statue
sword
take in
take off

tradition
turn out
turn up
worthless
worthwhile
youth/youthful

Unit 16

bare
brighten up
brownish
cheerful
cluttered
cold
cosy
dark/light
detached
do up
dreary
exotic
greeny
homely
impersonal
keep up
let go
mix up
modern
north/south-facing
pale
pick out
run down
stand out
strong
suburban
terraced
traditional
turn into
warm
well-cared for

Irregular verbs

Alternate forms are separated by /. The first form listed is the most commonly used.

Infinitive	Simple Past	Past Participle
arise	arose	arisen
awake	awakened/awoke	awakened/awoken
be	was, were	been
become	became	become
begin	began	begun
bite	bit	bitten
blow	blew	blown
break	broke	broken
breed	bred	bred
bring	brought	brought
build	built	built
burn	burned/burnt	burned/burnt
buy	bought	bought
catch	caught	caught
choose	chose	chosen
clothe	clothed/clad	clothed/clad
come	came	come
deal	dealt	dealt
do	did	done
draw	drew	drawn
dream	dreamed/dreamt	dreamed/dreamt
drink	drank	drunk
drive	drove	driven
eat	ate	eaten
fall	fell	fallen
feed	fed	fed
feel	felt	felt
fight	fought	fought
find	found	found
flee	fled	fled
fly	flew	flown
forbid	forbade	forbidden
foresee	foresaw	foreseen
forget	forgot	forgot/forgotten
forgive	forgave	forgiven
freeze	froze	frozen
get	got	got/gotten
give	gave	given
go	went	gone/been
grow	grew	grown
have	had	had
hear	heard	heard
hide	hid	hidden
hold	held	held
keep	kept	kept
know	knew	known

Infinitive	Simple Past	Past participle
lay	laid	laid
lead	led	led
lean	leaned	leaned
learn	learned/learnt	learned/learnt
leave	left	left
lend	lent	lent
lie	lay	lain
lie (not tell truth)	lied	lied
lose	lost	lost
make	made	made
mean	meant	meant
meet	met	met
mistake	mistook	mistaken
partake	partook	partaken
pay	paid	paid
plead	pleaded/pled	pleaded/pled
prove	proved	proven/proved
read	read (sounds like 'red')	read (sounds like 'red')
ride	rode	ridden
ring	rang	rung
rise	rose	risen
run	ran	run
say	said	said
see	saw	seen
seek	sought	sought
sell	sold	sold
send	sent	sent
shake	shook	shaken
shine	shone/shined	shined/shone
show	showed	shown/showed
sing	sang	sung
sink	sank/sunk	sunk/sunken
sit	sat	sat
sleep	slept	slept
speak	spoke	spoken
spell	spelled/spelt	spelled/spelt
spin	spun/span	spun
spit	spat/spit	spat/spit
spoil	spoiled/spoilt	spoiled/spoilt
steal	stole	stolen
strike	struck	stricken/struck
swear	swore	sworn
swim	swam	swum
take	took	taken
teach	taught	taught
tear	tore	torn
tell	told	told
think	thought	thought
throw	threw	thrown
tread	trod	trodden/trod
wear	wore	worn
weep	wept	wept
win	won	won
wind	wound	wound
withdraw	withdrew	withdrawn
write	wrote	written

Credits